An Introduction to
the Theory of Computation

PRINCIPLES OF COMPUTER SCIENCE SERIES

Series Editors
Alfred V. Aho, Bell Telephone Laboratories, Murray Hill, New Jersey
Jeffrey D. Ullman, Stanford University, Stanford, California

Computer Organization
Michael Andrews
Trends in Theoretical Computer Science
Egon Börger, Editor
Truth, Deduction, and Computation: An Introduction to Logic and Semantics for Computer Scientists
R. E. Davis
The Turing Omnibus
A. K. Dewdney
Formal Languages and Automata Theory
Vladimir Drobot
Advanced C: Food for the Educated Palate
Narain Gehani
C: An Advanced Introduction, ANSI C Version
Narain Gehani
C for Personal Computers: IBM PC, AT&T PC 6300, and Compatibles
Narain Gehani
An Introduction to the Theory of Computation
Eitan Gurari
Theory of Relational Databases
David Maier
An Introduction to Solid Modeling
Martti Mäntylä
Principles of Computer Design
Leonard R. Marino
UNIX: The Minimal Manual
Jim Moore
A Logical Language for Data and Knowledge Bases
Shamim Naqvi and Shalom Tsur
The Theory of Database Concurrency Control
Christos Papadimitriou
Algorithms for Graphics and Image Processing
Theo Pavlidis
Data Compression: Methods and Theory
James A. Storer
The Elements of Artificial Intelligence
Steven Tanimoto
Computational Aspects of VLSI
Jeffrey D. Ullman
Principles of Database and Knowledge-Base Systems, Volumes 1 and 2
Jeffrey D. Ullman
Algorithmic Studies in Mass Storage Systems
C. K. Wong

OTHER BOOKS OF INTEREST

Jewels of Formal Language Theory
Arto Salomaa
Fuzzy Sets, Natural Language Computations, and Risk Analysis
Kurt J. Schmucker
LISP: An Interactive Approach
Stuart C. Shapiro

An Introduction to
the Theory of Computation

Eitan Gurari

The Ohio State University

COMPUTER SCIENCE PRESS

Library of Congress Cataloging-in-Publication Data

Gurari, Eitan.
  An introduction to the theory of computation.

  (Principles of computer science series;   )
  Bibliography: p.
  Includes index.
    1. Electronic data processing.   I. Title.   II. Series.
  QA76.G828   1989   004   88-35285
  ISBN 0-7167-8182-4

64960

Printed in the United States of America

Computer Science Press
1803 Research Boulevard
Rockville, MD 20850

An imprint of W. H. Freeman and Company
41 Madison Avenue, New York NY 10010
20 Beaumont Street, Oxford OX1 2NQ, England

1 2 3 4 5 6 7 8 9 0   RRD   7 6 5 4 3 2 1 0 8 9

To Shaula,
Inbal, Itai, Erez,
Netta, and Danna

Contents

Preface

Computations are designed to solve problems. Programs are descriptions of computations written for execution on computers. The field of computer science is concerned with the development of methodologies for designing programs, and with the development of computers for executing programs. It is therefore of central importance for those involved in the field that the characteristics of programs, computers, problems, and computation be fully understood. Moreover, to clearly and accurately communicate intuitive thoughts about these subjects, a precise and well-defined terminology is required.

This book explores some of the more important terminologies and questions concerning programs, computers, problems, and computation. The exploration reduces in many cases to a study of mathematical theories, such as those of automata and formal languages; theories that are interesting also in their own right. These theories provide abstract models that are easier to explore, because their formalisms avoid irrelevant details.

Organized into seven chapters, the material in this book gradually increases in complexity. In many cases, new topics are treated as refinements of old ones, and their study is motivated through their association to programs.

Chapter 1 is concerned with the definition of some basic concepts. It starts by considering the notion of strings, and the role that strings have in presenting information. Then it relates the concept of languages to the notion of strings, and introduces grammars for characterizing languages. The chapter continues by introducing a class of programs. The choice is made for a class, which on one hand is general enough to model all programs, and on the other hand is primitive enough to simplify the specific investigation of programs. In particular, the notion of nondeterminism is introduced through programs. The chapter concludes by considering the notion of problems, the relationship between problems and programs, and some other related notions.

Chapter 2 studies finite-memory programs. The notion of a state is introduced as an abstraction for a location in a finite-memory program as well as an assignment to the variables of the program. The notion of state is used to show how finite-memory programs can be modeled by abstract computing machines, called finite-state transducers. The transducers are essentially sets of states with rules for transition between the states. The inputs that can be recognized by finite-memory programs are characterized in terms of a class of grammars, called regular grammars. The limitations of finite-memory programs, closure properties for simplifying the job of writing finite-memory programs, and decidable properties of such programs are also studied.

Chapter 3 considers the introduction of recursion to finite-memory programs. The treatment of the new programs, called recursive finite-domain programs, resembles that for finite-memory programs in Chapter 2. Specifically, the recursive finite-domain programs are modeled by abstract computing machines, called pushdown transducers. Each pushdown transducer is essentially a finite-state transducer that can access an auxiliary memory that behaves like a pushdown storage of unlimited size. The inputs that can be recognized by recursive finite-domain programs are characterized in terms of a generalization of regular grammars, called context-free grammars. Finally, limitations, closure properties, and decidable properties of recursive finite-domain programs are derived using techniques similar to those for finite-memory programs.

Chapter 4 deals with the general class of programs. Abstract computing machines, called Turing transducers, are introduced as generalizations of pushdown transducers that place no restriction on the auxiliary memory. The Turing transducers are proposed for characterizing the programs in general, and computability in particular. It is shown that a function is computable by a Turing transducer if and only if it is computable by a deterministic Turing transducer. In addition, it is shown that there exists a universal Turing transducer that can simulate any given deterministic Turing transducer. The limitations of Turing transducers are studied, and they are used to demonstrate some undecidable problems. A grammatical characterization for the inputs that Turing transducers recognize is also offered.

Chapter 5 considers the role of time and space in computations. It shows that problems can be classified into an infinite hierarchy according to their time requirements. It discusses the feasibility of those computations that can be carried out in "polynomial time" and the infeasibility of those computations that require "exponential time." Then it considers the role of "nondeterministic polynomial time." "Easiest" hard problems are identified, and their usefulness for detecting hard problems is exhibited. Finally, the relationship between time and space is examined.

Chapter 6 introduces instructions that allow random choices in programs. Deterministic programs with such instructions are called probabilistic programs. The usefulness of these programs is considered, and then probabilistic Turing transducers are introduced as abstractions of such programs. Finally, some interesting classes of problems that are solvable probabilistically in polynomial time are studied.

Chapter 7 is devoted to parallelism. It starts by considering parallel programs in which the communication cost is ignored. Then it introduces "high-level" abstractions for parallel programs, called PRAM's, which take into account the cost of communication. It continues by offering a class of "hardware-level" abstractions, called uniform families of circuits, which allow for a rigorous analysis of the complexity of parallel computations. The relationship between the two classes of abstractions is detailed, and the applicability of parallelism in speeding up sequential computations is considered.

The motivation for adding this text to the many already in the field originated from the desire to provide an approach that would be more appealing to readers with a background in programming. A unified treatment of the subject is therefore provided, which links the development of the mathematical theories to the study of programs.

The only cost of this approach occurs in the introduction of transducers, instead of restricting the attention to abstract computing machines that produce no output. The cost, however, is minimal because there is negligible variation between these corresponding kinds of computing machines.

On the other hand, the benefit is extensive. This approach helps considerably in illustrating the importance of the field, and it allows for a new treatment of some topics that is more attractive to those readers whose main background is in programming. For instance, the notions of nondeterminism, acceptance, and abstract computing machines are introduced here through programs in a natural way. Similarly, the characterization of pushdown automata in terms of context-free languages is shown here indirectly through recursive finite-domain programs, by a proof that is less tedious than the direct one.

The choice of topics for the text and their organization are generally in line with what is the standard in the field. The exposition, however, is not always standard. For instance, transition diagrams are offered as representations of pushdown transducers and Turing transducers. These representations enable a significant simplification in the design and analysis of such abstract machines, and consequently provide the opportunity to illustrate many more ideas using meaningful examples and exercises.

As a natural outcome, the text also treats the topics of probabilistic and parallel computations. These important topics have matured quite recently, and so far have not been treated in other texts.

The level of the material is intended to provide the reader with introductory tools for understanding and using formal specifications in computer science. As a result, in many cases ideas are stressed more than detailed argumentation, with the objective of developing the reader's intuition toward the subject as much as possible.

This book is intended for undergraduate students at advanced stages of their studies, and for graduate students. The reader is assumed to have some experience as a programmer, as well as in handling mathematical concepts. Otherwise no specific prerequisite is necessary.

The entire text represents a one-year course load. For a lighter load some of the material may be just sketched, or even skipped, without loss of continuity. For instance, most of the proofs in Section 2.6, the end of Section 3.5, and Section 3.6, may be so treated.

Theorems, Figures, Exercises, and other items in the text are labeled with triple numbers. An item that is labeled with a triple $i.j.k$ is assumed to be the kth item of its type in Section j of Chapter i.

Finally, I am indebted to Elizabeth Zwicky for helping me with the computer facilities at Ohio State University, and to Linda Davoli and Sonia DiVittorio for their editing work. I would like to thank my colleagues Ming Li, Tim Long, and Yaacov Yesha for helping me with the difficulties I had with some of the topics, for their useful comments, and for allowing me the opportunities to teach the material. I am also very grateful to an anonymous referee and to many students whose feedback guided me to the current exposition of the subject.

An Introduction to
the Theory of Computation

Chapter 1

GENERAL CONCEPTS

Computations are designed for processing information. They can be as simple as an estimation for driving time between cities, and as complex as a weather prediction.

The study of computation aims at providing an insight into the characteristics of computations. Such an insight can be used for predicting the complexity of desired computations, for choosing the approaches they should take, and for developing tools that facilitate their design.

The study of computation reveals that there are problems that cannot be solved. And of the problems that can be solved, there are some that require infeasible amount of resources (e.g., millions of years of computation time). These revelations might seem discouraging, but they have the benefit of warning against trying to solve such problems. Approaches for identifying such problems are also provided by the study of computation.

On an encouraging note, the study of computation provides tools for identifying problems that can feasibly be solved, as well as tools for designing such solutions. In addition, the study develops precise and well-defined terminology for communicating intuitive thoughts about computations.

The study of computation is conducted in this book through the medium of programs. Such an approach can be adopted because programs are descriptions of computations.

Any formal discussion about computation and programs requires a clear understanding of these notions, as well as of related notions. The purpose of this chapter is to define some of the basic concepts used in this book. The first section of this chapter considers the notion of strings, and the role that strings have in representing information. The second section relates the concept of languages to the notion of strings, and introduces grammars for characterizing languages. The third section deals with the notion of programs, and the concept of nondeterminism in programs. The fourth section formalizes the notion of problems, and discusses the relationship between problems and programs. The fifth section defines the notion of reducibility among problems.

1.1   Alphabets, Strings, and Representations

The ability to represent information is crucial to communicating and processing information. Human societies created spoken languages to communicate on a basic level, and developed writing to reach a more sophisticated level.

The English language, for instance, in its spoken form relies on some finite set of basic sounds as a set of primitives. The words are defined in term of finite sequences of such sounds. Sentences are derived from finite sequences of words. Conversations are achieved from finite sequences of sentences, and so forth.

Written English uses some finite set of symbols as a set of primitives. The words are defined by finite sequences of symbols. Sentences are derived from finite sequences of words. Paragraphs are obtained from finite sequences of sentences, and so forth.

Similar approaches have been developed also for representing elements of other sets. For instance, the natural number can be represented by finite sequences of decimal digits.

Computations, like natural languages, are expected to deal with information in its most general form. Consequently, computations function as manipulators of integers, graphs, programs, and many other kinds of entities. However, in reality computations only manipulate strings of symbols that represent the objects. The previous discussion necessitates the following definitions.

Alphabets and Strings

A finite, nonempty ordered set will be called an *alphabet* if its elements are *symbols*, or *characters* (i.e., elements with "primitive" graphical representations). A finite sequence of symbols from a given alphabet will be called a *string* over the alphabet. A string that consists of a sequence $a_1, a_2, \ldots, a_n$ of symbols will be denoted by the juxtaposition $a_1 a_2 \cdots a_n$. Strings that have zero symbols, called *empty strings*, will be denoted by ϵ.

Example 1.1.1 $\Sigma_1 = \{a, \ldots, z\}$ and $\Sigma_2 = \{0, \ldots, 9\}$ are alphabets. *abb* is a string over Σ_1, and 123 is a string over Σ_2. *ba*12 is not a string over Σ_1, because it contains symbols that are not in Σ_1. Similarly, $314\ldots$ is not a string over Σ_2, because it is not a finite sequence. On the other hand, ϵ is a string over any alphabet.

The empty set $\emptyset$ is not an alphabet because it contains no element. The set of natural numbers is not an alphabet, because it is not finite. The union $\Sigma_1 \cup \Sigma_2$ is an alphabet only if an ordering is placed on its symbols.   □

An alphabet of cardinality 2 is called a *binary alphabet*, and strings over a binary alphabet are called *binary strings*. Similarly, an alphabet of cardinality 1 is called a *unary alphabet*, and strings over a unary alphabet are called *unary strings*.

The *length* of a string α is denoted $|\alpha|$ and assumed to equal the number of symbols in the string.

Example 1.1.2 $\{0, 1\}$ is a binary alphabet, and $\{1\}$ is a unary alphabet. 11 is a binary string over the alphabet $\{0, 1\}$, and a unary string over the alphabet $\{1\}$.
    11 is a string of length 2, $|\epsilon| = 0$, and $|01| + |1| = 3$.   □

The string consisting of a sequence α followed by a sequence β is denoted $\alpha\beta$. The string $\alpha\beta$ is called the *concatenation* of α and β. The notation α^i is used for the string obtained by concatenating i copies of the string α.

Example 1.1.3 The concatenation of the string 01 with the string 100 gives the string 01100. The concatenation $\epsilon\alpha$ of ϵ with any string α, and the concatenation $\alpha\epsilon$ of any string α with ϵ give the string α. In particular, $\epsilon\epsilon = \epsilon$.
    If $\alpha = 01$, then $\alpha^0 = \epsilon$, $\alpha^1 = 01$, $\alpha^2 = 0101$, and $\alpha^3 = 010101$.   □

A string α is said to be a *substring* of a string β if $\beta = \gamma\alpha\rho$ for some γ and ρ. A substring α of a string β is said to be a *prefix* of β if $\beta = \alpha\rho$ for some ρ. The prefix is said to be a *proper prefix* of β if $\rho \neq \epsilon$. A substring α of a string β is said to be a *suffix* of β if $\beta = \gamma\alpha$ for some γ. The suffix is said to be a *proper suffix* of β if $\gamma \neq \epsilon$.

Example 1.1.4 ϵ, 0, 1, 01, 11, and 011 are the substrings of 011. ϵ, 0, and 01 are the proper prefixes of 011. ϵ, 1, and 11 are the proper suffixes of 011. 011 is a prefix and a suffix of 011.   □

If $\alpha = a_1 \cdots a_n$ for some symbols $a_1, \ldots, a_n$ then $a_n \cdots a_1$ is called the *reverse* of α, denoted α^{rev}. β is said to be a *permutation* of α if β can be obtained from α by reordering the symbols in α.

Example 1.1.5 Let α be the string 001. $\alpha^{\mathrm{rev}} = 100$. The strings 001, 010, and 100 are the permutations of α.   □

The set of all the strings over an alphabet Σ will be denoted by Σ^*. Σ^+ will denote the set $\Sigma^* - \{\epsilon\}$.

Ordering of Strings

Searching is probably the most commonly applied operation on information. Due to the importance of this operation, approaches for searching information and for organizing information to facilitate searching, receive special attention. Sequential search, binary search, insertion sort, quick sort, and merge sort are some examples of such approaches. These approaches rely in most cases on the existence of a relationship that defines an ordering of the entities in question.
    A frequently used relationship for strings is the one that compares them alphabetically, as reflected by the ordering of names in telephone books. The relationship and ordering can be defined in the following manner.
    Consider any alphabet Σ. A string α is said to be *alphabetically smaller* in Σ^* than a string β, or equivalently, β is said to be *alphabetically bigger* in Σ^* than α if α and β are in Σ^* and either of the following two cases holds.

a. α is a proper prefix of β.

b. For some γ in Σ^* and some a and b in Σ such that a precedes b in Σ, the string γa is a prefix of α and the string γb is a prefix of β.

An ordered subset of Σ^* is said to be *alphabetically ordered*, if β is not alphabetically smaller in Σ^* than α whenever α precedes β in the subset.

Example 1.1.6 Let Σ be the binary alphabet $\{0, 1\}$. The string 01 is alphabetically smaller in Σ^* than the string 01100, because 01 is a proper prefix of 01100. On the other hand, 01100 is alphabetically smaller than 0111, because both strings agree in their first three symbols and the fourth symbol in 01100 is smaller than the fourth symbol in 0111.

The set $\{\epsilon, 0, 00, 000, 001, 01, 010, 011, 1, 10, 100, 101, 11, 110, 111\}$, of those strings that have length not greater than 3, is given in alphabetical ordering.   □

Alphabetical ordering is satisfactory for finite sets, because each string in such an ordered set can eventually be reached. For similar reasons, alphabetical ordering is also satisfactory for infinite sets of unary strings. However, in some other cases alphabetical ordering is not satisfactory because it can result in some strings being preceded by an unbounded number of strings. For instance, such is the case for the string 1 in the alphabetically ordered set $\{0, 1\}^*$, that is, 1 is preceded by the strings 0, 00, 000, ... This deficiency motivates the following definition of canonical ordering for strings. In canonical ordering each string is preceded by a finite number of strings.

A string α is said to be *canonically smaller* or *lexicographically smaller* in Σ^* than a string β, or equivalently, β is said to be *canonically bigger* or *lexicographically bigger* in Σ^* than α if either of the following two cases holds.

a. α is shorter than β.

b. α and β are of identical length but α is alphabetically smaller than β.

An ordered subset of Σ^* is said to be *canonically ordered* or *lexicographically ordered*, if β is not canonically smaller in Σ^* than α whenever α precedes β in the subset.

Example 1.1.7 Consider the alphabet $\Sigma = \{0, 1\}$. The string 11 is canonically smaller in Σ^* than the string 000, because 11 is a shorter string than 000. On the other hand, 00 is canonically smaller than 11, because the strings are of equal length and 00 is alphabetically smaller than 11.

The set $\Sigma^* = \{\epsilon, 0, 1, 00, 01, 10, 11, 000, 001, \ldots\}$ is given in its canonical ordering.   □

Representations

Given the preceding definitions of alphabets and strings, representations of information can be viewed as the mapping of objects into strings in accordance with

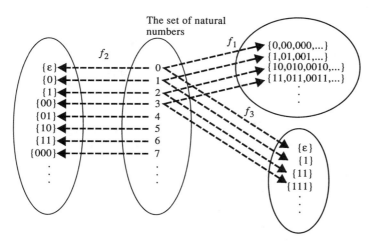

Figure 1.1.1 Representations for the natural numbers.

some rules. That is, formally speaking, a *representation* or *encoding* over an alphabet Σ of a set D is a function f from D to 2^{Σ^*} that satisfies the following condition: $f(e_1)$ and $f(e_2)$ are disjoint nonempty sets for each pair of distinct elements e_1 and e_2 in D.

If Σ is a unary alphabet, then the representation is said to be a *unary representation*. If Σ is a binary alphabet, then the representation is said to be a *binary representation*.

In what follows each element in $f(e)$ will be referred to as a representation, or encoding, of e.

Example 1.1.8 f_1 is a binary representation over $\{0, 1\}$ of the natural numbers if $f_1(0) = \{0, 00, 000, 0000, \ldots\}$, $f_1(1) = \{1, 01, 001, 0001, \ldots\}$, $f_1(2) = \{10, 010, 0010, 00010, \ldots\}$, and $f_1(3) = \{11, 011, 0011, 00011, \ldots\}$, and $f_1(4) = \{100, 0100, 00100, 000100, \ldots\}$, etc.

Similarly, f_2 is a binary representation over $\{0, 1\}$ of the natural numbers if it assigns to the ith natural number the set consisting of the ith canonically smallest binary string. In such a case, $f_2(0) = \{\epsilon\}$, $f_2(1) = \{0\}$, $f_2(2) = \{1\}$, $f_2(3) = \{00\}$, $f_2(4) = \{01\}$, $f_2(5) = \{10\}$, $f_2(6) = \{11\}$, $f_2(7) = \{000\}$, $f_2(8) = \{001\}$, $f_2(9) = \{010\}, \ldots$

On the other hand, f_3 is a unary representation over $\{1\}$ of the natural numbers if it assigns to the ith natural number the set consisting of the ith alphabetically (= canonically) smallest unary string. In such a case, $f_3(0) = \{\epsilon\}$, $f_3(1) = \{1\}$, $f_3(2) = \{11\}$, $f_3(3) = \{111\}$, $f_3(4) = \{1111\}, \ldots, f_3(i) = \{1^i\}, \ldots$

The three representations f_1, f_2, and f_3 are illustrated in Figure 1.1.1. $\square$

In the rest of the book, unless otherwise is stated, the function f_1 of Example 1.1.8 is assumed to be the binary representation of the natural numbers.

1.2   Formal Languages and Grammars

The universe of strings is a useful medium for the representation of information as long as there exists a function that provides the interpretation for the information carried by the strings. An interpretation is just the inverse of the mapping that a representation provides, that is, an *interpretation* is a function g from Σ^* to D for some alphabet Σ and some set D. The string 111, for instance, can be interpreted as the number one hundred and eleven represented by a decimal string, as the number seven represented by a binary string, and as the number three represented by a unary string.

The parties communicating a piece of information do the representing and interpreting. The representation is provided by the sender, and the interpretation is provided by the receiver. The process is the same no matter whether the parties are human beings or programs. Consequently, from the point of view of the parties involved, a language can be just a collection of strings because the parties embed the representation and interpretation functions in themselves.

Languages

In general, if Σ is an alphabet and L is a subset of Σ^*, then L is said to be a *language* over Σ, or simply a language if Σ is understood. Each element of L is said to be a *sentence* or a *word* or a *string* of the language.

Example 1.2.1 $\{0, 11, 001\}$, $\{\epsilon, 10\}$, and $\{0, 1\}^*$ are subsets of $\{0, 1\}^*$, and so they are languages over the alphabet $\{0, 1\}$.

The empty set $\emptyset$ and the set $\{\epsilon\}$ are languages over every alphabet. $\emptyset$ is a language that contains no string. $\{\epsilon\}$ is a language that contains just the empty string.   □

The *union* of two languages L_1 and L_2, denoted $L_1 \cup L_2$, refers to the language that consists of all the strings that are either in L_1 or in L_2, that is, to $\{x \mid x$ is in L_1 or x is in $L_2\}$. The *intersection* of L_1 and L_2, denoted $L_1 \cap L_2$, refers to the language that consists of all the strings that are both in L_1 and L_2, that is, to $\{x \mid x$ is in L_1 and in $L_2\}$. The *complementation* of a language L over Σ, or just the complementation of L when Σ is understood, denoted $\overline{L}$, refers to the language that consists of all the strings over Σ that are not in L, that is, to $\{x \mid x$ is in Σ^* but not in $L\}$.

Example 1.2.2 Consider the languages $L_1 = \{\epsilon, 0, 1\}$ and $L_2 = \{\epsilon, 01, 11\}$. The union of these languages is $L_1 \cup L_2 = \{\epsilon, 0, 1, 01, 11\}$, their intersection is $L_1 \cap L_2 = \{\epsilon\}$, and the complementation of L_1 is $\overline{L_1} = \{00, 01, 10, 11, 000, 001, \ldots\}$.

$\emptyset \cup L = L$ for each language L. Similarly, $\emptyset \cap L = \emptyset$ for each language L. On the other hand, $\overline{\emptyset} = \Sigma^*$ and $\overline{\Sigma^*} = \emptyset$ for each alphabet Σ.   □

The *difference* of L_1 and L_2, denoted $L_1 - L_2$, refers to the language that consists of all the strings that are in L_1 but not in L_2, that is, to $\{x \mid x$ is in L_1 but not in $L_2\}$. The *cross product* of L_1 and L_2, denoted $L_1 \times L_2$, refers to the set of all the pairs (x, y) of strings such that x is in L_1 and y is in L_2, that is, to the relation $\{(x, y) \mid x$ is in L_1 and y is in $L_2\}$. The *composition* of L_1 with L_2, denoted $L_1 L_2$, refers to the language $\{xy \mid x$ is in L_1 and y is in $L_2\}$.

Example 1.2.3 If $L_1 = \{\epsilon, 1, 01, 11\}$ and $L_2 = \{1, 01, 101\}$ then $L_1 - L_2 = \{\epsilon, 11\}$ and $L_2 - L_1 = \{101\}$.

On the other hand, if $L_1 = \{\epsilon, 0, 1\}$ and $L_2 = \{01, 11\}$, then the cross product of these languages is $L_1 \times L_2 = \{(\epsilon, 01), (\epsilon, 11), (0, 01), (0, 11), (1, 01), (1, 11)\}$, and their composition is $L_1 L_2 = \{01, 11, 001, 011, 101, 111\}$.

$L - \emptyset = L$, $\emptyset - L = \emptyset$, $\emptyset L = \emptyset$, and $\{\epsilon\} L = L$ for each language L. ☐

L^i will also be used to denote the composing of i copies of a language L, where L^0 is defined as $\{\epsilon\}$. The set $L^0 \cup L^1 \cup L^2 \cup L^3 \ldots$, called the *Kleene closure* or just the *closure* of L, will be denoted by L^*. The set $L^1 \cup L^2 \cup L^3 \cdots$, called the *positive closure* of L, will be denoted by L^+.

L^i consists of those strings that can be obtained by concatenating i strings from L. L^* consists of those strings that can be obtained by concatenating an arbitrary number of strings from L.

Example 1.2.4 Consider the pair of languages $L_1 = \{\epsilon, 0, 1\}$ and $L_2 = \{01, 11\}$. For these languages $L_1^2 = \{\epsilon, 0, 1, 00, 01, 10, 11\}$, and $L_2^3 = \{010101, 010111, 011101, 011111, 110101, 110111, 111101, 111111\}$. In addition, ϵ is in L_1^*, in L_1^+, and in L_2^* but not in L_2^+. ☐

The operations above apply in a similar way to relations in $\Sigma^* \times \Delta^*$, when Σ and Δ are alphabets. Specifically, the *union* of the relations R_1 and R_2, denoted $R_1 \cup R_2$, is the relation $\{(x, y) \mid (x, y)$ is in R_1 or in $R_2\}$. The *intersection* of R_1 and R_2, denoted $R_1 \cap R_2$, is the relation $\{(x, y) \mid (x, y)$ is in R_1 and in $R_2\}$. The *composition* of R_1 with R_2, denoted $R_1 R_2$, is the relation $\{(x_1 x_2, y_1 y_2) \mid (x_1, y_1)$ is in R_1 and (x_2, y_2) is in $R_2\}$.

Example 1.2.5 Consider the relations $R_1 = \{(\epsilon, 0), (10, 1)\}$ and $R_2 = \{(1, \epsilon), (0, 01)\}$. For these relations $R_1 \cup R_2 = \{(\epsilon, 0), (10, 1), (1, \epsilon), (0, 01)\}$, $R_1 \cap R_2 = \emptyset$, $R_1 R_2 = \{(1, 0), (0, 001), (101, 1), (100, 101)\}$, and $R_2 R_1 = \{(1, 0), (110, 1), (0, 010), (010, 011)\}$. ☐

The *complementation* of a relation R in $\Sigma^* \times \Delta^*$, or just the complementation of R when Σ and Δ are understood, denoted $\overline{R}$, is the relation $\{(x, y) \mid (x, y)$ is in $\Sigma^* \times \Delta^*$ but not in $R\}$. The *inverse* of R, denoted R^{-1}, is the relation $\{(y, x) \mid (x, y)$ is in $R\}$. $R^0 = \{(\epsilon, \epsilon)\}$. $R^i = R^{i-1} R$ for $i \geq 1$.

Example 1.2.6 If R is the relation $\{(\epsilon, \epsilon), (\epsilon, 01)\}$, then $R^{-1} = \{(\epsilon, \epsilon), (01, \epsilon)\}$, $R^0 = \{(\epsilon, \epsilon)\}$, and $R^2 = \{(\epsilon, \epsilon), (\epsilon, 01), (\epsilon, 0101)\}$. ☐

A language that can be defined by a formal system, that is, by a system that has a finite number of axioms and a finite number of inference rules, is said to be a *formal language*.

Grammars

It is often convenient to specify languages in terms of grammars. The advantage in doing so arises mainly from the usage of a small number of rules for describing a language with a large number of sentences. For instance, the possibility that an English sentence consists of a subject phrase followed by a predicate phrase can be expressed by a grammatical rule of the form $<sentence> \rightarrow <subject><predicate>$. (The names in angular brackets are assumed to belong to the grammar metalanguage.) Similarly, the possibility that the subject phrase consists of a noun phrase can be expressed by a grammatical rule of the form $<subject> \rightarrow <noun>$. In a similar manner it can also be deduced that "Mary sang a song" is a possible sentence in the language described by the following grammatical rules.

$$
\begin{aligned}
<sentence> &\rightarrow <subject><predicate> \\
<subject> &\rightarrow <noun> \\
<predicate> &\rightarrow <verb><article><noun> \\
<noun> &\rightarrow <name> \\
<noun> &\rightarrow <string> \\
<name> &\rightarrow <u\_character><string> \\
<string> &\rightarrow <string><character> \\
<string> &\rightarrow <character> \\
<character> &\rightarrow a \\
&\ \ \vdots \\
<character> &\rightarrow z \\
<u\_character> &\rightarrow A \\
&\ \ \vdots \\
<u\_character> &\rightarrow Z \\
<verb> &\rightarrow sang \\
<article> &\rightarrow a
\end{aligned}
$$

The grammatical rules above also allow English sentences of the form "Mary sang a song" for other names besides Mary. On the other hand, the rules imply non-English sentences like "Mary sang a Mary," and do not allow English sentences like "Mary read a song." Therefore, the set of grammatical rules above consists of an incomplete grammatical system for specifying the English language.

For the investigation conducted here it is sufficient to consider only grammars that consist of finite sets of grammatical rules of the previous form. Such grammars are called Type 0 grammars, or phrase structure grammars, and the formal languages that they generate are called Type 0 languages.

Strictly speaking, each *Type 0 grammar G* is defined as a mathematical system consisting of a quadruple $<N, \Sigma, P, S>$, where

N is an alphabet, whose elements are called *nonterminal* symbols.

Σ is an alphabet disjoint from N, whose elements are called *terminal* symbols.

P is a relation of finite cardinality on $(N \cup \Sigma)^*$, whose elements are called *production rules*. Moreover, each production rule (α, β) in P, denoted $\alpha \rightarrow \beta$, must have at least one nonterminal symbol in α. In each such production rule, α is said to be the *left-hand side* of the production rule, and β is said to be the *right-hand side* of the production rule.

S is a symbol in N called the *start*, or *sentence*, symbol.

Example 1.2.7 $<N, \Sigma, P, S>$ is a Type 0 grammar if $N = \{S\}$, $\Sigma = \{a, b\}$, and $P = \{S \rightarrow aSb, S \rightarrow \epsilon\}$. By definition, the grammar has a single nonterminal symbol S, two terminal symbols a and b, and two production rules $S \rightarrow aSb$ and $S \rightarrow \epsilon$. Both production rules have a left-hand side that consists only of the nonterminal symbol S. The right-hand side of the first production rule is aSb, and the right-hand side of the second production rule is ϵ.

$<N_1, \Sigma_1, P_1, S>$ is not a grammar if N_1 is the set of natural numbers, or Σ_1 is empty, because N_1 and Σ_1 have to be alphabets.

If $N_2 = \{S\}$, $\Sigma_2 = \{a, b\}$, and $P_2 = \{S \rightarrow aSb, S \rightarrow \epsilon, ab \rightarrow S\}$ then $<N_2, \Sigma_2, P_2, S>$ is not a grammar, because $ab \rightarrow S$ does not satisfy the requirement that each production rule must contain at least one nonterminal symbol on the left-hand side. $\square$

In general, the nonterminal symbols of a Type 0 grammar are denoted by S and by the first uppercase letters in the English alphabet A, B, C, D, and E. The start symbol is denoted by S. The terminal symbols are denoted by digits and by the first lowercase letters in the English alphabet a, b, c, d, and e. Symbols of insignificant nature are denoted by X, Y, and Z. Strings of terminal symbols are denoted by the last lowercase English characters u, v, w, x, y, and z. Strings that may consist of both terminal and nonterminal symbols are denoted by the first lowercase Greek symbols α, β, and γ. In addition, for convenience, sequences of production rules of the form

$$
\begin{aligned}
\alpha &\rightarrow \beta_1 \\
\alpha &\rightarrow \beta_2 \\
&\vdots \\
\alpha &\rightarrow \beta_n
\end{aligned}
$$

are denoted as

$$
\begin{aligned}
\alpha &\rightarrow \beta_1 \\
&\rightarrow \beta_2 \\
&\vdots \\
&\rightarrow \beta_n
\end{aligned}
$$

Example 1.2.8 $<N, \Sigma, P, S>$ is a Type 0 grammar if $N = \{S, B\}$, $\Sigma = \{a, b, c\}$, and P consists of the following production rules.

$$
\begin{aligned}
S &\rightarrow aBSc \\
&\rightarrow abc \\
&\rightarrow \epsilon \\
Ba &\rightarrow aB \\
Bb &\rightarrow bb
\end{aligned}
$$

The nonterminal symbol S is the left-hand side of the first three production rules. Ba is the left-hand side of the fourth production rule. Bb is the left-hand side of the fifth production rule.

The right-hand side $aBSc$ of the first production rule contains both terminal and nonterminal symbols. The right-hand side abc of the second production rule contains only terminal symbols. Except for the trivial case of the right-hand side ϵ of the third production rule, none of the right-hand sides of the production rules consists only of nonterminal symbols, even though they are allowed to be of such a form.   □

Derivations

Grammars generate languages by repeatedly modifying given strings. Each modification of a string is in accordance with some production rule of the grammar in question $G = <N, \Sigma, P, S>$. A modification to a string γ in accordance with production rule $\alpha \rightarrow \beta$ is derived by replacing a substring α in γ by β.

In general, a string γ is said to directly derive a string γ' if γ' can be obtained from γ by a single modification. Similarly, a string γ is said to derive γ' if γ' can be obtained from γ by a sequence of an arbitrary number of direct derivations.

Formally, a string γ is said to *directly derive* in G a string γ', denoted $\gamma \Rightarrow_G \gamma'$, if γ' can be obtained from γ by replacing a substring α with β, where $\alpha \rightarrow \beta$ is a production rule in G. That is, if $\gamma = \rho\alpha\delta$ and $\gamma' = \rho\beta\delta$ for some strings α, β, ρ, and δ such that $\alpha \rightarrow \beta$ is a production rule in G.

Example 1.2.9 If G is the grammar $<N, \Sigma, P, S>$ in Example 1.2.7, then both ϵ and aSb are directly derivable from S. Similarly, both ab and a^2Sb^2 are directly derivable from aSb. ϵ is directly derivable from S, and ab is directly derivable from aSb, in accordance with the production rule $S \rightarrow \epsilon$. aSb is directly derivable from S, and a^2Sb^2 is directly derivable from aSb, in accordance with the production rule $S \rightarrow aSb$.

On the other hand, if G is the grammar $<N, \Sigma, P, S>$ of Example 1.2.8, then $aBaBabccc \Rightarrow_G aaBBabccc$ and $aBaBabccc \Rightarrow_G aBaaBbccc$ in accordance with the production rule $Ba \rightarrow aB$. Moreover, no other string is directly derivable from $aBaBabccc$ in G.   □

γ is said to *derive* γ' in G, denoted $\gamma \Rightarrow_G^* \gamma'$, if $\gamma_0 \Rightarrow_G \cdots \Rightarrow_G \gamma'_n$ for some $\gamma_0, \ldots, \gamma_n$ such that $\gamma_0 = \gamma$ and $\gamma_n = \gamma'$. In such a case, the sequence $\gamma_0 \Rightarrow_G \cdots \Rightarrow_G \gamma_n$ is said to be a *derivation* of γ from γ' whose *length* is equal to n. $\gamma_0, \ldots, \gamma_n$ are said to be *sentential forms*, if $\gamma_0 = S$. A sentential form that contains no terminal symbols is said to be a *sentence*.

Example 1.2.10 If G is the grammar of Example 1.2.7, then a^4Sb^4 has a derivation from S. The derivation $S \Rightarrow_G^* a^4Sb^4$ has length 4, and it has the form $S \Rightarrow_G aSb \Rightarrow_G a^2Sb^2 \Rightarrow_G a^3Sb^3 \Rightarrow_G a^4Sb^4$.   □

A string is assumed to be in the language that the grammar G generates if and only if it is a string of terminal symbols that is derivable from the starting symbol. The language that is *generated* by G, denoted $L(G)$, is the set of all the strings of terminal symbols that can be derived from the start symbol, that is, the set $\{\, w \mid w$ is in Σ^*, and $S \Rightarrow_G^* w \,\}$. Each string in the language $L(G)$ is said to be generated by G.

Example 1.2.11 Consider the grammar G of Example 1.2.7. ϵ is in the language that G generates because of the existence of the derivation $S \Rightarrow_G \epsilon$. ab is in the language that G generates, because of the existence of the derivation $S \Rightarrow_G aSb \Rightarrow_G ab$. $a^2 b^2$ is in the language that G generates, because of the existence of the derivation $S \Rightarrow_G aSb \Rightarrow_G a^2Sb^2 \Rightarrow_G a^2b^2$.

The language $L(G)$ that G generates consists of all the strings of the form $a \cdots ab \cdots b$ in which the number of a's is equal to the number of b's, that is, $L(G) = \{\, a^i b^i \mid i$ is a natural number $\,\}$.

aSb is not in $L(G)$ because it contains a nonterminal symbol. a^2b is not in $L(G)$ because it cannot be derived from S in G.   □

In what follows, the notations $\gamma \Rightarrow \gamma'$ and $\gamma \Rightarrow^* \gamma'$ are used instead of $\gamma \Rightarrow_G \gamma'$ and $\gamma \Rightarrow_G^* \gamma'$, respectively, when G is understood. In addition, Type 0 grammars are referred to simply as grammars, and Type 0 languages are referred to simply as languages, when no confusion arises.

Example 1.2.12 If G is the grammar of Example 1.2.8, then the following is a derivation for $a^3 b^3 c^3$. The underlined and the overlined substrings are the left- and the right-hand sides, respectively, of those production rules used in the derivation.

$$
\begin{array}{rl}
\underline{S} & \Rightarrow \quad \overline{aB\underline{S}c} \\
& \Rightarrow \quad aBa\overline{B\underline{S}}cc \\
& \Rightarrow \quad aBa\underline{B}\overline{abc}cc \\
& \Rightarrow \quad aB\underline{aaB}\overline{b}ccc \\
& \Rightarrow \quad a\underline{B}aa\overline{bb}ccc \\
& \Rightarrow \quad aa\overline{B}abbccc \\
& \Rightarrow \quad aaa\overline{B}bbccc \\
& \Rightarrow \quad aaa\overline{bbb}ccc
\end{array}
$$

The language generated by the grammar G consists of all the strings of the form $a \cdots ab \cdots bc \cdots c$ in which there are equal numbers of a's, b's, and c's, that is, $L(G) = \{\, a^i b^i c^i \mid i$ is a natural number $\,\}$.

The first two production rules in G are used for generating sentential forms that have the pattern $aBaB \cdots aBabc \cdots c$. In each such sentential form the number of a's is equal to the number of c's and is greater by 1 than the number of B's.

The production rule $Ba \rightarrow aB$ is used for transporting the B's rightward in the sentential forms. The production rule $Bb \rightarrow bb$ is used for replacing the B's by b's, upon reaching their appropriate positions.   □

Derivation Graphs

Derivations of sentential forms in Type 0 grammars can be displayed by *derivation*, or *parse*, *graphs*. Each derivation graph is a rooted, ordered, acyclic, directed graph whose nodes are labeled. The label of each node is either a nonterminal symbol, a terminal symbol, or an empty string. The derivation graph that corresponds to a derivation $S \Rightarrow \gamma_1 \Rightarrow \cdots \Rightarrow \gamma_n$ is defined inductively in the following manner.

   a. The derivation graph D_0 that corresponds to S consists of a single node labeled by the start symbol S.

   b. If $\alpha \to \beta$ is the production rule used in the direct derivation $\gamma_i \Rightarrow \gamma_{i+1}$, $0 \le i < n$ and $\gamma_0 = S$, then the derivation graph D_{i+1} that corresponds to $\gamma_0 \Rightarrow \cdots \Rightarrow \gamma_{i+1}$ is obtained from D_i by the addition of $max(|\beta|, 1)$ new nodes. The new nodes are labeled by the characters of β, and are assigned as common successors to each of the nodes in D_i that corresponds to a character in α. Consequently, the leaves of the derivation graph D_{i+1} are labeled by γ_{i+1}.

Derivation graphs are also called *derivation trees* or *parse trees* when the directed graphs are trees.

Example 1.2.13 Figure 1.2.1(a) provides examples of derivation trees for derivations in the grammar of Example 1.2.7. Figure 1.2.1(b) provides examples of derivation graphs for derivations in the grammar of Example 1.2.8.   □

Leftmost Derivations

A derivation $\gamma_0 \Rightarrow \cdots \Rightarrow \gamma_n$ is said to be a *leftmost derivation* if α_1 is replaced before α_2 in the derivation whenever the following two conditions hold.

   a. α_1 appears to the left of α_2 in γ_i, $0 \le i < n$.

   b. α_1 and α_2 are replaced during the derivation in accordance with some production rules of the form $\alpha_1 \to \beta_1$ and $\alpha_2 \to \beta_2$, respectively.

Example 1.2.14 The derivation graph in Figure 1.2.2 indicates the order in which the production rules are used in the derivation of $a^3b^3c^3$ in Example 1.2.12. The substring $\alpha_1 = aB$ that is replaced in the seventh step of the derivation is in the same sentential form as the substring $\alpha_2 = Bb$ that is replaced in the sixth step of the derivation. The derivation is not a leftmost derivation because α_1 appears to the left of α_2 while it is being replaced after α_2.

On the other hand, the following derivation is a leftmost derivation for $a^3b^3c^3$ in G. The order in which the production rules are used is similar to that indicated in Figure 1.2.2. The only difference is that the indices 6 and 7 should be interchanged.

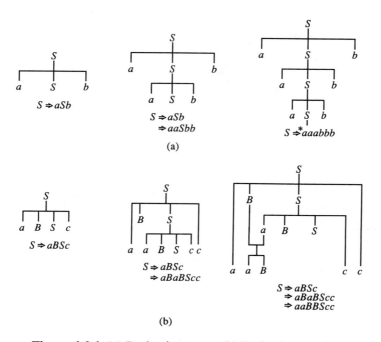

Figure 1.2.1 (a) Derivation trees. (b) Derivation graphs.

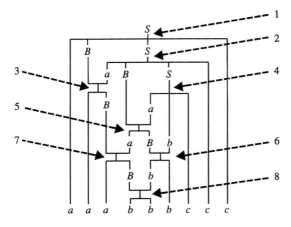

Figure 1.2.2 A derivation graph with ordering of the usage of production rules indicated with arrows.

$$
\begin{aligned}
\underline{S} &\Rightarrow \overline{a B \underline{S} c} \\
&\Rightarrow a \underline{Ba} B \underline{S} cc \\
&\Rightarrow a \overline{aa} B B \underline{S} cc \\
&\Rightarrow aa B \underline{B a} b ccc \\
&\Rightarrow aa \underline{Ba} \overline{B} b ccc \\
&\Rightarrow aaa \overline{B} B b ccc \\
&\Rightarrow aaa B \underline{\overline{bb}} b ccc \\
&\Rightarrow aaa \overline{b} b b ccc
\end{aligned}
$$

□

Hierarchy of Grammars

The following classes of grammars are obtained by gradually increasing the restrictions that the production rules have to obey.

A *Type* 1 *grammar* is a Type 0 grammar $<N, \Sigma, P, S>$ that satisfies the following two conditions.

   a. Each production rule $\alpha \to \beta$ in P satisfies $|\alpha| \leq |\beta|$ if it is not of the form $S \to \epsilon$.

   b. If $S \to \epsilon$ is in P, then S does not appear in the right-hand side of any production rule.

A language is said to be a *Type* 1 *language* if there exists a Type 1 grammar that generates the language.

Example 1.2.15 The grammar of Example 1.2.8 is not a Type 1 grammar, because it does not satisfy condition (b). The grammar can be modified to be of Type 1 by replacing its production rules with the following ones. E is assumed to be a new nonterminal symbol.

$$
\begin{aligned}
S &\to E \\
&\to \epsilon \\
E &\to a B E c \\
&\to abc \\
Ba &\to a B \\
Bb &\to bb
\end{aligned}
$$

An addition to the modified grammar of a production rule of the form $Bb \to b$ will result in a non-Type 1 grammar, because of a violation to condition (a).   □

A *Type* 2 *grammar* is a Type 1 grammar in which each production rule $\alpha \to \beta$ satisfies $|\alpha| = 1$, that is, α is a nonterminal symbol. A language is said to be a *Type* 2 *language* if there exists a Type 2 grammar that generates the language.

Example 1.2.16 The grammar of Example 1.2.7 is not a Type 1 grammar, and therefore also not a Type 2 grammar. The grammar can be modified to be a Type 2 grammar, by replacing its production rules with the following ones. E is assumed to be a new nonterminal symbol.

$$
\begin{aligned}
S &\rightarrow \epsilon \\
&\rightarrow E \\
E &\rightarrow aEb \\
&\rightarrow ab
\end{aligned}
$$

An addition of a production rule of the form $aE \rightarrow EaE$ to the grammar will result in a non-Type 2 grammar.   □

A *Type 3 grammar* is a Type 2 grammar $<N, \Sigma, P, S>$ in which each of the production rules $\alpha \rightarrow \beta$, which is not of the form $S \rightarrow \epsilon$, satisfies one of the following conditions.

a. β is a terminal symbol.

b. β is a terminal symbol followed by a nonterminal symbol.

A language is said to be a *Type 3 language* if there exists a Type 3 grammar that generates the language.

Example 1.2.17 The grammar $<N, \Sigma, P, S>$, which has the following production rules, is a Type 3.

$$
\begin{aligned}
S &\rightarrow \epsilon \\
&\rightarrow aA \\
&\rightarrow bB \\
&\rightarrow b \\
A &\rightarrow bB \\
&\rightarrow b \\
B &\rightarrow aA \\
&\rightarrow bB \\
&\rightarrow b
\end{aligned}
$$

An addition of a production rule of the form $A \rightarrow Ba$, or of the form $B \rightarrow bb$, to the grammar will result in a non-Type 3 grammar.   □

Figure 1.2.3 illustrates the hierarchy of the different types of grammars.

1.3 Programs

Our deep dependency on the processing of information brought about the deployment of programs in an ever increasing array of applications. Programs can be found at home, at work, and in businesses, libraries, hospitals, and schools. They

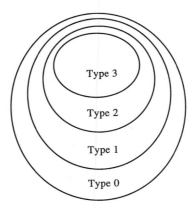

Figure 1.2.3 Hierarchy of grammars.

are used for learning, playing games, typesetting, directing telephone calls, providing medical diagnostics, forecasting weather, flying airplanes, and for many other purposes.

To facilitate the task of writing programs for the multitude of different applications, numerous programming languages have been developed. The diversity of programming languages reflects the different interpretations that can be given to information. However, from the perspective of their power to express computations, there is very little difference among them. Consequently, different programming languages can be used in the study of programs.

The study of programs can benefit, however, from fixing the programming language in use. This enables a unified discussion about programs. The choice, however, must be for a language that is general enough to be relevant to all programs but primitive enough to simplify the discussion.

Choice of a Programming Language

Here, a *program* is defined as a finite sequence of instructions over some domain D. The domain D, called the *domain of the variables*, is assumed to be a set of elements with a distinguished element, called the *initial value of the variables*. Each of the elements in D is assumed to be a possible assignment of a value to the variables of the program. The sequence of instructions is assumed to consist of instructions of the following form.

a. Read instructions of the form

$$\textbf{read } x$$

where x is a variable.

b. Write instructions of the form

$$\textbf{write } x$$

where x is a variable.

c. Deterministic assignment instructions of the form

$$y := f(x_1, \ldots, x_m)$$

where $x_1, \ldots, x_m$, and y are variables, and f is a function from D^m to D.

d. Conditional if instructions of the form

if $Q(x_1, \ldots, x_m)$ **then** I

where I is an instruction, $x_1, \ldots, x_m$ are variables, and Q is a predicate from D^m to $\{false, true\}$.

e. Deterministic looping instructions of the form

do
$$\alpha$$
until $Q(x_1, \ldots, x_m)$

where α is a nonempty sequence of instructions, $x_1, \ldots, x_m$ are variables, and Q is a predicate from D^m to $\{false, true\}$.

f. Conditional accept instructions of the form

if *eof* **then accept**

g. Reject instructions of the form

reject

h. Nondeterministic assignment instructions of the form

$$x := ?$$

where x is a variable.

i. Nondeterministic looping instructions of the form

do
$$\alpha_1$$
or
$$\alpha_2$$
or
$$\vdots$$
or
$$\alpha_k$$
until $Q(x_1, \ldots, x_m)$

where $k \geq 2$, each of $\alpha_1, \ldots, \alpha_k$ is a nonempty sequence of instructions, $x_1, \ldots, x_m$ are variables, and Q is a predicate from D^m to $\{false, true\}$.

In each program the domain D of the variables is assumed to have a representation over some alphabet. For instance, D can be the set of natural numbers, the set of integers, and any finite set of elements. The functions f and predicates Q are assumed to be from a given "built-in" set of computable functions and predicates (see Section 1.4 and Church's thesis in Section 4.1).

```
read x
y := 0
z := 1
do                                      do
    y := y + 1                              read x
    z := z + 1                          or
until z = x                                 y := ?
read y                                      write y
if eof then accept                      until y = x
reject                                  if eof then accept
```

(a)   (b)

Figure 1.3.1 (a) A deterministic program. (b) A nondeterministic program.

In what follows, the domains of the variables will not be explicitly noted when their nature is of little significance. In addition, expressions in infix notations will be used for specifying functions and predicates.

Programs without nondeterministic instructions are called *deterministic* programs, and programs with nondeterministic instructions are called *nondeterministic* programs.

Example 1.3.1 The program P_1 in Figure 1.3.1(a) is an example of a deterministic program, and the program P_2 in Figure 1.3.1(b) is an example of a nondeterministic program. The set of natural numbers is assumed for the domains of the variables, with 0 as initial value.

The program P_1 uses three variables, namely, x, y, and z. There are two functions in this program. The constant function $f_1() = 0$, and the unary function $f_2(n) = n+1$ of addition by one. The looping instruction uses the binary predicate of equality.

The program P_2 uses two nondeterministic instructions. One of the nondeterministic instructions is an assignment instruction of the form "$y := ?$"; the other is a looping instruction of the form "**do** $\cdots$ **or** $\cdots$ **until** $\cdots$"   □

An *input* of a given program is a sequence of elements from the domain of the variables of the program. Each element in an input of a program is called an *input value*.

Example 1.3.2 The programs of Example 1.3.1 (see Figure 1.3.1) can have any input that is a finite sequence of natural numbers. An input of the form "$1, 2, 3, 4$" consists of four input values, and an input of the form " " contains no input value.

The sequence "$1, 2, 3, \ldots$" cannot be an input for the programs because it is not a finite sequence.   □

An *execution sequence* of a given program is an execution on a given input of the instructions according to their semantics. The instructions are executed consecutively, starting with the first instruction. The variables initially hold the initial value of the variables.

Figure 1.3.2 Two deterministic programs.

Deterministic Programs

Deterministic programs have the property that no matter how many times they are executed on a given input, the executions are always in exactly the same manner. Each instruction of a deterministic program fully specifies the operations to be performed. In contrast, nondeterministic instructions provide only partial specifications for the actions.

An execution of a read instruction **read** x reads the next input value to x. An execution of a write instruction **write** x writes the value of x.

The deterministic assignment instructions and the conditional if instructions have the conventional semantics.

An execution of a deterministic looping instruction **do** α **until** $Q(x_1, \ldots, x_m)$ consists of repeatedly executing α and checking the value of $Q(x_1, \ldots, x_m)$. The execution of the looping instruction is terminated upon detecting that the predicate $Q(x_1, \ldots, x_m)$ has the value *true*. If $Q(x_1, \ldots, x_m)$ is the constant *true*, then only one iteration is executed. On the other hand, if $Q(x_1, \ldots, x_m)$ is the constant *false*, then the looping goes on forever, unless the execution terminates in α.

A conditional accept instruction causes an execution sequence to halt if executed after all the input is consumed, that is, after reaching the end of input file (*eof* for short). Otherwise the execution of the instruction causes the execution sequence to continue at the code following the instruction. Similarly, an execution sequence also halts upon executing a reject instruction, trying to read beyond the end of the input, trying to transfer the control beyond the end of the program, or trying to compute a value not in the domain of the variables (e.g., trying to divide by 0).

Example 1.3.3 Consider the two programs in Figure 1.3.2. Assume that the programs have the set of integers for the domains of their variables, with 0 as initial value.

For each input the program in Figure 1.3.2(a) has one execution sequence. In each execution sequence the program provides an output that is equal to the input. All the execution sequences of the program terminate due to the execution of the conditional accept instruction.

On input "1, 2" the execution sequence repeatedly executes for three times the body of the deterministic looping instruction. During the first iteration, the execution sequence determines that the predicate *eof* has the value *false*. Consequently, the execution sequence ignores the accept command and continues by reading the value 1 and writing it out. During the second iteration the execution sequence verifies again that the end of the input has not been reached yet, and then the execution sequence reads the input value 2 and writes it out. During the third iteration, the execution sequence terminates due to the accept command, after determining a *true* value for the predicate *eof* .

The execution sequences of the program in Figure 1.3.2(b) halt due to the conditional accept instruction, only on inputs that end with a negative value and have no negative values elsewhere (e.g., the input "$1, 2, -3$"). On inputs that contain no negative values at all, the execution sequences of the program halt due to trying to read beyond the end of the input (e.g., on input "$1, 2, 3$"). On inputs that have negative values before their end, the execution sequences of the program halt due to the transfer of control beyond the end of the program (e.g., on input "$-1, 2, -3$").   □

Intuitively, an **accept** can be viewed as a halt command that signals a successful completion of a program execution, where the **accept** can be executed only after the end of the input is reached. Similarly, a **reject** can be viewed as a halt instruction that signals an unsuccessful completion of a program execution.

The requirement that the accept commands be executed only after reading all the input values should cause no problem, because each program can be modified to satisfy this condition. Moreover, such a constraint seems to be natural, because it forces each program to check all its input values before signaling a success by an accept command. Similarly, the requirement that an execution sequence must halt upon trying to read beyond the end of an input seems to be natural. It should not matter whether the reading is due to a read instruction or to checking for the *eof* predicate.

It should be noted that the predicates $Q(x_1, \ldots, x_m)$ in the conditional if instructions and in the looping instructions cannot be of the form *eof* . The predicates are defined just in terms of the values of the variables $x_1, \ldots, x_m$, not in terms of the input.

Computations

Programs use finite sequences of instructions for describing sets of infinite numbers of computations. The descriptions of the computations are obtained by "unrolling" the sequences of instructions into execution sequences. In the case of deterministic programs, each execution sequence provides a description for a computation. On the other hand, as it will be seen below, in the case of nondeterministic programs some execution sequences might be considered as computations, whereas others might be considered noncomputations. To delineate this distinction we need the following definitions.

An execution sequence is said to be an *accepting computation* if it terminates due to an accept command. An execution sequence is said to be a *nonaccepting computation* or a *rejecting computation* if it is on input that has no accepting computations. An execution sequence is said to be a *computation* if it is an accepting computation or a nonaccepting computation.

```
read value
do
  write value
  value := value − 2
until value = 0
if eof then accept
```

Figure 1.3.3 A deterministic program.

A computation is said to be a *halting computation* if it is finite.

Example 1.3.4 Consider the program in Figure 1.3.3. Assume that the domain of the variables is the set of integers, with 0 as initial value.

On an input that consists of a single, even, positive integer, the program has an execution sequence that is an accepting computation (e.g., on input "4").

On an input that consists of more than one value and that starts with an even positive integer, the program has a halting execution sequence that is a nonaccepting computation (e.g., on input "4, 3, 2").

On the rest of the inputs the program has nonhalting execution sequences that are nonaccepting computations (e.g., on input "1"). □

An input is said to be *accepted*, or *recognized*, by a program if the program has an accepting computation on such an input. Otherwise the input is said to be *not accepted*, or *rejected*, by the program.

A program is said to have an *output y* on input *x* if it has an accepting computation on *x* with output *y*. The outputs of the nonaccepting computations are considered to be undefined, even though such computations may execute write instructions.

Example 1.3.5 The program in Example 1.3.4 (see Figure 1.3.3) accepts the inputs "2", "4", "6", ... On input "6" the program has the output "6, 4, 2", and on input "2" the program has the output "2".

The program does not accept the inputs "0", "1", and "4, 2". For these inputs the program has no output, that is, the output is undefined. □

A computation is said to be a *nondeterministic computation* if it involves the execution of a nondeterministic instruction. Otherwise the computation is said to be a *deterministic computation.*

Nondeterministic Programs

Different objectives create the need for nondeterministic instructions in programming languages. One of the objectives is to allow the programs to deal with problems that may have more than one solution. In such a case, nondeterministic instructions provide a natural method of selection (see, e.g., Example 1.3.6 below). Another objective is to simplify the task of programming (see, e.g., Example 1.3.9

```
counter := 0
/* Choose five input values. */
do
    read value
or
    read value
    write value
    counter := counter + 1
until counter = 5
/* Read the remainder of the input. */
do
    if eof then accept
    read value
until false
```

Figure 1.3.4 A nondeterministic program that chooses five input values.

below). Still another objective is to provide tools for identifying difficult problems (see Chapter 5) and for studying restricted classes of programs (see Chapter 2 and Chapter 3).

Implementation considerations should not bother the reader at this point. After all, one usually learns the semantics of new programming languages before learning, if one ever does, the implementation of such languages. Later on it will be shown how a nondeterministic program can be translated into a deterministic program that computes a related function (see Section 4.3).

Nondeterministic instructions are essentially instructions that can choose between some given options. Although one is often required to make choices in everyday life, the use of such instructions might seem strange within the context of programs.

The semantics of a nondeterministic looping instruction of the form **do** α_1 **or** α_2 **or** $\cdots$ **or** α_k **until** $Q(x_1, \ldots, x_m)$, are similar to those of a deterministic looping instruction of the form **do** α **until** $Q(x_1, \ldots, x_m)$. The only difference is that in the deterministic case a fixed code segment α is executed in each iteration, whereas in the nondeterministic case an arbitrary code segment from $\alpha_1, \ldots, \alpha_k$ is executed in each iteration. The choice of a code segment can differ from one iteration to another.

Example 1.3.6 The program in Figure 1.3.4 is nondeterministic. The set of natural numbers is assumed to be the domain of the variables, with 0 as initial value. Parenthetical remarks are enclosed between /* and */.

The program on input "1, 2, 3, 4, 5, 6" has an execution sequence of the following form. The execution sequence starts with an iteration of the nondeterministic looping instruction in which the first code segment is chosen. The execution of the code segment consists of reading the input value 1, while writing nothing and leaving `counter` with the value of 0. Then the execution sequence continues with five additional iterations of the nondeterministic looping instruction. In each of the additional iterations, the second code segment is chosen. Each execution of the second code segment reads an input value, outputs the value that has been read, and increases the value of `counter` by 1. When `counter` reaches the value of 5, the execution sequence exits the first looping instruction. During the first iteration of the second looping instruction, the execution sequence halts due to the execution of the conditional accept instruction. The execution sequence is an accepting computation with output "2, 3, 4, 5, 6".

The program on input "1, 2, 3, 4, 5, 6" has four additional execution sequences similar to the one above. The only difference is that the additional execution sequences, instead of ignoring the input value 1, ignore the input values 2, 3, 4, and 5, respectively. An execution sequence ignores an input value i by choosing to read the value in the first code segment of the nondeterministic looping instruction. The additional execution sequences are accepting computations with outputs "1, 3, 4, 5, 6", "1, 2, 4, 5, 6", "1, 2, 3, 5, 6", and "1, 2, 3, 4, 6", respectively.

The program on input "1, 2, 3, 4, 5, 6" also has an accepting computation of the following form. The computation starts with five iterations of the first looping instruction. In each of these iterations the second code segment of the nondeterministic looping instruction is executed. During each iteration an input value is read, that value is written into the output, and the value of `counter` is increased by 1. After five iterations of the nondeterministic looping instruction, `counter` reaches the value of 5, and the computation transfers to the deterministic looping instruction. The computation reads the input value 6 during the first iteration of the deterministic looping instruction, and terminates during the second iteration. The output of the computation is "1, 2, 3, 4, 5".

The program has $2^7 - 14$ execution sequences on input "1, 2, 3, 4, 5, 6" that are not computations. $2^6 - 7$ of these execution sequences terminate due to trying to read beyond the input end by the first read instruction, and $2^6 - 7$ of these execution sequences terminate due to trying to read beyond the input end by the second read instruction. In each of these execution sequences at least two input values are ignored by consuming the values in the first code segment of the nondeterministic looping instruction. The execution sequences differ in the input values they choose to ignore.

None of the execution sequences of the program on input "1, 2, 3, 4, 5, 6" is a nonaccepting computation, because the program has an accepting computation on such an input.

The program does not accept the input "1, 2, 3, 4". On such an input the program has 2^5 execution sequences all of which are nonaccepting computations.

The first nondeterministic looping instruction of the program is used for choosing the output values from the inputs. Upon choosing five values the execution sequences continue to consume the rest of the inputs in the second deterministic looping instruction.

On inputs with fewer than five values the execution sequences terminate in the first nondeterministic looping instruction, upon trying to read beyond the end of the inputs.

The variable `counter` records the number of values chosen at steps during

```
/* Nondeterministically find a value that
a. appears exactly once in the input, and
b. is the last value in the input.              */
last := ?
write last
/* Read the input values, until a value equal
to the one stored in last is reached.      */
do
    read value
until value = last
/* Check for end of input. */
if eof then accept
reject
```

Figure 1.3.5 A nondeterministic program for determining a single appearance of the last input value.

each execution sequence.   □

A deterministic program has exactly one execution sequence on each input, and each execution sequence of a deterministic program is a computation. On the other hand, the last example shows that a nondeterministic program might have more than one execution sequence on a given input, and that some of the execution sequences might not be computations of the program.

Nondeterministic looping instructions have been introduced to allow selections between code segments. The motivation for introducing nondeterministic assignment instructions is to allow selections between values. Specifically, a nondeterministic assignment instruction of the form $x := ?$ assigns to the variable x an arbitrary value from the domain of the variables. The choice of the assigned value can differ from one encounter of the instruction to another.

Example 1.3.7 The program in Figure 1.3.5 is nondeterministic. The set of natural numbers is assumed to be the domain of the variables. The initial value is assumed to be 0.

The program accepts a given input if and only if the last value in the input does not appear elsewhere in the input. Such a value is also the output of an accepting computation. For instance, on input "1, 2, 3" the program has the output "3". On the other hand, on input "1, 2, 1" no output is defined since the program does not accept the input.

On each input the program has infinitely many execution sequences. Each execution sequence corresponds to an assignment of a different value to last from the domain of the variables.

An assignment to last of a value that appears in the input, causes an execution sequence to exit the looping instruction upon reaching such a value in the input. With such an assignment, one of the following cases holds.

a. The execution sequence is an accepting computation if the value assigned
   to last appears only at the end of the input (e.g., an assignment of 3 to
   last on input "1, 2, 3").

b. The execution sequence is a nonaccepting computation if the value at the
   end of the input appears more than once in the input (e.g., an assignment of
   1 or 2 to last on input "1, 2, 1").

c. The execution sequence is not a computation if neither (a) nor (b) hold (e.g.,
   an assignment of 1 or 2 to last on input "1, 2, 3").

An assignment to last of a value that does not appear in the input causes an
execution sequence to terminate within the looping instruction upon trying to read
beyond the end of the input. With such an assignment, one of the following cases
hold.

a. The execution sequence is a nonaccepting computation if the value at the
   end of the input appears more than once in the input (e.g., an assignment to
   last of any natural number that differs from 1 and 2 on input "1, 2, 1").

b. The execution sequence is a nonaccepting computation if the input is empty
   (e.g., an assignment of any natural number to last on input " ").

c. The execution sequence is not a computation, if neither (a) nor (b) hold (e.g.,
   an assignment to last of any natural number that differs from 1, 2, and 3
   on input "1, 2, 3").   □

Intuitively, each program on each input defines "good" execution sequences,
and "bad" execution sequences. The good execution sequences terminate due to
the accept commands, and the bad execution sequences do not terminate due to
accept commands. The best execution sequences for a given input are the computations that the program has on the input. If there exist good execution sequences,
then the set of computations is identified with that set. Otherwise, the set of
computations is identified with the set of bad execution sequences.

The computations of a program on a given input are either all accepting computations or all nonaccepting computations. Moreover, some of the nonaccepting
computations may never halt. On inputs that are accepted the program might have
execution sequences that are not computations. On the other hand, on inputs that
are not accepted all the execution sequences are computations.

Guessing in Programs

The semantics of each program are characterized by the computations of the program. In the case of deterministic programs the semantics of a given program are
directly related to the semantics of its instructions. That is, each execution of the
instructions keeps the program within the course of a computation.

In the case of nondeterministic programs a distinction is made between execution sequences and computations, and so the semantics of a given program are

related only in a restricted manner to the semantics of its instructions. That is, although each computation of the program can be achieved by executing the instructions, some of the execution sequences do not correspond to any computation of the program. The source for this phenomenon is the ability of the nondeterministic instructions to make arbitrary choices.

Each program can be viewed as having an imaginary agent with magical power that executes the program. On a given input, the task of the imaginary agent is to follow any of the computations the program has on the input. The case of deterministic programs can be considered as a lesser and restricted example in which the agent is left with no freedom. That is, the outcome of the execution of each deterministic instruction is completely determined for the agent by the semantics of the instruction. On the other hand, when executing a nondeterministic instruction the agent must satisfy not only the local semantics of the instruction, but also the global goal of reaching an accept command whenever the global goal is achievable.

Specifically, the local semantics of a nondeterministic looping instruction of the form **do** α_1 **or** $\cdots$ **or** α_k **until** $Q(x_1, \ldots, x_m)$ require that in each iteration exactly one of the code segments $\alpha_1, \ldots, \alpha_k$ will be chosen in an arbitrary fashion by the agent. The global semantics of a program require that the choice be made for a code segment which can lead the execution sequence to halt due to a conditional accept instruction, whenever such is possible.

Similarly, the local semantics of a nondeterministic assignment instruction of the form $x := ?$ require that each assigned value of x be chosen by the agent in an arbitrary fashion from the domain of the variables. The global semantics of the program require that the choice be made for a value that halts the execution sequence due to a conditional accept instruction, whenever such is possible.

From the discussion above it follows that the approach of "first guess a solution and then check for its validity" can be used when writing a program. This approach simplifies the task of the programmer whenever checking for the validity of a solution is simpler than the derivation of the solution. In such a case, the burden of determining a correct "guess" is forced on the agent performing the computations.

It should be emphasized that from the point of view of the agent, a guess is correct if and only if it leads an execution sequence along a computation of the program. The agent knows nothing about the problem that the program intends to solve. The only thing that drives the agent is the objective of reaching the execution of a conditional accept instruction at the end of the input. Consequently, it is still up to the programmer to fully specify the constraints that must be satisfied by the correct guesses.

Example 1.3.8 The program of Figure 1.3.6 outputs a value that does not appear in the input. The program starts each computation by guessing a value and storing it in x. Then the program reads the input and checks that each of the input values differs from the value stored in x.   □

The notion of an imaginary agent provides an appealing approach for explaining nondeterminism. Nevertheless, the notion should be used with caution to avoid

```
/* Guess the output value. */
x := ?
write x
/* Check for the correctness
of the guessed value.        */
do
    if eof then accept
    read y
until y = x
```

Figure 1.3.6 A nondeterministic program that outputs a noninput value.

```
sum1 := 0
sum2 := 0
do
  if eof then accept
  do          /* Guess where the next input value belongs. */
    read x
    sum1 := sum1 + x
  or
    read x
    write x
    sum2 := sum2 + x
  until sum1 = sum2     /* Check for the correctness of the
                          guesses, with respect to the portion
                          of the input consumed so far.     */
until false
```

Figure 1.3.7 A nondeterministic program for partitioning the input into two subsets of equal sums of elements.

misconceptions. In particular, an imaginary agent should be employed only on full programs. The definitions leave no room for one imaginary agent to be employed by other agents. For instance, an imaginary agent that is given the program P in the following example cannot be employed by other agents to derive the acceptance of exactly those inputs that the agent rejects.

Example 1.3.9 Consider the program P in Figure 1.3.7. On a given input, P outputs an arbitrary choice of input values, whose sum equals the sum of the non-chosen input values. The values have the same relative ordering in the output as in the input.

For instance, on input "2, 1, 3, 4, 2" the possible outputs are "2, 1, 3", "1, 3, 2", "2, 4", and "4, 2". On the other hand, no output is defined for input "2, 3".

In each iteration of the nested looping instruction the program guesses whether

```
median := ?      /* Guess the median. */
write median
count := 0
do
   /* Find the difference between the num-
   ber of values greater than and those
   smaller than the guessed median.    */
   do
      read x
      if x > median then
         count := count + 1
      if x < median then
         count := count − 1
      if x = median then
         do
            count := count + 1
         or
            count := count − 1
         until true
   until 0 ≤ count ≤ 1
   /* The median is correct for the portion
   of the input consumed so far.        */
   if eof then accept
until false
```

Figure 1.3.8 A nondeterministic program that finds the median of the input values.

the next input value is to be among the chosen ones. If it is to be chosen then $sum2$ is increased by the magnitude of the input value. Otherwise, $sum1$ is increased by the magnitude of the input value. The program checks that the sum of the nonchosen input values equals the sum of the chosen input values by comparing the value in $sum1$ with the value in $sum2$.   □

Example 1.3.10 The program of Figure 1.3.8 outputs the median of its input values, that is, the $\lceil n/2 \rceil$th smallest input value for the case that the input consists of n values. On input "$1, 3, 2$" the program has the output "2", and on input "$2, 1, 3, 3$" the program has the output "3".

The program starts each computation by storing in median a guess for the value of the median. Then the program reads the input values and determines in count the difference between the number of input values that are greater than the one stored in median and the number of input values that are smaller than the one stored in median.

For those input values that are equal to the value stored in median, the program guesses whether they should be considered as bigger values or smaller values.

The program checks that the guesses are correct by verifying that count holds either the value 0 or the value 1.   □

The *relation computed* by a program P, denoted $R(P)$, is the set $\{(x, y) \mid P$ has an accepting computation on input x with output $y\}$. When P is a deterministic program, the relation $R(P)$ is a function.

Example 1.3.11 Consider the program P in Figure 1.3.6. Assume the set of natural numbers for the domain of the variables. The relation $R(P)$ that P computes is $\{(\alpha, a) \mid \alpha$ is a sequence of natural numbers, and a is a natural number that does not appear in $\alpha\}$.   □

The language that a program P accepts is denoted by $L(P)$ and it consists of all the inputs that P accepts.

Configurations of Programs

An execution of a program on a given input is a discrete process in which the input is consumed, an output is generated, the variables change their values, and the program traverses its instructions. Each stage in the process depends on the outcome of the previous stage, but not on the history of the stages. The outcome of each stage is a configuration of the program that indicates the instruction being reached, the values stored in the variables, the portion of the input left to be read, and the output that has been generated so far. Consequently, the process can be described by a sequence of moves between configurations of the program.

Formally, a segment of a program is said to be an *instruction segment* if it is of any of the following forms.

a. Read instruction

b. Write instruction

c. Assignment instruction

d. **if** $Q(x_1, \ldots, x_m)$ **then** portion of a conditional if instruction

e. **do** portion of a looping instruction

f. **until** $Q(x_1, \ldots, x_m)$ portion of a looping instruction

g. Conditional accept instruction

h. Reject instruction

Consider a program P that has k instruction segments, m variables, and a domain of variables that is denoted by D. A *configuration*, or *instantaneous description*, of P is a five-tuple (i, x, u, v, w), where $1 \leq i \leq k$, x is a sequence of m values from D, and u, v, and w are sequences of values from D.

Intuitively, a configuration (i, x, u, v, w) says that P is in its ith instruction segment, its jth variable contains the jth value of x, u is the portion of the input

```
last := ?                          /* I₁ */
write last                         /* I₂ */
do                                 /* I₃ */
    read value                     /* I₄ */
until value = last                 /* I₅ */
if eof then accept                 /* I₆ */
reject                             /* I₇ */
```

Figure 1.3.9 A program consisting of seven instruction segments.

that has already been read, the leftover of the input is v, and the output so far is w. (The component u is not needed in the definition of a configuration. It is inserted here for reasons of compatibility with future definitions that require such a component.)

Example 1.3.12 Consider the program in Figure 1.3.9. Assume the set of natural numbers for the domain D of the variables, with 0 as initial value. Each line I_i in the program is an instruction segment. The program has $k = 7$ instruction segments, and $m = 2$ variables.

In each configuration (i, x, u, v, w) of the program i is a natural number between 1 and 7, and x is a pair $<last, value>$ of natural numbers that corresponds to a possible assignment of $last$ and $value$ in the variables last and value, respectively. Similarly, u, v, and w are sequences of natural numbers.

The configuration $(1, <0, 0>, <>, <1, 2, 3>, <>)$ states that the program is in the first instruction segment, the variables hold the value 0, no input value has been read so far, the rest of the input is "$1, 2, 3$", and the output is empty.

The configuration $(5, <3, 2>, <1, 2>, <3>, <3>)$ states that the program is in the fifth instruction segment, the variable last holds the value 3, the variable value holds the value 2, "$1, 2$" is the portion of the input consumed so far, the rest of the input contains just the value 3, and the output so far contains only the value 3. □

A configuration (i, x, u, v, w) of P is called an *initial configuration* if $i = 1$, x is a sequence of m initial values, u is an empty sequence, and w is an empty sequence. The configuration is said to be an *accepting configuration* if the ith instruction segment of P is a conditional accept instruction and v is an empty sequence.

A direct move of P from configuration C_1 to configuration C_2 is denoted $C_1 \vdash_P C_2$, or simply $C_1 \vdash C_2$ if P is understood. A sequence of unspecified number of moves of P from configuration C_1 to configuration C_2 is denoted $C_1 \vdash_P^* C_2$, or simply $C_1 \vdash^* C_2$ if P is understood.

Example 1.3.13 Consider the program in Figure 1.3.9. On input "$1, 2, 3$" it has an accepting computation that goes through the following sequence of moves between configurations. The first configuration in the sequence is the initial configuration of the program on input "$1, 2, 3$", and the last configuration in the sequence is an accepting configuration of the program. In each configuration (i, x, u, v, w) the pair $x = <last, value>$ corresponds to the assignment of *last* and *value* in the variables `last` and `value`, respectively.

$$(1, <0, 0>, <>, <1, 2, 3>, <>) \quad \vdash \quad (2, <3, 0>, <>, <1, 2, 3>, <>)$$
$$\vdash \quad (3, <3, 0>, <>, <1, 2, 3>, <3>)$$
$$\vdash \quad (4, <3, 0>, <>, <1, 2, 3>, <3>)$$
$$\vdash \quad (5, <3, 1>, <1>, <2, 3>, <3>)$$
$$\vdash \quad (3, <3, 1>, <1>, <2, 3>, <3>)$$
$$\vdash \quad (4, <3, 1>, <1>, <2, 3>, <3>)$$
$$\vdash \quad (5, <3, 2>, <1, 2>, <3>, <3>)$$
$$\vdash \quad (3, <3, 2>, <1, 2>, <3>, <3>)$$
$$\vdash \quad (4, <3, 2>, <1, 2>, <3>, <3>)$$
$$\vdash \quad (5, <3, 3>, <1, 2, 3>, <>, <3>)$$
$$\vdash \quad (6, <3, 3>, <1, 2, 3>, <>, <3>)$$

The subcomputation

$$(1, <0, 0>, <>, <1, 2, 3>, <>) \quad \vdash^* \quad (1, <0, 0>, <>, <1, 2, 3>, <>)$$

consists of zero moves, and the subcomputation

$$(1, <0, 0>, <>, <1, 2, 3>, <>) \quad \vdash^* \quad (6, <3, 3>, <1, 2, 3>, <>, <3>)$$

consists of eleven moves. □

1.4   Problems

The first two sections of this chapter treated different aspects of information. The third section considered programs. The purpose of the rest of this chapter is to deal with the motivation for writing programs for manipulating information, that is, with problems.

Each *problem K* is a pair consisting of a set and a question, where the question can be applied to each element in the set. The set is called the *domain* of the problem, and its elements are called the *instances* of the problem.

Example 1.4.1 Consider the problem K_1 defined by the following domain and question.

Domain: $\{ <a, b> \mid a$ and b are natural numbers $\}$.

Question: What is the integer part y of a divided by b for the given instance $x = <a, b>$?

The domain of the problem contains the instances $<0, 0>$, $<5, 0>$, $<3, 8>$, $<24, 6>$, and $<27, 8>$. On the other hand, $<-5, 3>$ is not an instance of the problem.

For the instance $<27, 8>$ the problem asks what is the integer part of 27 divided by 8. Similarly, for the instance $<0, 0>$ the problem asks what is the integer part of 0 divided by 0. □

```
        read a
        read b
        ans := 0
        if a ≥ b then                               read a
           do                                       read b
              a := a - b                            do
              ans := ans + 1                           if a = b then
           until a<b                                      if eof then accept
        write ans                                     a := a - b
        if eof then accept                         until false

             (a)                                        (b)
```

Figure 1.4.1 (a) A program that partially solves the problem of dividing natural numbers. (b) A program that partially decides the problem of divisibility of natural numbers.

An answer to the question that the problem K poses for a given instance is said to be a *solution* for the problem at the given instance. The *relation induced by the problem*, denoted $R(K)$, is the set $\{ (x, y) \mid x$ is an instance of the problem, and y is a solution for the problem at $x \}$. The problem is said to be a *decision problem* if for each instance the problem has either a *yes* or a *no* solution.

Example 1.4.2 Consider the problem K_1 in Example 1.4.1. The problem has the solution 3 at instance $<27, 8>$, and an undefined solution at instance $<0, 0>$. K_1 induces the relation $R(K_1) = \{(<0, 1>, 0), (<0, 2>, 0), (<1, 1>, 1), (<0, 3>, 0), (<1, 2>, 0), (<2, 1>, 2), (<0, 3>, 0), \ldots \}$.

The problem K_1 is not a decision problem. But the problem K_2 defined by the following pair is.

Domain: $\{ <a, b> \mid a$ and b are natural numbers $\}$.

Question: Does b divide a, for the given instance $<a, b>$? □

Partial Solvability and Solvability

A program P is said to *partially solve* a given problem K if it provides the answer for each instance of the problem, that is, if $R(P) = R(K)$. If, in addition, all the computations of the program are halting computations, then the program is said to *solve* the problem.

Example 1.4.3 Consider the program P_1 in Figure 1.4.1(a). The domain of the variables is assumed to equal the set of natural numbers. The program partially solves the problem K_1 of Example 1.4.1.

On input "27, 8" the program halts in an accepting configuration with the answer 3 in the output. On input "0, 0" the program never halts, and so the program has undefined output on such an input. On input "27" and input "27, 8, 2" the program halts in rejecting configurations and does not define an output.

The program P₁ does not solve K_1 because it does not halt when the input value for b is 0. P₁ can be modified to a program P that solves K_1 by letting P check for a 0 assignment to b. □

A program is said to *partially decide* a problem if the following two conditions are satisfied.

a. The problem is a decision problem; and

b. The program accepts a given input if and only if the problem has an answer *yes* for the input, that is, the program accepts the language $\{ x \mid x$ is an instance of the problem, and the problem has the answer *yes* at $x \}$.

A program is said to *decide* a problem if it partially decides the problem and all its computations are halting computations.

Example 1.4.4 It is meaningless to talk about the partial decidability or decidability of the problem K_1 of Example 1.4.1 by a program, because the problem is not a decision problem. On the other hand, the problem K_2 of Example 1.4.2 is a decision problem. The latter problem is partially decidable by the program P₂ in Figure 1.4.1(b). □

The main difference between a program P₁ that partially solves (partially decides) a problem, and a program P₂ that solves (decides) the same problem, is that P₁ might reject an input by a nonhalting computation, whereas P₂ can reject the input only by a halting computation. (Recall that on an input that is accepted by a program, the program has only accepting computations, and all these computations are halting computations. But on an input that is not accepted the program might have more than one computation, of which some may never halt.)

The notions of partial solvability, solvability, partial decidability, and decidability of a problem by a program can be intuitively generalized in a straightforward manner by considering effective (i.e., strictly mechanical) procedures instead of programs. However, formalizing the generalizations requires that the intuitive notion of effective procedure be formalized. In any case, under such intuitively understood generalizations a problem is said to be *partially solvable, solvable, partially decidable*, and *decidable* if it can be partially solved, solved, partially decided, and decided by an effective procedure, respectively.

In what follows effective procedures will also be called *algorithms*.

Example 1.4.5 The program P₁ of Example 1.4.3 describes how the problem K_1 of Example 1.4.1 can be solved. The program P₂ of Example 1.4.4 describes how the problem K_2 of Example 1.4.2 can be solved. □

A problem is said to be *unsolvable* if no algorithm can solve it. The problem is said to be *undecidable* if it is a decision problem and no algorithm can decide

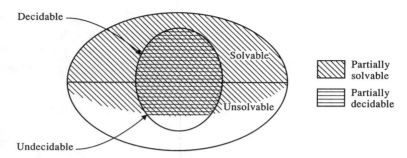

Figure 1.4.2 Classification of the set of problems.

it. The relationship between the different classes of problems is illustrated in the Venn diagram of Figure 1.4.2.

It should be noted that an unsolvable problem might be partially solvable by an algorithm that makes an exhaustive search for a solution. In such a case the solution is eventually found whenever it is defined, but the search might continue forever whenever the solution is undefined. Similarly, an undecidable problem might also be partially decidable by an algorithm that makes an exhaustive search. However, here the solution is eventually found whenever it has the value *yes*, but the search might continue forever whenever it has the value *no*.

Example 1.4.6 The empty-word membership problem for grammars is the problem consisting of the following domain and question.

Domain: $\{ G \mid G$ is a grammar $\}$.

Question: Is the empty word ϵ in $L(G)$ for the given grammar G?

It is possible to show that the problem is undecidable (e.g., see Theorem 4.6.2 and Exercise 4.5.7). On the other hand, the problem is partially decidable because given an instance $G = <N, \Sigma, P, S>$ one can exhaustively search for a derivation of the form $S = \gamma_0 \Rightarrow \gamma_1 \Rightarrow \cdots \Rightarrow \gamma_{n-1} \Rightarrow \gamma_n = \epsilon$, by considering all derivations of length n for $n = 1, 2, \ldots$ With such an algorithm the desired derivation will eventually be found if ϵ is in $L(G)$. However, if ϵ is not in $L(G)$, then the search might never terminate.

For the grammar $G = <N, \Sigma, P, S>$, whose production rules are listed below, the algorithm will proceed in the following manner.

$$
\begin{aligned}
S & \rightarrow aBS \\
  & \rightarrow Ba \\
aB & \rightarrow SB \\
BS & \rightarrow \epsilon
\end{aligned}
$$

The algorithm will start by determining the set of all the derivations $\Psi_1 = \{S \Rightarrow aBS, S \Rightarrow Ba\}$ of length $n = 1$. After determining that none of the derivations in Ψ_1 provides the empty string ϵ, the algorithm determines the set of all the derivations $\Psi_2 = \{S \Rightarrow aBS \Rightarrow aBaBS, S \Rightarrow aBS \Rightarrow aBBa, S \Rightarrow aBS \Rightarrow SBS, S \Rightarrow aBS, S \Rightarrow a\}$ of length $n = 2$. Then the algorithm continues by determining the set Ψ_3 of all the derivations of length 3, the set Ψ_4 of all the derivations of length 4, and so forth. The algorithm stops (with the answer *yes*) when, and only when, it finds a set Ψ_n of derivations of length n that includes a derivation for ϵ. Such a set Ψ_n exists for $n = 5$ because of the derivation $S \Rightarrow aBS \Rightarrow SBS \Rightarrow BaBS \Rightarrow BSBS \Rightarrow BS \Rightarrow \epsilon$.

On the other hand, for the grammar $G = <N, \Sigma, P, S>$, whose production rules are listed below, the algorithm never stops.

$$
\begin{aligned}
S &\rightarrow aSb \\
&\rightarrow aAb \\
A &\rightarrow \epsilon
\end{aligned}
$$
□

The unsolvability of a problem does not mean that a solution cannot be found at some of its instances. It just means that no algorithm can uniformly find a solution for every given instance. Consequently, an unsolvable problem might have simplified versions that are solvable. The simplifications can be in the question being asked and in the domain being considered.

Example 1.4.7 The empty-word membership problem for Type 1 grammars is the problem consisting of the following domain and question.

Domain: $\{G \mid G$ is a Type 1 grammar$\}$.

Question: Is the empty word ϵ in $L(G)$ for the given grammar G?

The problem is decidable because ϵ is in $L(G)$ for a given Type 1 grammar $G = <N, \Sigma, P, S>$ if and only if $S \rightarrow \epsilon$ is a production rule of G.   □

A function f is said to be *computable* (respectively, *partially computable*, *noncomputable*) if the problem defined by the following domain and question is solvable (respectively, partially solvable, unsolvable).

Domain: The domain of f.

Question: What is the value of $f(x)$ at the given instance x?

Problems concerning Programs

Although programs are written to solve problems, there are also interesting problems that are concerned with programs. The following are some examples of such decision problems.

Uniform halting problem for programs

Domain: Set of all programs.

Question: Does the given program halt on each of its inputs, that is, are all the computations of the program halting computations?

Halting problem for programs

Domain: $\{(P, x) \mid P$ is a program and x is an input for $P\}$.

Question: For the given instance (P, x) does P halt on x, that is, are all the computations of P on input x halting computations?

Recognition/acceptance problem for programs

Domain: $\{(P, x) \mid P$ is a program and x is an input for $P\}$.

Question: For the given instance (P, x) does P accept x?

Membership problem for programs

Domain: $\{(P, x, y) \mid P$ is a program, and x and y are sequences of values from the domain of the variables of $P\}$.

Question: Is (x, y) in the relation $R(P)$ for the given instance (P, x, y), that is, does P have an accepting computation on x with output y?

Emptiness problem for programs

Domain: Set of all programs.

Question: Does the given program accept an empty language, that is, does the program accept no input?

Ambiguity problem for programs

Domain: Set of all programs.

Question: Does the given program have two or more accepting computations that define the same output for some input?

Single-valuedness problem for programs

Domain: Set of all programs.

Question: Does the given program define a function, that is, does the given program for each input have at most one output?

Equivalence problem for programs

Domain: $\{(P_1, P_2) \mid P_1$ and P_2 are programs$\}$.

Question: Does the given pair (P_1, P_2) of programs define the same relation, that is, does $R(P_1) = R(P_2)$?

Example 1.4.8 The two programs P_1 and P of Example 1.4.3 are equivalent, but only P_2 halts on all inputs. □

The nonuniform halting problem, the unambiguity problem, the inequivalence problem, and so forth are defined similarly for programs as the uniform halting problem, the ambiguity problem, the equivalence problem, and so forth, respectively. The only difference is that the questions are phrased so that the solutions to the new problems are the complementation of the old ones, that is, *yes* becomes *no* and *no* becomes *yes*.

It turns out that nontrivial questions about programs are difficult, if not impossible, to answer. It is natural to expect these problems to become easier when the programs under consideration are "appropriately" restricted. The extent to which the programs have to be restricted, as well as the loss in their expressibility power, and the increase in the resources they require due to such restrictions, are interesting questions on their own.

Problems concerning Grammars

Some of the problems concerned with programs can in a similar way be defined also for grammars. The following are some examples of such problems.

Membership problem for grammars

  Domain: $\{ (G, x) \mid G$ is a grammar $<N, \Sigma, P, S>$ and x is a string in $\Sigma^* \}$.

  Question: Is x in $L(G)$ for the given instance (G, x)?

Emptiness problem for grammars

  Domain: $\{ G \mid G$ is a grammar $\}$.

  Question: Does the given grammar define an empty language?

Ambiguity problem for grammars

  Domain: $\{ G \mid G$ is a grammar $\}$.

  Question: Does the given grammar G have two or more different derivation graphs for some string in $L(G)$?

Equivalence problem for grammars,

  Domain: $\{ (G_1, G_2) \mid G_1$ and G_2 are grammars $\}$.

  Question: Does the given pair of grammars generate the same language?

1.5 Reducibility among Problems

A common approach in solving problems is to transform them to different problems, solve the new ones, and derive the solutions for the original problems from those for the new ones. This approach is useful when the new problems are simpler to solve, or when they already have known algorithms for solving them. A similar approach is also very useful in the classification of problems according to their complexity.

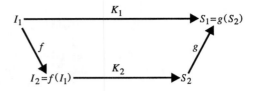

Figure 1.5.1 Reducibility from problem K_1 to problem K_2.

A problem K_1, which can be transformed to another problem K_2, is said to be reducible to the new problem. Specifically, a problem K_1 is said to be *reducible* to a problem K_2 if there exist computable total functions f and g with the following properties (see Figure 1.5.1).

If I_1 is an instance of K_1, then

  a. $I_2 = f(I_1)$ is an instance of K_2.

  b. K_1 has a solution S_1 at I_1 if and only if K_2 has a solution S_2 at $I_2 = f(I_1)$ such that $S_1 = g(S_2)$.

Example 1.5.1 Let Ψ be the set $\{ m \mid m = 2^i$ for some integer $i \}$. The problem of exponentiation of numbers from Ψ is reducible to the problem of multiplication of integer numbers. The reducibility is implied from the equalities $x^y = (2^{\log x})^y = 2^{y \cdot \log x}$, which allow the choice of $f(x, y) = (y, \log x)$ and $g(z) = 2^z$ for f and g, respectively.[1]   □

Example 1.5.2 Let $K_\emptyset$ and $K_\equiv$ be the emptiness problem and the equivalence problem for programs, respectively. Then $K_\emptyset$ is reducible to $K_\equiv$ by functions f and g of the following form. f is a function whose value at program P is the pair of programs $(\text{P}, \text{P}_\emptyset)$. $\text{P}_\emptyset$ is a program that accepts no input, for example, the program that consists only of the instruction **reject**. g is the identity function, that is, $g(yes) = yes$ and $g(no) = no$.   □

If K_1 is a problem that is reducible to a problem K_2 by total functions f and g that are computable by algorithms T_f and T_g, respectively, and K_2 is solvable by an algorithm A, then one can also get an algorithm B for solving K_1 (see Figure 1.5.2). Given an input I, the algorithm B starts by running T_f on I. Then B gives the output I' of T_f to A. Finally B gives the output S' of A to T_g, and assumes the same output S as the one obtained from T_g.

Exercises

1.1.1   a. Find all the alphabets that use only symbols from the set $\{a, b, c\}$. Which of the alphabets is unary? Which is binary?

---

[1] Throughout the text, unless otherwise is stated, *log* stands for logarithm base 2.

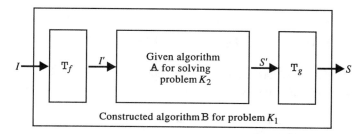

Figure 1.5.2 Reduction of problem K_1 to problem K_2.

b. Let S be a set of t symbols. How many unary alphabets can be constructed from the symbols of S? How many binary alphabets?

1.1.2 For each of the following conditions find all the strings α over the alphabet $\{a, b\}$ that satisfy the condition.

   a. No symbol is repeated in α.

   b. The length of α is 3, that is, $|\alpha| = 3$.

1.1.3 a. Find $\alpha\beta$, $\beta\alpha$, α^2, $\alpha^0\beta^2$, and $\alpha^2\beta^2\epsilon$ for the case that $\alpha = a$ and $\beta = ab$.

   b. Find all the pairs of strings α and β over the alphabet $\{a, b\}$ that satisfy $\alpha\beta = abb$.

1.1.4 Let α be the string 011.

   a. Find all the proper prefixes of α^2.

   b. Find all the substrings β of $\alpha\alpha^{\text{rev}}$ that satisfy $\beta = \beta^{\text{rev}}$.

1.1.5 How many strings of length t are in Σ^* if Σ is an alphabet of cardinality r.

1.1.6 For each of the following cases give the first 20 strings in $\{a, b, c\}^*$.

   a. $\{a, b, c\}^*$ is given in alphabetical ordering.

   b. $\{a, b, c\}^*$ is given in canonical ordering.

1.1.7 Let S be the set of all the strings over the alphabet $\{a, b, c\}$, that is, $S = \{a, b, c\}^*$. Let S_1 and S_2 be subsets of S. Which are the strings that appear both in S_1 and in S_2 in each of the following cases?

   a. S_1 contains the t alphabetically smallest strings in S, and S_2 contains all the strings in S of length t at most.

   b. S_1 contains the 127 alphabetically smallest strings in S, and S_2 contains the 127 canonically smallest strings in S.

1.1.8 Show that if Σ is an alphabet, then Σ^* has the following representations.

   a. Binary representation

b. Unary representation

1.1.9 Find a binary representation for the set of rational numbers.

1.1.10 Show that if D has a binary representation f_1, then it also has a binary representation f_2, such that $f_2(e)$ is an infinite set for each element e of D.

1.1.11 Let f_1 and f_2 be binary representations for D_1 and D_2, respectively. Find a binary representation f for each of the following sets.

    a. $D_1 \cup D_2$

    b. $D_1 \times D_2$

    c. D_1^*

1.1.12 Show that the set of real numbers does not have a binary representation.

1.2.1 Let L be the language $\{\epsilon, 0, 10\}$ over $\{0, 1\}$. Determine the following sets.

    a. $L \cup \overline{L}$

    b. $L \cap \overline{L}$

    c. $L\overline{L}$

    d. $\overline{L}L$

    e. L^2

    f. $L \times L$

1.2.2 Let $G = <N, \Sigma, P, S>$ be a grammar in which $N = \{S\}$, $\Sigma = \{a\}$, and each production rule contains at most 3 symbols. What are the possible production rules in P?

1.2.3 Let G be the grammar $<N, \Sigma, P, S>$, where $N = \{S\}$, $\Sigma = \{a, b\}$, and $P = \{S \rightarrow \epsilon, S \rightarrow aSbS\}$.

    a. Find all the strings that are directly derivable from SaS in G.

    b. Find all the derivations in G that start at S and end at ab.

    c. Find all the sentential forms of G of length 4 at most.

1.2.4 Find all the derivations of length 3 at most that start at S in the grammar $<N, \Sigma, P, S>$ whose production rules are listed below.

$$
\begin{aligned}
S &\rightarrow AS \\
aS &\rightarrow bb \\
A &\rightarrow aa
\end{aligned}
$$

1.2.5 For each of the following sets of production rules P find all the strings of length 4 or less in the language generated by the grammar $<N, \Sigma, P, S>$.

$$
\begin{aligned}
S &\rightarrow aSA \\
&\rightarrow bSB \\
&\rightarrow X \\
aA &\rightarrow Aa \\
bA &\rightarrow Ab \\
aB &\rightarrow Ba \\
bB &\rightarrow Bb \\
XA &\rightarrow Xa \\
&\rightarrow a \\
XB &\rightarrow Xb \\
&\rightarrow b
\end{aligned}
$$

$$
\begin{aligned}
S &\rightarrow aa \\
&\rightarrow bb \\
&\rightarrow aSa \\
&\rightarrow bSb \\
&\rightarrow SS
\end{aligned}
$$

(a)   (b)

1.2.6 Give two parse trees for the string $aababb$ in the grammar $G = <N, \Sigma, P, S>$, whose production rules are listed below.

$$
\begin{aligned}
S &\rightarrow b \\
&\rightarrow aA \\
&\rightarrow aS \\
A &\rightarrow Ab \\
&\rightarrow Sa \\
&\rightarrow a
\end{aligned}
$$

1.2.7 Consider the grammar $G = <N, \Sigma, P, E>$ for arithmetic expressions, where $N = \{E, T, F\}$, $\Sigma = \{+, *, (,), a\}$, and P is the set consisting of the following production rules.

$$
\begin{aligned}
E &\rightarrow E + T \\
E &\rightarrow T \\
T &\rightarrow T * F \\
&\rightarrow F \\
F &\rightarrow (E) \\
&\rightarrow a
\end{aligned}
$$

Give the derivation tree for the expression $a * (a + a)$ in G.

1.2.8 Let $G = <N, \Sigma, P, S>$ be the grammar with the following production rules. Find the derivation graph for the string $a^3 b^3 c^3$ in G.

$$
\begin{aligned}
S &\rightarrow aSBc \\
&\rightarrow \epsilon \\
cB &\rightarrow Bc \\
aB &\rightarrow ab \\
bB &\rightarrow bb
\end{aligned}
$$

1.2.9 For each of the following languages give a grammar that generates the language.

    a. $\{\, x01 \mid x \text{ is in } \{0, 1\}^* \,\}$

    b. $\{01, 10\}^*$

    c. $\{\, x \mid x \text{ is in } \{a, b\}^*, \text{ and the number of } a\text{'s in } x \text{ or the number of } b\text{'s in } x \text{ is equal to } 1 \,\}$

    d. $\{\, 0^i 1^j \mid i \geq j \,\}$

    e. $\{\, x \mid x \text{ is in } \{0, 1\}^*, \text{ and } x = x^{\text{rev}} \,\}$

    f. $\{\, x \mid x \text{ is in } \{0, 1\}^*, \text{ and each } 01 \text{ in } x \text{ is followed by } 10 \,\}$

    g. $\{\, x \mid x \text{ is in } \{0, 1\}^*, \text{ and the length of } x \text{ is not divisible by } 3 \,\}$

    h. $\{\, x \mid x \text{ is in } \{a, b\}^*, \text{ and } x \text{ is of odd length if and only if it ends with } b \,\}$

    i. $\{\, x \mid x \text{ is in } \{a, b\}^*, \text{ and } abb \text{ is not a substring of } x \,\}$

    j. $\{\, x\#y \mid x \text{ is in } \{a, b\}^*, \text{ and } y \text{ is a permutation of } x \,\}$

    k. $\{\, a^i b^i c^i d^i \mid i \text{ is a natural number} \,\}$

    l. $\{\, a^{i_1} \# a^{i_2} \# a^{i_3} \# \cdots \# a^{i_n} \mid n \geq 2 \text{ and } i_j = i_k \text{ for some } 1 \leq j < k \leq n \,\}$

    m. $\{\, aba^2 b^2 a^3 b^3 \cdots a^n b^n \mid n \text{ is a natural number} \,\}$

1.2.10 For each of the following conditions show how, from any arbitrary given pair of grammars $G_1 = <N_1, \Sigma_1, P_1, S_1>$ and $G_2 = <N_2, \Sigma_2, P_2, S_2>$, a grammar $G_3 = <N_3, \Sigma_3, P_3, S_3>$ that satisfies the condition can be constructed.

    a. $L(G_3) = \{\, w \mid w^{\text{rev}} \text{ is in } L(G_1) \,\}$

    b. $L(G_3) = L(G_1) \cup L(G_2)$

    c. $L(G_3) = L(G_1)L(G_2)$

    d. $L(G_3) = (L(G_1))^*$

    e. $L(G_3) = L(G_1) \cap L(G_2)$

1.2.11 Show that from each grammar $G_1 = <N, \Sigma, P_1, S>$ a two-nonterminal-symbols grammar $G_2 = <\{S, A\}, \Sigma, P_2, S>$ can be constructed such that $L(G_1) = L(G_2)$.

1.2.12 Give the leftmost derivation and a nonleftmost derivation for the string $abbabb$ in the grammar of Exercise 1.2.5.

1.2.13 For each of the following cases find all the possible grammars G that satisfy the case, where $G = <N, \Sigma, P, S>$ with $N = \{S, A\}$, $\Sigma = \{a, b\}$, and P being a subset of $\{S \to \epsilon, S \to abAS, S \to ab, bA \to aS\}$.

    a. G is a Type 3 grammar.

```
          sum1 := 0
          sum2 := 0
          do
             if eof then accept
             do
                read x
                sum1 := sum1 + x                          x := ?
             or                                           write x
                read x                                    do
                write x                                      if eof then accept
                sum2 := sum2 + x                             read y
             until sum1 ≠ sum2                            until x ≠ y
          until false

                 (a)                                            (b)
```

Figure 1.E.1

b. G is a Type 2 grammar, but not of Type 3.

c. G is a Type 1 grammar, but not of Type 2.

1.3.1 Consider the program P in Figure 1.E.1(a). What are the outputs of P on input "2, 2"? On input "3, 2"?

1.3.2 Consider the program P in Figure 1.E.1(b). Assume that P has the domain of variables $\{0, 1, 2, 3, 4, 5\}$. What are the outputs of P on input "2, 2"? On input "3, 2"?

1.3.3 For each of the following cases write a program that corresponds to the case. Assume that the variables have the set of natural numbers as the domain of the variables, and 0 as an initial value.

a. The program outputs an input value v such that $v + 2$ does not appear in the input.

   Example: On input "1, 4, 2, 3" the program should have an accepting computation with output "3", and an accepting computation with output "4". Moreover, each accepting computation of the program should provide either the output "3" or the output "4".

b. The program outputs an input value v such that $v + 2$ also appears in the input.

   Example: On input "1, 4, 3, 2" the program should have an accepting computation with output "1", and an accepting computation with output "2". Moreover, each accepting computation of the program should provide either the output "1" or the output "2".

c. The program outputs a value that does not appear exactly twice in the input.

Example: On input "$1, 4, 1, 4, 3, 1$" the program should have for each $i \neq 4$ an accepting computation with output i (i.e., $i = 0$, 1, 2, 3, 5, 6, ...). Moreover, each accepting computation of the program should provide one of these outputs.

d. The program outputs an input value v that appears as the vth value in the input.

Example: On input "$3, 2, 1, 2, 5, 3$" the program should have an accepting computation with output "2", and an accepting computation with output "5". Moreover, each accepting computation of the program should provide either of these outputs.

e. The program outputs an input value v that appears exactly v times in the input.

Example: On input "$3, 2, 1, 2, 5, 3$" the program should have an accepting computation with output "1", and an accepting computation with output "2". Moreover, each accepting computation of the program should provide either of these outputs.

f. The program accepts exactly those inputs whose values cannot be sorted into a sequence of consecutive numbers.

Example: The program should accept the input "$1, 2, 1$", and the input "$1, 4, 2$". On the other hand, the program should reject the input "$1, 3, 2$".

1.3.4 For each of the following cases write a program that computes the given relation.

a. $\{ (x, y) \mid$ There is a value in the domain of the variables that does not appear in x and does not appear in $y \}$.

Example: With the domain of variables $\{1, 2, 3, 4, 5, 6\}$ on input "$1, 2, 4, 5, 6$" the program can have any output that does not contain the value 3.

b. $\{ (x, y) \mid x$ is not empty, and the first value in x is equal to the first value in $y \}$.

1.3.5 Let P_1 and P_2 be any two given programs. Find a program P_3 that computes the union $R(P_1) \cup R(P_2)$.

1.3.6 Let P be the program in Example 1.3.13. Give the sequence of moves between the configurations of P in the computation of P on input "$1, 2, 1$" that has the minimal number of moves.

1.4.1 Consider the following problem K_1.

Domain: $\{ (a, b) \mid a, b$ are natural numbers $\}$.

Question: What is the value of the natural number c that satisfies the equality $a^2 + b^2 = c^2$?

Find a decision problem K_2 whose solutions are defined at the same instances as for K_1.

1.4.2 Let K be the following decision problem.

Domain: $\{(a, b, c) \mid a, b, c$ are natural numbers $\}$.

Question: Is there a pair of natural numbers x and y such that the equality $ax^2 + by = c$ holds?

a. Write a program that decides K.

b. Write a program that partially decides K, but does not decide K.

1.4.3 Show that the following problems are partially decidable for Type 0 grammars.

a. Membership problem

b. Nonemptiness problem

1.4.4 Show that the membership problem is decidable for Type 1 grammars.

1.4.5 Show that the inequivalence problem is partially decidable for Type 1 grammars.

1.4.6 Which of the following statements is correct?

a. If the emptiness problem is decidable for Type 3 grammars, then it is also decidable for Type 0 grammars.

b. If the emptiness problem is undecidable for Type 3 grammars, then it is also undecidable for Type 0 grammars.

c. If the emptiness problem is decidable for Type 0 grammars, then it is also decidable for Type 3 grammars.

d. If the emptiness problem is undecidable for Type 0 grammars, then it is also undecidable for Type 3 grammars.

A *polynomial expression over the natural numbers*, or simply a *polynomial expression* when the natural numbers are understood, is an expression defined recursively in the following manner.

a. Each natural number is a polynomial expression of degree 0.

b. Each variable is a polynomial expression of degree 1.

c. If E_1 and E_2 are polynomial expressions of degree d_1 and d_2, respectively, then

   i. $(E_1 + E_2)$ and $(E_1 - E_2)$ are polynomial expressions of degree $max(d_1, d_2)$.

   ii. $(E_1 * E_2)$ is a polynomial expression of degree $d_1 + d_2$.

A polynomial is called a *Diophantine polynomial* if it can be is represented by a polynomial expression, and its variables are over the natural numbers. *Hilbert's tenth problem* is the problem of determining for any given Diophantine polynomial $Q(x_1, \ldots, x_n)$ with variables $x_1, \ldots, x_n$ whether or not there exist $\hat{x}_1, \ldots, \hat{x}_n$ such that $Q(\hat{x}_1, \ldots, \hat{x}_n) = 0$.

A *LOOP program* is a program that consists only of instructions of the form x ← 0, x ← y, x ← x + 1, and **do** x α **end**. The variables can hold only natural numbers. α can be any sequence of instructions. An execution of **do** x α **end** causes the execution of α for a number of times equal to the value of x upon encountering the **do**. Each *LOOP* program has a distinct set of variables that are initialized to hold the input values. Similarly, each *LOOP* program has a distinct set of variables, called the output variables, that upon halting hold the output values of the program. Two *LOOP* programs are said to be *equivalent* if on identical input values they produce the same output values.

1.4.7 The following problems are known to be undecidable. Can you show that they are partially decidable?

    a. Hilbert's tenth problem

    b. The inequivalence problem for *LOOP* programs

1.5.1 Let Ψ be the set $\{ m \mid m = 2^i$ for some integer $i \}$. Show that the problem of multiplication of numbers from Ψ is reducible to the problem of addition of integer numbers.

1.5.2 Show that the nonemptiness problem for programs is reducible to the acceptance problem for programs.

1.5.3 Show that Hilbert's tenth problem is reducible to the nonemptiness problem for programs.

1.5.4 Show that the problem of determining the existence of solutions over the natural numbers for systems of Diophantine equations of the following form is reducible to Hilbert's tenth problem. Each $Q_i(x_1, \ldots, x_n)$ is assumed to be a Diophantine polynomial.

$$
\begin{aligned}
Q_1(x_1, \ldots, x_n) &= 0 \\
&\vdots \\
Q_m(x_1, \ldots, x_n) &= 0
\end{aligned}
$$

1.5.5 For each of the following cases show that K_1 is reducible to K_2.

    a. K_1 is the emptiness problem for Type 0 grammars, and K_2 is the equivalence problem for Type 0 grammars.

    b. K_1 is the membership problem for Type 0 grammars, and K_2 is the equivalence problem for Type 0 grammars.

Bibliographic Notes

The hierarchy of grammars in Section 1.2 is due to Chomsky (1959). In the classification Chomsky (1959) used an equivalent class of grammars, called context-sensitive grammars, instead of the Type 1 grammars. Type 1 grammars are due to Kuroda (1964). Harrison (1978) provides an extensive treatment for grammars and formal languages.

Nondeterminism was introduced in Rabin and Scott (1959) and applied to programs in Floyd (1967).

The study of undecidability originated in Turing (1936) and Church (1936). Hilbert's tenth problem is due to Hilbert (1901), and its undecidability to Matijasevic (1970). *LOOP* programs and the undecidability of the equivalence problem for them are due to Ritchie (1963) and Meyer and Ritchie (1967).

Chapter 2

FINITE-MEMORY PROGRAMS

Finite-memory programs are probably one of the simplest classes of programs for which our study would be meaningful. The first section of this chapter motivates the investigation of this class. The second section introduces the mathematical systems of finite-state transducers, and shows that they model the computations of finite-memory programs. The third section provides grammatical characterizations for the languages that finite-memory programs accept, and the fourth section considers the limitations of those programs. The fifth section discusses the importance of closure properties in the design of programs, and their applicability for finite-memory programs. And the last section considers properties that are decidable for finite-memory programs.

2.1 Motivation

It is often useful when developing knowledge in a new field to start by considering restricted cases and then gradually expand to the general case. Such an approach allows a gradual increase in the complexity of the argumentation. In particular, it is a quite common strategy in the investigation of infinite systems to start by considering finite subsystems. We take a similar approach here by using programs with finite domains of variables, called *finite-memory programs* or *finite-domain programs*, first.

However, it should be mentioned that finite-memory programs are also important on their own merit. They are applicable in the design and analysis of some common types of computer programs.

For instance, in compilers (i.e., in programs that translate programs written in high-level languages to equivalent programs written in machine languages) the lexical analyzers are basically designed as finite-memory programs. The main task of a lexical analyzer is to scan the given inputs and locate the symbols that belong to each of the tokens.

```
char := "  "
do
  /* Find the first character of the next token. */
  if char = "  " then
    do
      if eof then accept
      read char
    until char ≠ "  "
  /* Determine the class of the token. */
  charClass := class(char)
  write className(charClass)
  /* Determine the remaining characters of the token. */
  do
    write char
    if eof then accept
    oldCharClass := charClass
    read char
    charClass := M(charClass, char)
  until charClass ≠ oldCharClass
until false
```

(a)

class

" "	0
"A"	1
⋮	⋮
"Z"	1
"0"	2
⋮	⋮
"9"	2

M

	" "	"A"	⋯	"Z"	"0"	⋯	"9"
1	0	1	⋯	1	1	⋯	1
2	0	0	⋯	0	2	⋯	2

className

1	"identifier"
2	"natural number"

(b)

Figure 2.1.1 (a) A lexical analyzer. (b) Tables for the lexical analyzer.

Example 2.1.1 Let LEXANL be the finite-memory program in Figure 2.1.1(a). The domain of the variables is assumed to equal {" ", "A", . . . , "Z", "0", . . . , "9", $0, 1, 2$}, with " " as initial value. The functions *class*, *className*, and M are defined by the tables of Figure 2.1.1(b).

LEXANL is a lexical analyzer that determines the tokens in the given inputs, and classifies them into identifiers and natural numbers. Each identifier is represented by a letter followed by an arbitrary number of letters and digits. Each natural number is represented by one or more digits. Each pair of consecutive tokens, except for a natural number followed by an identifier, must be separated by one or more blanks.

LEXANL can be easily modified to recognize a different class of tokens, by just redefining *class*, *className*, and M.   □

Protocols for communicating processes are also examples of systems that are frequently designed as finite-memory programs. In such systems, each process is represented by a finite-memory program. Each channel from one process to another is abstracted by an implicit queue, that is, by a first-in-first-out memory. At each instance the queue holds those messages that have been sent through the channel but not received yet. Each sending of a message is represented by the writing of the message to the appropriate channel. Each receiving of a message is represented by the reading of the message from the appropriate channel.

In Section 2.6 it is shown that finite-memory programs have some interesting decidable properties. Such decidable properties make the finite-memory programs also attractive as tools for showing the complexity of some seemingly unrelated problems.

Example 2.1.2 Consider the problem K of deciding the existence of solutions over the natural numbers for systems of linear Diophantine equations, that is, for systems of equations of the following form. The a_{ij}'s and b_i's are assumed to be integers.

$$a_{11}x_1 + \cdots + a_{1n}x_n = b_1$$
$$\vdots$$
$$a_{m1}x_1 + \cdots + a_{mn}x_n = b_m$$

No straightforward algorithm seems to be evident for deciding the problem, though one can easily partially decide the problem by exhaustively searching for an assignment to the variables that satisfies the given system.

For each instance I of K, a finite-memory program P_I can be constructed to accept some input if and only if I has a solution over the natural numbers. Consequently, the problem K is reducible to the emptiness problem for finite-memory programs. The decidability of K is then implied by the decidability of the emptiness problem for finite-memory programs (Theorem 2.6.1).

In fact, the proof of Theorem 2.6.1 implies that a system I has a solution over the natural numbers if and only if the system has a solution in which the values of $x_1, \ldots, x_n$ are no greater than some bound that depends only on the a_{ij}'s, b_i's, m and n.   □

Computer programs that use no auxiliary memory, except for holding the input and output values, are by definition examples of finite-memory programs. However, such programs can deal with domains of high cardinality (i.e., 2^k for computers with k bits per word), and as a result their designs are generally not affected by the finiteness of their domains. Consequently, such programs should not generally be considered as "natural" finite-memory programs.

```
x := ?                          /* I₁  */
write x                         /* I₂  */
do                              /* I₃  */
    do                          /* I₄  */
        read y                  /* I₅  */
    until x = y                 /* I₆  */
    if eof then accept          /* I₇  */
    do                          /* I₈  */
        x := x − 1              /* I₉  */
    or
        y := y + 1              /* I₁₀ */
    until x ≠ y                 /* I₁₁ */
until false                     /* I₁₂ */
```

Figure 2.2.1 A finite-memory program with $\{0, 1\}$ as the domain of the variables.

2.2 Finite-State Transducers

Central to the investigation of finite-memory programs is the observation that the set of all the states reachable in the computations of each such program is finite. As a result, the computations of each finite-memory program can be characterized by a finite set of states and a finite set of rules for transitions between those states.

Abstracted Finite-Memory Programs

Specifically, let P be a finite-memory program with m variables $x_1, \ldots, x_m$, and k instruction segments $I_1, \ldots, I_k$. Denote the initial value of the variables of P with $\odot$.

Each *state* of P is an $(m+1)$-tuple $[i, v_1, \ldots, v_m]$, where i is an integer between 1 and k, and $v_1, \ldots, v_m$ are values from the domain of the variables. Intuitively, a state $[i, v_1, \ldots, v_m]$ indicates that the program reached instruction segment I_i with values $v_1, \ldots, v_m$ in the variables $x_1, \ldots, x_m$, respectively.

Example 2.2.1 Let P be the program in Figure 2.2.1. The domain of the variables is assumed to equal $\{0, 1\}$, and the initial value is assumed to be 0. Let $[i, x, y]$ denote the state of P that corresponds to the ith instruction segment I_i, the value x in x, and the value y in y.

The state $[1, 0, 0]$ indicates that the program reached the first instruction segment with the value 0 in x and y. The state $[5, 1, 0]$ indicates that the program reached the fifth instruction segment with the value 1 in x and the value 0 in y.

From state $[5, 1, 0]$ the program can reach either state $[6, 1, 0]$ or state $[6, 1, 1]$. In the transition from state $[5, 1, 0]$ to state $[6, 1, 0]$ the program reads the value 0 and writes nothing. In the transition from state $[5, 1, 0]$ to state $[6, 1, 1]$ the program reads the value 1 and writes nothing.   □

The computational behavior of P can be abstracted by a formal system $<Q, \Sigma,$ $\Delta, \delta, q_0, F>$, which is defined through the algorithm below. In the formal system

Q represents the set of states that P can reach.

δ represents the set of transitions that P can take between its states.

Σ represents the set of input values that P can read.

Δ represents the set of output values that P can write.

q_0 represents the initial state of P.

F represents the set of accepting states that P can reach.

The algorithm determines the sets Q, Σ, Δ, δ, and F by conducting a search for the elements of the sets.

Step 1 Initiate Q to the set containing just $q_0 = [1, \odot, \ldots, \odot]$, and δ to be an empty set. q_0 is called the *initial state* of P, and δ is called the *transition table* of P.

Step 2 Add the state $p = [j, u_1, \ldots, u_m]$ of P to Q, if for some state $q = [i, v_1, \ldots, v_m]$ in Q the following condition holds: P can, by executing I_i with values $v_1, \ldots, v_m$ in its variables, reach I_j with $u_1, \ldots, u_m$ in its variables, respectively.

Step 3 Add $(q, \alpha, (p, \rho))$ to δ, if P, by executing a single instruction segment, can go from state q in Q to state p in Q while reading α and writing ρ. For notational convenience, in what follows $(q, \alpha, (p, \rho))$ will be written as (q, α, p, ρ). Each tuple in δ is called a *transition rule* of P.

Step 4 Repeat Steps 2 and 3 as long as more states can be added to Q or more transition rules can be added to δ.

Step 5 Initialize Σ, Δ, and F to be empty sets.

Step 6 If (q, α, p, ρ) is a transition rule in δ and $\alpha \neq \epsilon$ then add α to Σ. Similarly, if (q, α, p, ρ) is a transition rule in δ and $\rho \neq \epsilon$, then add ρ to Δ. Each α in Σ is called an *input symbol* of P, and Σ is called the *input alphabet* of P. Similarly, each ρ in Δ is called an *output symbol* of P, and Δ is called the *output alphabet* of P.

Step 7 Insert to F each state $[i, v_1, \ldots, v_m]$ in Q for which I_i is a conditional accept instruction. The states in F are called the *accepting*, or the *final*, states of P.

By definition δ is a relation from $Q \times (\Sigma \cup \{\epsilon\})$ to $Q \times (\Delta \cup \{\epsilon\})$. Moreover, the sets Q, Σ, Δ, δ, and F are all finite because the number of instruction segments in P, the number of variables in P, and the domain of the variables of P are all finite.

Example 2.2.2 Assume the notations of Example 2.2.1. The initial state of the program P is $[1, 0, 0]$. By executing the first instruction, the program can move from state $[1, 0, 0]$ and either enter the state $[2, 0, 0]$ or the state $[2, 1, 0]$. In both cases, no input symbol is read and no output symbol is written during the transition between the states. Hence, the transition table δ for P contains the transition rules $([1, 0, 0], \epsilon, [2, 0, 0], \epsilon)$ and $([1, 0, 0], \epsilon, [2, 1, 0], \epsilon)$.

Similarly, by executing its second instruction, the program P must move from state $[2, 1, 0]$ and enter state $[3, 1, 0]$ while reading nothing and writing 1. Hence, δ contains also the transition rule $([2, 1, 0], \epsilon, [3, 1, 0], 1)$.

The number of states in Q is no greater than $12 \times 2 \times 2$. $\{0, 1\}$ is the input and the output alphabet for the program P. $\{[7, 0, 0], [7, 1, 1]\}$ is the set of accepting states for P. $\qquad\square$

Finite-State Transducers

In general, a formal system M consisting of a six-tuple $<Q, \Sigma, \Delta, \delta, q_0, F>$ is called a *finite-state transducer* if it satisfies the following conditions.

Q is a finite set, whose members are called the *states* of M.

Σ is an alphabet, called the *input alphabet* of M. Each symbol in Σ is called an *input symbol* of M.

Δ is an alphabet, called the *output alphabet* of M. Each symbol in Δ is called an *output symbol* of M.

δ is a relation from $Q \times (\Sigma \cup \{\epsilon\})$ to $Q \times (\Delta \cup \{\epsilon\})$, called the *transition table* of M. Each tuple $(q, \alpha, (p, \rho))$, or simply (q, α, p, ρ), in δ is called a *transition rule* of M.

q_0 is a state in Q, called the *initial state* of M.

F is a subset of Q, whose states are called the *accepting*, or the *final*, states of M.

Example 2.2.3 The tuple $M = <\{q_0, q_1\}, \{a, b\}, \{1\}, \{(q_0, a, q_1, 1), (q_0, b, q_1, \epsilon), (q_1, b, q_1, 1), (q_1, a, q_0, \epsilon)\}, q_0, \{q_0\}>$ is a finite-state transducer. The finite-state transducer has the states q_0 and q_1. The input alphabet of M consists of two symbols a and b. The output alphabet of M consists of a single symbol 1. The finite-state transducer M has four transition rules. q_0 is the initial state of M, and the only accepting state of M.

The transition rule $(q_0, a, q_1, 1)$ of M uses the input symbol a and the output symbol 1. The transition rule (q_1, a, q_0, ϵ) of M uses the input symbol a and no output symbol. $\qquad\square$

Each finite-state transducer $<Q, \Sigma, \Delta, \delta, q_0, F>$ can be graphically represented by a *transition diagram* of the following form. For each state in Q the transition diagram has a corresponding node, which is shown by a circle. The initial state is

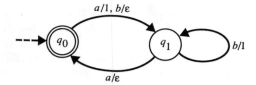

Figure 2.2.2 Transition diagram of a finite-state transducer.

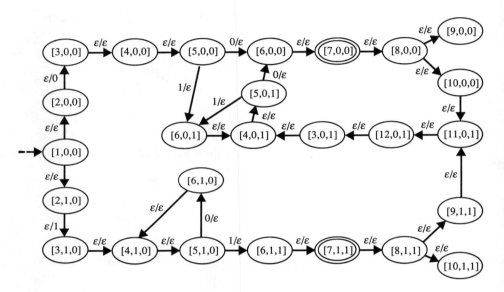

Figure 2.2.3 Transition diagram for the program of Figure 2.2.1.

identified by an arrow from nowhere that points to the corresponding node. Each accepting state is identified by a double circle. Each transition rule (q, α, p, ρ) in δ is represented by an edge labeled with α/ρ, from the node labeled by state q to the node labeled by state p. For notational convenience edges that agree in their origin and destination are merged, and their labels are separated by commas.

Example 2.2.4 The transition diagram in Figure 2.2.2 represents the finite-state transducer M of Example 2.2.3. The label $a/1$ on the edge from state q_0 to state q_1 in the transition diagram corresponds to the transition rule $(q_0, a, q_1, 1)$ of M. The label b/ϵ on the edge from state q_0 to state q_1 corresponds to the transition rule (q_0, b, q_1, ϵ). The label $b/1$ on the edge from state q_1 to itself corresponds to the transition rule $(q_1, b, q_1, 1)$.   □

Example 2.2.5 The transition diagram in Figure 2.2.3 represents the finite-state transducer that characterizes the program of Example 2.2.1.   □

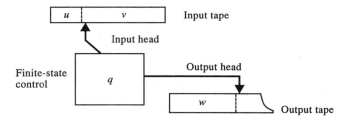

Figure 2.2.4 A view of a finite-state transducer as an abstract computing machine.

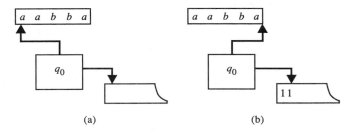

Figure 2.2.5 Configurations of the finite-state transducer of Figure 2.2.2.

Configurations and Moves of Finite-State Transducers

Intuitively, a finite-state transducer $M = <Q, \Sigma, \Delta, \delta, q_0, F>$ can be viewed as an abstract computing machine. The computing machine consists of a *finite-state control*, an *input tape*, a read-only *input head*, an *output tape*, and a write-only *output head* (see Figure 2.2.4). Each tape is divided into cells, which can each hold exactly one symbol.

The input tape is used for holding the input uv of M. The input head is used for accessing the input tape. The output tape is used for holding the output w of M, and the output head is used for accessing the output tape. The finite-state control is used for recording the state of M.

On each input $a_1 \cdots a_n$ from Σ^*, the computing machine M has some set of possible configurations. Each *configuration*, or *instantaneous description*, of M is a pair (uqv, w), where q is a state in Q, $uv = a_1 \cdots a_n$, and w is a string in Δ^*. Intuitively, a configuration (uqv, w) says that M on input uv reached state q after reading u and writing w. With no loss of generality it is assumed that Q and Σ are mutually disjoint.

Example 2.2.6 Let M be the finite-state transducer of Example 2.2.3 (see Figure 2.2.2). The configuration $(aabq_1ba, 1)$ of M says that M reached the state q_1 after reading $u = aab$ from the input tape and writing $w = 1$ into the output tape. In addition, the configuration says that $v = ba$ is the remainder of the input (see Figure 2.2.5(a)).

The configuration $(q_0 aabba, \epsilon)$ of M says that M reached the state q_0 after reading nothing (i.e., $u = \epsilon$) from the input tape and writing nothing (i.e., $w = \epsilon$) into the output tape. In addition, the configuration says that $v = aabba$ is the input to be consumed (see Figure 2.2.5(b)).

The configuration $(aabbaq_0, 1)$ of M says that M reached state q_0 after reading all the input (i.e., $v = \epsilon$) and writing $w = 11$. In addition, the configuration says that the input that has been read is $u = aabba$.   □

A configuration (uqv, w) of M is said to be an *initial configuration* if $q = q_0$ and $u = w = \epsilon$. An initial configuration says that the input head is placed at the start (leftmost position) of the input, the output tape is empty, and the finite-state control is set to the initial state.

A configuration (uqv, w) of M is said to be an *accepting configuration* if $v = \epsilon$ and q is an accepting state in F. An accepting configuration says that M reached an accepting state after reading all the input.

Example 2.2.7 The finite-state transducer M of Example 2.2.3 (see Figure 2.2.2) has the initial configuration $(q_0 aabba, \epsilon)$, and the accepting configuration $(aabbaq_0, 11)$ on input $aabba$ (see Figure 2.2.5(a) and Figure 2.2.5(b), respectively).

$(aabbaq_0, \epsilon)$ and $(aabbaq_0, 111)$ are also accepting configurations of M on input $aabba$. On the other hand, $(q_0 aabba, \epsilon)$ is the only initial configuration of M on input $aabba$.   □

The transition rules of M are used for defining the possible moves of M. Each move uses some transition rule. A *move* on transition rule (q, α, p, ρ) consists of changing the state of the finite-state control from q to p, of reading α from the input tape, of writing ρ to the output tape, and of moving the input and the output heads, $|\alpha|$ and $|\rho|$ positions to the right, respectively.

A move of M from configuration C_1 to configuration C_2 is denoted $C_1 \vdash_M C_2$, or simply $C_1 \vdash C_2$ if M is understood. A sequence of zero or more moves of M from configuration C_1 to configuration C_2 is denoted $C_1 \vdash_M^* C_2$, or simply $C_1 \vdash^* C_2$, if M is understood.

Example 2.2.8 Let M be the finite-state transducer of Example 2.2.3 (see Figure 2.2.2). On input $aabba$, M can have the following sequence $(q_0 aabba, \epsilon) \vdash^*$ $(aabbaq_0, 11)$ of moves between configurations (see Figure 2.2.6): $(q_0 aabba, \epsilon) \vdash$ $(aq_1 abba, 1) \vdash (aaq_0 bba, 1) \vdash (aabq_1 ba, 1) \vdash (aabbq_1 a, 11) \vdash (aabbaq_0, 11)$.

The sequence consists of five moves. It starts with a move $(q_0 aabba, \epsilon) \vdash$ $(aq_1 abba, 1)$ on the first transition rule $(q_0, a, q_1, 1)$ of M. During the move, M makes a transition from state q_0 to state q_1 while reading a and writing 1.

The second move $(aq_1 abba, 1) \vdash (aaq_0 bba, 1)$ is on the fourth transition rule (q_1, a, q_0, ϵ) of M. During the move, M makes a transition from state q_1 to state q_0 while reading a and writing nothing.

The sequence continues by a move on the second transition rule (q_0, b, q_1, ϵ), followed by a move on the third transition rule $(q_1, b, q_1, 1)$, and it terminates after an additional move on the fourth transition rule (q_1, a, q_0, ϵ).

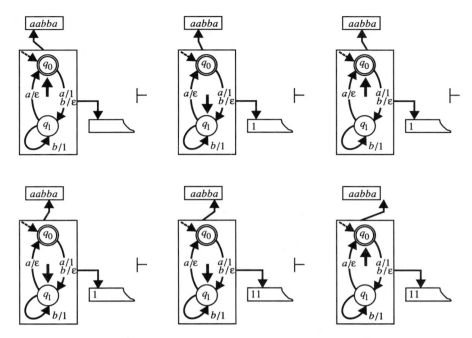

Figure 2.2.6 Sequence of moves between configurations of a finite-state transducer.

The sequence of moves is the only one that can start at the initial configuration and end at an accepting configuration for the input $aabba$. □

By definition, $|\alpha| = 0$ or $|\alpha| = 1$ in each transition rule (q, α, p, ρ). $|\alpha| = 0$ if no input symbol is read during the moves that use the transition rule (i.e., $\alpha = \epsilon$), and $|\alpha| = 1$ if exactly one input symbol is read during the moves. Similarly, $|\rho| = 0$ or $|\rho| = 1$, depending on whether nothing is written during the moves or exactly one symbol is written, respectively.

Determinism and Nondeterminism in Finite-State Transducers

A finite-state transducer $M = <Q, \Sigma, \Delta, \delta, q_0, F>$ is said to be *deterministic* if, for each state q in Q and each input symbol a in Σ, the union $\delta(q, a) \cup \delta(q, \epsilon)$ is a multiset that contains at most one element.

Intuitively, M is deterministic if each state of M fully determines whether an input symbol is to be read on a move from the state, and the state together with the input to be consumed in the move fully determine the transition rule to be used.

A finite-state transducer is said to be *nondeterministic* if the previous conditions do not hold.

Example 2.2.9 The finite-state transducer M_1, whose transition diagram is given in Figure 2.2.2, is deterministic. In each of its moves M_1 reads an input symbol.

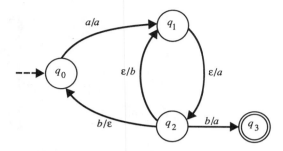

Figure 2.2.7 A nondeterministic Turing transducer.

The transition rule to be used in each move is uniquely determined by the state and the input symbol being read.

If M_1 reads the input symbol a in the move from state q_0, then M_1 must use the transition rule $(q_0, a, q_1, 1)$ in the move. If M_1 reads the input symbol b in the move from state q_0 then M_1 must use the transition rule (q_0, b, q_1, ϵ) in the move.

On the other hand, consider the finite-state transducer M_2, which satisfies $M_2 = <Q, \Sigma, \Delta, \delta, q_0, F>$ for $Q = \{q_0, q_1, q_2, q_3\}$, $\Sigma = \{a, b\}$, $\Delta = \{a, b\}$, $\delta = \{(q_0, a, q_1, a), (q_1, \epsilon, q_2, a), (q_2, \epsilon, q_1, b), (q_2, b, q_0, \epsilon), (q_2, b, q_3, a)\}$, and $F = \{q_3\}$. The transition diagram of M_2 is given in Figure 2.2.7. M_2 is a nondeterministic finite-state transducer.

On moving from state q_0, the finite-state transducer M_2 must read an input symbol. On moving from state q_1, the finite-state transducer M_2 does not read an input symbol. The transition rules that M_2 can use on moving from states q_0 and q_1 are uniquely determined by the states, and, therefore, these states are not the source for the nondeterminism of M_2.

The source for the nondeterminism of M_2 is in the transition rules that origi-nate at state q_2. The transition rules do not determine whether M_2 has to read a symbol in moving from state q_2, nor do they specify which of the transition rules is to be used on the moves that read the symbol b.   □

Computations of Finite-State Transducers

The computations of the finite-state transducers are defined in a manner similar to that for the programs. An *accepting computation* of a finite-state transducer M is a sequence of moves of M that starts at an initial configuration and ends at an accepting configuration. A *nonaccepting*, or *rejecting*, *computation* of M is a sequence of moves on an input x for which the following conditions hold.

a. The sequence starts from the initial configuration of M on x.

b. If the sequence is finite, then it ends at a configuration from which no move is possible.

c. M has no accepting computation on x.

Each accepting computation and each nonaccepting computation of M is said to be a *computation* of M.

A computation is said to be a *halting computation* if it consists of a finite number of moves.

Example 2.2.10 Let M be the finite-state transducer of Example 2.2.3 (see Figure 2.2.2). On input $aabba$ the finite-state transducer M has a computation that is given by the sequence of moves in Example 2.2.8 (see Figure 2.2.6). The computation is an accepting one.

Alternatively, on input aab the finite-state transducer M has the following sequence of moves: $(q_0aab, \epsilon) \vdash (aq_1ab, 1) \vdash (aaq_0b, 1) \vdash (aabq_1, 1)$. This sequence is the only one possible from the initial configuration of M on input abb; it is a nonaccepting computation of M.

The two computations in the example are halting computations of M. $\qquad\square$

By definition, on inputs that are accepted by a finite-state transducer the finite-state transducer may have also executable sequences of transition rules which are not considered to be computations.

Example 2.2.11 Consider the finite-state transducer M whose transition diagram is given in Figure 2.2.7. On input ab, M has the accepting computation that moves along the sequence of states q_0, q_1, q_2, q_3. Similarly, on input ab, M also has an accepting computation that moves along the sequence of states $q_0, q_1, q_2, q_1, q_2, q_3$. However, on input ab across the states q_0, q_1, q_2, q_0, M's sequence of moves is not a computation of M.

On input a the finite-state transducer has only one computation. The computation is a nonhalting computation that goes along the sequence of states $q_0, q_1, q_2, q_1, q_2, \ldots$ On the other hand, on input aba the Turing transducer has infinitely many halting computations and infinitely many nonhalting computations. All the computations on input aba are nonaccepting computations.

The halting computations of M on input aba consume just the prefix ab of M and move through the sequences $q_0, q_1, q_2, q_1, q_2, \ldots, q_1, q_2, q_3$ of states. The nonhalting computations of M on input aba consume the input until its end and move through the sequences $q_0, q_1, q_2, q_1, q_2, \ldots, q_1, q_2, q_0, q_1, q_2, q_1, q_2, \ldots$ of states. $\qquad\square$

By definition, each move in each computation must be on a transition rule that allows the computation to eventually read all the input and thereafter reach an accepting state. Whenever more than one such alternative exists in the set of feasible transition rules, any of these alternatives can be chosen. Similarly, whenever none of the feasible transition rules satisfy the conditions above, then any of these transition rules can be chosen. This fact suggests that we view the computations of the finite-state transducers as being executed by imaginary agents with magical power.

An input x is said to be *accepted*, or *recognized*, by a finite-state transducer M if M has an accepting computation on x. An accepting computation that terminates in an accepting configuration (xq_f, y) is said to have an *output* y. The output of a nonaccepting computation is assumed to be *undefined*.

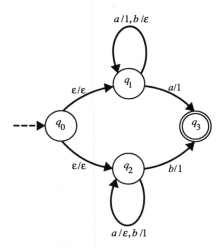

Figure 2.2.8 A nondeterministic finite-state transducer.

A finite-state transducer M is said to have an *output* y on input x if it has an accepting computation on x with output y. M is said to *halt* on x if all the computations of M on input x are halting computations.

Example 2.2.12 The finite-state transducer M whose transition diagram is given in Figure 2.2.8 has, on input $baabb$, a sequence of moves that goes through the states q_0, q_1, q_1, q_1, q_1, q_1; a sequence of moves that goes through the states q_0, q_2, q_2, q_2, q_2, q_2; and a sequence of moves that goes through the states q_0, q_2, q_2, q_2, q_2, q_3. The sequence of moves that goes through the states q_0, q_2, q_2, q_2, q_2, q_3 is the only computation of M on input $baabb$. The computation is an accepting computation that provides the output 111.

M accepts all inputs. However, the finite-state transducer of Example 2.2.11 accepts exactly those inputs that have the form $ababa \cdots bab$.   □

As in the case of programs, the semantics of the finite-state transducers are characterized by their computations. Consequently, the behavior of these transducers are labeled with respect to their computations.

For instance, a finite-state transducer M is said *to move* from configuration C_1 to configuration C_2 on x if C_2 follows C_1 in the considered computation of M on x. Similarly, M is said *to read* α from its input if α is consumed from the input in the considered computation of M.

Example 2.2.13 The finite-state transducer whose transition diagram is given in Figure 2.2.8 on input $baabb$ starts its computation with a move that takes M from state q_0 to state q_2. M then makes four moves, which consume $baab$ and leave M in state q_2. Finally, M moves from state q_2 to state q_3 while reading b.   □

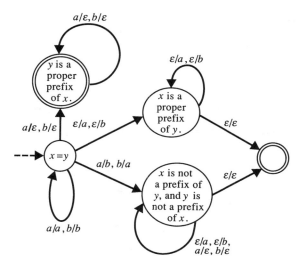

Figure 2.2.9 A finite-state transducer that computes the relation $R(M) = \{ (x,y) \mid x \text{ and } y \text{ are in } \{a,b\}^*, \text{ and } y \neq x \}$.

Relations and Languages of Finite-State Transducers

The relation *computed* by a finite-state transducer $M = <Q, \Sigma, \Delta, \delta, q_0, F>$, denoted $R(M)$, is the set $\{ (x,y) \mid (q_0 x, \epsilon) \vdash^* (x q_f, y) \text{ for some } q_f \text{ in } F \}$. That is, the relation computed by M is the set of all the pairs (x, y) such that M has an accepting computation on input x with output y.

The language *accepted*, or *recognized*, by M, denoted $L(M)$, is the set of all the inputs that M accepts, that is, the set $\{ x \mid (x,y) \text{ is in } R(M) \text{ for some } y \}$. The language is said to be *decided* by M if, in addition, M halts on all inputs, that is, on all x in Σ^*.

The language *generated* by M is the set of all the outputs that M has on its inputs, that is, the set $\{ y \mid (x,y) \text{ is in } R(M) \text{ for some } x \}$.

Example 2.2.14 The nondeterministic finite-state transducer M whose transition diagram is given in Figure 2.2.8 computes the relation $R(M) = \{ (x, 1^i) \mid x \text{ is in} \{a,b\}^*, i = \text{number of } a\text{'s in } x \text{ if the last symbol in } x \text{ is } a, \text{ and } i = \text{number of } b\text{'s in } x \text{ if the last symbol in } x \text{ is } b \}$. The finite-state automaton M accepts the language $L(M) = \{a,b\}^*$. □

Example 2.2.15 The nondeterministic finite-state transducer M whose transition diagram is given in Figure 2.2.9 computes the relation $R(M) = \{ (x,y) \mid x \text{ and } y \text{ are in } \{a,b\}^*, \text{ and } y \neq x \}$.

As long as M is in its initial state "$x = y$" the output of M is equal to the portion of the input consumed so far.

If M wants to provide an output that is a proper prefix of its input, then upon reaching the end of the output, M must move from the initial state to state "y is proper prefix of x."

```
state := q₀
do
    /* Accept if an accepting state of M is reached at the end
    of the input.                                             */
    if F(state) then
        if eof then accept
    /* Nondeterministically find the entries of the transition
    rule (q, α, p, ρ) used in the next simulated move.        */
    do in := e or read in until true        /* in := α */
    next_state := ?                    /* next_state := p */
    out := ?                                /* out := ρ */
    if not δ(state, in, next_state, out) then reject
    /* Simulate the move. */
    if out ≠ e then
        write out
    state := next_state
until false
```

Figure 2.2.10 A table-driven finite-memory program for simulating a finite-state transducer.

If M wants its input to be a proper prefix of its output, then M must move to state "x is a proper prefix of y" upon reaching the end of the input.

Otherwise, at some nondeterministically chosen instance of the computation, M must move to state "x is not a prefix of y, and y is not a prefix of x," to create a discrepancy between a pair of corresponding input and output symbols.   □

From Finite-State Transducers to Finite-Memory Programs

The previous discussion shows us that there is an algorithm that translates any given finite-memory program into an equivalent finite-state transducer, that is, into a finite-state transducer that computes the same relation as the program. Conversely, there is also an algorithm that derives an equivalent finite-memory program from any given finite-state transducer. The program can be a "table-driven" program that simulates a given finite-state transducer $M = <Q, \Sigma, \Delta, \delta, q_0, F>$ in the manner described in Figure 2.2.10.

The program uses a variable `state` for recording M's state in a given move, a variable `in` for recording the input M consumes in a given move, a variable `next_state` for recording the state M enters in a given move, and a variable `out` for recording the output M writes in a given move.

The program starts a simulation of M by initializing the variable `state` to the initial state q_0 of M. Then M enters an infinite loop.

The program starts each iteration of the loop by checking whether an accepting state of M has been reached at the end of the input. If such is the case, the program halts in an accepting configuration. Otherwise, the program simulates a

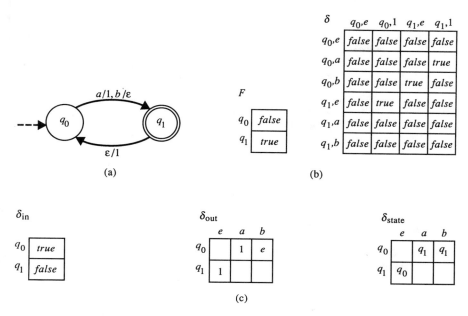

Figure 2.2.11 (a) A finite-state transducer M. (b) Tables for a table-driven program that simulates M. (c) Tables for a deterministic table-driven program that simulates M.

single move of M. The predicate F is used to determine whether state holds an accepting state.

The simulation of each move of M is done in a nondeterministic manner. The program guesses the value for variable in that has to be read in the simulated move, the state for variable next_state that M enters in the simulated move, and the value for variable out that the program writes in the simulated move. Then the program uses the predicate δ to verify that the guessed values are appropriate and continues according to the outcome of the verification.

The domain of the variables of the program is assumed to equal $Q \cup \Sigma \cup \Delta \cup \{e\}$, where e is assumed to be a new symbol not in $Q \cup \Sigma \cup \Delta$, used for denoting the empty string ϵ.

In the table-driven program, F is a predicate that assumes a *true* value when, and only when, its parameter is an accepting state. Similarly, δ is a predicate that assumes a *true* value when, and only when, its entries correspond to a transition rule of M.

The programs that correspond to different finite-state transducers differ in the domains of their variables and in the truth assignments for the predicates F and δ.

The algorithm can be easily modified to give a deterministic finite-memory program whenever the finite-state transducer M is deterministic.

Example 2.2.16 For the finite-state transducer M of Figure 2.2.11(a), the program

```
state := q_0
do
    if F(state) then
        if eof then accept
    if not δ_in(state) then
        in := e
    if δ_in(state) then
        read in
    next_state := δ_state(state, in)
    out := δ_out(state, in)
    if out ≠ e then
        write out
    state := next_state
until false
```

Figure 2.2.12 A table-driven, deterministic finite-memory program for simulating a deterministic finite-state transducer.

in Figure 2.2.10 has the domain of variables $\{a, b, 1, q_0, q_1, e\}$. The truth values of the predicates F and δ are defined by the corresponding tables of Figure 2.2.11(b).

The program also allows that for F and δ there are parameters that differ from those specified in the tables. On such parameters the predicates are assumed to be undefined.

The finite-state transducer can be simulated also by the deterministic table-driven program in Figure 2.2.12. F is assumed to be a predicate as before, and δ_{in}, δ_{out}, and δ_{state} are assumed to be defined by the corresponding tables in Figure 2.2.11(c).

The predicate δ_{in} determines whether an input symbol is to be read on moving from a given state. The function δ_{out} determines the output to be written in each simulated move, and δ_{state} determines the state to be reached in each simulated state.

The deterministic finite-state transducer can be simulated also by a non-table-driven finite-memory program of the form shown in Figure 2.2.13. In such a case, through conditional if instructions, the program explicitly records the effect of F, δ_{in}, δ_{out}, and δ_{state}. $\qquad\qquad\square$

It follows that the finite-state transducers characterize the finite-memory programs, and so they can be used for designing and analyzing finite-memory programs. As a result, the study conducted below for finite-state transducers applies also for finite-memory programs.

Finite-state transducers offer advantages in

a. Their straightforward graphic representations, which are in many instances more "natural" than finite-memory programs.

b. Their succinctness, because finite-state transducers are abstractions that ignore those details irrelevant to the study undertaken.

```
state := q₀
do
  if state = q₀ then
  do
    read in
    if in = a then
    do
      state := q₁
      out := 1
      write out
    until true
    if in = b then
      state := q₁
  until true
  if state = q₁ then
  do
    if eof then accept
    state := q₀
    out := 1
    write out
  until true
until false
```

Figure 2.2.13 A non-table-driven deterministic finite-memory program that simulates the deterministic finite-state transducer of Figure 2.2.11(a).

c. The close dependency of the outputs on the inputs.

2.3 Finite-State Automata and Regular Languages

The computations of programs are driven by their inputs. The outputs are just the results of the computations, and they have no influence on the course that the computations take. Consequently, it seems that much can be studied about finite-state transducers, or equivalently, about finite-memory programs even when their outputs are ignored. The advantage of conducting a study of such stripped-down finite-state transducers is in the simplified argumentation that they allow.

Finite-State Automata

A finite-state transducer whose output components are ignored is called a finite-state automaton. Formally, a *finite-state automaton* M is a tuple $<Q, \Sigma, \delta, q_0, F>$, where Q, Σ, q_0, and F are defined as for finite-state transducers, and the transition table δ is a relation from $Q \times (\Sigma \cup \{\epsilon\})$ to Q.

Transition diagrams similar to those used for representing finite-state transducers can also be used to represent finite-state automata. The only difference is that

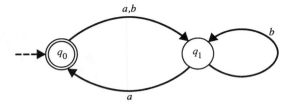

Figure 2.3.1 A finite-state automaton that corresponds to the finite-state transducer of Figure 2.2.2.

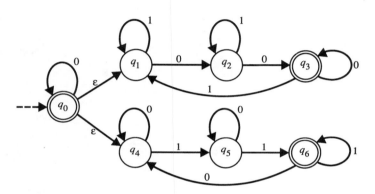

Figure 2.3.2 A nondeterministic finite-state automaton.

in the case of finite-state automata, an edge that corresponds to a transition rule (p, α, p) is labeled by the string α.

Example 2.3.1 The finite-state automaton that is induced by the finite-state transducer of Figure 2.2.2 is $<Q, \Sigma, \delta, q_0, F>$, where $Q = \{q_0, q_1\}$, $\Sigma = \{a, b\}$, $\delta = \{(q_0, a, q_1), (q_0, b, q_1), (q_1, b, q_1), (q_1, a, q_0)\}$, and $F = \{q_0\}$.

The transition diagram in Figure 2.3.1 represents the finite-state automaton. □

The finite-state automaton M is said to be *deterministic* if, for each state q in Q and for each input symbol a in Σ, the union $\delta(q, a) \cup \delta(q, \epsilon)$ is a multiset that contains at most one element. The finite-state automaton is said to be *nondeterministic* if it is not a deterministic finite-state automaton.

A transition rule (q, α, p) of the finite-state automaton is said to be an ϵ *transition rule* if $\alpha = \epsilon$. A finite-state automaton with no ϵ transition rules is said to be an ϵ-*free* finite-state automaton.

Example 2.3.2 Consider the finite-state automaton $M_1 = <\{q_0, \ldots, q_6\}, \{0, 1\}, \{(q_0, 0, q_0), (q_0, \epsilon, q_1), (q_0, \epsilon, q_4), (q_1, 0, q_2), (q_1, 1, q_1), (q_2, 0, q_3), (q_2, 1, q_2), (q_3, 0, q_3), (q_3, 1, q_1), (q_4, 0, q_4), (q_4, 1, q_5), (q_5, 0, q_5), (q_5, 1, q_6), (q_6, 1, q_6), (q_6, 0, q_4)\}$, $q_0, \{q_0, q_3, q_6\}>$. The transition diagram of M_1 is given in Figure 2.3.2.

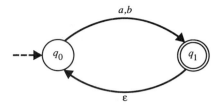

Figure 2.3.3 A deterministic finite-state automaton.

M_1 is nondeterministic owing to the transition rules that originate at state q_0. One of the transition rules requires that an input value be read, whereas the other two transition rules require that no input value be read. Moreover, M_1 is also nondeterministic when the transition rule $(q_0, 0, q_0)$ is ignored, because M_1 cannot determine locally which of the other transition rules to follow on the moves that originate at state q_0.

The finite-state automaton M_2 in Figure 2.3.3 is a deterministic finite-state automaton.

M_1 has two ϵ transition rules, and M_2 has one. ☐

A *configuration*, or an *instantaneous description*, of the finite-state automaton is a singleton uqv, where q is a state in Q, and uv is a string in Σ^*. The configuration is said to be an *initial configuration* if $u = \epsilon$ and q is the initial state. The configuration is said to be an *accepting*, or *final*, *configuration* if $v = \epsilon$ and q is an accepting state. With no loss of generality it is assumed that Q and Σ are mutually disjoint.

Other definitions, like those of $\vdash_M$, $\vdash$, $\vdash_M^*$, $\vdash^*$, and acceptance, recognition, and decidability of a language by a finite-state automaton, are similar to those given for finite-state transducers.

Nondeterminism versus Determinism in Finite-State Automata

By the following theorem, nondeterminism does not add to the recognition power of finite-state automata, even though it might add to their succinctness. The proof of the theorem provides an algorithm for constructing, from any given n-state finite-state automaton, an equivalent deterministic finite-state automaton of at most 2^n states.

Theorem 2.3.1 If a language is accepted by a finite-state automaton, then it is also decided by a deterministic finite-state automaton that has no ϵ transition rules.

Proof Consider any finite-state automaton $M = <Q, \Sigma, \delta, q_0, F>$. Let A_x denote the set of all the states that M can reach from its initial state q_0, by the sequences of moves that consume the string x, that is, the set $\{ q \mid q_0 x \vdash^* xq \}$. Then an input w is accepted by M if and only if A_w contains an accepting state.

The proof relies on the observation that A_{xa} contains exactly those states that can be reached from the states in A_x, by the sequences of transition rules that consume a, that is, $A_{xa} = \{ p \mid q \text{ is in } A_x, \text{ and } qa \vdash^* ap \}$.

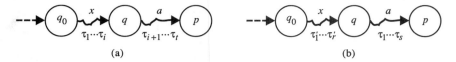

Figure 2.3.4 Sequences of transition rules that consume xa.

Specifically, if p is a state in A_{xa}, then by definition there is a sequence of transition rules $\tau_1, \ldots, \tau_t$ that takes M from the initial state q_0 to state p while consuming xa. This sequence must have a prefix $\tau_1, \ldots, \tau_i$ that takes M from q_0 to some state q while consuming x (see Figure 2.3.4(a)). Consequently, q is in A_x and the subsequence $\tau_{i+1}, \ldots, \tau_t$ of transition rules takes M from state q to state p while consuming a.

On the other hand, if q is in A_x and if p is a state that is reachable from state q by a sequence $\tau_1, \ldots, \tau_s$ of transition rules that consumes a, then the state p is in A_{xa}. In such a case, if $\tau'_1, \ldots, \tau'_r$ is a sequence of transition rules that takes M from the initial state q_0 to state q while consuming x, then M can reach the state p from state q_0 by the sequence $\tau'_1, \ldots, \tau'_r, \tau_1, \ldots, \tau_s$ of transition rules that consumes xa (see Figure 2.3.4(b)).

As a result, to determine if $a_1 \cdots a_n$ is accepted by M, one needs only to follow the sequence $A_\epsilon, A_{a_1}, A_{a_1 a_2}, \ldots, A_{a_1 \cdots a_n}$ of sets of states, where each $A_{a_1 \cdots a_{i+1}}$ is uniquely determined from $A_{a_1 \cdots a_i}$ and a_{i+1}. Therefore, a deterministic finite-state automaton M' of the following form decides the language that is accepted by M.

The set of states of M' is equal to $\{ A \mid A$ is a subset of Q, and $A = A_x$ for some x in $\Sigma^* \}$. Since Q is finite, it follows that Q has only a finite number of subsets A, and consequently M' has also only a finite number of states. The initial state of M' is the subset of Q that is equal to A_ϵ. The accepting states of M' are those states of M' that contain at least one accepting state of M. The transition table of M' is the set $\{ (A, a, A') \mid A$ and A' are states of M', a is in Σ, and A' is the set of states that the finite-state automaton M can reach by consuming a from those states that are in $A \}$.

By definition, M' has no ϵ transition rules. Moreover, M' is deterministic because, for each x in Σ^* and each a in Σ, the set A_{xa} is uniquely defined from the set A_x and the symbol a. $\square$

Example 2.3.3 Let M be the finite-state automaton whose transition diagram is given in Figure 2.3.2. The transition diagram in Figure 2.3.5 represents an ϵ-free, deterministic finite-state automaton that is equivalent to M. Using the terminology of the proof of Theorem 2.3.1 $A_\epsilon = \{q_0, q_1, q_4\}$, $A_0 = \{q_0, q_1, q_2, q_4\}$, and $A_{00} = A_{000} = \cdots = A_{0\cdots 0} = \{q_0, q_1, q_2, q_3, q_4\}$.

A_ϵ is the set of all the states that M can reach without reading any input. q_0 is in A_ϵ because it is the initial state of M. q_1 and q_2 are in A_ϵ because M has ϵ transition rules that leave the initial state q_0 and enter states q_1 and q_2, respectively.

A_0 is the set of all the states that M can reach just by reading 0 from those states that are in A_ϵ. q_0 is in A_0 because q_0 is in A_ϵ and M has the transition

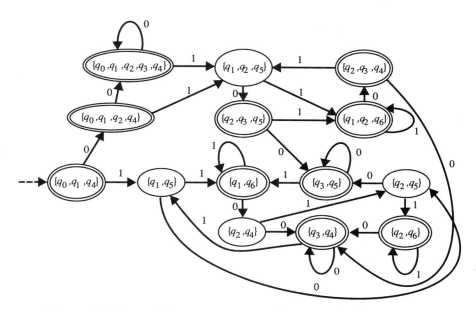

Figure 2.3.5 A transition diagram of an ϵ-free, deterministic finite-state automaton that is equivalent to the finite-state automaton whose transition diagram is given in Figure 2.3.2.

rule $(q_0, 0, q_0)$. q_1 is in A_0 because q_0 is in A_ϵ and M can use the pair $(q_0, 0, q_0)$ and (q_0, ϵ, q_1) of transition rules to reach q_1 from q_0 just by reading 0. q_2 is in A_0 because q_0 is in A_ϵ and M can use the pair (q_0, ϵ, q_1) and $(q_1, 0, q_2)$ of transition rules to reach q_2 from q_0 just by reading 0. $\qquad\square$

The result of the last theorem cannot be generalized to finite-state transducers, because deterministic finite-state transducers can only compute functions, whereas nondeterministic finite-state transducers can also compute relations which are not functions, for example, the relation $\{(a, b), (a, c)\}$. In fact, there are also functions that can be computed by nondeterministic finite-state transducers but that cannot be computed by deterministic finite-state transducers. $R = \{(x0, 0^{|x|}) \mid x$ is a string in $\{0, 1\}^*\} \cup \{(x1, 1^{|x|}) \mid x$ is a string in $\{0, 1\}^*\}$ is an example of such a function. The function cannot be computed by a deterministic finite-state transducer because each deterministic finite-state transducer M satisfies the following condition, which is not shared by the function: if x_1 is a prefix of x_2 and M accepts x_1 and x_2, then the output of M on input x_1 is a prefix of the output of M on input x_2 (Exercise 2.2.5).

Finite-State Automata and Type 3 Grammars

The following two results imply that a language is accepted by a finite-state automaton if and only if it is a Type 3 language. The proof of the first result shows how Type 3 grammars can simulate the computations of finite-state automata.

Theorem 2.3.2 Finite-state automata accept only Type 3 languages.

Proof Consider any finite-state automaton $M = <Q, \Sigma, \delta, q_0, F>$. By Theorem 2.3.1 it can be assumed that M is an ϵ-free, finite-state automaton. With no loss of generality, it can also be assumed that no transition rule takes M to its initial state when that state is an accepting one. (If such is not the case, then one can add a new state q_0' to Q, make the new state q_0' both an initial and an accepting state, and add a new transition rule (q_0', α, q) to δ for each transition rule of the form (q_0, α, q) that is in δ.)

Let $G = <N, \Sigma, P, [q_0]>$ be a Type 3 grammar, where N has a nonterminal symbol $[q]$ for each state q in Q and P has the following production rules.

a. A production rule of the form $[q] \rightarrow a[p]$ for each transition rule (q, a, p) in the transition table δ.

b. A production rule of the form $[q] \rightarrow a$ for each transition rule (q, a, p) in δ such that p is an accepting state in F.

c. A production rule of the form $[q_0] \rightarrow \epsilon$ if the initial state q_0 is an accepting state in F.

The grammar G is constructed to simulate the computations of the finite-state automaton M. G records the states of M through the nonterminal symbols. In particular, G uses its start symbol $[q_0]$ to initiate a simulation of M at state q_0. G uses a production rule of the form $[q] \rightarrow a[p]$ to simulate a move of M from state q to state p. In using such a production rule, G generates the symbol a that M reads in the corresponding move. G uses a production rule of the form $[q] \rightarrow a$ instead of the production rule of the form $[q] \rightarrow a[p]$, when it wants to terminate a simulation at an accepting state p.

By induction on n it follows that a string $a_1 a_2 \cdots a_n$ has a derivation in G of the form $[q] \Rightarrow a_1[q_1] \Rightarrow a_1 a_2 [q_2] \Rightarrow \cdots \Rightarrow a_1 a_2 \cdots a_{n-1}[q_{n-1}] \Rightarrow a_1 a_2 \cdots a_n$ if and only if M has a sequence of moves of the form $q a_1 a_2 \cdots a_n \vdash a_1 q_1 a_2 \cdots a_n \vdash a_1 a_2 q_2 a_3 \cdots a_n \vdash \cdots \vdash a_1 \cdots a_{n-1} q_{n-1} a_n \vdash a_1 a_2 \cdots a_n q_n$ for some accepting state q_n. In particular the correspondence above holds for $q = q_0$. Therefore $L(G) = L(M)$.   ☐

Example 2.3.4 The finite-state automaton M_1, whose transition diagram is given in Figure 2.3.6(b), is an ϵ-free, deterministic finite-state automaton. M_1 is not suitable for a direct simulation by a Type 3 grammar because its initial state q_0 is both an accepting state and a destination of a transition rule. Without modifications to M_1 the algorithm that constructs the grammar G will produce the production rule $[q_0] \rightarrow \epsilon$ because q_0 is an accepting state, and the production rule $[q_1] \rightarrow b[q_0]$ because of the transition rule (q_1, b, q_0). Such a pair of production rules cannot coexist in a Type 3 grammar.

M_1 is equivalent to the finite-state automaton M_2, whose transition diagram is given in Figure 2.3.6(a). The Type 3 grammar $G = <N, \Sigma, P, [q_0']>$ generates

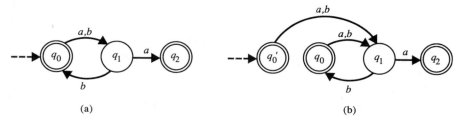

Figure 2.3.6 Two equivalent finite-state automata.

the language $L(M_2)$, if $N = \{[q_0'], [q_0], [q_1], [q_2]\}$, $\Sigma = \{a, b\}$, and P consists of the following production rules.

$$
\begin{aligned}
[q_0'] &\to \epsilon \\
&\to a[q_1] \\
&\to b[q_1] \\
[q_0] &\to a[q_1] \\
&\to b[q_1] \\
[q_1] &\to b[q_0] \\
&\to b \\
&\to a[q_2] \\
&\to a
\end{aligned}
$$

The accepting computation $q_0' abaa \vdash a q_1 baa \vdash ab q_0 aa \vdash abaq_1 a \vdash abaa q_2$ of M_2 on input $abaa$ is simulated by the derivation $[q_0'] \Rightarrow a[q_1] \Rightarrow ab[q_0] \Rightarrow aba[q_1] \Rightarrow abaa$ of the grammar.

The production rule $[q_1] \to a[q_2]$ can be eliminated from the grammar without affecting the generated language. □

The next theorem shows that the converse of Theorem 2.3.2 also holds. The proof shows how finite-state automata can trace the derivations of Type 3 grammars.

Theorem 2.3.3 Each Type 3 language is accepted by a finite-state automaton.

Proof Consider any Type 3 grammar $G = <N, \Sigma, P, S>$. The finite-state automaton $M = <Q, \Sigma, \delta, q_S, F>$ accepts the language that G generates if Q, δ, q_S, and F are as defined below.

M has a state q_A in Q for each nonterminal symbol A in N. In addition, Q also has a distinguished state named q_f. The state q_S of M, which corresponds to the start symbol S, is designated as the initial state of M. The state q_f of M is designated to be the only accepting state of M, that is, $F = \{q_f\}$.

M has a transition rule in δ if and only if the transition rule corresponds to a production rule of G. Each transition rule of the form (q_A, a, q_B) in δ corresponds to a production rule of the form $A \to aB$ in G. Each transition rule of the form

(q_A, a, q_f) in δ corresponds to a production rule of the form $A \rightarrow a$ in G. Each transition rule of the form (q_S, ϵ, q_f) in δ corresponds to a production rule of the form $S \rightarrow \epsilon$ in G.

The finite-state automaton M is constructed so as to trace the derivations of the grammar G in its computations. M uses its states to keep track of the nonterminal symbols in use in the sentential forms of G. M uses its transition rules to consume the input symbols that G generates in the direct derivations that use the corresponding production rules.

By induction on n, the constructed finite-state automaton M has a sequence $q_{A_0} x \vdash u_1 q_{A_1} v_1 \vdash u_2 q_{A_2} v_2 \vdash \cdots \vdash u_{n-1} q_{A_{n-1}} v_{n-1} \vdash x q_{A_n}$ of n moves if and only if the grammar G has a derivation of length n of the form $A_0 \Rightarrow u_1 A_1 \Rightarrow u_2 A_2 \Rightarrow \cdots \Rightarrow u_{n-1} A_{n-1} \Rightarrow x$. In particular, such correspondence holds for $A_0 = S$. Consequently, x is in $L(M)$ if and only if it is in $L(G)$. $\qquad\square$

Example 2.3.5 Consider the Type 3 grammar $G = <\{S, A, B\}, \{a, b\}, P, S>$, where P consists of the following transition rules.

$$
\begin{array}{rcl}
S & \rightarrow & \epsilon \\
  & \rightarrow & aA \\
  & \rightarrow & bB \\
A & \rightarrow & aA \\
  & \rightarrow & b \\
B & \rightarrow & bB \\
  & \rightarrow & a
\end{array}
$$

The transition diagram in Figure 2.3.7 represents a finite-state automaton that accepts the language $L(G)$. The derivation $S \Rightarrow aA \Rightarrow aaA \Rightarrow aab$ in G is traced by the computation $q_S aab \vdash a q_A ab \vdash aa q_A b \vdash aab q_f$ of M. $\qquad\square$

It turns out that finite-state automata and Type 3 grammars are quite similar mathematical systems. The states in the automata play a role similar to the nonterminal symbols in the grammars, and the transition rules in the automata play a role similar to the production rules in the grammars.

Type 3 Grammars and Regular Grammars

Type 3 grammars seem to be minimal in the sense that placing further meaningful restrictions on them results in grammars that cannot generate all the Type 3 languages. On the other hand, some of the restrictions placed on Type 3 grammars can be relaxed without increasing the class of languages that they can generate.

Specifically, a grammar $G = <N, \Sigma, P, S>$ is said to be a *right-linear grammar* if each of its production rules is either of the form $A \rightarrow xB$ or of the form $A \rightarrow x$, where A and B are nonterminal symbols in N and x is a string of terminal symbols in Σ^*.

The grammar is said to be a *left-linear grammar* if each of its production rules is either of the form $A \rightarrow Bx$ or of the form $A \rightarrow x$, where A and B are nonterminal symbols in N and x is a string of terminal symbols in Σ^*.

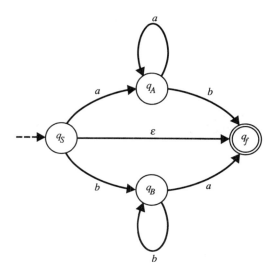

Figure 2.3.7 A finite-state automaton that accepts $L(G)$, where G is the grammar of Example 2.3.5.

The grammar is said to be a *regular grammar* if it is either a right-linear grammar or a left-linear grammar. A language is said to be a *regular language* if it is generated by a regular grammar.

By Exercise 2.3.5 a language is a Type 3 language if and only if it is regular.

Regular Languages and Regular Expressions

Regular languages can also be defined, from the empty set and from some finite number of singleton sets, by the operations of union, composition, and Kleene closure. Specifically, consider any alphabet Σ. Then a *regular set* over Σ is defined in the following way.

  a. The empty set $\emptyset$, the set $\{\epsilon\}$ containing only the empty string, and the set $\{a\}$ for each symbol a in Σ, are regular sets.

  b. If L_1 and L_2 are regular sets, then so are the union $L_1 \cup L_2$, the composition $L_1 L_2$, and the Kleene closure L_1^*.

  c. No other set is regular.

By Exercise 2.3.6 the following characterization holds.

Theorem 2.3.4 A set is a regular set if and only if it is accepted by a finite-state automaton.

Regular sets of the form $\emptyset$, $\{\epsilon\}$, $\{a\}$, $L_\alpha \cup L_\beta$, $L_\alpha L_\beta$, and L_α^* are quite often denoted by the expressions $\emptyset$, ϵ, a, $(\alpha) + (\beta)$, $(\alpha)(\beta)$, and $(\alpha)^*$, respectively.

α and β are assumed to be the expressions that denote L_α and L_β in a similar manner, respectively. a is assumed to be a symbol from the alphabet. Expressions that denote regular sets in this manner are called *regular expressions*.

Some parentheses can be omitted from regular expressions, if a precedence relation between the operations of Kleene closure, composition, and union in the given order is assumed. The omission of parentheses in regular expressions is similar to that in arithmetic expressions, where closure, composition, and union in regular expressions play a role similar to exponentiation, multiplication, and addition in arithmetic expressions.

Example 2.3.6 The regular expression $0^*(1^*01^*00^*(11^*01^*00^*)^* + 0^*10^*11^* (00^*10^*11^*)^*)$ denotes the language that is recognized by the finite-state automaton whose transition diagram is given in Figure 2.3.2. The expression indicates that each string starts with an arbitrary number of 0's. Then the string continues with a string in $1^*01^*00^*(11^*01^*00^*)^*$ or with a string in $10^*11^*(00^*10^*11^*)^*$. In the first case, the string continues with an arbitrary number of 1's, followed by 0, followed by an arbitrary number of 1's, followed by one or more 0's, followed by an arbitrary number of strings in $11^*01^*00^*$.   □

By the previous discussion, nondeterministic finite-state automata, deterministic finite-state automata, regular grammars, and regular expressions are all characterizations of the languages that finite-memory programs accept. Moreover, there are effective procedures for moving between the different characterizations. These procedures provide the foundation for many systems that produce finite-memory-based programs from characterizations of the previous nature. For instance, one of the best known systems, called LEX, gets inputs that are generalizations of regular expressions and provides outputs that are scanners. The advantage of such systems is obviously in the reduced effort they require for obtaining the desired programs.

Figure 2.3.8 illustrates the structural and functional hierarchies for some descriptive systems. The structural hierarchies are shown by the directed acyclic graphs. The functional hierarchy is shown by the Venn diagram.

2.4   Limitations of Finite-Memory Programs

It can be intuitively argued that there are computations that finite-memory programs cannot carry out, because of the limitations imposed on the amount of memory the programs can use. For instance, it can be argued that $\{ a^n b^n \mid n \geq 0 \}$ is not recognizable by any finite-memory program. The reasoning here is that upon reaching the first b in a given input, the program must remember how many a's it read. Moreover, the argument continues that each finite-memory program has an upper bound on the number of values that it can record, whereas no such bound exists on the number of a's that the inputs can contain. As a result, one can conclude that each finite-memory program can recognize only a finite number of strings in the set $\{ a^n b^n \mid n \geq 0 \}$.

The purposes of this section are to show that there are computations that cannot be carried out by finite-memory programs, and to provide formal tools for identi-

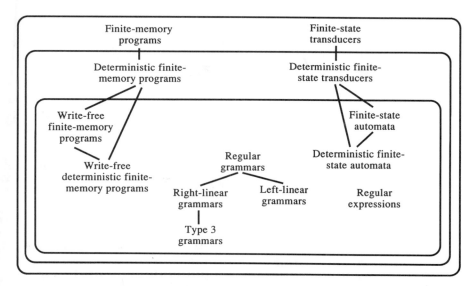

Figure 2.3.8 The structural and functional relationships between some descriptive systems.

fying such computations. The proofs rely on abstractions of the intuitive argument above. However, it should be mentioned that the problem of determining for any given language, whether the language is recognizable by a finite-memory program, can be shown to be undecidable (see Theorem 4.5.6). Therefore, no tool can be expected to provide an algorithm that decides the problem in its general form.

A Pumping Lemma for Regular Languages

The following theorem provides necessary conditions for a language to be decidable by a finite-memory program. The proof of the theorem relies on the observations that the finite-memory programs must repeat a state on long inputs, and that the subcomputations between the repetitions of the states can be pumped.

Theorem 2.4.1 (*Pumping lemma for regular languages*) Every regular language L has a number m for which the following conditions hold. If w is in L and $|w| \geq m$, then w can be written as xyz, where $xy^k z$ is in L for each $k \geq 0$. Moreover, $|xy| \leq m$, and $|y| > 0$.

Proof Consider any regular language L. Let M be a finite-state automaton that recognizes L. By Theorem 2.3.1 it can be assumed that M has no ϵ transition rules. Denote by m the number of states of M.

On input $w = a_1 \cdots a_n$ from L the finite-state automaton M has a computation of the form

$$p_0 a_1 \cdots a_n \vdash a_1 p_1 a_2 \cdots a_n \vdash \cdots \vdash a_1 \cdots a_i p_i a_{i+1} \cdots a_n \vdash \cdots \vdash$$
$$a_1 \cdots a_j p_j a_{j+1} \cdots a_n \vdash \cdots \vdash a_1 \cdots a_n p_n$$

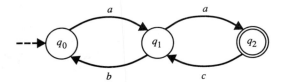

Figure 2.4.1 A finite-state automaton.

The computation goes through some sequence p_0, p_1, ..., p_n of $n + 1$ states, where p_0 is the initial state of M and p_n is an accepting state of M. In each move of the computation exactly one input symbol is being read.

If the length n of the input is equal at least to the number m of states of M, then the computation consists of m or more moves and some state q must be repeated within the first m moves. That is, if $n \geq m$ then $p_i = p_j$ for some i and j such that $0 \leq i < j \leq m$. In such a case, take $x = a_1 \cdots a_i$, $y = a_{i+1} \cdots a_j$, and $z = a_{j+1} \cdots a_n$.

With such a decomposition xyz of w the above computation of M takes the form

$$p_0 xyz \vdash^* xqyz \vdash^* xyqz \vdash^* xyzp_n$$

During the computation the state $q = p_i = p_j$ of M is repeated. The string x is consumed before reaching the state q that is repeated. The string y is consumed between the repetition of the state q. The string z is consumed after the repetition of state q.

Consequently, M also has an accepting computation of the form

$$p_0 xy^k z \vdash^* xqy^k z \vdash^* xyqy^{k-1}z \vdash^* \cdots \vdash^* xy^k qz \vdash^* xy^k zp_n$$

for each $k \geq 0$. That is, M has an accepting computation on $xy^k z$ for each $k \geq 0$, where M starts and ends consuming each y in state q.

The substring y that is consumed between the repetition of state q is not empty, because by assumption M has no ϵ transition rules.   □

Example 2.4.1 Let L be the regular language accepted by the finite-state automaton of Figure 2.4.1. Using the terminology in the proof of the pumping lemma (Theorem 2.4.1), L has the constant $m = 3$.

On input $w = ababaa$, the finite-state automaton goes through the sequence q_0, q_1, q_0, q_1, q_0, q_1, q_2 of states. For such an input the pumping lemma provides the decomposition $x = \epsilon$, $y = ab$, $z = abaa$; and the decomposition $x = a$, $y = ba$, $z = baa$. The first decomposition is due to the first repetition of state q_0; the second is a result of to the first repetition of state q_1.

For each string w of a minimum length 3, the pumping lemma implies a decomposition xyz in which the string y must be either ab or ba or ac. If $y = ab$, then $x = \epsilon$ and the repetition of q_0 is assumed. If $y = ba$, then $x = a$ and the repetition of q_1 is assumed. If $y = ac$, then $x = a$ and the repetition of q_1 is assumed.   □

Applications of the Pumping Lemma

For proving that a given language L is not regular, the pumping lemma implies the following schema of reduction to contradiction.

a. For the purpose of the proof assume that L is a regular language.

b. Let m denote the constant implied by the pumping lemma for L, under the assumption in (a) that L is regular.

c. Find a string w in L, whose length is at least m. Require that w implies a k, for each decomposition xyz of w, such that $xy^k z$ is not in L. That is, find a w that implies, by using the pumping lemma, that a string not in L must, in fact, be there.

d. Use the contradiction in (c) to conclude that the pumping lemma does not apply for L.

e. Use the conclusion in (d) to imply that the assumption in (a), that L is regular, is false.

It should be emphasized that in the previous schema the pumping lemma implies only the existence of a constant m for the assumed regular language L, and the existence of a decomposition xyz for the chosen string w. This lemma does not provide any information about the specific values of m, x, y, and z besides the restriction that they satisfy the conditions $|xy| \leq m$ and $|y| > 0$. The importance for the schema of the condition $|xy| \leq m$ lies in allowing some limitation on the possible decompositions that are to be considered for the chosen w. The importance of the restriction $|y| > 0$ is in enabling a proper change in the pumped string.

Example 2.4.2 Consider the nonregular language $L = \{\, 0^n 1^n \mid n \geq 0 \,\}$. To prove that L is nonregular assume to the contrary that it is regular. From the assumption that L is regular deduce the existence of a fixed constant m that satisfies the conditions of the pumping lemma for L.

Choose the string $w = 0^m 1^m$ in L. By the pumping lemma, $0^m 1^m$ has a decomposition of the form xyz, where $|xy| \leq m$, $|y| > 0$, and $xy^k z$ is in L for each $k \geq 0$. That is, the decomposition must be of the form $x = 0^i$, $y = 0^j$, and $z = 0^{m-i-j} 1^m$ for some i and j such that $j > 0$. (Note that the values of i, j, and m cannot be chosen arbitrarily.) Moreover, $xy^0 z$ must be in L. However, $xy^0 z = 0^{m-j} 1^m$ cannot be in L because $j > 0$. It follows that the pumping lemma does not apply for L, consequently contradicting the assumption that L is regular.

Other choices of w can also be used to show that L is not regular. However, they might result in a more complex analysis. For instance, for $w = 0^{m-1} 1^{m-1}$ the pumping lemma provides three possible forms of decompositions:

a. $x = 0^i$, $y = 0^j$, $z = 0^{m-i-j-1} 1^{m-1}$ for some $j > 0$.

b. $x = 0^{m-1-j}$, $y = 0^j 1$, $z = 1^{m-2}$ for some $j > 0$.

   c. $x = 0^{m-1}$, $y = 1$, $z = 1^{m-2}$.

In such a case, each of the three forms of decompositions must be shown to be inappropriate to conclude that the pumping lemma does not apply to w. For (a) the choice of $k = 0$ provides $xy^0z = 0^{m-1-j}1^{m-1}$ not in L. For (b) the choice of $k = 2$ provides $xy^2z = 0^{m-1}10^j1^{m-1}$ not in L. For (c) the choice of $c = 0$ provides $xy^0z = 0^{m-1}1^{m-2}$ not in L. $\square$

Example 2.4.3 Consider the nonregular language $L = \{\, \alpha\alpha^{\text{rev}} \mid \alpha \text{ is in } \{a,b\}^* \,\}$. To prove that L is not regular assume to the contrary that it is regular. Then deduce the existence of a fixed constant m that satisfies the conditions of the pumping lemma for L.

   Choose $w = a^m b b a^m$ in L. By the pumping lemma, $a^m b b a^m = xyz$ for some x, y, and z such that $|xy| \le m$, $|y| > 0$ and xy^kz is in L for each $k \ge 0$. That is, $x = a^i$, $y = a^j$, and $z = a^{m-i-j}bba^m$ for some i and j such that $j > 0$. However, $xy^0z = a^{m-j}bba^m$ is not in L, therefore contradicting the assumption that L is regular.

   It should be noted that not every choice for w implies the desired contradiction. For instance, consider the choice of a^{2m} for w. By the pumping lemma, a^{2m} has a decomposition xyz in which $x = a^i$, $y = a^j$, and $z = a^{2m-i-j}$ for some i and j such that $j > 0$. With such a decomposition, $xy^kz = a^{2m+(k-1)j}$ is not in L if and only if $2m + (k-1)j$ is an odd integer. On the other hand, $2m + (k-1)j$ is an odd integer if and only if k is an even number and j is an odd number. However, although k can arbitrarily be chosen to equal any value, such is not the case with j. Consequently, the choice of a^{2m} for w does not guarantee the desired contradiction. $\square$

A Generalization to the Pumping Lemma

The proof of the pumping lemma is based on the observation that a state is repeated in each computation on a "long" input, with a portion of the input being consumed between the repetition. The repetition of the state allows the pumping of the subcomputation between the repetition to obtain new accepting computations on different inputs. The proof of the pumping lemma with minor modifications also holds for the following more general theorem.

Theorem 2.4.2 For each relation R that is computable by a finite-state transducer, there exists a constant m that satisfies the following conditions. If (v, w) is in R and $|v| + |w| \ge m$, then v can be written as $x_v y_v z_v$ and w can be written as $x_w y_w z_w$, where $(x_v y_v^k z_v, x_w y_w^k z_w)$ is in R for each $k \ge 0$. Moreover, $|x_v y_v| + |x_w y_w| \le m$, and $|y_v| + |y_w| > 0$.

   A schema, similar to the one that uses the pumping lemma for determining nonregular languages, can utilize Theorem 2.4.2 for determining relations that are not computable by finite-state transducers.

Example 2.4.4 The relation $R = \{(u, u^{\text{rev}}) \mid u \text{ is in } \{0,1\}^*\}$ is not computable by a finite-state transducer. If R were computable by a finite-state transducer, then there would be a constant m that satisfies the conditions of Theorem 2.4.2 for R. In such a case, since $(0^m 1^m, 1^m 0^m)$ is in R, then $u = 0^m 1^m$ could be written as $x_v y_v z_v$ and $u^{\text{rev}} = 1^m 0^m$ could be written as $x_w y_w z_w$, where $x_v = 0^{i_v}$, $y_v = 0^{j_v}$, $z_v = 0^{m-i_v-j_v} 1^m$, $x_w = 1^{i_w}$, $y_w = 1^{j_w}$, $z_w = 1^{m-i_w-j_w} 0^m$, and $j_v + j_w > 0$. Moreover, it would be implied that $(x_v y_v^0 z_v, x_w y_w^0 z_w) = (0^{m-j_v} 1^m, 1^{m-j_w} 0^m)$ must also be in R, which is not the case. □

2.5 Closure Properties for Finite-Memory Programs

A helpful approach in simplifying the task of programming is to divide the given problem into subproblems, design subprograms to solve the subproblems, and then combine the subprograms into a program that solves the original problem. To allow for a similar approach in designing finite-state transducers (and finite-memory programs), it is useful to determine those operations that preserve the set of relations that are computable by finite-state transducers. Such knowledge can then be used in deciding how to decompose given problems to simpler subproblems, as well as in preparing tools for automating the combining of subprograms into programs.

In general, a set is said to be *closed* under a particular operation if each application of the operation on elements of the set results in an element of the set.

Example 2.5.1 The set of natural numbers is closed under addition, but it is not closed under subtraction. The set of integers is closed under addition and subtraction, but not under division. The set $\{S \mid S \text{ is a set of five or more integers}\}$ is closed under union, but not under intersection or complementation. The set $\{S \mid S \text{ is a set of at most five integer numbers}\}$ is closed under intersection, but not under union or complementation. □

The first theorem in this section is concerned with closure under the operation of union.

Theorem 2.5.1 The class of relations computable by finite-state transducers is closed under union.

Proof Consider any two finite-state transducers $M_1 = \langle Q_1, \Sigma_1, \Delta_1, \delta_1, q_{01}, F_1 \rangle$ and $M_2 = \langle Q_2, \Sigma_2, \Delta_2, \delta_2, q_{02}, F_2 \rangle$. With no loss of generality assume that the sets q_1 and q_2 of states are mutually disjoint, and that neither of them contains q_0.

Let M_3 be the finite-state transducer $\langle Q_3, \Sigma_3, \Delta_3, \delta_3, q_0, F_3 \rangle$, where $Q_3 = Q_1 \cup Q_2 \cup \{q_0\}$, $\Sigma_3 = \Sigma_1 \cup \Sigma_2$, $\delta_3 = \delta_1 \cup \delta_2 \cup \{(q_0, \epsilon, q_{01}, \epsilon), (q_0, \epsilon, q_{02}, \epsilon)\}$, and $F_3 = F_1 \cup F_2$ (see Figure 2.5.1).

Intuitively, M_3 is a finite-state transducer that at the start of each computation nondeterministically chooses to trace either a computation of M_1 or a computation of M_2.

By construction, $R(M_3) = R(M_1) \cup R(M_2)$. □

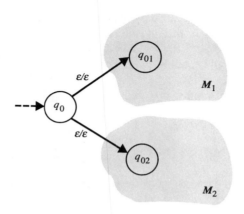

Figure 2.5.1 A schema of a finite-state transducer M_3 that computes $R(M_1) \cup R(M_2)$.

Besides their usefulness in simplifying the task of programming, closure properties can also be used to identify relations that cannot be computed by finite-state transducers.

Example 2.5.2 The union of the languages $L_1 = \{\epsilon\}$ and $L_2 = \{0^i 1^i \mid i \geq 1\}$ is equal to the language $L_3 = \{0^i 1^i \mid i \geq 0\}$. By Theorem 2.5.1 the union $L_3 = L_1 \cup L_2$ of L_1 and L_2 is a regular language if L_1 and L_2 are regular languages. Since $L_1 = \{\epsilon\}$ is a regular language, it follows that L_3 is a regular language if L_2 is a regular language. However, by Example 2.4.2 the language $L_3 = \{0^i 1^i \mid i \geq 0\}$ is not regular. Consequently, is also $L_2 = \{0^i 1^i \mid i \geq 1\}$ not regular. $\square$

The relations $R_1 = \{(0^i 1^j, c^i) \mid i, j \geq 1\}$ and $R_2 = \{(0^i 1^j, c^j) \mid i, j \geq 1\}$ are computable by deterministic finite-state transducers. The pair $(0^i 1^j, c^k)$ is in R_1 if and only if $k = i$, and it is in R_2 if and only if $k = j$. The intersection $R_1 \cap R_2$ contains all the pairs $(0^i 1^j, c^k)$ that satisfy $k = i = j$, that is, $R_1 \cap R_2$ is the relation $\{(0^n 1^n, c^n) \mid n \geq 1\}$.

If $R_1 \cap R_2$ is computable by a finite-state transducer then the language $\{0^n 1^n \mid n \geq 1\}$ must be regular. However, by Example 2.4.2 the language is not regular. Therefore, the class of the relations that are computable by finite-state transducers is not closed under intersection.

The class of the relations computable by the finite-state transducers is also not closed under complementation. An assumption to the contrary would imply that the nonregular language $R_1 \cap R_2$ is regular, because by DeMorgan's law $R_1 \cap R_2 = (\overline{\overline{R_1} \cup \overline{R_2}})$. That is, an assumed closure under complementation would imply that $\overline{R_1}$ and $\overline{R_2}$ are computable by finite-state transducers. Theorem 2.5.1 would then imply that the union $\overline{R_1} \cup \overline{R_2}$ is computable by finite-state transducers. Finally, another application of the assumption would imply that $\overline{(\overline{R_1} \cup \overline{R_2})} = R_1 \cap R_2$ is also computable by a finite-state transducer.

The choice of R_1 and R_2 also implies the nonclosure, under intersection, of the class of relations computable by deterministic finite-state transducers. The nonclosure under union and complementation, of the class of relations computable by deterministic finite-state transducers, is implied by the choice of the relations $\{(1, 1)\}$ and $\{(1, 11)\}$.

For regular languages the following theorem holds.

Theorem 2.5.2 Regular languages are closed under union, intersection, and complementation.

Proof By DeMorgan's law and the closure of regular languages under union (see Theorem 2.5.1), it is sufficient to show that regular languages are closed under complementation.

For the purpose of this proof consider any finite-state automaton $M = <Q, \Sigma, \delta, q_0, F>$. By Theorem 2.3.1 it can be assumed that M is deterministic, and contains no ϵ transition rules.

Let M_{eof} be M with a newly added, nonaccepting "trap" state, say, q_{trap} and the following newly added transition rules.

a. (q, a, q_{trap}) for each pair (q, a) — of a state q in Q and of an input symbol a in Σ — for which no move is defined in M. That is, for each (q, a) for which no p exists in Q such that (q, a, p) is in δ.

b. (q_{trap}, a, q_{trap}) for each input symbol a in Σ.

By construction M_{eof} is a deterministic finite-state automaton equivalent to M. Moreover, M_{eof} consumes all the inputs until their end, and it has no ϵ transition rules.

The complementation of the language $L(M)$ is accepted by the finite-state automaton $M_{complement}$ that is obtained from M_{eof} by interchanging the roles of the accepting and nonaccepting states.

For each given input $a_1 \cdots a_n$ the finite-state automaton $M_{complement}$ has a unique path that consumes $a_1 \cdots a_n$ until its end. The path corresponds to the sequence of moves that M_{eof} takes on such an input. Therefore, $M_{complement}$ reaches an accepting state on a given input if and only if M_{eof} does not reach an accepting state on the the input. $\square$

Example 2.5.3 Let M be the finite-state automaton whose transition diagram is given in Figure 2.5.2(a). The complementation of $L(M)$ is accepted by the finite-state automaton whose transition diagram is given in Figure 2.5.2(b).

Without the trap state q_{trap}, neither M nor $M_{complement}$ would be able to accept the input 011, because none of them would be able to consume the whole input.

Without the requirement that the algorithm has to be applied only on deterministic finite-state automata, $M_{complement}$ could end up accepting an input that M also accepts. For instance, by adding the transition rule $(q_1, 1, q_1)$ to M and $M_{complement}$, on input 01 each of the finite-state automata can end up either in state q_0 or in state q_1. In such a case, M would accept 01 because it can reach state q_1, and $M_{complement}$ would accept 01 because it can reach state q_0. $\square$

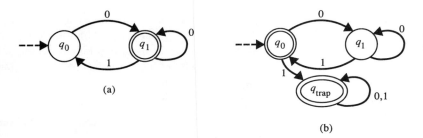

Figure 2.5.2 The finite-state automaton in (b) accepts the complementation of the language that the finite-state automaton in (a) accepts.

2.6   Decidable Properties for Finite-Memory Programs

The emptiness problem, the equivalence problem, the halting problem, and other decision problems for finite-memory programs or, equivalently, for finite-state transducers are defined in a similar manner as for the general class of programs.

For instance, the equivalence problem for finite-state transducers asks for any given pair of finite-state transducers whether or not the transducers compute the same relation.

Similarly, the halting problem for finite-state transducers asks for any given pair (M, x), of a finite-state transducer M and of an input x for M, whether or not M has only halting computations on x.

In this section, some properties of finite-state transducers are shown to be decidable. The proofs are constructive in nature and they therefore imply effective algorithms for determining the properties in discourse. The first theorem is interesting mainly for its applications (see Example 2.1.2). It is concerned with the problem of determining whether an arbitrarily given finite-state automaton accepts no input.

Theorem 2.6.1 The emptiness problem is decidable for finite-state automata.

Proof   Consider any finite-state automaton M. M accepts some input if and only if there is a path in its transition diagram from the node that corresponds to the initial state to a node that corresponds to an accepting state. The existence of such a path can be determined by the following algorithm.

Step 1 Mark in the transition diagram the node that corresponds to the initial state of M.

Step 2 Repeatedly mark those unmarked nodes in the transition diagram that are reachable by an edge from a marked node. Terminate the process when no additional nodes can be marked.

Step 3 If the transition diagram contains a marked node that corresponds to an accepting state, then determine that $L(M)$ is not empty. Otherwise, determine that $L(M)$ is empty.   □

By definition, a program has only halting computations on inputs that it accepts. On the other hand, on each input that it does not accept, the program may have some computations that never terminate.

An important general determination about programs is whether they halt on all inputs. The proof of the following theorem indicates how, in the case of finite-memory programs, the uniform halting problem can be reduced to the emptiness problem.

Theorem 2.6.2 The uniform halting problem is decidable for finite-state automata.

Proof Consider any finite-state automaton $M = <Q, \Sigma, \delta, q_0, F>$. With no loss of generality, assume that the symbol c is not in Σ, and that Q has n states. In addition, assume that every state from which M can reach an accepting state by reading nothing is also an accepting state. Let A be a finite-state automaton obtained from M by replacing each ϵ transition rule of the form (q, ϵ, p) with a transition rule of the form (q, c, p). Let B be a finite-state automaton that accepts the language $\{ x \mid x$ is in $(\Sigma \cup \{c\})^*$, and c^n is a substring of $x \}$.

M has a nonhalting computation on a given input if and only if the following two conditions hold.

    a. The input is not accepted by M.

    b. On the given input M can reach a state that can be repeated without reading any input symbol.

Consequently, M has a nonhalting computation if and only if A accepts some input that has c^n as a substring.

By the proof of Theorem 2.5.2, a finite-state automaton C can be constructed to accept the complementation of $L(A)$. By that same proof, a finite-state automaton D can also be constructed to accept the intersection of $L(B)$ and $L(C)$.

By construction, D is a finite-state automaton that accepts exactly those inputs that have c^n as a substring and that are not accepted by A. That is, D accepts no input if and only if M halts on all inputs. The theorem thus follows from Theorem 2.6.1.   □

For finite-memory programs that need not halt on all inputs, the proof of the following result implies an algorithm to decide whether or not they halt on specifically given inputs.

Theorem 2.6.3 The halting problem is decidable for finite-state automata.

Proof Consider any finite-state automaton M and any input $a_1 \cdots a_n$ for M. As in the proof of Theorem 2.3.1, one can derive for each $i = 1, \ldots, n$ the set $A_{a_1 \cdots a_i}$ of all the states that can be reached by consuming $a_1 \cdots a_i$. Then M is determined to halt on $a_1 \cdots a_n$ if and only if either of the following two conditions hold.

    a. $A_{a_1 \cdots a_n}$ contains an accepting state.

```
x := ?
do
    read y
until y ≠ x
do
    y := y + x
    write y
or
    if eof then accept
    reject
until false
```

Figure 2.E.1

b. For no integer i such that $1 \le i \le n$ the set $A_{a_1 \cdots a_i}$ contains a state that can be reached from itself by a sequence of one or more moves on ϵ transition rules.   □

There are many other properties that are decidable for finite-memory programs. This section concludes with the following theorem.

Theorem 2.6.4 The equivalence problem is decidable for finite-state automata.

Proof Two finite-state automata M_1 and M_2 are equivalent if and only if the relation $(L(M_1) \cap \overline{L(M_2)}) \cup (\overline{L(M_1)} \cap L(M_2)) = \emptyset$ holds, where $\overline{L(M_i)}$ denotes the complementation of $L(M_i)$ for $i = 1$, 2. The result then follows from the proof of Theorem 2.5.2 and from Theorem 2.6.1.   □

The result in Theorem 2.6.4 can be shown to hold also for deterministic finite-state transducers (see Corollary 3.6.1). However, for the general class of finite-state transducers the equivalence problem can be shown to be undecidable (see Corollary 4.7.1).

Exercises

2.2.1 Let P be a program with k instruction segments and a domain of variables of cardinality m. Determine an upper bound on the number of states of P, and an upper bound on the number of possible transitions between these states.

2.2.2 Determine the diagram representation of a finite-state transducer that models the computations of the program in Figure 2.E.1. Assume that the domain of the variables is $\{0, 1\}$, and that 0 is the initial value in the domain. Denote each node in the transition diagram with the corresponding state of the program.

2.2.3 For each of the following relations give a finite-state transducer that computes the relation.

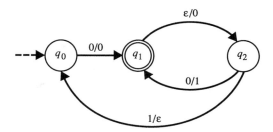

Figure 2.E.2

a. $\{(x\#y, a^i b^j) \mid x$ and y are in $\{a, b\}^*$, $i =$ (number of a's in x), and $j =$ (number of b's in y)$\}$

b. $\{(x, c^i) \mid x$ is in $\{a, b\}^*$, and $i =$ (number of appearances of the substring abb's in x)$\}$

c. $\{(x, c^i) \mid x$ is in $\{a, b\}^*$, and $i =$ (number of appearances of the substring aba's in x)$\}$

d. $\{(1^i, 1^j) \mid i$ and j are natural numbers and $i \geq j\}$

e. $\{(x, a) \mid x$ is in $\{0, 1\}^*$, a is in $\{0, 1\}$, and a appears at least twice in the string $x\}$

f. $\{(xy, a^i b^j) \mid x$ and y are in $\{a, b\}^*$, $i =$ (the number of a's in x), and $j =$ (the number of b's in y)$\}$

g. $\{(x, y) \mid x$ and y are in $\{a, b\}^*$, and either x is a substring of y or y is a substring of $x\}$

h. $\{(x, y) \mid x$ is in $\{a, b\}^*$, y is a substring of x, and the first and last symbols in y are of distinct values$\}$

i. $\{(x, y) \mid x$ and y are in $\{a, b\}^*$, and the substring ab has the same number of appearances in x and $y\}$

j. $\{(1^i, 1^j) \mid i = 2j$ or $i = 3j\}$

k. $\{(1^i, 1^j) \mid i \neq 2j\}$

l. $\{(x, y) \mid x$ and y are in $\{a, b\}^*$, and the number of a's in x differs from the number of b's in $y\}$

m. $\{(x, y) \mid x$ and y are in $\{0, 1\}^*$, and (the natural number represented by y) $= 3$(the natural number represented by x)$\}$

n. $\{(\binom{x_1}{y_1}) \cdots (\binom{x_n}{y_n}), z_1 \cdots z_n) \mid x_1, \ldots, x_n, y_1, \ldots, y_n, z_1, \ldots, z_n$ are in $\{0, 1\}$, and (the natural number represented by $x_1 \cdots x_n$) $-$ (the natural number represented by $y_1 \cdots y_n$) $=$ (the natural number represented by $z_1 \cdots z_n$)$\}$

2.2.4 Let $M = <Q, \Sigma, \Delta, \delta, q_0, F>$ be the deterministic finite-state transducer whose transition diagram is given in Figure 2.E.2. For each of the following relations find a finite-state transducer that computes the relation.

a. $\{(x, y) \mid x$ is in $L(M)$, and y is in $\Delta^*\}$.

b. $\{(x, y) \mid x$ is in $L(M)$, y is in Δ^*, and (x, y) is not in $R(M)\}$.

2.2.5 Show that if a deterministic finite-state transducer M accepts inputs x_1 and x_2 such that x_1 is a prefix of x_2, then on these inputs M outputs y_1 and y_2, respectively, such that y_1 is a prefix of y_2.

2.2.6 Determine the sequence of configurations in the computation that the finite-state transducer $<\{q_0, q_1, q_2\}, \{0, 1\}, \{a, b\}, \{(q_0, 0, q_1, a), (q_1, 1, q_0, a), (q_1, 1, q_2, \epsilon), (q_2, \epsilon, q_1, b)\}, q_0, \{q_2\}>$ has on input 0101.

2.2.7 Modify Example 2.2.16 for the case that M is the finite-state transducer whose transition diagram is given in Figure 2.2.2.

2.3.1 For each of the following languages construct a finite-state automaton that accepts the language.

a. $\{x \mid x$ is in $\{0, 1\}^*$, and no two 0's are adjacent in $x\}$

b. $\{x \mid x$ is in $\{a, b, c\}^*$, and none of the adjacent symbols in x are equal $\}$

c. $\{x \mid x$ is in $\{0, 1\}^*$, and each substring of length 3 in x contains at least two 1's$\}$

d. $\{1^z \mid z = 3x + 5y$ for some natural numbers x and $y\}$

e. $\{x \mid x$ is in $\{a, b\}^*$, and x contains an even number of a's and an even number of b's$\}$

f. $\{x \mid x$ is in $\{0, 1\}^*$, and the number of 1's between every two 0's in x is even$\}$

g. $\{x \mid x$ is in $\{0, 1\}^*$, and the number of 1's between every two substrings of the form 00 in x is even$\}$

h. $\{x \mid x$ is in $\{0, 1\}^*$, but not in $\{10, 01\}^*\}$

i. $\{x \mid x$ is in $\{a, b, c\}^*$, and a substring of x is accepted by the finite-state automaton of Figure 2.4.1$\}$

2.3.2 Find a deterministic finite-state automaton that is equivalent to the finite-state automaton whose transition diagram is given in Figure 2.E.3.

2.3.3 Find a Type 3 grammar that generates the language accepted by the finite-state automaton whose transition diagram is given in Figure 2.E.4.

2.3.4 Find a finite-state automaton that accepts the language $L(G)$, for the case that $G = <N, \Sigma, P, S>$ is the Type 3 grammar whose production rules are

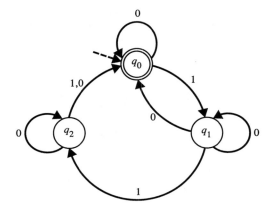

Figure 2.E.3

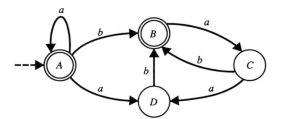

Figure 2.E.4

listed below.

$$
\begin{aligned}
S &\rightarrow aA \\
&\rightarrow bB \\
&\rightarrow b \\
A &\rightarrow aS \\
&\rightarrow bC \\
B &\rightarrow bS \\
&\rightarrow aC \\
&\rightarrow bA \\
C &\rightarrow aB
\end{aligned}
$$

2.3.5 Show that a language is generated by a Type 3 grammar if and only if it is generated by a right-linear grammar, and if and only if it is generated by a left-linear grammar.

2.3.6 Prove that a set is regular if and only if it is accepted by a finite-state automaton.

2.4.1 Let M be the finite-state automaton whose transition diagram is given in Figure 2.E.5. Using the notation of the proof of the pumping lemma for

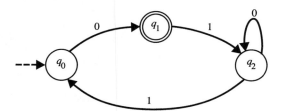

Figure 2.E.5

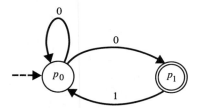

Figure 2.E.6

regular languages (Theorem 2.4.1), what are the possible values of m, x, and y for each w in $L(M)$?

2.4.2 Use the pumping lemma for regular languages to show that none of the following languages is regular.

a. $\{\, a^n b^t \mid n > t \,\}$

b. $\{\, v \mid v$ is in $\{a, b\}^*$, and v has fewer a's than b's $\}$

c. $\{\, x \mid x$ is in $\{a, b\}^*$, and $x = x^{\mathrm{rev}} \,\}$

d. $\{\, vv^{\mathrm{rev}} \mid v$ is accepted by the finite-state automaton of Figure 2.E.6 $\}$

e. $\{\, a^{n^2} \mid n \geq 1 \,\}$

f. $\{\, a^n b^t \mid n \neq t \,\}$

g. $\{\, x \mid x$ is in $\{a, b\}^*$, and $x \neq x^{\mathrm{rev}} \,\}$

2.4.3 Show that each relation R computable by a finite-state transducer has a fixed integer m such that the following holds for all (v, w) in R. If $|w| > m \cdot max(1, |v|)$, then $w = xyz$ for some x, y, z such that $(v, xy^k z)$ is in R for all $k \geq 0$. Moreover, $0 < |y| \leq m$.

2.4.4 Prove that the relation $\{\, (a^i b^j, c^k) \mid i$ and j are natural numbers and $k = i \cdot j \,\}$ is not computable by a finite-state transducer.

2.5.1 Let M_1 be the finite-state automaton given in Figure 2.E.3, and M_2 be the finite-state automaton given in Figure 2.E.6. Give a finite-state automaton that accepts the relation $R(M_1) \cap R(M_2)$.

2.5.2 For each of the following cases show that regular sets are closed under the operation Ψ.

    a. $\Psi(L) = \{\, x \mid x$ is in L, and a proper prefix of L is in $L \,\}$.

    b. $\Psi(L_1, L_2) = \{\, xyzw \mid xz$ is in L_1, and yw is in $L_2 \,\}$.

2.5.3 Let Ψ be a permutation operation on languages defined as $\Psi(L) = \{\, x \mid x$ is a permutation of some y in $L \,\}$. Show that regular sets are not closed under Ψ.

2.5.4 Show that the set of relations that finite-state transducers compute is closed under each of the following operations Ψ.

    a. Inverse, that is, $\Psi(R) = R^{-1} = \{\, (y, x) \mid (x, y)$ is in $R \,\}$.

    b. Closure, that is, $\Psi(R) = \cup_{i \geq 0} R^i$.

    c. Composition, that is, $\Psi(R_1, R_2) = \{\, (x, y) \mid x = x_1 x_2$ and $y = y_1 y_2$ for some (x_1, y_1) in R_1, and some (x_2, y_2) in $R_2 \,\}$.

    d. Cascade composition, that is, $\Psi(R_1, R_2) = \{\, (x, z) \mid (x, y)$ is in R_1 and (y, z) is in R_2 for some $y \,\}$.

2.5.5 Show that the set of the relations computed by deterministic finite-state transducers is not closed under composition.

2.5.6 Let M be the finite-state automaton whose transition diagram is given in Figure 2.E.3. Give a finite-state automaton that accepts the complementation of $L(M)$.

2.5.7 Show that the complementation of a relation computable by a deterministic finite-state transducer, is computable by a finite-state transducer.

2.6.1 Show that the problem defined by the following pair is decidable.

    Domain: $\{\, M \mid M$ is a finite-state automaton $\}$

    Question: Is $L(M)$ a set of infinite cardinality for the given instance M?

Bibliographic Notes

Finite-memory programs and their relationship to finite-state transducers have been studied in Jones and Muchnick (1977). Their applicability in designing lexical analyzers can be seen in Aho, Sethi, and Ullman (1986). Their applicability in designing communication protocols is discussed in Danthine (1980). Their usefulness for solving systems of linear Diophantine equations follows from Büchi (1960).

    Finite-state transducers were introduced by Sheperdson (1959). Deterministic finite-state automata originated in McCulloch and Pitts (1943). Rabin and Scott (1959) introduced nondeterminism to finite-state automata, and showed the equivalency of nondeterministic finite-state automata to deterministic finite-state automata. The representation of finite-state transducers by transition diagrams is due to Myhill (1957).

Chomsky and Miller (1958) showed the equivalency of the class of languages accepted by finite-state automata and the class of Type 3 languages. Kleene (1956) showed that the languages that finite-state automata accept are characterized by regular expressions. LEX is due to Lesk (1975).

The pumping lemma for regular languages is due to Bar-Hillel, Perles, and Shamir (1961). Beauquier (see Ehrenfeucht, Parikh, and Rozenberg, 1981) showed the existence of a nonregular language that certifies the conditions of the pumping lemma.

The decidability of the emptiness and equivalence problems for finite-state automata, as well as Exercise 2.6.1, have been shown by Moore (1956).

Hopcroft and Ullman (1979) is a good source for additional coverage of these topics.

Chapter 3

RECURSIVE FINITE-DOMAIN PROGRAMS

Recursion is an important programming tool that deserves an investigation on its own merits. However, it takes on additional importance here by providing an intermediate class of programs — between the restricted class of finite-memory programs and the general class of programs. This intermediate class is obtained by introducing recursion into finite-domain programs.

The first section of this chapter considers the notion of recursion in programs. The second section shows that recursive finite-domain programs are characterized by finite-state transducers that are augmented by pushdown memory. A grammatical characterization for the recursive finite-domain programs is provided in the third section. The fourth section considers the limitations of recursive finite-domain programs. And the fifth and sixth sections consider closure and decidable properties of recursive finite-domain programs, respectively.

3.1   Recursion

The task of programming is in many cases easier when recursion is allowed. However, although recursion does not in general increase the set of functions that the programs can compute, in the specific case of finite-domain programs such an increase is achieved.

Here recursion is introduced to programs by

a. Pseudoinstructions of the following form. These are used for defining procedures. Each list of formal parameters consists of variable names that are all distinct, and each procedure body consists of an arbitrary sequence of instructions.

> **procedure** <procedure name> (<list of formal parameters>)
>   <procedure body>
> **end**

b. Call instructions of the following form. These are used for activating the
execution of procedures. Each list of actual parameters is equal in size to the
corresponding list of formal parameters, and it consists of variable names
that are all distinct.

> **call** <procedure name>(<list of actual parameters>)

c. Return instructions of the following form. These are used for deactivating
the execution of procedures. The instructions are restricted to appearing only
inside procedure bodies.

> **return**

Finite-domain programs that allow recursion are called *recursive finite-domain
programs.*

An execution of a call instruction activates the execution of the procedure that
is invoked. The activation consists of copying the values from the variables in
the list of actual parameters to the corresponding variables in the list of formal
parameters, and of transferring the control to the first instruction in the body of
the procedure.

An execution of a return instruction causes the deactivation of the last of those
activations of the procedures that are still in effect. The deactivation causes the
transfer of control to the instruction immediately following the call instruction that
was responsible for this last activation. Upon the transfer of control, the values
from the variables in the list of formal parameters are copied to the corresponding
variables in the list of actual parameters. In addition, the variables that do not
appear in the list of actual parameters are restored to their values just as before
the call instruction was executed.

All the variables of a program are assumed to be recognized throughout the
full scope of the program, and each of them is allowed to appear in an arbitrary
number of lists of formal and actual variables.

Any attempt to enter or leave a procedure without using a call instruction or a
return instruction, respectively, causes the program to abort execution in a rejecting
configuration.

In what follows, each call instruction and each return instruction is considered
to be an instruction segment.

Example 3.1.1 Let P be the recursive finite-domain program in Figure 3.1.1. The
variables are assumed to have the domain $\{0, 1\}$, with 0 as initial value. The
program P accepts exactly those inputs in which the number of 0's is equal to the
number of 1's. On each such input the program outputs those input values that
are preceded by the same number of 0's as 1's.

On input 00111001 the program starts by reading the first input value 0 in I_3,
writing 0 in I_4, and transferring the control to RP in I_5. Upon entering RP $x =$

```
do                              /* I_1  */
    if eof then accept          /* I_2  */
    read x                      /* I_3  */
    write x                     /* I_4  */
    call RP(x)                  /* I_5  */
until false                     /* I_6  */
procedure RP(y)
    do                          /* I_7  */
        read z                  /* I_8  */
        if z ≠ y then           /* I_9  */
            return              /* I_10 */
        call RP(z)              /* I_11 */
    until false                 /* I_12 */
end
```

Figure 3.1.1 A recursive finite-domain program.

$y = z = 0$. In RP the program uses instruction segment I_8 to read the second input value 0, and then it calls RP recursively in I_{11}.

The embedded activation of RP reads the first 1 in the input and then executes the return instruction, to resume in I_{12} with $x = y = z = 0$ the execution of the first activation of RP. The procedure continues by reading the second 1 of the input into z, and then returns to resume the execution of the main program in I_6 with $x = y = z = 0$. The main program reads 1 into x, prints out that value, and invokes RP.

Upon entering RP $x = y = 1$ and $z = 0$. The procedure reads 0 and then returns the control to the main program. The main program reads into x the last 0 of the input, prints the value out, and calls RP again. RP reads the last input value and returns the control to the main program, where the computation is terminated at I_2.

The table in Figure 3.1.2 shows the flow of data upon the activation and deactivation of RP.   □

The definition given here for recursion is not standard, but can be shown to be equivalent to standard definitions. The sole motivation for choosing the nonstandard definition is because it simplifies the notion of states of recursive programs. The convention that the variables of a program are recognizable throughout the full scope of the program is introduced to allow uniformity in the definition of states. The convention — that upon the execution of a return instruction the variables that do not appear in the list of actual parameters are restored to their values just before the execution of the corresponding call instructions — is introduced to show a resemblance to the notion of local variables in procedures.

Example 3.1.2 The recursive finite-domain program in Figure 3.1.3 computes the relation $\{ (ww^{rev}, w) \mid w$ is a string of even length in $\{0, 1\}^* \}$. The domain of the variables is assumed to equal $\{0, 1\}$, with 0 as initial value. On input 00111100

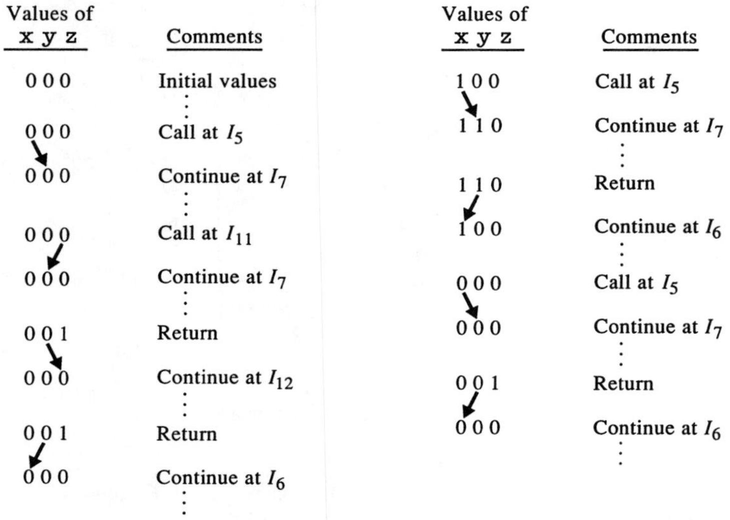

Values of x y z	Comments	Values of x y z	Comments
0 0 0	Initial values	1 0 0	Call at I_5
⋮			
0 0 0	Call at I_5	1 1 0	Continue at I_7
↘		⋮	
0 0 0	Continue at I_7	1 1 0	Return
⋮		↙	
0 0 0	Call at I_{11}	1 0 0	Continue at I_6
↙		⋮	
0 0 0	Continue at I_7	0 0 0	Call at I_5
⋮		↘	
0 0 1	Return	0 0 0	Continue at I_7
↘		⋮	
0 0 0	Continue at I_{12}	0 0 1	Return
⋮		↙	
0 0 1	Return	0 0 0	Continue at I_6
↙		⋮	
0 0 0	Continue at I_6		
⋮			

Figure 3.1.2 Flow of data in the program of Figure 3.1.1 on input 00111001.

```
call RP(parity)
if parity = 0 then
   if eof then accept
reject
procedure RP(parity)
   do    /* Process the next symbol in w. */
      read x
      write x
      parity := 1 − parity
      call RP(parity)
   or        /* Leave w and go to w^rev. */
      return
   until true
   /* Process the next symbol in w^rev. */
   read y
   if y ≠ x then reject
   return
end
```

Figure 3.1.3 A recursive finite-domain program.

the program has a unique computation that gives the output 0011. The program makes five calls to the procedure RP while reading 0011. Then it proceeds with five returns while reading 1100. □

It turns out that an approach similar to the one used for studying finite-memory programs can also be used for studying recursive finite-domain programs. The main difference between the two cases is in the complexity of the argumentation.

Moreover, as in the case of finite-memory programs, it should be emphasized here that recursive finite-domain programs are important not only as a vehicle for investigating the general class of programs but also on their own merits. For instance, in many compilers the syntax analyzers are basically designed as recursive finite-domain programs. (The central task of a syntax analyzer is to group together, according to some grammatical rules, the tokens in the program that is compiled. Such a grouping enables the compiler to detect the structure of the program, and therefore to generate the object code.)

3.2 Pushdown Transducers

In general, recursion in programs is implemented by means of a pushdown store, that is, a last-in-first-out memory. Thus, it is only natural to suspect that recursion in finite-domain programs implicitly allows an access to some auxiliary memory. Moreover, the observation makes it also unsurprising that the computations of recursive finite-domain programs can be characterized by finite-state transducers that are augmented with a pushdown store. Such transducers are called pushdown transducers.

Pushdown Transducers

Each pushdown transducer M can be viewed as an abstract computing machine that consists of a *finite-state control*, an *input tape*, a read-only *input head*, a *pushdown tape* or *pushdown store*, a read-write *pushdown head*, an *output tape*, and a write-only *output head* (see Figure 3.2.1). Each move of M is determined by the state of M, the input to be consumed, and the content on the top of the pushdown store. Each move of M consists of changing the state of M, reading at most one input symbol, changing the content on top of the pushdown store, and writing at most one symbol into the output.

Example 3.2.1 A pushdown transducer M can compute the relation $\{ (a^i b^i, c^i) \mid i \geq 1 \}$ by checking that each input has the form $a \cdots a b \cdots b$ with the same number of a's as b's, and writing that many c's. The computations of M can be in the following manner (see Figure 3.2.2).

Initially the pushdown store is assumed to contain just one symbol, say, Z_0 to mark the bottom of the pushdown store. M starts each computation by reading the a's from the input tape while pushing them into the pushdown store. The symbols are read one at a time from the input.

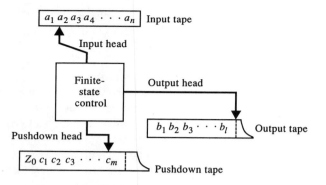

Figure 3.2.1 Schema of a pushdown transducer.

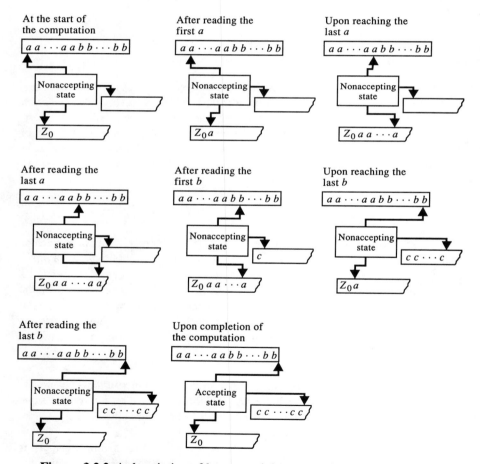

Figure 3.2.2 A description of how a pushdown transducer can compute the relation $\{(a^i b^i, c^i) \mid i \geq 1\}$.

Once M is done reading the a's from the input, it starts reading the b's. As M reads the b's it retrieves, or pops, one a from the pushdown store for each symbol b that it reads from the input. In addition, M writes one c to the output for each symbol b that it reads from the input.

M accepts the input if and only if it reaches the end of the input at the same time as it reaches the symbol Z_0 in the pushdown store. M rejects the input if it reaches the symbol Z_0 in the pushdown store before reaching the end of the input, because in such a case the input contains more b's than a's. M rejects the input if it reaches the end of the input before reaching the symbol Z_0 in the pushdown store, because in such a case the input contains more a's than b's. □

Formally, a mathematical system M consisting of an eight-tuple $<Q, \Sigma, \Gamma, \Delta, \delta, q_0, Z_0, F>$ is called a *pushdown transducer* if it satisfies the following conditions.

Q is a finite set, where the elements of Q are called the *states* of M.

Σ, Γ and Δ are alphabets. Σ is called the *input alphabet* of M, and its elements are called the *input symbols* of M. Γ is called the *pushdown alphabet* of M, and its elements are called the *pushdown symbols* of M. Δ is called the *output alphabet* of M, the elements of which are called the *output symbols* of M.

δ is a relation from $Q \times (\Sigma \cup \{\epsilon\}) \times (\Gamma \cup \{\epsilon\})$ to $Q \times \Gamma^* \times (\Delta \cup \{\epsilon\})$. δ is called the *transition table* of M, the elements of which are called the *transition rules* of M.

q_0 is an element in Q, called the *initial state* of M.

Z_0 is an element in Γ, called the *bottom pushdown symbol* of M.

F is a subset of Q. The states in the subset F are called the *accepting*, or *final*, *states* of M.

In what follows, each transition rule $(q, \alpha, \beta, (p, \gamma, \rho))$ of a pushdown transducer will be written as $(q, \alpha, \beta, p, \gamma, \rho)$.

Example 3.2.2 $M = <Q, \Sigma, \Gamma, \Delta, \delta, q_0, Z_0, F>$ is a pushdown transducer if $Q = \{q_0, q_1, q_2\}$; $\Sigma = \{a, b\}$; $\Delta = \{a, b\}$; $\Gamma = \{Z_0, c\}$; $\delta = \{(q_0, a, \epsilon, q_0, c, \epsilon), (q_0, b, \epsilon, q_0, c, \epsilon), (q_0, \epsilon, \epsilon, q_1, \epsilon, \epsilon), (q_1, a, c, q_1, \epsilon, a), (q_1, b, c, q_1, \epsilon, b), (q_1, \epsilon, Z_0, q_2, Z_0, \epsilon)\}$; and $F = \{q_2\}$. □

By definition, in each transition rule $(q, \alpha, \beta, p, \gamma, \rho)$ the entries q and p are states in Q, α is either an input symbol or an empty string, β is either a pushdown symbol or an empty string, γ is a string of pushdown symbols, and ρ is either an output symbol or an empty string.

Each pushdown transducer $M = <Q, \Sigma, \Gamma, \Delta, \delta, q_0, Z_0, F>$ can be graphically represented by a *transition diagram* of the following form. For each state in Q the transition diagram has a corresponding node drawn as a circle. The initial state is identified by an arrow from nowhere that points to the corresponding node. Each

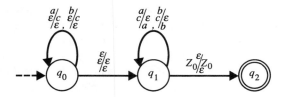

Figure 3.2.3 A transition diagram of a pushdown transducer.

accepting state is identified by a double circle. Each transition rule $(q, \alpha, \beta, p, \gamma, \rho)$ is represented by an edge from the node that corresponds to state q to the node that corresponds to state p. In addition, the edge is labeled with

$$\frac{\frac{\alpha}{}}{\frac{\beta}{}\frac{\gamma}{\rho}} \; .$$

For notational convenience, edges that agree in their origin and destination are merged, and their labels are separated by commas.

Example 3.2.3 Figure 3.2.3 gives the transition diagram for the pushdown transducer of Example 3.2.2. The label

$$\frac{\frac{a}{}}{\frac{\epsilon}{\epsilon}}$$

on the edge that starts and ends at state q_0 corresponds to the transition rule $(q_0, a, \epsilon, q_0, \epsilon, \epsilon)$. The label

$$\frac{\frac{\epsilon}{}}{\frac{\epsilon}{\epsilon}}$$

on the edge that starts at state q_0 and ends at state q_1 corresponds to the transition rule $(q_0, \epsilon, \epsilon, q_1, \epsilon, \epsilon)$.   □

The top row "$\alpha/$" in the label

$$\frac{\frac{\alpha}{}}{\frac{\beta}{}\frac{\gamma}{\rho}}$$

corresponds to the input tape. The middle row "β/γ" corresponds to the pushdown tape. The bottom row "$/\rho$" corresponds to the output tape.

Throughout the text the following conventions are assumed for each production rule $(q, \alpha, \beta, p, \gamma, \rho)$ of a pushdown transducer. The conventions do not affect the power of the pushdown transducers, and they are introduced to simplify the investigation of the pushdown transducers.

a. If $\beta = Z_0$, then Z_0 is a prefix of γ.

b. γ is a string of length 2 at most.

c. If γ is a string of length 2, the β is equal to the first symbol in γ.

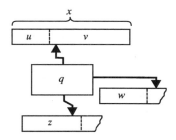

Figure 3.2.4 A configuration of a pushdown transducer.

Configurations and Moves of Pushdown Transducers

On each input x from Σ^* the pushdown transducer M has some set of possible configurations (see Figure 3.2.4). Each *configuration*, or *instantaneous description*, of M is a triplet (uqv, z, w), where q is a state of M, $uv = x$ is the input of M, z is a string from Γ^* of pushdown symbols, and w is a string from Δ^* of output symbols. Intuitively, a configuration (uqv, z, w) says that M on input x can reach state q with z in its pushdown store, after reading u and writing w. With no loss of generality it is assumed that Σ and Q are mutually disjoint.

The configuration is said to be an *initial configuration* if $q = q_0$, $u = w = \epsilon$, and $z = Z_0$. Such an initial configuration says that M is in its initial state q_0, with none of the input symbols being read yet (i.e., $u = \epsilon$), with the output being still empty (i.e., $w = \epsilon$), and the pushdown being still in its original stage (i.e., $z = Z_0$). In addition, the configuration says that M is given the input v.

The configuration is said to be an *accepting configuration* if $v = \epsilon$ and q is an accepting state. Such an accepting configuration says that M reached an accepting state after reading all the input (i.e., $v = \epsilon$) and writing w. In addition, the configuration says that the input M has consumed is equal to v.

Example 3.2.4 Consider the pushdown transducer M whose transition diagram is given in Figure 3.2.3. (q_0abbb, Z_0, ϵ) is the initial configuration of M on input $abbb$. The configuration $(abq_1bb, Z_0cc, \epsilon)$ of M says that M consumed already $u = ab$ from the input, the remainder of the input is $v = bb$, M has reached state q_1 with the string Z_0cc in the pushdown store, and the output so far is empty. The configurations are illustrated in Figure 3.2.5(a) and Figure 3.2.5(b), respectively.

$(abbbq_2, Z_0, bb)$ and $(abq_2bb, Z_0cc, \epsilon)$ are also configurations of M_0. The first configuration is accepting. The second, however, is not an accepting configuration despite its being in an accepting state, because the input has not been consumed until its end. $\qquad\qquad\square$

The transition rules of M are used for defining the possible moves of M. Each move is in accordance with some transition rule. A *move* on transition rule $(q, \alpha, \beta, p, \gamma, \rho)$ changes the state of the finite-state control from q to p; reads α from the input tape, moving the input head $|\alpha|$ positions to the right; writes ρ in the output tape, moving the output head $|\rho|$ positions to the right; and replaces on

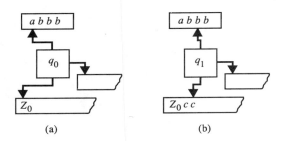

Figure 3.2.5 Configurations of the pushdown transducer of Figure 3.2.3.

top of the pushdown store (i.e., from the location of the pushdown head to its left) the string β with the string γ, moving the pushdown head $|\gamma| - |\beta|$ positions to the right. The move is said to be a *pop* move if $|\gamma| < |\beta|$. The move is said to be a *push* move if $|\beta| < |\gamma|$. The symbol under the pushdown head is called the *top symbol* of the pushdown store.

A move of M from configuration C_1 to configuration C_2 is denoted $C_1 \vdash_M C_2$, or simply $C_1 \vdash C_2$ if M is understood. A sequence of zero or more moves of M from configuration C_1 to configuration C_2 is denoted $C_1 \vdash_M^* C_2$, or simply $C_1 \vdash^* C_2$, if M is understood.

Example 3.2.5 The pushdown transducer whose transition diagram is given in Figure 3.2.3, has a sequence of moves on input $abbb$ that is given by the following sequence of configurations: $(q_0 abbb, Z_0, \epsilon) \vdash (aq_0 bbb, Z_0 c, \epsilon) \vdash (abq_0 bb, Z_0 cc, \epsilon) \vdash (abq_1 bb, Z_0 cc, \epsilon) \vdash (abbq_1 b, Z_0 c, b) \vdash (abbbq_1, Z_0, bb) \vdash (abbbq_2, Z_0, bb)$. This sequence is the only one that can start at the initial configuration and end at an accepting configuration for the input $abbb$. The sequence of configurations is depicted graphically in Figure 3.2.6.

All the moves of M on the transition rules that both start and end at state q_0 are push moves. All the moves of M on the transition rules that both start and end at state q_1 are pop moves. $\square$

A string in the pushdown store that starts at the bottom symbol and ends at the top symbol, excluding the bottom symbol, is called the *content* of the pushdown store. The pushdown store is said to be *empty* if its content is empty.

Example 3.2.6 Let M be the pushdown transducer of Figure 3.2.3. Consider the computation of M on input $abbb$ (see Figure 3.2.6). M starts with an empty pushdown store, adding c to the store during the first move. After the second move, the content of the pushdown store is cc. The content of the pushdown store does not change during the third move. $\square$

Determinism and Nondeterminism in Pushdown Transducers

The definitions of determinism and nondeterminism in pushdown transducers are, in principal, similar to those provided for finite-state transducers. The difference

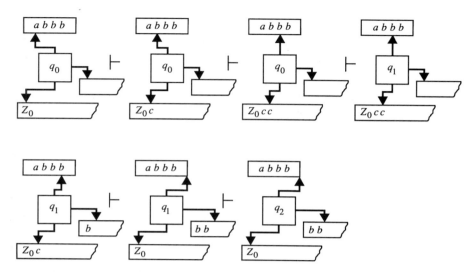

Figure 3.2.6 Transition between configurations of the pushdown transducer of Figure 3.2.3.

arises only in the details.

A pushdown transducer $M = <Q, \Sigma, \Gamma, \Delta, \delta, q_0, Z_0, F>$ is said to be *deterministic* if for each state q in Q; each input symbol a in Σ; and each pushdown symbol Z in Γ, the union $\delta(q, a, Z) \cup \delta(q, a, \epsilon) \cup \delta(q, \epsilon, Z) \cup \delta(q, \epsilon, \epsilon)$, is a multiset that contains at most one element.

Intuitively, M is deterministic if the state and the top pushdown symbol are sufficient for determining whether or not a symbol is to be read from the input, and the state, the top pushdown symbol, and the input to be read are sufficient for determining which transition rule is to be used.

A pushdown transducer is said to be *nondeterministic* if it is not a deterministic pushdown transducer.

Example 3.2.7 Let M_1 be the pushdown transducer whose transition diagram is given in Figure 3.2.3.

In a move from state q_1, the pushdown transducer M_1 reads an input symbol if and only if the topmost pushdown symbol is not Z_0. If the symbol is not Z_0, then the next symbol in the input uniquely determines which transition rule is to be used in the move. If the topmost pushdown symbol is Z_0, then M_1 must use the transition rule that leads to q_2. Consequently, the moves that originate at state q_1 can be fully determined "locally."

On the other hand, the moves from state q_0 cannot be determined locally, because the topmost pushdown symbol is not sufficient for determining if an input symbol is to be read in the move.

It follows that M_1 is a nondeterministic pushdown transducer. However, the pushdown transducer M_2 whose transition diagram is given in Figure 3.2.7 is deterministic.

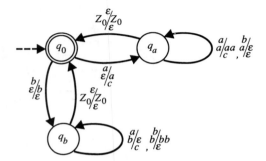

Figure 3.2.7 A deterministic pushdown transducer.

To move from state q_0 the pushdown transducer M_2 has to read an input symbol. If it reads the symbol a, then the move takes M_2 to state q_a. If it reads the symbol b, then the move takes M_2 to state q_b.

The topmost symbol in the pushdown store determines whether M_2 must enter state q_0 or state q_a on a move that originates at state q_a. If the topmost symbol is Z_0, then M moves to state q_0. If the topmost symbol is a, then M moves to state q_a. In the latter case M uses the transition rule (q_a, a, a, q_a, aa, c) if the input symbol to be read is a, and it uses the transition rule $(q_a, b, a, q_a, \epsilon, \epsilon)$ if the symbol to be read is b. $\square$

Computations of Pushdown Transducers

The computations of the pushdown transducers are also defined like the computations of the finite-state transducers. An *accepting computation* of a pushdown transducer M is a sequence of moves of M that starts at an initial configuration and ends at an accepting one. A *nonaccepting*, or *rejecting*, computation of M is a sequence of moves on an input x, for which the following conditions hold.

a. The sequence starts from the initial configuration of M on input x.

b. If the sequence is finite, it ends at a configuration from which no move is possible.

c. M has no accepting computation on input x.

Each accepting computation and each nonaccepting computation of M is said to be a *computation* of M.

A computation is said to be a *halting computation* if it consists of a finite number of moves.

Example 3.2.8 Consider the pushdown transducer M whose transition diagram is given in Figure 3.2.7. The pushdown transducer has accepting computations only on those inputs that have the same number of a's as b's. On each input w in which the pushdown transducer has an accepting computation, it writes the string c^i onto the output tape, where $i =$ (the number of a's in w) = (the number of b's in w).

The pushdown transducer enters state q_0 whenever the portion of the input read so far contains the same number of a's and b's. The pushdown transducer enters state q_a whenever the portion of the input read so far contains more a's than b's. Similarly, the pushdown transducer enters state q_b whenever the portion of the input read so far contains more b's than a's. The pushdown store is used for recording the difference between the number of a's and the number of b's, at any given instant of a computation.

On input $aabbba$ the pushdown transducer M has only one computation. M starts the computation by moving from state q_0 to state q_a, while reading a, writing c, and pushing a into the pushdown store. In the second move M reads a, writes c, pushes a into the pushdown store, and goes back to q_a. In the third and fourth moves M reads b, pops a from the pushdown store, and goes back to state q_a. In the fifth move M goes to state q_0 without reading, writing, or changing the content of the pushdown store. In the sixth move M reads b, pushes b into the pushdown store, and moves to state q_b. In its seventh move M reads a, pops b from the pushdown store, writes c, and goes back to q_b. The computation terminates in an accepting configuration by a move from state q_b to state q_0 in which no input is read, no output is written, and no change is made in the content of the pushdown store. □

By definition, each move in each computation must be on a transition rule that keeps the computation in a path, that eventually causes the computation to read all the input and halt in an accepting state. Whenever more than one such alternative in the set of feasible transition rules exists, then any of these alternatives can be chosen. Similarly, whenever none of the feasible transition rules satisfies the conditions above, then any of these transition rules can be chosen. This observation suggests that we view the computations of the pushdown transducers as also being executed by imaginary agents with magical power.

An input x is said to be *accepted*, or *recognized*, by a pushdown transducer M if M has an accepting computation on x. An accepting computation on x that terminates in a configuration of the form $(x q_f, z, w)$ is said to have an *output w*. The output of a nonaccepting computation is assumed to be undefined.

Example 3.2.9 Consider the pushdown transducer M, whose transition diagram is given in Figure 3.2.3. The pushdown transducer accepts exactly those inputs that have even length. In each accepting computation the pushdown transducer outputs the second half of the input.

As long as the pushdown transducer is in state q_0, it repeatedly reads an input symbol and stores c in the pushdown store. Alternatively, as long as the pushdown transducer is in state q_1, it repeatedly reads an input symbol and pops c from the pushdown store.

Upon reaching an empty pushdown store, the pushdown transducer makes a transition from state q_1 to state q_2 to verify that the end of the input has been reached. Consequently, in its accepting computations, the pushdown transducer must make a transition from state q_0 to state q_1 upon reaching the middle of its inputs.

On input $abbb$ the pushdown transducer starts (its computation) with two moves, reading the first two input symbols, pushing two c's into the pushdown store, and returning to state q_0. In its third move the pushdown transducer makes a transition from state q_0 to state q_1.

The pushdown transducer continues with two moves, reading the last two symbols in the input, popping two c's from the pushdown store, and copying the input being read onto the output tape.

The pushdown concludes its computation on input $abbb$ by moving from state q_1 to state q_2.

If M on input $abbb$ reads more than two input symbols in the moves that originate at state q_0, it halts in state q_1 because of an excess of symbols in the pushdown store. If M on input $abbb$ reads fewer than two input symbols in the moves that originates at state q_1, it halts in state q_1 because of a lack of symbols in the pushdown store. In either case the sequences of moves do not define computations of M.   □

This example shows that, on inputs accepted by a pushdown transducer, the transducer may also have executable sequences of transition rules which are not considered to be computations.

Other definitions, such as those of the relations computable by pushdown transducers, the languages accepted by pushdown transducers, and the languages decided by pushdown transducers, are similar to those given for finite-state transducers in Section 2.2.

Example 3.2.10 The pushdown transducer M_1, whose transition diagram is given in Figure 3.2.3, computes the relation $\{ (xy, y) \mid xy$ is in $\{a, b\}^*$, and $|x| = |y| \}$.

The pushdown transducer M_2, whose transition diagram is given in Figure 3.2.7 computes the relation $\{ (x, c^i) \mid x$ is in $\{a, b\}^*$, and $i =$ (number of a's in x) = (number of b's in x)$\}$.   □

From Recursive Finite-Domain Programs to Pushdown Transducers

The simulation of recursive finite-domain programs by pushdown transducers is similar to the simulation of the finite-memory programs by the finite-state transducers, as long as no call and return instructions are encountered. In such a case the pushdown transducers just trace across the states of the programs without using the pushdown store.

Upon reaching the call instructions, the pushdown transducers use their store to record the states from which the calls originate. Upon reaching the return instructions, the pushdown transducers retrieve from the store the states that activated the corresponding calls, and use this information to simulate the return instructions.

Specifically, consider any recursive finite-domain program P. Assume that P has m variables $x_1, \ldots, x_m$, and k instruction segments $I_1, \ldots, I_k$. Denote the initial value with $\odot$ in the domain of the variables of P. Let a *state* of P be an

$(m + 1)$-tuple $[i, v_1, \ldots, v_m]$, where i is a positive integer no greater than k and $v_1, \ldots, v_m$ are values from the domain of the variables of P.

The computational behavior of P can be modeled by a pushdown transducer $M = <Q, \Sigma, \Gamma, \Delta, \delta, q_0, Z_0, F>$ whose states are used for recording the states of P, whose transition rules are used for simulating the transitions between the states of P, and whose pushdown store is used for recording the states of P which activated those executions of the procedures that have not been deactivated yet. Q, Σ, Γ, Δ, δ, q_0, Z_0, and F are defined in the following manner.

Q is a set containing of all those states that P can reach.

Σ is a set consisting of all those input values that P can read.

Γ is a set containing Z_0 and all the call states in Q. Z_0 is assumed to be a new element not in Q, and a call state is assumed to be a state that corresponds to a call instruction.

Δ is a set containing all the output values that P can write.

q_0 denotes the state $[1, \odot, \ldots, \odot]$ of P.

F denotes the set of all those states in Q corresponding to an instruction of the form **if** *eof* **then accept**.

δ contains a transition rule of the form $(q, \alpha, \beta, p, \gamma, \rho)$ if and only if $q = [i, u_1, \ldots, u_m]$ and $p = [j, v_1, \ldots, v_m]$ are states in Q that satisfy the following conditions.

    a. By executing the instruction segment I_i, the program P (with values $u_1, \ldots, u_m$ in its variables $x_1, \ldots, x_m$, respectively) can read α, write ρ, and reach instruction segment I_j with respective values $v_1, \ldots, v_m$ in its variables.

    b. If I_i is neither a call instruction nor a return instruction, then $\beta = \gamma = \epsilon$. That is, the pushdown store is ignored.

    c. If I_i is a call instruction, then $\beta = \epsilon$ and $\gamma = q$. That is, the state q of P prior to invoking the procedure is pushed on top of the store. The state is recorded to allow the simulation of a return instruction that deactivates the procedure's activation caused by I_i.

    d. If I_i is a return, instruction then β is assumed to be a state of P, and the transition from state q to state p is assumed to deactivate a call made at state β. In such a case $\gamma = \epsilon$.

Example 3.2.11 Consider the recursive finite-domain program P in Figure 3.1.1 with $\{0, 1\}$ as the domain of its variables. The program is abstracted by the pushdown transducer whose transition diagram is given in Figure 3.2.8. In the transition diagram, a state $[i, x, y, z]$ corresponds to instruction segment I_i with values x, y, and z in the variables x, y, and z, respectively.

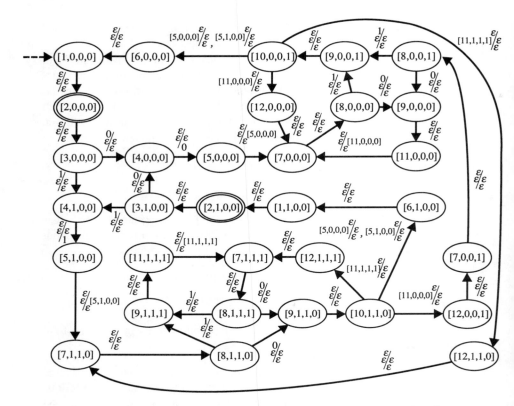

Figure 3.2.8 The transition diagram of a pushdown transducer that characterizes the recursive finite-domain program of Figure 3.1.1.

On moving from state $[3, 0, 0, 0]$ to state $[4, 0, 0, 0]$, the pushdown transducer reads the value 0 into x. On moving from state $[3, 0, 0, 0]$ to state $[4, 1, 0, 0]$, the pushdown transducer reads the value 1 into x.

Each move from state $[5, 1, 0, 0]$ to state $[7, 1, 1, 0]$ corresponds to a call instruction, and each such move stores the state $[5, 1, 0, 0]$ in the pushdown store. In each such move, the value of y in state $[7, 1, 1, 0]$ is determined by the value of x in state $[5, 1, 0, 0]$, and the values of x and z in $[7, 1, 1, 0]$ are determined by the values of x and z in state $[5, 1, 0, 0]$.

Each move from state $[10, 1, 1, 0]$ to state $[6, 1, 0, 0]$ that uses the transition rule $([10, 1, 1, 0], \epsilon, [5, 1, 0, 0], [6, 1, 0, 0], \epsilon, \epsilon, \epsilon)$ corresponds to an execution of a return instruction for a call that has been originated in state $[5, 1, 0, 0]$. The value of x in state $[6, 1, 0, 0]$ is determined by the value of y in state $[10, 1, 1, 0]$. The values of y and z state $[6, 1, 0, 0]$ are determined by values of y and z in state $[5, 1, 0, 0]$.

The pushdown transducer has the following computation on input 0011.

$$([1, 0, 0, 0]0011, Z_0, \epsilon) \vdash ([2, 0, 0, 0]0011, Z_0, \epsilon)$$
$$\vdash ([3, 0, 0, 0]0011, Z_0, \epsilon)$$
$$\vdash (0[4, 0, 0, 0]011, Z_0, \epsilon)$$

$\vdash$ $(0[5,0,0,0]011, Z_0, 0)$
$\vdash$ $(0[7,0,0,0]011, Z_0[5,0,0,0], 0)$
$\vdash$ $(0[8,0,0,0]011, Z_0[5,0,0,0], 0)$
$\vdash$ $(00[9,0,0,0]11, Z_0[5,0,0,0], 0)$
$\vdash$ $(00[11,0,0,0]11, Z_0[5,0,0,0], 0)$
$\vdash$ $(00[7,0,0,0]11, Z_0[5,0,0,0][11,0,0,0], 0)$
$\vdash$ $(00[8,0,0,0]11, Z_0[5,0,0,0][11,0,0,0], 0)$
$\vdash$ $(001[9,0,0,1]1, Z_0[5,0,0,0][11,0,0,0], 0)$
$\vdash$ $(001[10,0,0,1]1, Z_0[5,0,0,0][11,0,0,0], 0)$
$\vdash$ $(001[12,0,0,0]1, Z_0[5,0,0,0], 0)$
$\vdash$ $(001[7,0,0,0]1, Z_0[5,0,0,0], 0)$
$\vdash$ $(001[8,0,0,0]1, Z_0[5,0,0,0], 0)$
$\vdash$ $(0011[9,0,0,1], Z_0[5,0,0,0], 0)$
$\vdash$ $(0011[10,0,0,1], Z_0[5,0,0,0], 0)$
$\vdash$ $(0011[6,0,0,0], Z_0, 0)$
$\vdash$ $(0011[1,0,0,0], Z_0, 0)$
$\vdash$ $(0011[2,0,0,0], Z_0, 0).$ $\square$

From Pushdown Transducers to Recursive Finite-Domain Programs

Using the previous discussion, we conclude that there is an algorithm that translates any given recursive finite-domain program into an equivalent pushdown transducer. Conversely, there is also an algorithm that derives an equivalent recursive finite-domain program from any given pushdown transducer $M = <Q, \Sigma, \Gamma, \Delta, \delta, q_0, Z_0, F>$. The recursive finite-domain program can be a table-driven program of the form shown in Figure 3.2.9. The program simulates the pushdown transducer in a manner similar to that of simulating a finite-state transducer by a finite-memory program as shown in Section 2.2. The main difference is in simulating the effect of the pushdown store.

The program uses the variable state for recording the states that M leaves in its moves, the variable top for recording the topmost symbol in the pushdown store, the variable in for recording inputs that M consumes in its moves, the variable next_state for recording the states that M enters in its moves, the variable pop for recording the substrings that are replaced on top of the pushdown store, the variable push for recording the changes that have to be made on top of the pushdown store, and a variable out for recording the outputs that have to be written in the moves of M.

The content of the pushdown store is recorded indirectly through recursion. Each pushing of a symbol is simulated by a recursive call, and each popping of a symbol is simulated by a return.

The main program initializes the variable state to q_0, and calls RP to record a pushdown store containing only Z_0.

The body of the recursive procedure RP consists of an infinite loop. Each iteration of the loop starts by checking whether an accepting state of M has been reached at the end of the input. If such is the case, the program halts in an accepting configuration. Otherwise, the program simulates a single move of M. The predicate F is used to determine whether state holds an accepting state.

The simulation of each move of M is done in a nondeterministic manner. The

```
state := q₀
do
   top := Z₀
   call RP(top)              /* Record the bottom pushdown symbol Z₀. */
until false
procedure RP(top)
   do
      /* Accept if an accepting state of M is reached at the end of the
      input.                                                          */
      if F(state) then
         if eof then accept
      /* Nondeterministically find the entries of the transition rule
      (q, α, β, p, γ, ρ) that M uses in the next simulated move.      */
      do in := e or read in until true      /*            in := α */
      do pop := e or pop := top until true   /*           pop := β */
      next_state := ?                        /* next_state := p */
      push := ?                              /*          push := γ */
      out := ?                               /*           out := ρ */
      if not δ(state, in, pop, next_state, push, out) then reject
      /* Simulate the next move of M. */
      state := next_state
      if out ≠ e then write out
      if pop ≠ e then return
      if push ≠ e then call RP(push)
   until false
end
```

Figure 3.2.9 A table-driven recursive finite-domain program for simulating pushdown transducers.

program guesses the input to be read, the top portion of the pushdown store to be replaced, the state to be reached, the replacement to the top of the store, and the output to be written. Then the program uses the predicate δ for determining the appropriateness of the guessed values. The program aborts the simulation if it determines that the guesses are inappropriate. Otherwise, the program records the changes that have to be done as a result of the guessed transition rule.

The variables of the program are assumed to have the domain $Q \cup \Sigma \cup \Gamma \cup \Delta \cup \{e\}$, with e being a new symbol. In addition, with no loss of generality, it is assumed that each transition rule $(q, \alpha, \beta, p, \gamma, \rho)$ of M satisfies either $|\beta| + |\gamma| = 1$ or $\beta = \gamma = Z_0$. The latter assumptions are made to avoid the situation in which both a removal and an addition of a symbol in the pushdown store are to be simulated for the same move of M.

Example 3.2.12 For the pushdown transducer of Figure 3.2.3 the table-driven program has the domain of variables equal to $\{a, b, Z_0, c, q_0, q_1, q_2, e\}$. The truth

δ

F			q_0,c,ε	$q_1,\varepsilon,\varepsilon$	q_1,ε,a	q_1,ε,b	q_2,Z_0,ε
q_0	false	$q_0,\varepsilon,\varepsilon$	false	true	false	false	false
q_1	false	q_0,a,ε	true	false	false	false	false
q_2	true	q_0,b,ε	true	false	false	false	false
		q_1,a,c	false	false	true	false	false
		q_1,b,c	false	false	false	true	false
		q_1,ε,Z_0	false	false	false	false	true

Figure 3.2.10 Tables for a table-driven recursive finite-domain program that simulates the pushdown transducer of Figure 3.2.3.

values of the predicates F and δ are defined by the corresponding tables in Figure 3.2.10. (F and δ are assumed to have the value *false* for arguments that are not specified in the tables.)

The pushdown transducer can be simulated also by the non-table-driven program of Figure 3.2.11. $\qquad\square$

In a manner similar to the one discussed in Section 2.2 for finite-state transducers, the recursive finite-domain program can be modified to be deterministic whenever the given pushdown transducer is deterministic.

A formalization of the previous discussion implies the following theorem.

Theorem 3.2.1 A relation is computable by a nondeterministic (respectively, deterministic) recursive finite-domain program if and only if it is computable by a nondeterministic (respectively, deterministic) pushdown transducer.

Pushdown Automata

Pushdown transducers whose output components are ignored are called pushdown automata. Formally, a *pushdown automaton* is a tuple $<Q, \Sigma, \Gamma, \delta, q_0, Z_0, F>$, where Q, Σ, Γ, q_0, Z_0, and F are defined as for pushdown transducers, and δ is a relation from $Q \times (\Sigma \cup \{\epsilon\}) \times (\Gamma \cup \{\epsilon\})$ to $Q \times \Gamma^*$.

As in the case for pushdown transducers, the following conditions are assumed for each transition rule $(q, \alpha, \beta, p, \gamma)$ of a pushdown automaton.

a. If $\beta = Z_0$, then Z_0 is a prefix of γ.

b. γ is a string of length 2 at most.

c. If γ is a string of length 2, then β is equal to the first symbol in γ.

Transition diagrams similar to those used for representing pushdown transducers can be used to represent pushdown automata. The only difference is that the labels of the edges do not contain entries for outputs.

```
state := q_0
next_top := Z_0
call RP(next_top)
procedure RP(top)
   do
      if state = q_0 then
         do
            read in
            if (in ≠ a) and (in ≠ b) then reject
            next_top := c
            call RP(next_top)
         or
            state := q_1
         until true
      if state = q_1 then
         do
            if top = Z_0 then state := q_2
            if top = c then
               do
                  read in
                  if (in ≠ a) and (in ≠ b) then reject
                  write in
                  return
               until true
         until false
      if state = q_2 then
         if eof then accept
   until false
end
```

Figure 3.2.11 A non-table-driven recursive finite-domain program for simulating the pushdown transducer of Figure 3.2.3.

Example 3.2.13 The pushdown automaton M that is induced by the pushdown transducer of Figure 3.2.3 is $<Q, \Sigma, \delta, q_0, F>$, where $Q = \{q_0, q_1, q_2\}$, $\Sigma = \{a, b\}$, $\Gamma = \{Z_0, c\}$, $\delta = \{(q_0, a, \epsilon, q_0, c), (q_0, b, \epsilon, q_0, c), (q_0, \epsilon, \epsilon, q_1, \epsilon), (q_1, a, c, q_1, \epsilon), (q_1, b, c, q_1, \epsilon), (q_1, \epsilon, Z_0, q_2, Z_0)\}$, and $F = \{q_2\}$. The pushdown automaton is represented by the transition diagram of Figure 3.2.12.   □

The pushdown automaton is said to be *deterministic* if for each state q in Q, each input symbol a in Σ, and each pushdown symbol Z in Γ the union $\delta(q, a, Z) \cup \delta(q, a, \epsilon) \cup \delta(q, \epsilon, Z) \cup \delta(q, \epsilon, \epsilon)$ is a multiset that contains at most one element. The pushdown automaton is said to be *nondeterministic* if it is not a deterministic pushdown automaton.

A *configuration*, or an *instantaneous description*, of the pushdown automaton is a pair (uqv, z), where q is a state in Q, uv is a string in Σ^*, and z is a string

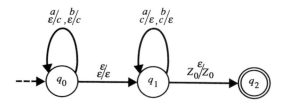

Figure 3.2.12 A transition diagram of a pushdown automaton.

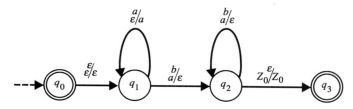

Figure 3.2.13 Transition diagram of a deterministic pushdown automaton that accepts $\{ a^i b^i \mid i \geq 0 \}$.

in Γ^*. Other definitions, such as those for initial and final configurations, $\vdash_M$, $\vdash$, $\vdash_M^*$, $\vdash^*$; and acceptance, recognition, and decidability of a language by a pushdown automaton, are similar to those given for pushdown transducers.

Example 3.2.14 The transition diagram in Figure 3.2.13 represents the deterministic pushdown automaton $<\{q_0, q_1, q_2, q_3\}, \{a, b\}, \{a, Z_0\}, \{(q_0, \epsilon, \epsilon, q_1, \epsilon), (q_1, a, \epsilon, q_1, a), (q_1, b, a, q_2, \epsilon), (q_2, b, a, q_2, \epsilon), (q_2, \epsilon, Z_0, q_3, Z_0)\}, q_0, Z_0, \{q_3\}>$. The pushdown automaton accepts the language $\{ a^i b^i \mid i \geq 0 \}$. The pushdown automaton reads the a's from the input and pushes them into the pushdown store as long as it is in state q_1. Then, it reads the b's from the input, while removing one a from the pushdown store for each b that is read. As long as it reads b's, the pushdown automaton stays in state q_2. The pushdown automaton enters the accepting state q_3 once it has read the same number of b's as a's.

The transition diagram in Figure 3.2.14 is of a nondeterministic pushdown automaton that accepts the language $\{ ww^{\text{rev}} \mid w \text{ is in } \{a, b\}^* \}$. In state q_0 the pushdown automaton reads w and records it in the pushdown store in reverse order. On the other hand, in state q_1 the pushdown automaton reads w^{rev} and compares it with the string recorded in the pushdown store. $\square$

3.3 Context-Free Languages

Pushdown automata can be characterized by Type 2 grammars or, equivalently, by context-free grammars.

Specifically, a Type 0 grammar $G = <N, \Sigma, P, S>$ is said to be *context-free* if each of its production rules has exactly one nonterminal symbol on its left hand

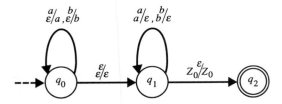

Figure 3.2.14 Transition diagram of a nondeterministic pushdown automaton that accepts $\{\, ww^{\text{rev}} \mid w$ is in $\{a, b\}^*\,\}$.

side, that is, if each of its production rules is of the form $A \rightarrow \alpha$.

The grammar is called context-free because it provides no mechanism to restrict the usage of a production rule $A \rightarrow \alpha$ within some specific context. However, in a Type 0 grammar such a restriction can be achieved by using a production rule of the form $\beta A \gamma \rightarrow \beta \alpha \gamma$ to specify that $A \rightarrow \alpha$ is to be used only within the context of β and γ.

The languages that context-free grammars generate are called *context-free languages*.

Example 3.3.1 The language $\{\, a^{i_1} b^{i_1} a^{i_2} b^{i_2} \cdots a^{i_n} b^{i_n} \mid n, i_1, \ldots, i_n \geq 0 \,\}$ is generated by the context-free grammar $<N, \Sigma, P, S>$, whose production rules are given below.

$$
\begin{aligned}
S &\rightarrow SS \\
&\rightarrow A \\
&\rightarrow \epsilon \\
A &\rightarrow aAb \\
&\rightarrow ab
\end{aligned}
$$

$\square$

From Context-Free Grammars to Type 2 Grammars

Recall that a Type 2 grammar is a context-free grammar $G = <N, \Sigma, P, S>$ in which $A \rightarrow \epsilon$ in P implies that $A = S$ and that no right-hand side of the production rules contains S. By the following theorem it follows that context-free grammars and Type 2 grammars act as "maximal" and "minimal" grammars for the same class of languages.

Theorem 3.3.1 Each context-free language is also a Type 2 language.

Proof Consider any context-free grammar $G_1 = <N, \Sigma, P_1, S_1>$. A Type 2 grammar $G_2 = <N \cup \{S_2\}, \Sigma, P_2, S_2>$ satisfies $L(G_2) = L(G_1)$, if S_2 is a new symbol and P_2 is obtained from P_1 in the following way.

Initialize P_2 to equal $P_1 \cup \{S_2 \rightarrow S_1\}$. Then, as long as P_2 contains a production rule of the form $A \rightarrow \epsilon$ for some $A \neq S_2$, modify P_2 as follows.

a. Delete the production rule $A \rightarrow \epsilon$ from P_2.

b. Add a production rule to P_2 of the form $B \to \alpha_A$ as long as such new production rules can be formed. α_A is assumed to be the string α with one appearance of A omitted in it, and α is assumed to be the right-hand side of a production rule of the form $B \to \alpha$ that is already in P_2. If $\alpha_A = \epsilon$ and the production rule $B \to \epsilon$ has been removed earlier from P_2, then the production rule is not reinserted to P_2.

No addition of a production rule of the form $B \to \alpha_A$ to P_2 changes the generated language, because any usage of the production rule can be simulated by the pair $B \to \alpha$ and $A \to \epsilon$ of production rules.

Similarly, no deletion of a production rule $A \to \epsilon$ from P_2 affects the generated language, because each subderivation $C \Rightarrow \beta_1 A \beta_2 \Rightarrow^* \gamma_1 A \gamma_2 \Rightarrow \gamma_1 \gamma_2$ which uses $A \to \epsilon$ can be replaced with an equivalent subderivation of the form $C \Rightarrow \beta_1 \beta_2 \Rightarrow^* \gamma_1 \gamma_2$. $\qquad \square$

Example 3.3.2 Let G_1 be the context-free grammar whose production rules are listed below.

$$
\begin{aligned}
S_1 &\to \epsilon \\
&\to S_1 a C C \\
C &\to \epsilon \\
&\to Dab \\
D &\to S_1
\end{aligned}
$$

The construction in the proof of Theorem 3.3.1 implies the following equivalent grammars, where G_2 is a Type 2 grammar.

G'_1	G'_2	G'_3	G_2
Added $S_2 \to S_1$	Removed $S_1 \to \epsilon$	Removed $C \to \epsilon$	Removed $D \to \epsilon$
$S_2 \to S_1$	$S_2 \to S_1$	$S_2 \to S_1$	$S_2 \to S_1$
$S_1 \to \epsilon$	$\to \epsilon$	$\to \epsilon$	$\to \epsilon$
$\to S_1 a C C$	$S_1 \to S_1 a C C$	$S_1 \to S_1 a C C$	$S_1 \to S_1 a C C$
$C \to \epsilon$	$\to a C C$	$\to S_1 a C$	$\to S_1 a C$
$\to Dab$	$C \to \epsilon$	$\to S_1 a$	$\to S_1 a$
$D \to S_1$	$\to Dab$	$\to a C C$	$\to a C C$
	$D \to S_1$	$\to a C$	$\to a C$
	$\to \epsilon$	$\to a$	$\to a$
		$C \to Dab$	$C \to Dab$
		$D \to S_1$	$\to ab$
		$\to \epsilon$	$D \to S_1$ $\quad \square$

From Context-Free Grammars to Pushdown Automata

Pushdown automata and recursive finite-domain programs process their inputs from left to right. To enable such entities to trace derivations of context-free grammars, the following lemma considers a similar property in the derivations of context-free grammars.

Lemma 3.3.1 If a nonterminal symbol A derives a string ρ of terminal symbols in a context-free grammar G, then ρ has a leftmost derivation from A in G.

Proof The proof is by contradiction. Recall that in context-free grammars the leftmost derivations $\rho_1 \Rightarrow \rho_2 \Rightarrow \cdots \Rightarrow \rho_n$ replace the leftmost nonterminal symbol in each sentential form ρ_i, $i = 1, 2, \ldots, n - 1$.

The proof relies on the observation that the ordering in which the nonterminal symbols are replaced in the sentential forms is of no importance for the derivations in context-free grammars. Each nonterminal symbol in each sentential form is expanded without any correlation to its context in the sentential form.

Consider any context-free grammar G. For the purpose of the proof assume that a string ρ of terminal symbols has a derivation of length n from a nonterminal symbol A. In addition, assume that ρ has no leftmost derivation from A.

Let $A \Rightarrow \rho_1 \Rightarrow \cdots \Rightarrow \rho_m \Rightarrow \cdots \Rightarrow \rho_n = \rho$ be a derivation of length n in which $A \Rightarrow \rho_1 \Rightarrow \cdots \Rightarrow \rho_m$ is a leftmost subderivation. In addition, assume that m is maximized over the derivations $A \Rightarrow^* \rho$ of length n. By the assumption that ρ has no leftmost derivation from A, it follows that $m < n - 1$.

The derivation in question satisfies $\rho_m = wB\hat{\rho}_m$, $\rho_{m+1} = wB\hat{\rho}_{m+1}, \ldots, \rho_k = wB\hat{\rho}_k$, $\rho_{k+1} = w\beta\hat{\rho}_k$ for some string w of terminal symbols, production rule $B \to \beta$, $m < k < n$, and $\hat{\rho}_m, \ldots, \hat{\rho}_k$. Thus $A \Rightarrow \rho_1 \Rightarrow \cdots \Rightarrow \rho_{m-1} \Rightarrow \rho_m = wB\hat{\rho}_m \Rightarrow w\beta\hat{\rho}_m \Rightarrow w\beta\hat{\rho}_{m+1} \Rightarrow \cdots \Rightarrow w\beta\hat{\rho}_k = \rho_{k+1} \Rightarrow \cdots \Rightarrow \rho_n = \rho$ is also a derivation of ρ from A of length n.

However, in this new derivation $A \Rightarrow \rho_1 \Rightarrow \cdots \Rightarrow \rho_m \Rightarrow w\beta\hat{\rho}_m$ is a leftmost subderivation of length $m + 1$. Consequently, contradicting the existence of a maximal m as implied above, from the assumption that ρ has only nonleftmost derivations from A.

As a result, the assumption that ρ has no leftmost derivation from A is also contradicted. $\square$

The proof of the following theorem shows how pushdown automata can trace the derivations of context-free grammars.

Theorem 3.3.2 Each context-free language is accepted by a pushdown automaton.

Proof Consider any context-free grammar $G = <N, \Sigma, P, S>$. With no loss of generality assume that Z_0 is not in $N \cup \Sigma$. $L(G)$ is accepted by the pushdown automaton $M = <Q, \Sigma, N \cup \Sigma \cup \{Z_0\}, \delta, q_0, Z_0, \{q_f\}>$ whose transition table δ consists of the following derivation rules.

    a. A transition rule of the form $(q_0, \epsilon, \epsilon, q_1, S)$.

    b. A sequence of transition rules for each $A \to \alpha$ in P. Each such sequence starts and ends at state q_1, and replaces a nonterminal symbol A on top of the pushdown store with the string α in reverse order.

    c. A transition rule of the form $(q_1, a, a, q_1, \epsilon)$, for each terminal symbol a in the alphabet Σ.

d. A transition rule of the form $(q_1, \epsilon, Z_0, q_f, Z_0)$.

Intuitively, we know that on a given input x the pushdown automaton M nondeterministically traces a leftmost derivation in G that starts at S and ends at x. At each stage of the tracing, the portion of the input that has already been read together with the content of the pushdown store in reverse order, record the sentential form in the corresponding stage of the derivation.

The transition rule in (a) is used for pushing the first sentential form S into the pushdown store. The transition rules in (b) are used for replacing the leftmost nonterminal symbol in a given sentential form with the right-hand side of an appropriate production rule. The transition rules in (c) are used for matching the leading terminal symbols in the sentential forms with the corresponding symbols in the given input x. The purpose of the production rule in (d) is to move the pushdown automaton into an accepting state upon reaching the end of a derivation.

By induction on n it can be verified that x has a leftmost derivation in G if and only if M has an accepting computation on x, where the derivation and the computation have the following forms with $u_i v_i = x$ for $1 \leq i < n$.

$$
\begin{aligned}
S & & (q_0 x, Z_0) &\vdash (q_1 x, Z_0 S) \\
\Rightarrow\ & u_1 A_1 \rho_1 & \vdash^* & (u_1 q_1 v_1, Z_0 \rho_1^{\text{rev}} A_1) \\
\Rightarrow\ & u_2 A_2 \rho_2 & \vdash^* & (u_2 q_1 v_2, Z_0 \rho_2^{\text{rev}} A_2) \\
\Rightarrow\ & \cdots & \vdash^* & \cdots \\
\Rightarrow\ & u_{n-1} A_{n-1} \rho_{n-1} & \vdash^* & (u_{n-1} q_1 v_{n-1}, Z_0 \rho_{n-1}^{\text{rev}} A_{n-1}) \\
\Rightarrow\ & x & \vdash^* & (x q_1, Z_0) \vdash (x q_f, Z_0) \quad\square
\end{aligned}
$$

Example 3.3.3 If G is the context-free grammar of Example 3.3.1, then the language $L(G)$ is accepted by the pushdown automaton M, whose transition diagram is given in Figure 3.3.1(a).

$aabbab$ has the leftmost derivation $S \Rightarrow SS \Rightarrow AS \Rightarrow aAbS \Rightarrow aabbS \Rightarrow aabbA \Rightarrow aabbab$ in G. Figure 3.3.1(b) shows the corresponding configurations of M in its computation on such an input. $\quad\square$

From Context-Free Grammars to Recursive Finite-Domain Programs

By Theorems 3.2.1 and 3.3.2 each context-free language is accepted by a recursive finite-domain program. For a given context-free grammar $G = <N, \Sigma, P, S>$, the recursive finite-domain program T that accepts $L(G)$ can be of the following form.

T on a given input x nondeterministically traces a leftmost derivation that starts at S. If the leftmost derivation provides the string x, then T accepts its input. Otherwise, T rejects the input.

T has one procedure for each nonterminal symbol in N, and one procedure for each terminal symbol in Σ. A procedure that corresponds to a nonterminal symbol A is responsible for initiating a tracing of a leftmost subderivation that starts at A. The procedure does so by nondeterministically choosing a production rule of the form $A \rightarrow X_1 \cdots X_m$, and then calling the procedures that correspond to $X_1, \ldots, X_m$ in the given order. On the other hand, each procedure that

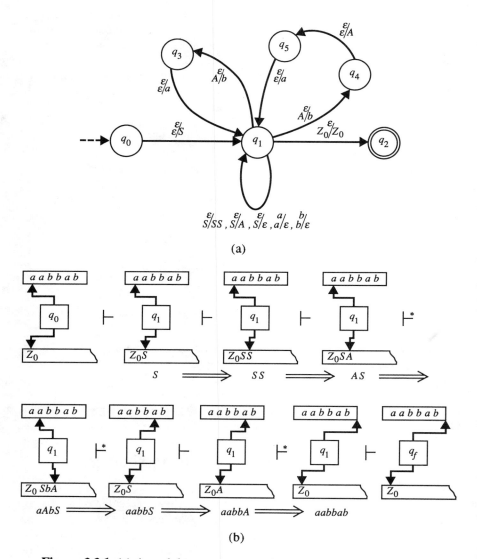

Figure 3.3.1 (a) A pushdown automaton that accepts the language generated by the grammar of Example 3.3.3. (b) A leftmost derivation in the grammar and the corresponding computation by the pushdown automaton.

```
                call S()
                if eof then accept
                reject

                procedure A()  /* For each nonterminal symbol A. */
                   do
                      ⋮
                   or              /* For each production rule of the form
                                        A → X₁ ··· Xₘ.                    */
                     call X₁() ··· call Xₘ()
                     return
                   or
                      ⋮
                   until true
                end

                procedure a()       /* For each terminal symbol a. */
                   read symbol
                   if symbol = a then return
                   reject
                end
```

Figure 3.3.2 A scheme of recursive finite-domain programs that simulate context-free grammars.

corresponds to a terminal symbol is responsible for reading an input symbol and verifying that the symbol is equal to its corresponding terminal symbol.

Each of the procedures above returns the control to the point of invocation, upon successfully completing the given responsibilities. However, each of the procedures terminates the computation at a nonaccepting configuration upon determining that the given responsibility cannot be carried out.

The main program starts a computation by invoking the procedure that corresponds to the start symbol S. Upon the return of control the main program terminates the computation, where the termination is in an accepting configuration if and only if the remainder of the input is empty.

The recursive finite-domain program T can be as depicted in Figure 3.3.2.

Example 3.3.4 If G is the context-free grammar of Example 3.3.1, then $L(G)$ is accepted by the recursive finite-domain program in Figure 3.3.3.

On input $aabbab$ the recursive finite-domain program traces the derivation $S \Rightarrow SS \Rightarrow AS \Rightarrow aAbS \Rightarrow aabbS \Rightarrow aabbA \Rightarrow aabbab$ by calling its procedures in the order indicated in Figure 3.3.4.   □

```
call S()
if eof then accept
reject

procedure S()
    do                                  /* S → SS  */
        call S() call S() return
    or                                  /* S → A    */
        call A() return
    or                                  /* S → ε    */
        return
    until true
end

procedure A()
    do                                  /* A → aAb */
        call a() call A() call b() return
    or                                  /* A → ab   */
        call a() call b() return
    until true
end

procedure a()
    read symbol
    if symbol = a then return
    reject
end

procedure b()
    read symbol
    if symbol = b then return
    reject
end
```

Figure 3.3.3 A recursive finite-domain program for the grammar of Example 3.3.1.

From Recursive Finite-Domain Programs to Context-Free Grammars

A close look at the proof of Theorem 2.3.2 indicates how a given finite-memory program P can be simulated by a Type 3 grammar $G = <N, \Sigma, P, S>$.

The grammar uses its nonterminal symbols to record the states of P. Each production rule of the form $A \rightarrow aB$ in the grammar is used to simulate a sub-computation of P that starts at the state recorded by A, ends at the state recorded

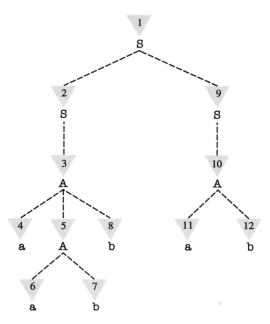

Figure 3.3.4 The calls to procedures that the program of Figure 3.3.3 makes on input $aabbab$.

by B, and reads an input symbol a. However, each production rule of the form $A \rightarrow a$ in the grammar is used to simulate a subcomputation of P that starts at the state that is recorded by A, ends at an accepting state, and reads an input symbol a. The start symbol S of G is used to record the initial state of P. The production rule $S \rightarrow \epsilon$ is used to simulate an accepting computation of P in which no input value is read.

The proof of the following theorem relies on a similar approach.

Theorem 3.3.3 Every language that is accepted by a recursive finite-domain program is a context-free language.

Proof Consider any recursive finite-domain program P. With no loss of generality it can be assumed that the program has no write instructions. The language that is accepted by P can be generated by a context-free grammar G that simulates the computations of P. The nonterminal symbols of G are used to indicate the start and end states of subcomputations of P that have to be simulated, and the production rules of G are used for simulating transitions between states of P.

The Nonterminal Symbols of G

Specifically, the nonterminal symbols of G consist of

a. A nonterminal symbol A_q, for each state q of P. Each such nonterminal symbol A_q is used for indicating that a subcomputation of P, which starts at state q

and ends at an accepting state, has to be simulated. Moreover, each execution of a return instruction in the subcomputation must be for a call that is made previously during the subcomputation.

The start symbol of G is the nonterminal symbol A_{q_0} that corresponds to the initial state q_0 of P.

b. A nonterminal symbol $A_{q,p}$, for each pair of states q and p corresponding to instruction segments that are in the same procedure of P. Each such nonterminal symbol $A_{q,p}$ is introduced for indicating that a subcomputation, which starts at state q and ends at state p, has to be simulated. In the subcomputation the number of executions of return instructions has to equal the number of executions of call instructions. Moreover, each execution of a return instruction in the subcomputation must be for a call that is made previously during the subcomputation.

The Production Rules of G

The production rules of G consist of

a. A production rule of the form $A_q \rightarrow \alpha A_r$, and a production rule of the form $A_{q.p} \rightarrow \alpha A_{r,p}$, for each q, r, p, and α that satisfy the following condition. The instruction segment that corresponds to state q is neither a call instruction nor a return instruction, and its execution can take the program from state q to state r while reading α.

A production rule of the form $A_q \rightarrow \alpha A_r$ replaces the objective of reaching an accepting state from state q with the objective of reaching an accepting state from state r.

A production rule of the form $A_{q,p} \rightarrow \alpha A_{r,p}$ replaces the objective of reaching state p from state q with the objective of reaching state p from state r.

b. A production rule of the form $A_q \rightarrow \epsilon$, for each state q that corresponds to an **if** *eof* **then accept** instruction.

c. A production rule of the form $A_q \rightarrow A_r$, for each state q that corresponds to a call instruction, where r is the state reached from q. Each such production rule simulates an execution of a **call** which is not matched by an execution of **a return**.

d. A production rule of the form $A_q \rightarrow A_{r,s} A_t$, and a production rule of the form $A_{q.p} \rightarrow A_{r,s} A_{t,p}$, for each q, r, s, t, and p such that the following conditions hold.

   1. State q corresponds to a call instruction whose execution at such a state causes the program to enter state r.

   2. State s corresponds to a return instruction in the called procedure, and the execution of the return instruction at such a state takes the program to state t that is compatible with r.

That is, the subcomputation that starts at state q is decomposed into two sub-computations. One is to be performed by an invoked procedure, starting at state r and ending at state s; the other takes on from the instant that the control returns from the invoked procedure, starting at state t.

e. A production rule of the form $A_{q,q} \rightarrow \epsilon$ for each state q that corresponds to a **return** instruction.

Each of the production rules above is used for terminating a successful simulation of a subcomputation performed by an invoked procedure.

$L(G)$ is Contained in $L(\mathrm{P})$

A proof by induction can be used to show that the construction above implies $L(G) = L(\mathrm{P})$.

To show that $L(G)$, is contained in $L(\mathrm{P})$ it is sufficient to show that the following two conditions hold for each string α of terminal symbols.

a. If $A_q \Rightarrow^* \alpha$ in G then P can reach from state q an accepting state while reading α, and in any prefix of the subexecution sequence there must be at least as many executions of call instructions as executions of return instructions.

b. If $A_{q,p} \Rightarrow^* \alpha$ in G, then P can reach state p from state q while reading α. In the subexecution sequence the number of executions of return instructions must equal the number of executions of call instructions, and in any prefix of the subexecution sequence there must be at least as many executions of call instructions as executions of return instructions.

The proof can be by induction on the number of steps i in the derivations. For $i = 1$, the only feasible derivations are those that have either the form $A_q \Rightarrow \epsilon$ or the form $A_{p,p} \Rightarrow \epsilon$. In the first case q corresponds to an accept instruction, and in the second case p corresponds to a return instruction. In both cases the subexecution sequences of the program are empty.

For $i > 1$ the derivations must have either of the following forms.

a. $A_q \Rightarrow \alpha_1 A_r \Rightarrow^* \alpha_1 \alpha_2 = \alpha$, or $A_{q,p} \Rightarrow \alpha_1 A_{r,p} \Rightarrow^* \alpha_1 \alpha_2 = \alpha$. In either case, by definition $A_q \Rightarrow \alpha_1 A_r$ and $A_{q,p} \Rightarrow \alpha_1 A_{r,p}$ correspond to subexecution sequences that start at state q, end at state r, consume the input α_1, and execute neither a call instruction nor a return instruction. However, by the induction hypothesis $A_r \Rightarrow^* \alpha_2$ and $A_{r,p} \Rightarrow^* \alpha_2$ correspond to subexecution sequences that have the desired properties. Consequently, $A_q \Rightarrow^* \alpha$ and $A_{q,p} \Rightarrow^* \alpha$ also correspond to subexecution sequences that have the desired properties.

b. $A_q \Rightarrow A_{r,s} A_t \Rightarrow^* \alpha_1 \alpha_2$, or $A_{q,p} \Rightarrow A_{r,s} A_{t,p} \Rightarrow^* \alpha_1 \alpha_2$, where $A_{r,s} \Rightarrow^* \alpha_1$. In either case, by definition q corresponds to a call instruction, r is the state that P reaches from state q, s corresponds to a return instruction, and t is the state that P reaches from state s. However, by the induction hypothesis $A_{r,s} \Rightarrow^* \alpha_1$, $A_t \Rightarrow^* \alpha_2$, and $A_{t,p} \Rightarrow^* \alpha_2$ correspond to subexecution sequences that have the desired properties. Consequently, $A_q \Rightarrow^* \alpha_1 \alpha_2$ and $A_{q,p} \Rightarrow^* \alpha_1 \alpha_2$ also correspond to subexecution sequences that have the desired properties.

$L(\mathrm{P})$ is Contained in $L(G)$

To show that $L(\mathrm{P})$ is contained in $L(G)$ it is sufficient to show that either of the following conditions holds for each subexecution sequence that reads α, starts at state q, ends at state p, and has at least as many executions of return instructions as of call instructions in each of the prefixes.

a. If p corresponds to an accepting state, then G has a derivation of the form $A_q \Rightarrow^* \alpha$.

b. If p corresponds to a return instruction and the subexecution sequence has as many executions of call instructions as of return instructions, then G has a derivation of the form $A_{q,p} \Rightarrow^* \alpha$.

The proof is by induction on the number of moves i in the subexecution sequences. For $i = 0$ the subexecution sequences consume no input, and for them G has the corresponding derivations $A_p \Rightarrow \epsilon$ and $A_{p,p} \Rightarrow \epsilon$, respectively.

For $i > 0$ either of the following cases must hold.

a. q does not correspond to a call instruction, or q corresponds to a call instruction that is not matched in the subexecution sequence by a return instruction. In such a case, by executing a single instruction segment the subexecution sequences in question enter some state r from state q while consuming some input α_1.

Consequently, by definition, the grammar G has a production rule of the form $A_q \rightarrow \alpha_1 A_r$ if p is an accepting state, and a production rule of the form $A_{q,p} \rightarrow \alpha_1 A_{r,p}$ if p corresponds to a return instruction.

However, by the induction hypothesis the $i - 1$ moves that start in state r have in G a corresponding derivation of the form $A_r \Rightarrow^* \alpha_2$ if p is an accepting state, and of the form $A_{r,p} \Rightarrow^* \alpha_2$ if p corresponds to a return instruction. α_2 is assumed to satisfy $\alpha_1 \alpha_2 = \alpha$.

b. q corresponds to a call instruction that is matched in the subexecution sequence by a return instruction. In such a case the subexecution sequence from state q enters some state r by executing the call instruction that corresponds to state q. Moreover, the subexecution sequence has a corresponding execution of a return instruction that takes the subexecution sequence from some state s to some state t.

Consequently, by definition, the grammar G has a production rule of the form $A_q \rightarrow A_{r,s} A_t$ if p is an accepting state, and a production rule of the form $A_{q,p} \rightarrow A_{r,s} A_{t,p}$ if p corresponds to a return instruction.

However, by the induction hypothesis, the grammar G has a derivation of the form $A_{r,s} \Rightarrow^* \alpha_1$ for the input α_1 that the subexecution sequence consumes between states r and s. In addition, G has either a derivation of the form $A_t \Rightarrow^* \alpha_2$ or a derivation of the form $A_{t,p} \Rightarrow^* \alpha_2$, respectively, for the input α_2 that the subexecution sequence consumes between states t and p, depending on whether p is an accepting state or not.   □

Example 3.3.5 Let P be the recursive finite-domain program in Figure 3.3.5(a), with $\{a, b\}$ as a domain of the variables and a as initial value.

$L(\text{P})$ is generated by the grammar G, which has the production rules in Figure 3.3.5(b). $[i, x]$ denotes a state of P that corresponds to the instruction segment I_i, and value x in x.

The derivation tree for the string abb in the grammar G, and the corresponding transitions between the states of the program P on input "a, b, b", are shown in Figure 3.3.6. The symbol $A_{[1,a]}$ states that the computation of P has to start at state $[1, a]$ and end at an accepting state. The production rule $A_{[1,a]} \rightarrow A_{[4,a][5,b]} A_{[2,b]}$ corresponds to a call to f which returns the value b.   □

Context-free grammars do not resemble pushdown automata, the way Type 3 grammars resemble finite-state automata. The difference arises because derivations in context-free grammars are recursive in nature, whereas computations of pushdown automata are iterative.

Consequently, some context-free languages can be more easily characterized by context-free grammars, and other context-free languages can be more easily characterized by pushdown automata.

3.4 Limitations of Recursive Finite-Domain Programs

The study of the limitations of finite-memory programs in Section 2.4 relied on the following observation: A subcomputation of an accepting computation of a finite-memory program can be pumped to obtain new accepting computations if the subcomputation starts and ends at the same state. For recursive finite-domain programs similar, but somewhat more complex, conditions are needed to allow pumping of subcomputations.

A Pumping Lemma for Context-Free Languages

The proof of the following theorem uses the abstraction of context-free grammars to provide conditions under which subcomputations of recursive finite-domain programs can be pumped. The corresponding theorem for the degenerated case of finite-memory programs is implied by the choice of $u = v = \epsilon$.

Theorem 3.4.1 (*Pumping lemma for context-free languages*) Every context-free language L has a positive integer constant m with the following property. If w is in L and $|w| \geq m$, then w can be written as $uvxyz$, where $uv^k xy^k z$ is in L for each $k \geq 0$. Moreover, $|vxy| \leq m$ and $|vy| > 0$.

```
call f(x)              /* I₁ */
if eof then accept     /* I₂ */
reject                 /* I₃ */
procedure f(x)
    do                 /* I₄ */
        return         /* I₅ */
    or
        read x         /* I₆ */
        call f(x)      /* I₇ */
    until x = a        /* I₈ */
end
```

(a)

$$A_{[1,a]} \rightarrow A_{[4,a]}$$
$$\rightarrow A_{[4,a],[5,a]} A_{[2,a]}$$
$$\rightarrow A_{[4,a],[5,b]} A_{[2,b]}$$
$$A_{[2,a]} \rightarrow \epsilon$$
$$\rightarrow A_{[3,a]}$$
$$A_{[2,b]} \rightarrow \epsilon$$
$$\rightarrow A_{[3,b]}$$
$$A_{[4,a]} \rightarrow A_{[5,a]}$$
$$\rightarrow A_{[6,a]}$$
$$A_{[4,b]} \rightarrow A_{[5,b]}$$
$$\rightarrow A_{[6,b]}$$
$$A_{[6,a]} \rightarrow a A_{[7,a]}$$
$$\rightarrow b A_{[7,b]}$$
$$A_{[6,b]} \rightarrow a A_{[7,a]}$$
$$\rightarrow b A_{[7,b]}$$
$$A_{[7,a]} \rightarrow A_{[4,a],[5,a]} A_{[8,a]}$$
$$\rightarrow A_{[4,a],[5,b]} A_{[8,b]}$$
$$A_{[7,b]} \rightarrow A_{[4,b],[5,a]} A_{[8,a]}$$
$$\rightarrow A_{[4,b],[5,b]} A_{[8,b]}$$
$$A_{[8,b]} \rightarrow A_{[4,b]}$$
$$A_{[4,a],[5,a]} \rightarrow A_{[5,a],[5,a]}$$
$$\rightarrow A_{[6,a],[5,a]}$$
$$A_{[4,a],[5,b]} \rightarrow A_{[5,a],[5,b]}$$
$$\rightarrow A_{[6,a],[5,b]}$$

$$A_{[4,b],[5,a]} \rightarrow A_{[5,b],[5,a]}$$
$$\rightarrow A_{[6,b],[5,a]}$$
$$A_{[4,b],[5,b]} \rightarrow A_{[5,b],[5,b]}$$
$$\rightarrow A_{[6,b],[5,b]}$$
$$A_{[5,a],[5,a]} \rightarrow \epsilon$$
$$A_{[5,b],[5,b]} \rightarrow \epsilon$$
$$A_{[6,a],[5,a]} \rightarrow a A_{[7,a],[5,a]}$$
$$\rightarrow b A_{[7,b],[5,a]}$$
$$A_{[6,a],[5,b]} \rightarrow a A_{[7,a],[5,b]}$$
$$\rightarrow b A_{[7,b],[5,b]}$$
$$A_{[6,b],[5,a]} \rightarrow a A_{[7,a],[5,a]}$$
$$\rightarrow b A_{[7,b],[5,a]}$$
$$A_{[6,b],[5,b]} \rightarrow a A_{[7,a],[5,b]}$$
$$\rightarrow b A_{[7,b],[5,b]}$$
$$A_{[7,a],[5,a]} \rightarrow A_{[4,a],[5,a]} A_{[8,a],[5,a]}$$
$$\rightarrow A_{[4,a],[5,b]} A_{[8,b],[5,a]}$$
$$A_{[7,a],[5,b]} \rightarrow A_{[4,a],[5,a]} A_{[8,a],[5,b]}$$
$$\rightarrow A_{[4,a],[5,b]} A_{[8,b],[5,b]}$$
$$A_{[7,b],[5,a]} \rightarrow A_{[4,b],[5,a]} A_{[8,a],[5,a]}$$
$$\rightarrow A_{[4,b],[5,b]} A_{[8,b],[5,a]}$$
$$A_{[7,b],[5,b]} \rightarrow A_{[4,b],[5,a]} A_{[8,a],[5,b]}$$
$$\rightarrow A_{[4,b],[5,b]} A_{[8,b],[5,b]}$$
$$A_{[8,b],[5,a]} \rightarrow A_{[4,b],[5,a]}$$
$$A_{[8,b],[5,b]} \rightarrow A_{[4,b],[5,b]}$$

(b)

Figure 3.3.5 The grammar in (b) generates the language accepted by the program in (a).

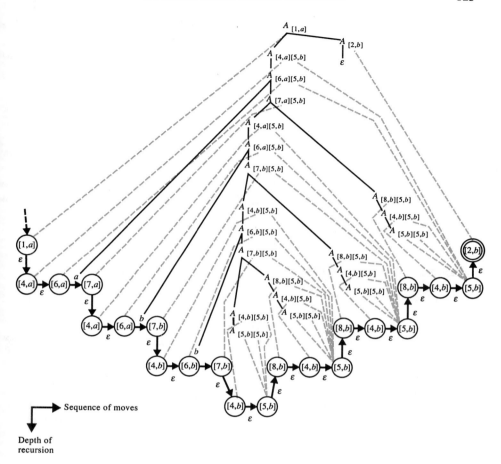

Figure 3.3.6 A correspondence between a derivation tree and a computation of a recursive finite-domain program.

Proof Let $G = <N, \Sigma, P, S>$ be any context-free grammar. Use t to denote the number of symbols in the longest right-hand side of the production rules of G. With no loss of generality assume that $t \geq 2$. Use $|N|$ to denote the number of nonterminal symbols in N. Choose m to equal $t^{|N|+1}$.

Consider any w in $L(G)$ such that $|w| \geq m$. Let T denote a derivation tree for w that is minimal for w in the number of nodes. Let π be a longest path from the root to a leaf in T. Let n denote the number of nodes in π.

The number of leaves in T is at most t^{n-1}. Thus, $t^{n-1} \geq |w|$ and $|w| \geq m = t^{|N|+1}$ imply that $n \geq |N| + 2$. That is, the path π must have two nodes whose corresponding nonterminal symbols, say E and F, are equal. As a result, w can be written as $uvxyz$, where vxy and x are the strings that correspond to the leaves of the subtrees of T with roots E and F, respectively (see Figure 3.4.1(a)).

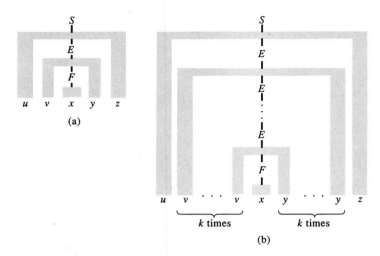

Figure 3.4.1 (a) A derivation tree T with $E = F$. (b) The derivation tree T_k.

Let T_k be the derivation tree T modified so that the subtree of E, excluding the subtree of F, is pumped k times (see Figure 3.4.1(b)). Then T_k is also a derivation tree in G for each $k \geq 0$. It follows that $uv^k xy^k z$, which corresponds to the leaves of T_k, is also in $L(G)$ for each $k \geq 0$.

A choice of E and F from the last $|N| + 1$ nonterminal symbols in the path π implies that $|vxy| \leq t^{|N|+1} = m$, because each path from E to a leaf contains at most $|N| + 2$ nodes. However, $|vy| \neq 0$, because otherwise T_0 would also be a derivation tree for w, contradicting the assumption that T is a minimal derivation tree for w.   □

Example 3.4.1 Let $G = <N, \Sigma, P, S>$ be the context-free grammar whose production rules are listed below.

$$
\begin{aligned}
S &\rightarrow AA \\
&\rightarrow ab \\
A &\rightarrow SS \\
&\rightarrow a
\end{aligned}
$$

For G, using the terminology of the proof of the previous theorem, $t = 2$, $|N| = 2$, and $m = 8$. The string $w = (ab)^3 a(ab)^2$ has the derivation tree given in Figure 3.4.2(a). A longest path in the tree, from the root to a leaf, contains six nodes.

w has two decompositions that satisfy the constraints of the proof of the pumping lemma. One is of the form $u = ab$, $v = \epsilon$, $x = ab$, $y = aba$, $z = abab$; the other is of the form $u = ab$, $v = ab$, $x = ab$, $y = a$, $z = abab$.

$(ab)^2(aba)^k(ab)^2$ and $ab(ab)^k aba^k(ab)^2$ are the new strings in the language for $k \geq 0$, that the proof implies for w by pumping. Figures 3.4.2(b) and 3.4.2(c), respectively, show the derivation trees T_k for these strings.   □

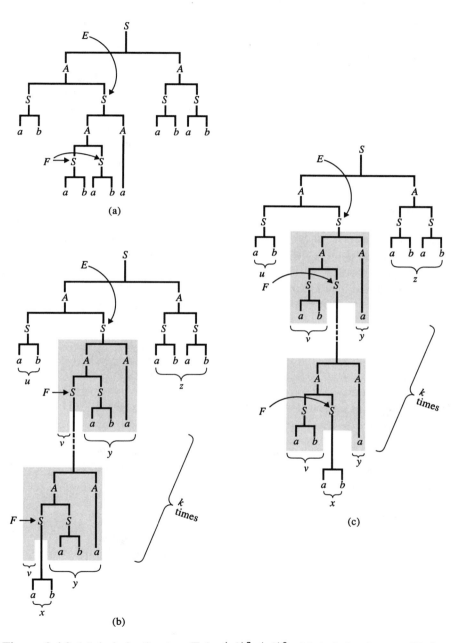

Figure 3.4.2 (a) A derivation tree T for $(ab)^3 a(ab)^2$. (b) A derivation tree T_k for $(ab)^2(aba)^k(ab)^2$. (c) A derivation tree T_k for $ab(ab)^k aba^k(ab)^2$.

Applications of the Pumping Lemma

The pumping lemma for context-free languages can be used to show that a language is not context-free. The method is similar to that for using the pumping lemma for regular languages to show that a language is not regular.

Example 3.4.2 Let L be the language $\{ a^n b^n c^n \mid n \geq 0 \}$. To show that L is not a context-free language, assume to the contrary that L is context-free. Consider the choice of $w = a^m b^m c^m$, where m is the constant implied by the pumping lemma for L.

By the lemma, $a^m b^m c^m$ can be written as $uvxyz$, where $|vxy| \leq m$, $|vy| > 0$, and the decomposition satisfies the following conditions.

    a. vy contains a's or b's but not c's.

    b. vy contains a's or c's but not b's.

    c. vy contains b's or c's but not a's.

Moreover, by the pumping lemma, $uv^k xy^k z$ is also in L for each $k \geq 0$. However, for (a) the choice of $k = 0$ implies $uv^0 xy^0 z$ not in L because of too many c's. Similarly, for (b) the choice of $k = 0$ implies $uv^0 xy^0 z$ not in L because of too many b's, and for (c) the choice of $k = 0$ implies $uv^0 xy^0 z$ not in L because of too many a's.

Since the pumping lemma does not hold for $a^m b^m c^m$, it also does not hold for L. It follows, therefore, that the assumption that L is a context-free language is false.   ☐

As in the case of the pumping lemma for regular languages the choice of the string w is of critical importance when trying to show that a language is not context-free.

Example 3.4.3 Consider the language $L = \{ \alpha\alpha \mid \alpha \text{ is in } \{a, b\}^* \}$. To show that L is not a context-free language assume the contrary. Let m be the constant implied by the pumping lemma for L.

For the choice $w = a^m b^m a^m b^m$ the pumping lemma implies a decomposition $uvxyz$ such that $|vxy| \leq m$ and $|vy| > 0$. For such a choice $uv^0 xy^0 z = uxz = a^i b^j a^s b^t$ with either $i \neq s$ or $j \neq t$. In either case, uxz is not in L. As a result, L cannot be context-free.

On the other hand, for the choice $w = a^m ba^m b$ a decomposition $uvxyz$ that satisfies $|vxy| \leq m$ and $|vy| > 0$ might be of the form $v = y = a^j$ with b in x for some $j > 0$. With such a decomposition $uv^k xy^k z = a^{m+(k-1)j} ba^{m+(k-1)j} b$ is also in L for all $k \geq 0$. Consequently the latter choice for w does not imply the desired contradiction.   ☐

A Generalization for the Pumping Lemma

The pumping lemma for context-free languages can be generalized to relations that are computable by pushdown transducers. This generalized pumping lemma,

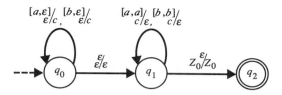

Figure 3.4.3 A pushdown automaton that "encodes" the pushdown transducer of Figure 3.2.3.

in turn, can be used to determine relations that cannot be computed by pushdown transducers.

Theorem 3.4.2 For each relation R that is computable by a pushdown transducer, there exists a constant m such that the following holds for each (w_1, w_2) in R. If $|w_1| + |w_2| \geq m$, then w_1 can be written as $u_1v_1x_1y_1z_1$ and w_2 can be written as $u_2v_2x_2y_2z_2$, where $(u_1v_1^kx_1y_1^kz_1, u_2v_2^kx_2y_2^kz_2)$ is also in R for each $k \geq 0$. Moreover, $|v_1x_1y_1| + |v_2x_2y_2| \leq m$ and $|v_1y_1| + |v_2y_2| > 0$.

Proof Consider any pushdown transducer M_1. Let M_2 be the pushdown automaton obtained from M_1 by replacing each transition rule of the form $(q, \alpha, \beta, p, \gamma, \rho)$ with a transition rule of the form $(q, [\alpha, \rho], \beta, p, \gamma)$ if the inequality $[\alpha, \rho] \neq [\epsilon, \epsilon]$ hols, and with a transition rule of the form $(q, \epsilon, \beta, p, \gamma)$ if the equality $[\alpha, \rho] = [\epsilon, \epsilon]$ holds. Let h_1 and h_2 be the projection functions defined in the following way: $h_1(\epsilon) = h_2(\epsilon) = \epsilon$, $h_1([\alpha, \rho]) = \alpha$, $h_2([\alpha, \rho]) = \rho$, $h_1([\alpha, \rho]w) = h_1([\alpha, \rho])h_1(w)$, and $h_2([\alpha, \rho]w) = h_2([\alpha, \rho])h_2(w)$.

By construction M_2 encodes in its inputs the inputs and outputs of M_1. h_1 and h_2, respectively, determine the values of these encoded inputs and outputs. As a result, (w_1, w_2) is in $R(M_1)$ if and only if w is in $L(M_2)$ for some w such that $h_1(w) = w_1$ and $h_2(w) = w_2$. Use m' to denote the constant implied by the pumping lemma for context-free languages for $L(M_2)$, and choose $m = 2m'$.

Consider any (w_1, w_2) in the relation $R(M_1)$ such that $|w_1| + |w_2| \geq m$. Then there is some w in the language $L(M_2)$ such that $h_1(w) = w_1$, $h_2(w) = w_2$, and $|w| \geq m/2 = m'$. By the pumping lemma for context-free languages w can be written as $uvxyz$, where $|vxy| \leq m'$, $|vy| > 0$, and uv^kxy^kz is in $L(M_2)$ for each $k \geq 0$. The result then follows if one chooses $u_1 = h_1(u)$, $u_2 = h_2(u)$, $v_1 = h_1(v)$, $v_2 = h_2(v)$, $x_1 = h_1(x)$, $x_2 = h_2(x)$, $y_1 = h_1(y)$, $y_2 = h_2(y)$, $z_1 = h_1(z)$, and $z_2 = k_2(z)$. $\square$

Example 3.4.4 Let M_1 be the pushdown transducer whose transition diagram is given in Figure 3.2.3. Using the terminology of the proof of Theorem 3.4.2, M_2 is the pushdown automaton whose transition diagram is given in Figure 3.4.3. The computation of M_1 on input $aabbaa$ gives the output baa. The computation of M_1 on input $aabbaa$ corresponds to the computation of M_2 on input $[a, \epsilon][a, \epsilon]$ $[b, \epsilon][b, b][a, a][a, a]$. $\square$

3.5   Closure Properties for Recursive Finite-Domain Programs

By a proof similar to that for Theorem 2.5.1, the class of the relations computable by pushdown transducers, and consequently the class of context-free languages, are closed under union. However, these classes are not closed under intersection and complementation. For instance, the language $\{ a^n b^n c^n \mid n \geq 0 \}$, which is not context-free, is the intersection of the context-free languages $\{ a^i b^i c^j \mid i, j \geq 0 \}$ and $\{ a^i b^j c^j \mid i, j \geq 0 \}$.

Similarly, the class of relations computable by pushdown transducers is not closed under intersection with the relations computable by finite-state transducers. For instance, $\{ (a^i b^i c^j, d^i) \mid i, j \geq 0 \}$ is computable by a pushdown transducer and $\{ (a^i b^j c^k, d^k) \mid i, j, k \geq 0 \}$ is computable by a finite-state transducer. However, the intersection $\{ (a^n b^n c^n, d^n) \mid n \geq 0 \}$ of these two relations cannot be computed by a pushdown transducer.

For context-free languages the following theorem holds.

Theorem 3.5.1 The class of context-free languages is closed under intersection with regular languages.

Proof   Consider any pushdown automaton $M_1 = \,<Q_1, \Sigma, \Gamma, \delta_1, q_{01}, Z_0, F_1>$, and any finite-state automaton $M_2 = \,<Q_2, \Sigma, \delta_2, q_{02}, F_2>$. With no loss of generality assume that M_2 is ϵ free and deterministic (see Theorem 2.3.1).

The intersection of $L(M_1)$ and $L(M_2)$ is accepted by the pushdown automaton $M_3 = \,<Q_1 \times Q_2, \Sigma, \Gamma, \delta_3, [q_{01}, q_{02}], Z_0, F_1 \times F_2>$. The transition table δ_3 contains $([q, q'], \alpha, \beta, [p, p'], \gamma)$ if and only if $(q, \alpha, \beta, p, \gamma)$ is in δ_1, and M_2 in zero or one moves can reach state p' from state q' by reading α.

Intuitively, M_3 is a pushdown automaton that simulates the computations of M_1 and M_2 in parallel, where the simulated computations are synchronized to read each symbol of the inputs to M_1 and M_2 together.

By induction on n it can be shown that M_3 accepts an input $a_1 \cdots a_n$ if and only if both M_1 and M_2 accept it.   □

Example 3.5.1 The pushdown automaton M_3, whose transition diagram is given in Figure 3.5.1(c), accepts the intersection of the language accepted by the pushdown automaton M_1, whose transition diagram is given in Figure 3.5.1(a), and the language accepted by the finite-state automaton M_2, whose transition diagram is given in Figure 3.5.1(b).

The computation of M_3 on input $abba$ is illustrated in Figure 3.5.1(d).   □

The languages $\{ a^i b^i c^j \mid i, j \geq 0 \}$ and $\{ a^i b^j c^j \mid i, j \geq 0 \}$ are accepted by deterministic pushdown automata, and the intersection $\{ a^n b^n c^n \mid n \geq 0 \}$ of these languages is not context-free. Consequently, the class of the languages that deterministic pushdown automata accept is not closed under intersection. However, the next theorem will show that the class is closed under complementation. The proof of the theorem uses the following lemma.

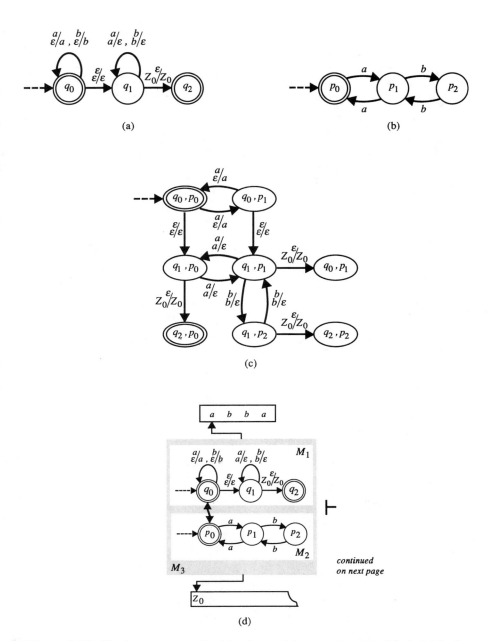

continued
on next page

Figure 3.5.1 The language accepted by the pushdown automaton M_3 in (c) is the intersection of the language accepted by the pushdown automaton M_1 in (a), and the language accepted by the finite-state automaton M_2 in (b). The computation of M_3 on input $abba$ is illustrated in (d).

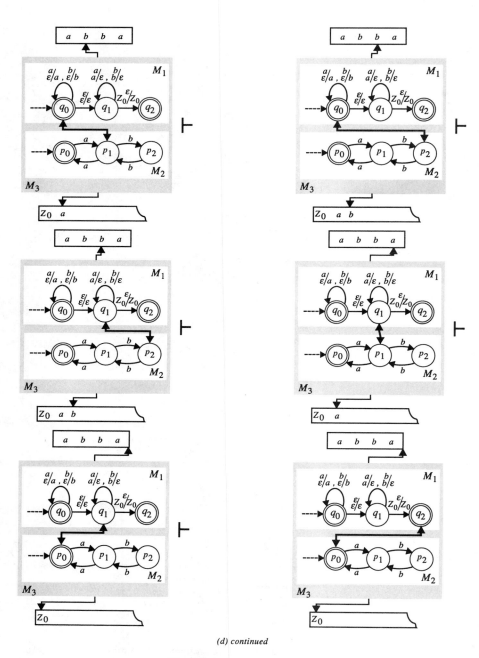

(d) continued

Figure 3.5.1 (continued)

Definition A sequence of moves $(uq_1v, z_1) \vdash \cdots \vdash (uq_kv, z_k)$ of a pushdown automaton M is said to be a *loop* if $k > 1$, M can move from configuration (uq_1v, z_1) on the same transition rules as from configuration (uq_kv, z_k), and z_1 is a prefix of z_i for $i = 2, \ldots, k$. The loop is said to be a *simple loop*, if it contains no loop except itself.

Lemma 3.5.1 Each deterministic pushdown automaton M_1 has an equivalent deterministic pushdown automaton M_2 that halts on all inputs.

Proof Let M_1 be any deterministic pushdown automaton. Let t denote the number of transition rules of M_1. M_1 does not halt on a given input x if and only if it enters a simple loop on x. Moreover, each simple loop of M_1 consists of no more than t^t moves. The desired pushdown automaton M_2 can be constructed from M_1 by employing this observation.

Specifically, M_2 is just M_1 modified to use "marked" symbols in its pushdown store, as well as a counter, say, C in its finite-state control. M_2 marks the topmost symbol in its pushdown store and sets C to zero at the start of each computation, immediately after reading an input symbol, and immediately after removing a marked symbol from the pushdown store. On the other hand, M_2 increases the value of C by one whenever it simulates a move of M_1. Upon reaching a value of $t^t + 1$ in C, the pushdown automaton M_2 determines that M_1 entered a simple loop, and so M_2 halts in a nonaccepting configuration. $\qquad\square$

The proof of the following theorem is a refinement of that provided for Theorem 2.5.2, to show that the class of regular languages is closed under complementation.

Theorem 3.5.2 The class of languages that the deterministic pushdown automata accept is closed under complementation.

Proof Consider any deterministic pushdown automaton M. By Lemma 3.5.1 it can be assumed that M has only halting computations, and with no loss of generality it can be assumed that $|\gamma| \leq 1$ in each transition rule $(q, \alpha, \beta, p, \gamma)$.

From M to M_{eof}
Let M_{eof} be a deterministic pushdown automaton that accepts $L(M)$, and that in each of its computations halts after consuming all the input. M_{eof} can be constructed from M in the following manner. Let M_{eof} be M initially with an added trap state q_{trap}, and added transition rule of the form $(q_{\mathrm{trap}}, a, \epsilon, q_{\mathrm{trap}}, \epsilon)$ for each input symbol a. Then repeatedly add to M_{eof} a new transition rule of the form $(q, \alpha, \beta, q_{\mathrm{trap}}, \beta)$, as long as M_{eof} does not have a next move from state q on input α and topmost pushdown content β.

Elimination of Mixed States
Call a state q of a pushdown automaton a *reading state*, if α is an input symbol in each transition rule $(q, \alpha, \beta, p, \gamma)$ that originates at state q. Call the state q an

ϵ *state*, if $\alpha = \epsilon$ in each transition rule $(q, \alpha, \beta, p, \gamma)$ that originates at state q. If the state q is neither a reading state nor an ϵ state then call it a *mixed state*.

If q is a mixed state of M_{eof}, then each of the transition rules $(q, \alpha, \beta, p, \gamma)$ of M that satisfies $|\alpha| = 1$, can be replaced by a pair of transition rules $(q, \epsilon, \beta, q_\beta, \epsilon)$ and $(q_\beta, \alpha, \epsilon, p, \gamma)$, where q_β is a new intermediate, nonaccepting state. Using such transformations M_{eof} can be modified to include no mixed states.

A Modification to M_{eof}

M_{eof} can be further modified to obtain a similar deterministic pushdown automaton M_{eof_max}, with the only difference being that upon halting, M_{eof_max} is in a reading state. The modification can be done in the following way.

  a. Let M_{eof_max} initially be M_{eof}.

  b. Rename each state q of M to $[q, accept]$ if it is an accepting state, and to $[q, reject]$ if it is a nonaccepting state.

  c. As long as the pushdown automaton M_{eof_max} has a transition rule of the form $([q, accept], \epsilon, \beta, [p, reject], \gamma)$, replace it with a transition rule of the form $([q, accept], \epsilon, \beta, [p, accept], \gamma)$. In addition, if $[p, accept]$ is a new state, then for each transition rule of the form $([p, reject], \alpha, \beta', p', \gamma')$ add also

   1. A transition rule of the form $([p, accept], \alpha, \beta', p', \gamma')$ if $p' \neq [p, reject]$ or $\alpha \neq \epsilon$.

   2. A transition rule of the form $([p, accept], \alpha, \beta', [p, accept], \gamma')$, if $p' = [p, reject]$ and $\alpha = \epsilon$.

  d. Let a state of M_{eof_max} be an accepting state if and only if it is a reading state of the form $[q, accept]$.

The above transformations propagate the "accepting property" of ϵ states until their "blocking" reading states.

A Pushdown Automaton That Accepts the Complementation of $L(M)$

The constructed pushdown automaton M_{eof_max} on a given input has a unique sequence of moves that ends at a reading state after consuming all the input. The sequence of moves remains the same, even when a different subset of the set of reading states is chosen to be the set of accepting states. Thus, the deterministic pushdown automaton that accepts the complementation of $L(M)$ can be obtained from M_{eof_max}, by requiring that the reading states of the form $[q, reject]$ become the accepting states.   □

Example 3.5.2 Let M be the deterministic pushdown automaton whose transition diagram is given in Figure 3.5.2(a). Using the terminology in the proof of Theorem 3.5.2, the state q_0 of M is an ϵ state, the state q is a reading state, and the state p is a mixed state.

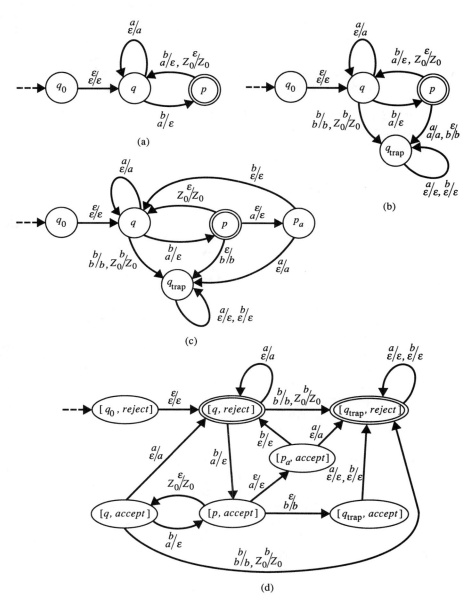

Figure 3.5.2 (a) A pushdown automaton M. (b) The complementation M_{eof} for M. (c) M_{eof} modified to include no mixed states. (d) A pushdown automaton that accepts the complementation of $L(M)$.

The transition diagram of M_{cof} is given in Figure 3.5.2(b). The transition diagram of M_{cof} modified to include no mixed states, is given in Figure 3.5.2(c). The transition diagram in Figure 3.5.2(d) is of a deterministic pushdown automaton that accepts the complementation of $L(M)$. □

The closure under complementation of the class of the languages that deterministic pushdown automata accept, the nonclosure of the class under intersection, and DeMorgan's law all imply the nonclosure of the class under union.

Corollary 3.5.1 There are languages that are accepted by nondeterministic pushdown automata, but that cannot be accepted by any deterministic pushdown automata.

3.6   Decidable Properties for Recursive Finite-Domain Programs

The first theorem of this section provides a generalization of the decidability of the emptiness problem for finite-state automata.

Theorem 3.6.1 The emptiness problem is decidable for pushdown automata.

Proof   Consider any pushdown automaton $M_1 = <Q, \Sigma, \Gamma, \delta_1, q_0, Z_0, F>$. Let c be a new symbol not in Σ. Let δ_2 be δ_1 with each transition rule of the form $(q, \epsilon, \beta, p, \gamma)$ being replaced with a transition rule of the form (q, c, β, p, γ). Let M_2 be the pushdown automaton $<Q, \Sigma \cup \{c\}, \Gamma, \delta_2, q_0, Z_0, F>$.

Intuitively, we see that M_2 is the pushdown automaton M_1 modified to read the symbol c whenever M_1 is to make a move that reads no input symbol. By construction, M_1 can reach configuration (uqv, w) in t moves if and only if there exists u_c such that M_2 can reach configuration $(u_c qv, w)$ in t moves, where u_c is a string obtained from u by insertion of some c's and $|u_c| = t$. Thus, $T(M_1) = \emptyset$ if and only if $T(M_2) = \emptyset$.

Denote m as the constant that the pumping lemma for context-free languages implies for $L(M_2)$. The shortest string x in $L(M_2)$ cannot be longer than m. Otherwise, a contradiction would arise because by the pumping lemma if x is in $L(M_2)$ and if its length is at least m, then a shorter string is also in $L(M_2)$.

On input x the pushdown automaton M_2 can have at most $|x|$ moves. Consequently, the emptiness of $L(M_2)$ or, equivalently, of $L(M_1)$ can be checked by considering all the possible execution sequences of M_2 or, equivalently, of M_1 that consist of no more than m moves. □

The decidability of the emptiness problem for pushdown automata can be used for showing the decidability of some problems for finite-state transducers. One such example is the decidability of the equivalence problem for deterministic finite-state transducers. For the general class of finite-state transducers as well as the class of pushdown automata the problem is undecidable (Corollary 4.7.1 and Corollary 4.7.2, respectively). On the other hand, for deterministic pushdown automata and for deterministic pushdown transducers the problem is open.

Corollary 3.6.1 The equivalence problem is decidable for deterministic finite-state transducers.

Proof Consider any two deterministic finite-state transducers M_1 and M_2. From M_1 and M_2 a finite-state automaton M_3 can be constructed such that M_3 accepts the empty set if and only if $L(M_1) = L(M_2)$. The construction can be as in the proof of Theorem 2.6.4.

On the other hand, one can also construct from M_1 and M_2 a pushdown automaton M_4 that accepts a given input if and only if both M_1 and M_2 accept it, while providing different outputs. That is, M_4 accepts the empty set if and only if M_1 and M_2 agree in their outputs on the inputs that they both accept.

A computation of M_4 on a given input consists of simulating in parallel, as in the proof of Theorem 3.5.1, the computations of M_1 and M_2 on such an input. The simulation is in accordance with either of the following cases, where the choice is made nondeterministically.

Case 1 M_4 simulates accepting computations of M_1 and M_2 that provide outputs of different lengths. During the simulation, M_4 ignores the outputs of M_1 and M_2. However, at each instant of the simulation, the pushdown store of M_4 holds the absolute value of the difference between the length of the outputs produced so far by M_1 and M_2. M_4 accepts the input if and only if it reaches accepting states of M_1 and M_2 at the end of the input, with a nonempty pushdown store.

Case 2 M_4 simulates accepting computations of M_1 and M_2 that provide outputs differing in their jth symbol, for some j that is no greater than their lengths. The simulation is similar to that in Case 1. The main difference is that M_4 records in the pushdown store the changes in the length of the output of M_i only until it establishes (nondeterministically) that M_i reached its jth output symbol, $i = 1, 2$. In addition, M_4 records in its finite-state control the jth output symbols of M_1 and M_2. Upon completing the simulation, M_4 accepts the input if and only if its pushdown is empty and the recorded symbols in the finite-state control are distinct.

Given M_3 and M_4, a pushdown automaton M_5 can then be constructed to accept $L(M_3) \cup L(M_4)$. M_5 accepts the empty set if and only if M_1 and M_2 are equivalent. The result thus follows from Theorem 3.6.1. $\qquad\square$

The uniform halting problem is undecidable for pushdown automata (Corollary 4.7.3). However, the decidability of the emptiness problem for pushdown automata can be used to show the decidability of the uniform halting problem for deterministic pushdown automata.

Theorem 3.6.2 The uniform halting problem is decidable for deterministic pushdown automata.

Proof Consider any deterministic pushdown automaton M_1. From M_1 a deterministic pushdown automaton M_2, similar to that in the proof of Lemma 3.5.1, can be constructed. The only difference is that here M_2 accepts a given input if and only if it determines that M_1 reaches a simple loop. By construction, M_2 accepts an empty set if and only if M_1 halts on all inputs. $\qquad\square$

The proof of the last theorem fails for nondeterministic pushdown automata because accepting computations of nondeterministic pushdown automata can include simple loops, without being forced to enter an infinite loop.

Theorem 3.6.3 The halting problem is decidable for pushdown automata.

Proof Consider any pair (M, x) of a pushdown automaton M and of an input x for M. From x, a finite-state automaton M_x can be constructed that accepts only the input x. However, from M, a pushdown automaton M_1 can be constructed to accept a given input if and only if M has a sequence of transition rules that leads M to a simple loop on the input. The construction can be similar to the proof of Theorem 3.6.2.

From M and M_x, a pushdown automaton $M_{a,x}$ can be constructed that accepts the intersection of $L(M)$ with $L(M_x)$ (see Theorem 3.5.1). By construction, $M_{a,x}$ accepts a nonempty set if and only if M accepts x. By Theorem 3.6.1 it can be determined if $M_{a,x}$ accepts a nonempty set. If so, then M is determined to halt on input x. Otherwise, in a similar way, a pushdown automaton $M_{1,x}$ can be constructed to accept the intersection of $L(M_1)$ and $L(M_x)$. By construction, $M_{1,x}$ accepts the empty set if and only if M has only halting computations on input x. The result then follows from Theorem 3.6.1. $\qquad\square$

Exercises

3.1.1 For each of the following relations give a recursive finite-domain program that computes the relation.

    a. $\{ (a^i b^i, c^i) \mid i \geq 0 \}$

    b. $\{ (xy, x) \mid xy$ is in $\{a, b\}^*$ and $|x| = |y| \}$

    c. $\{ (x, y) \mid x$ and y are in $\{0, 1\}^*$, $|x| = |y|$, and $y \neq x^{\text{rev}} \}$

3.2.1 For each of the following relations give a (deterministic, if possible) pushdown transducer that computes the relation.

    a. $\{ (a^i b^j, a^j b^i) \mid i, j \geq 0 \}$

    b. $\{ (x, a^i b^j) \mid x$ is in $\{a, b\}^*$, $i = $ (number of a's in x), and $j = $ (number of b's in x) $\}$

    c. $\{ (xyz, xy^{\text{rev}}z) \mid xyz$ is in $\{a, b\}^* \}$

    d. $\{ (a^i b^j, c^k) \mid i \leq k \leq j \}$

    e. $\{ (a^i b^j, c^k) \mid k = min(i, j) \}$

```
call RP(x)                     /* I₁ */
if eof then accept             /* I₂ */
reject                         /* I₃ */
procedure RP(y)
    read x                     /* I₄ */
    if x ≠ y then              /* I₅ */
        call RP(x)             /* I₆ */
    write y                    /* I₇ */
    return                     /* I₈ */
end
```

Figure 3.E.1

f. $\{(w, c^k) \mid w$ is in $\{a, b\}^*$, and $k = min($number of a's in w, number of b's in $w)\}$

g. $\{(xy, yx^{rev}) \mid x$ and y are in $\{a, b\}^*\}$

h. $\{(x, x^{rev}x) \mid x$ is in $\{a, b\}^*\}$

i. $\{(x, y) \mid x$ and y are in $\{a, b\}^*$, and y is a permutation of $x\}$

3.2.2 Find a pushdown transducer that simulates the computations of the recursive finite-domain program of Figure 3.E.1. Assume that the variables have the domain $\{0, 1\}$, and the initial value 0.

3.2.3 For each of the following languages find a (deterministic, if possible) pushdown automaton that accepts the language.

a. $\{vww^{rev} \mid v$ and w are in $\{a, b\}^*$, and $|w| > 0\}$

b. $\{x \mid x$ is in $\{a, b\}^*$ and each prefix of x has at least as many a's as b's$\}$

c. $\{a^i b^j a^j b^i \mid i, j > 0\}$

d. $\{w \mid w$ is in $\{a, b\}^*$, and $w \neq w^{rev}\}$

e. $\{xx^{rev} \mid x$ is accepted by the finite-state automaton of Figure 3.E.2$\}$

f. $\{x \mid x = x^{rev}$ and x is accepted by the finite-state automaton of Figure 3.E.2$\}$

3.3.1 For each of the following languages construct a context-free grammar that generates the language.

a. $\{x\#y \mid x$ and y are in $\{a, b\}^*$ and have the same number of a's$\}$

b. $\{a^i b^j c^k \mid i \neq j$ or $j \neq k\}$

c. $\{x \mid x$ is in $\{a, b\}^*$ and each prefix of x has at least as many a's as b's$\}$

d. $\{x\#y \mid x$ and y are in $\{a, b\}^*$ and y is not a permutation of $x\}$

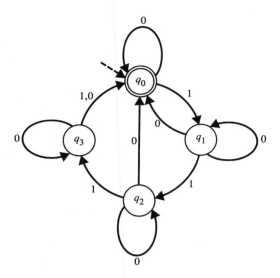

Figure 3.E.2

$$
\begin{array}{llll}
S & \rightarrow & CD & \\
  & \rightarrow & a & S \rightarrow AB \\
C & \rightarrow & \epsilon & A \rightarrow BAB & S \rightarrow aASa \\
  & \rightarrow & SC & \rightarrow a & \rightarrow b & S \rightarrow aA \\
  & \rightarrow & b & B \rightarrow ABA & A \rightarrow aAa & A \rightarrow Sb \\
D & \rightarrow & CC & \rightarrow b & \rightarrow b & \rightarrow ab \\
\end{array}
$$

(a)   (b)   (c)   (d)

Figure 3.E.3

    e. $\{\, x \# y \mid x \text{ and } y \text{ are in } \{a, b\}^* \text{ and } x \neq y \,\}$

3.3.2 Find a Type 2 grammar that is equivalent to the context-free grammar $G = \langle N, \Sigma, P, S \rangle$, whose production rules are given in Figure 3.E.3(a).

3.3.3 Let $G = \langle N, \Sigma, P, S \rangle$ be the context-free grammar whose production rules are listed in Figure 3.E.3(b). Find a recursive finite-domain program and a pushdown automaton that accept the language generated by G.

3.3.4 Let M be the pushdown automaton whose transition diagram is given in Figure 3.E.4. Find a context-free grammar that generates $L(M)$.

3.3.5 Find a deterministic pushdown automaton that accepts the language generated by the grammar $G = \langle N, \Sigma, P, S \rangle$, whose production rules are given in Figure 3.E.3(c).

3.3.6 Let the program P and the grammar G be as in Example 3.3.5. Find a derivation in G that corresponds to an accepting computation of P on input

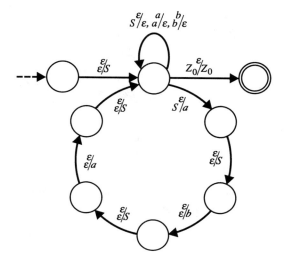

Figure 3.E.4

```
do                         /* I₁ */
    call f(x)              /* I₂ */
    if eof then accept     /* I₃ */
until false                /* I₄ */
procedure f(x)
    if x = b then          /* I₅ */
        return             /* I₆ */
    read x                 /* I₇ */
    call f(x)              /* I₈ */
    return                 /* I₉ */
end
```

Figure 3.E.5

bab.

3.3.7 Find the context-free grammar that accepts the same language as the program P in Figure 3.E.5, according to the proof of Theorem 3.3.3. Assume that the domain of the variables is equal to $\{a, b\}$, with a as initial value.

3.4.1 Redo Example 3.4.1 for the case that G has the production rules listed in Figure 3.E.3(d) and $w = a^5 b^4$.

3.4.2 Show that each of the following sets is not a context-free language.

    a. $\{ a^n b^l c^t \mid t > l > n > 0 \}$

    b. $\{ \alpha \alpha^{\text{rev}} \alpha \mid \alpha$ is in $\{a, b\}^* \}$

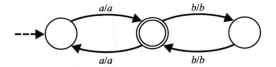

Figure 3.E.6

   c. $\{\alpha\beta\alpha^{\mathrm{rev}}\beta^{\mathrm{rev}} \mid \alpha \text{ and } \beta \text{ are in } \{a, b\}^*\}$

   d. $\{a^n\alpha a^n\alpha \mid \alpha \text{ is in } \{a, b\}^*, \text{ and } n = (\text{the number of } a\text{'s in } \alpha)\}$

   e. $\{\alpha\#\beta \mid \alpha \text{ and } \beta \text{ are in } \{a, b\}^* \text{ and } \beta \text{ is a permutation of } \alpha\}$

   f. $\{\alpha\beta \mid$ The finite-state transducer whose transition diagram is given in Figure 3.E.6 has output β on input $\alpha\}$

   g. $\{a^{n!} \mid n \geq 1\}$

3.4.3 Show that the relation $\{(x, d^n) \mid x \text{ is in } \{a, b, c\}^* \text{ and } n = min(\text{number of } a\text{'s in } x, \text{ number of } b\text{'s in } x, \text{ number of } c\text{'s in } x)\}$ is not computable by a pushdown transducer.

3.5.1 Show that the class of the relations computable by pushdown transducers is closed under each of the following operations Ψ.

   a. Inverse, that is, $\Psi(R) = R^{-1} = \{(y, x) \mid (x, y) \text{ is in } R\}$.

   b. Composition, that is, $\Psi(R_1, R_2) = \{(x, y) \mid x = x_1 x_2 \text{ and } y = y_1 y_2 \text{ for some } (x_1, y_1) \text{ in } R_1 \text{ and some } (x_2, y_2) \text{ in } R_2\}$.

   c. Reversal, that is, $\Psi = \{(x^{\mathrm{rev}}, y^{\mathrm{rev}}) \mid (x, y) \text{ is in } R\}$.

3.5.2 Show that the class of context-free languages is not closed under the operation $\Psi(L_1, L_2) = \{xyzw \mid xz \text{ is in } L_1 \text{ and } yw \text{ is in } L_2\}$.

3.5.3 Find a pushdown automaton that accepts the intersection of the language accepted by the pushdown automaton whose transition diagram is given in Figure 3.E.7(a), and the language accepted by the finite-state automaton whose transition diagram is given in Figure 3.5.1(b).

3.5.4 Let M be the deterministic pushdown automaton given in Figure 3.E.7(b). Find the pushdown automaton that accepts the complementation of $L(M)$ in accordance with the proof of Theorem 3.5.2.

3.5.5 Show that if a relation is computable by a deterministic pushdown transducer, then its complementation is computable by a pushdown transducer.

3.6.1 Show that the membership problem is decidable for pushdown automata.

3.6.2 Show that the single valuedness problem is decidable for finite-state transducers.

3.6.3 Show that the equivalence problem for finite-state transducers is reducible to the equivalence problem for pushdown automata.

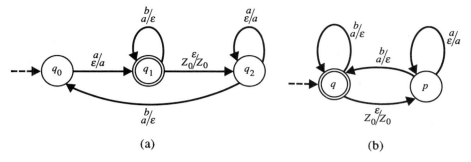

Figure 3.E.7

Bibliographic Notes

McCarthy (1963) introduced recursion to programs. Recursive finite-domain programs and their relationship to pushdown transducers were considered in Jones and Muchnick (1978).

The pushdown automata were introduced by Oettinger (1961) and Schutzenberger (1963). Evey (1963) introduced the pushdown transducers. The equivalence of pushdown automata to context-free languages were observed by Chomsky (1962) and Evey (1963).

The pumping lemma for context-free languages is from Bar-Hillel, Perles, and Shamir (1961). Scheinberg (1960) used similar arguments to show that $\{ a^n b^n c^n \mid n \geq 1 \}$ is not context-free.

The closure of context-free languages under union, and their nonclosure under intersection and complementation, were noticed by Scheinberg (1960). The closure of the class of context-free languages under composition and under intersection with regular languages is due to Bar-Hillel, Perles, and Shamir (1961). Schutzenberger (1963) showed the closure under complementation of the class of languages that are accepted by the deterministic pushdown automata (Theorem 3.5.2). Bar-Hillel, Perles, and Shamir (1961) showed the closure of context-free languages under reversal (see Exercise 3.5.1(c)).

The decidability of the emptiness problem for context-free grammars is also due to Bar-Hillel, Perles, and Shamir (1961). The decidability of the equivalence problem for the deterministic finite-state transducers in Corollary 3.6.1 follows from Bird (1973). The proof technique used here is from Gurari (1979). This proof technique coupled with proof techniques of Valiant (1973) were used by Ibarra and Rosier (1981) to show the decidability of the equivalence problem for some subclasses of deterministic pushdown transducers.

Greibach (1981) and Hopcroft and Ullman (1979) provide additional insight into the subject.

Chapter 4

GENERAL PROGRAMS

Our study of programs has so far concentrated on two subclasses, namely, the finite-memory programs and the recursive finite-domain programs. In this chapter the study is extended to the general class of programs. The first section introduces the mathematical systems of Turing transducers as a generalization to pushdown transducers, and offers the systems for characterizing the notion of computation. The second section considers the relationship between the general class of programs and the Turing transducers. Section 3 considers the relationship between determinism and nondeterminism in Turing transducers. Section 4 shows the existence of a Turing transducer, called a universal Turing transducer, that can be programmed to compute any computable function. The fifth section deals with the limitations of Turing transducers and proves the undecidability of some problems, and the sixth section shows that Turing transducers accept exactly the class of Type 0 languages. The chapter concludes with Section 7, which introduces the Post's correspondence problem, demonstrates its undecidability, and exhibits its usefulness in exploring undecidable problems.

4.1 Turing Transducers

The study of finite-memory programs and recursive finite-domain programs benefited considerably from the introduction of the mathematical systems of finite-state transducers and pushdown transducers, respectively. The usefulness of these mathematical systems stemmed from the abstraction they lend to the primitive computing machines that simulate the behavior of the programs. With this in mind it is only natural to try to follow a similar approach in studying the general class of programs.

Recursive finite-domain programs have been introduced as a generalization of finite-memory programs. In parallel, pushdown transducers have been introduced as a generalization of finite-state transducers. Going to the most general class of programs, therefore, suggests trying a similar generalization to the corresponding transducers.

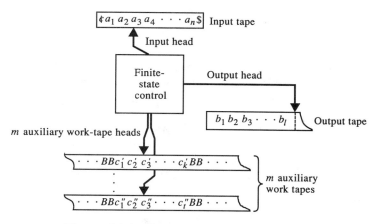

Figure 4.1.1 Schema of a Turing transducer.

Turing Transducers

Among the most general models of transducers that come to mind are probably those that allow more than one auxiliary work tape, unrestricted auxiliary work tapes, two-way input heads, inputs enclosed between endmarkers, and acceptance anywhere in the inputs. A class of such models, called Turing transducers, is introduced below.

Each Turing transducer M can be viewed as an abstract computing machine that consists of a *finite-state control*, an *input tape*, a read-only *input head*, m *auxiliary work tapes* for some $m \geq 0$, a read-write *auxiliary work-tape head* for each auxiliary work tape, an *output tape*, and a write-only *output head* (see Figure 4.1.1).

Each move of M is determined by the state of M, the symbol under the input head, and the symbols under the heads of the auxiliary work tapes. Each move of M consists of changing the state of M, changing the symbol under the head of each auxiliary work tape, relocating each head by at most one position in any direction, and writing at most one symbol onto the output tape.

Initially M is assumed to have its input $a_1 \cdots a_n$ stored on the input tape between a left endmarker ¢ and a right endmarker \$. In addition, the input head is assumed to be located at the start of the input, the auxiliary work tapes are assumed to contain just blank symbols B, and the output tape is assumed to be empty.

Example 4.1.1 A one auxiliary-work-tape Turing transducer M can compute the relation $\{ (x, x^{\text{rev}}) \mid x$ is in $\{a, b\}^*$ and $x = x^{\text{rev}} \}$ by checking that each input $a_1 \cdots a_n$ satisfies the equality $a_1 \cdots a_n = a_n \cdots a_1$. The computations of M can be in the following manner (see Figure 4.1.2).

M starts each computation by moving forward along the input tape and the auxiliary work tape simultaneously, one location at the time until the right endmarker \$ is encountered on the input tape. As M moves along the tapes it copies

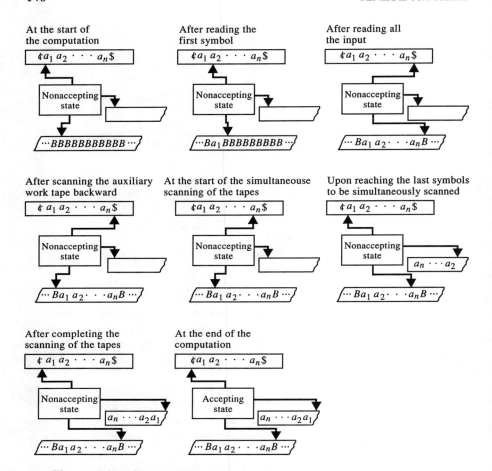

Figure 4.1.2 A description of how a Turing transducer computes the relation $\{ (x, x^{\mathrm{rev}}) \mid x$ is in $\{a, b\}^*$ and $x = x^{\mathrm{rev}} \}$.

onto the auxiliary work tape the symbols being read from the input. Then M scans the auxiliary work tape backward, and locates the first nonblank symbol. Finally, M scans the input tape backward, and the auxiliary work tape forward simultaneously, symbol by symbol. As M scans the two tapes it checks for the equality of the symbols being read at each move.   ☐

Formally, a mathematical system M consisting of an eight-tuple $<Q, \Sigma, \Gamma, \Delta, \delta, q_0, B, F>$ is called an m *auxiliary-work-tape Turing transducer* for $m \geq 0$ if the following conditions hold.

Q is a finite set, and the elements of Q are called the *states* of M.

Σ, Γ, Δ are alphabets that do not include the symbols ¢ and \$. Σ is called the *input alphabet* of M, and the elements of Σ are called the *input symbols* of M. Γ is called the *auxiliary work-tape alphabet* of M, and the elements of

Γ are called the *auxiliary work-tape symbols* of M. Δ is called the *output alphabet* of M, and the elements of Δ are called the *output symbols* of M.

δ is a relation from $Q \times (\Sigma \cup \{\math3c, \$\}) \times \Gamma^m$ to $Q \times \{-1, 0, +1\} \times (\Gamma \times \{-1, 0, +1\})^m \times (\Delta \cup \{\epsilon\})$. δ is called the *transition table* of M, and the elements $(q, a, b_1, b_2, \ldots, b_m, (p, d_0, c_1, d_1, c_2, d_2, \ldots, c_m, d_m, \rho))$, or simply $(q, a, b_1, b_2, \ldots, b_m, p, d_0, c_1, d_1, c_2, d_2, \ldots, c_m, d_m, \rho)$, of the transition table δ are called the *transition rules* of M.

q_0 is an element in Q, called the *initial state* of M.

B is a symbol in Γ, called the *blank symbol* of M.

F is a subset of Q, and the states in F are called the *accepting*, or *final*, states of M.

$\math3c$ is a symbol called *left endmarker*, and $\$$ is a symbol called *right endmarker*.

Example 4.1.2 $M = <Q, \Sigma, \Gamma, \Delta, \delta, q_0, B, F>$ is a one auxiliary-work-tape Turing transducer if $Q = \{q_0, q_1, q_2, q_3, q_4\}$, $\Sigma = \Delta = \{a, b\}$, $\Gamma = \{a, b, B\}$, $F = \{q_4\}$, and $\delta = \{(q_0, a, B, q_1, +1, a, +1, a), (q_0, b, B, q_1, +1, b, +1, b),$
$(q_0, \$, B, q_4, 0, B, 0, \epsilon),$ $(q_1, a, B, q_1, +1, a, +1, a),$ $(q_1, b, B, q_1, +1, b, +1, b),$
$(q_1, a, B, q_2, 0, B, -1, \epsilon),$ $(q_1, b, B, q_2, 0, B, -1, \epsilon),$ $(q_2, a, a, q_2, 0, a, -1, \epsilon),$
$(q_2, b, a, q_2, 0, a, -1, \epsilon),$ $(q_2, a, b, q_2, 0, b, -1, \epsilon),$ $(q_2, b, b, q_2, 0, b, -1, \epsilon),$
$(q_2, a, B, q_3, 0, B, +1, \epsilon),$ $(q_2, b, B, q_3, 0, B, +1, \epsilon),$ $(q_3, a, a, q_3, +1, a, +1, \epsilon),$
$(q_3, b, b, q_3, +1, b, +1, \epsilon), (q_3, \$, B, q_4, 0, B, 0, \epsilon)\}$.

The Turing transducer M has five states and 16 transition rules. M uses the state q_0 as an initial state, and the state q_4 as an accepting state. The symbol B is considered to be the blank symbol of M. $\square$

A mathematical system M is called a *Turing transducer* if it is an m auxiliary-work-tape Turing transducer for some $m \geq 0$.

Each Turing transducer $M = <Q, \Sigma, \Gamma, \Delta, \delta, q_0, B, F>$ can be graphically represented by a *transition diagram* of the following form. For each state in Q the transition diagram has a corresponding node drawn as a circle. The initial state is identified by an arrow from nowhere that points to the node. Each accepting state is identified by a double circle. Each transition rule $(q, a, b_1, b_2, \ldots, b_m, p, d_0, c_1, d_1, c_2, d_2, \ldots, c_m, d_m, \rho)$ in δ is represented by an edge from the node that corresponds to state q to the node that corresponds to state p, where the edge carries a label of the following form.

$$
\begin{array}{c}
a/d_0 \\
b_1/c_1, d_1 \\
\vdots / \vdots \\
b_m/c_m, d_m \\
/\rho
\end{array}
$$

In the label the top row "a/d_0" corresponds to the input tape, the bottom row "$/\rho$" corresponds to the output tape, and row "$b_i/c_i, d_i$" corresponds to the ith auxiliary work tape.

For notational convenience, edges that agree in their origin and destination are merged, and their labels are separated by commas.

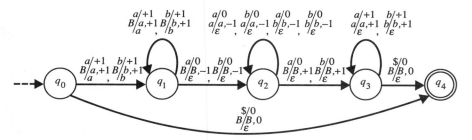

Figure 4.1.3 A one auxiliary-work-tape Turing transducer.

Example 4.1.3 The transition diagram in Figure 4.1.3 is a representation of the Turing transducer of Example 4.1.2. The transition rule $(q_0, a, B, q_1, +1, a, +1, a)$ of M is represented in the transition diagram by an edge from state q_0 to state q_1 that carries the label

$$\begin{array}{c} a/+1 \\ B/a, +1 \\ /a \end{array}.$$

The transition rule $(q_1, a, B, q_1, +1, a, +1, a)$ of M is represented in the transition diagram by an edge that starts and ends at state q_1 and carries a similar label. $\square$

Configurations and Moves of Turing Transducers

On each input x from Σ^* the Turing transducer M has some set of possible configurations. Each *configuration*, or *instantaneous description*, of the Turing transducer M is an $(m + 2)$-tuple $(uqv, u_1qv_1, \ldots, u_mqv_m, w)$, where q is a state of M, $uv = \mathcal{c}x\$$, u_iv_i is a string in Γ^* for each $1 \leq i \leq m$, and w is a string in Δ^*. Intuitively, we see that a configuration $(uqv, u_1qv_1, \ldots, u_mqv_m, w)$ says that M is in state q, with the input head at the first symbol of v, with the ith auxiliary work tape holding $\cdots Bu_iv_iB \cdots$, with the ith auxiliary work-tape head at the first symbol of v_iB, and with the output tape holding w (see Figure 4.1.4). With no loss of generality it is assumed that Q and $\Sigma \cup \Gamma \cup \{\mathcal{c}, \$\}$ are mutually disjoint.

The configuration is said to be an *initial configuration* if $q = q_0$, $u = \mathcal{c}$, $w = \epsilon$, and $u_iv_i = \epsilon$ for each $1 \leq i \leq m$. The initial configuration says that at the start of a computation the input is stored on the input tape, delimited by the endmarker $\mathcal{c}$ at its left and the endmarker $\$$ at its right. The input head is placed on the symbol to the right of $\mathcal{c}$, that is, on the leftmost symbol of the input when the input is not empty, and on the right endmarker $\$$ when the input is empty. The auxiliary work tapes are set to contain B's only, and the finite-state control is set at the initial state.

The configuration is said to be an *accepting configuration* if q is an accepting state in F.

Example 4.1.4 Let M_1 be the one auxiliary-work-tape Turing transducer of Figure 4.1.3. $(\mathcal{c}q_0aabaab\$, q_0, \epsilon)$ is the initial configuration of M_1 on input $aabaab$.

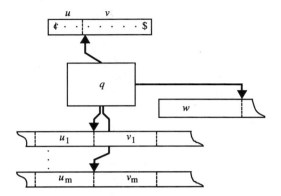

Figure 4.1.4 A configuration of a Turing transducer.

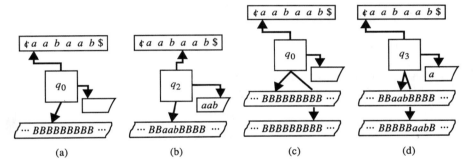

Figure 4.1.5 Configurations of Turing transducers.

On such an input M_1 also has the configuration $(\not caabq_2aab\$, aq_2ab, aab)$. The configurations are shown in Figure 4.1.5(a) and Figure 4.1.5(b), respectively.

Let M_2 be the two auxiliary-work-tape Turing transducer of Figure 4.1.6. On input $aabaab$ the Turing transducer has the initial configuration $(\not cq_0aabaab\$, q_0, q_0, \epsilon)$. Similarly, $(q_3\not caabaab\$, aq_3ab, q_3Baab, a)$ is also a configuration of M_2 on such an input. The configurations are shown in Figure 4.1.5(c) and Figure 4.1.5(d), respectively. □

The transition rules of the Turing transducer M are used for defining the possible moves of M. Each move is in accordance with some transition rule. A *move* on transition rule $(q, a, b_1, b_2, \ldots, b_m, p, d_0, c_1, d_1, c_2, d_2, \ldots, c_m, d_m, \rho)$ changes the state of the finite-state control from q to p, scans a in the input tape, moves the input head d_0 positions to the right, writes ρ on the output tape, moves the output head $|\rho|$ positions to the right, scans the symbol b_i on the ith auxiliary work tape, replaces b_i with the symbol c_i, and moves the ith auxiliary work-tape head d_i positions to the right, for $1 \le i \le m$.

A move of M from configuration C_1 to configuration C_2 is denoted $C_1 \vdash_M C_2$, or simply $C_1 \vdash C_2$ if M is understood. A sequence of zero or more moves

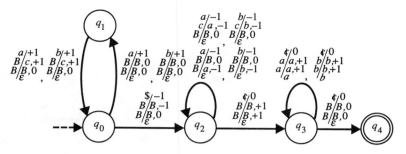

Figure 4.1.6 A two auxiliary-work-tape Turing transducer.

of M from configuration C_1 to configuration C_2 is denoted $C_1 \vdash_M^* C_2$, or simply $C_1 \vdash^* C_2$, if M is understood.

Example 4.1.5 The Turing transducer whose transition diagram is given in Figure 4.1.3, on input $aabaab$ has the following sequence of moves between configurations (see Figure 4.1.7).

$$
\begin{aligned}
(\rlap{$\mathcal{c}$}q_0 aabaab\$, q_0, \epsilon) \;\;&\vdash\;\; (\rlap{$\mathcal{c}$}aq_1 abaab\$, aq_1, a) \\
&\vdash\;\; (\rlap{$\mathcal{c}$}aaq_1 baab\$, aaq_1, aa) \\
&\vdash\;\; (\rlap{$\mathcal{c}$}aabq_1 aab\$, aabq_1, aab) \\
&\vdash\;\; (\rlap{$\mathcal{c}$}aabq_2 aab\$, aaq_2 b, aab) \\
&\vdash\;\; (\rlap{$\mathcal{c}$}aabq_2 aab\$, aq_2 ab, aab) \\
&\vdash\;\; (\rlap{$\mathcal{c}$}aabq_2 aab\$, q_2 aab, aab) \\
&\vdash\;\; (\rlap{$\mathcal{c}$}aabq_2 aab\$, q_2 Baab, aab) \\
&\vdash\;\; (\rlap{$\mathcal{c}$}aabq_3 aab\$, q_3 aab, aab) \\
&\vdash\;\; (\rlap{$\mathcal{c}$}aabaq_3 ab\$, aq_3 ab, aab) \\
&\vdash\;\; (\rlap{$\mathcal{c}$}aabaaq_3 b\$, aaq_3 b, aab) \\
&\vdash\;\; (\rlap{$\mathcal{c}$}aabaabq_3 \$, aabq_3, aab) \\
&\vdash\;\; (\rlap{$\mathcal{c}$}aabaabq_4 \$, aabq_4, aab).
\end{aligned}
$$

The sequence is the only one that can start at the initial configuration and end at an accepting configuration for the input $aabaab$.   □

Determinism and Nondeterminism in Turing Transducers

The nature of determinism and nondeterminism in Turing transducers is similar to that in pushdown transducers and in finite-state transducers. However, defining these properties is simpler for Turing transducers, because the transition rules scan exactly one symbol in each tape at each move. In the case of the finite-state transducers and the pushdown transducers, the heads can scan zero or one symbols in each move.

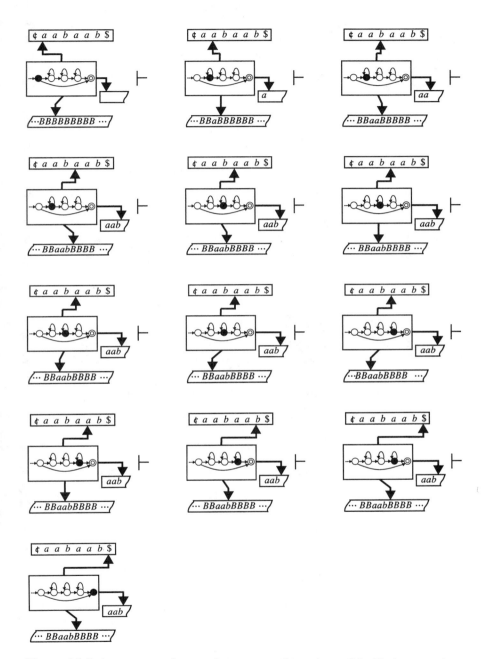

Figure 4.1.7 A sequence of moves between configurations of the Turing transducer of Figure 4.1.3.

Intuitively, we say that a Turing transducer is deterministic if each pair of transition rules that originate at the same state do not agree on the symbols they scan in the tapes. On the other hand, a Turing transducer is nondeterministic if it has a pair of transition rules that originate at the same state and that agree on the symbols they scan in the corresponding tapes.

Formally, a Turing transducer $M = <Q, \Sigma, \Gamma, \Delta, \delta, q_0, B, F>$ is said to be *deterministic* if there is no pair of transition rules

$$(q, a, b_1, \ldots, b_m, p, d_0, c_1, d_1, \ldots, c_m, d_m, \rho)$$

and

$$(q', a', b'_1, \ldots, b'_m, p', d'_0, c'_1, d'_1, \ldots, c'_m, d'_m, \rho')$$

in δ such that $(q, a, b_1, \ldots, b_m) = (q', a', b'_1, \ldots, b'_m)$. A Turing transducer is said to be *nondeterministic* if it is not a deterministic Turing transducer.

Example 4.1.6 The Turing transducer of Example 4.1.2 (see Figure 4.1.3) is a nondeterministic Turing transducer. The pair of transition rules

$$(q_1, a, B, q_1, +1, a, +1, a) \quad \text{and} \quad (q_1, a, B, q_2, 0, B, -1, \epsilon)$$

and the pair

$$(q_1, b, B, q_1, +1, b, +1, b) \quad \text{and} \quad (q_1, b, B, q_2, 0, B, -1, \epsilon),$$

are the cause for the nondeterminism of the Turing transducer. The first pair of transition rules agree in the prefix (q, a, B), and the second pair agree in the prefix (q, b, B).

However, the Turing transducer in Figure 4.1.6 is deterministic. None of the transition rules that originate at the same state agree in the symbols that they scan under the corresponding heads. For instance, the pair

$$(q_0, a, B, B, q_1, +1, B, 0, B, 0, \epsilon) \quad \text{and} \quad (q_0, b, B, B, q_1, +1, B, 0, B, 0, \epsilon)$$

of transition rules disagree in the symbols that they scan in the input tape, and the pair

$$(q_3, \mathcent, a, a, q_3, 0, b, +1, b, +1, b) \quad \text{and} \quad (q_3, \mathcent, b, b, q_3, 0, a, +1, a, +1, a)$$

of transition rules disagree in the symbols that they scan in their auxiliary work tapes. □

Computations of Turing Transducers

The definitions of computations for finite-state transducers and pushdown transducers also apply for Turing transducers. Specifically, an *accepting computation* of a Turing transducer M is a sequence of moves of M that starts at an initial configuration and ends at an accepting configuration. A *nonaccepting*, or *rejecting*, *computation* of M is a sequence of moves on an input x for which the following conditions hold.

    a. The sequence starts from the initial configuration of M on input x.

b. If the sequence is finite, then it ends at a configuration from which no move is possible.

c. M has no accepting computation on input x.

Each accepting computation and each nonaccepting computation of M is said to be a *computation* of M.

A computation is said to be a *halting computation* if it consists of a finite number of moves.

Example 4.1.7 Consider the deterministic Turing transducer whose transition diagram is given in Figure 4.1.6. The Turing transducer has an accepting computation on a given input if and only if the input is of the form ww for some string w in $\{a, b\}^*$. On an input of the form ww the Turing transducer writes the string w onto the output tape.

Each computation of the Turing transducer starts by reading the input. Upon reading the odd symbols from the input, it moves from state q_0 to state q_1, while leaving the auxiliary work tapes unchanged. Upon reading the even symbols from the input, the Turing transducer moves from state q_1 to state q_0, while writing c in the first auxiliary work tape.

On inputs of odd length the Turing transducer halts in state q_1 when it reaches the right endmarker \$. On the other hand, on inputs of even length the Turing transducer enters state q_2 when it reaches the right endmarker \$. On moving from state q_0 to state q_2 the number of c's in the second auxiliary work tape equals half of the length of the input.

In state q_2, the Turing transducer reads backward an input of the form xy which satisfies $|x| = |y|$. As the Turing transducer reads y backward it replaces the content $c^{|y|}$ of the first auxiliary work tape with the string y. Then the Turing transducer reads x backward and writes it onto the second auxiliary work tape.

Upon reaching the left endmarker ¢, the Turing transducer makes a transition from state q_2 to state q_3. In state q_3 it scans the two auxiliary work tapes to check that $x = y$. If the equality holds then the Turing transducer moves from state q_3 to state q_4. Otherwise, it halts in state q_3.

The computation that the Turing transducer has on input $aabaab$ is shown in Figure 4.1.8. ☐

By definition, each move in each computation must be on a transition rule that eventually causes the computation to halt in an accepting state. Whenever more than one such transition rule is possible for a given move, any of the alternatives can be chosen. Similarly, whenever none of the feasible transition rules for a given move can lead the computation to halt in an accepting state, then again any of the feasible transition rules can be chosen.

An input x is said to be *accepted*, or *recognized*, by a Turing transducer M if M has an accepting computation on input x. An accepting computation on input x that terminates in a configuration of the form $(uqv, u_1qv_1, \ldots, u_mqv_m, w)$ is said to have an *output* w. The output of a nonaccepting computation is assumed to be undefined.

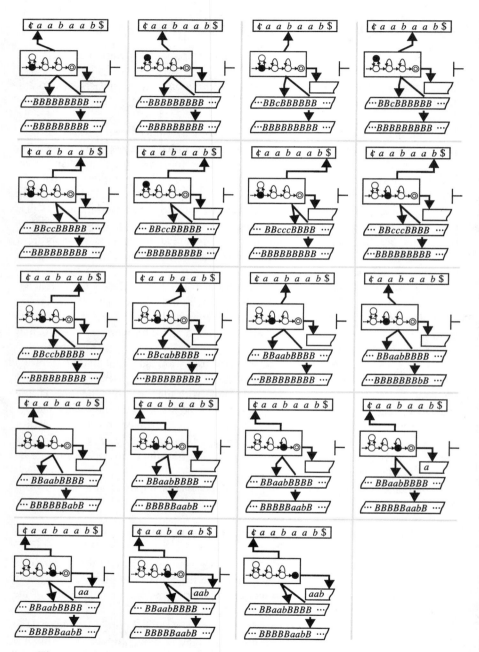

Figure 4.1.8 A computation of the Turing transducer of Figure 4.1.6.

As in the cases of finite-state transducers and pushdown transducers, a Turing transducer may have sequences of moves on inputs that are accepted that are not considered to be computations.

Example 4.1.8 Consider the nondeterministic Turing transducer whose transition diagram is given in Figure 4.1.3. The Turing transducer accepts an input if and only if it is of the form ww for some w in $\{a, b\}^*$. On such an input ww it provides the output w.

Each computation of M_1 on a nonempty input xy starts by reading x. As M_1 reads x from the input tape it writes the string onto the auxiliary work tape. At the end of x, which is found nondeterministically, M_1 switches from state q_1 to state q_2.

In state q_2, the Turing transducer M_1 moves backward across the copy of x that is stored in the auxiliary work tape until it locates the first symbol in the string. Then M_1 switches to state q_3.

In state q_3, M_1 checks that the remainder y of the input is equal to the string x stored on the auxiliary work tape. The Turing transducer accepts the input if and only if it determines that $x = y$. □

Other definitions, such as the relations that Turing transducers compute, the languages accepted by them, and the languages decidable by them, are similar to those given for finite-state transducers in Section 2.2, and for pushdown transducers in Section 3.2.

Example 4.1.9 The nondeterministic Turing transducer M_1, whose transition diagram is given in Figure 4.1.3, and the deterministic Turing transducer M_2, whose transition diagram is given in Figure 4.1.6, compute the relation $\{(ww, w) \mid w$ is in $\{a, b\}^*\}$. □

A language is said to be a *recursively enumerable language* if it is acceptable by a Turing transducer. The language is said to be *recursive* if it is decidable by a Turing transducer.

Turing Machines

Turing transducers whose output components are ignored are called *Turing machines*. Formally, for $m \geq 0$ an m *auxiliary-work-tape Turing machine* is a seven-tuple $<Q, \Sigma, \Gamma, \delta, q_0, B, F>$, where $Q, \Sigma, \Gamma, q_0, B$, and F are defined as for Turing transducers, and δ is a relation from $Q \times (\Sigma \cup \{\mathbb{c}, \$\}) \times \Gamma^m$ to $Q \times \{-1, 0, +1\} \times (\Gamma \times \{-1, 0, +1\})^m$. A mathematical system M is said to be a *Turing machine* if it is an m auxiliary-work-tape Turing machine for some m.

Transition diagrams similar to those used for representing Turing transducers can also be used to represent Turing machines. The only difference is that the labels of the edges do not contain entries for outputs.

Example 4.1.10 The Turing machine that is induced from the Turing transducer of Figure 4.1.3 is shown in Figure 4.1.9. □

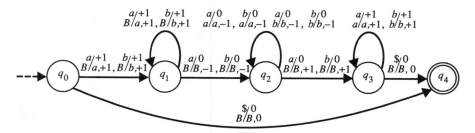

Figure 4.1.9 An one auxiliary-work-tape Turing machine.

A Turing machine is called a *linear bounded automaton* or just an LBA, if for each given input x the Turing machine visits at most $max(|x|, 1)$ locations in each of the auxiliary work tapes.

Other definitions, such as those for deterministic and nondeterministic Turing machines, their configurations, and the moves between these configurations, are similar to those given for Turing transducers.

Church's Thesis

Over the years, various characterizations have been offered to describe the concept of computability. These characterizations were derived using different approaches, including the models of deterministic Turing transducers. However, it turned out that all these characterizations are equivalent in the sense that one can effectively go from one characterization to another. The equivalency of the different characterizations suggests the following conjecture (which traditionally is stated in terms of Turing transducers).

Church's Thesis   A function is computable (respectively, partially computable) if and only if it is computable (respectively, partially computable) by a deterministic Turing transducer.

One cannot expect to be able to prove the correctness of Church's thesis, because of the lack of a precise specification for the intuitive notion of computability. The best one can expect is an increase in confidence, due to the failure of finding counter examples.

4.2   Programs and Turing Transducers

The definition of a program relies on the notion of computability of functions and predicates. In the cases of finite-memory programs and recursive finite-domain programs, the computability of the program's functions and predicates is implied by the finiteness of the domains of the variables. On the other hand, for the general class of programs the issue of the computability of the functions and predicates needs to be resolved explicitly.

do
    y := ?
or
    if x ≠ y **then**
        reject
    write y
    read x
until x = 0
if *eof* **then accept**

Figure 4.2.1 A program.

From Programs to Turing Transducers

By Church's thesis a program's functions and predicates can be assumed to be computable by deterministic Turing transducers. Consequently, a similar assumption can be used when showing that programs can be simulated by Turing transducers.

Consider any program P. Let D denote the domain of the variables of P and E be a binary representation for D. Then P can be simulated by a Turing transducer M of the following form.

M dedicates one auxiliary work tape for each of the variables of the program P. Each input "$v_1, \ldots, v_n$" of the program P is presented to M by a string of the form $E(v_1)\# \cdots \# E(v_n)$. Each output "$w_1, \ldots, w_t$" of P is represented in M by a string of the form $\# E(w_1)\# \cdots \# E(w_t)$. $E(u)$ stands for the binary representation of u.

For each instruction of the form **read** x, the Turing transducer M has a component that reads the representation $E(v)$ of the next input value v of P and stores it in the auxiliary work tape that corresponds to x. Similarly, for each instruction of the form **write** x the Turing transducer M has a component that copies onto the output tape the content of the auxiliary work tape that corresponds to x.

For each instruction of the form y := $f(x_1, \ldots, x_m)$ the Turing transducer has a component similar to the deterministic Turing transducer that computes the function $f(x_1, \ldots, x_m)$. The main difference is that the component gets the values of $x_1, \ldots, x_m$ from the auxiliary work tapes that correspond to the variables instead of from the input, and instead of writing onto the output tape the component writes the value of the function onto the auxiliary work tape that corresponds to y.

In a similar manner M has a component corresponding to each of the other instruction segments in P, as well as a component for recording the initial values of the variables of P. Moreover, the components are arranged in M in the same order as in P.

By construction, the Turing transducer M is deterministic when the program P is deterministic.

Example 4.2.1 Let P be the program in Figure 4.2.1. Assume the set of natural numbers for the domain of the variables of the program, with 0 as an initial value. Figure 4.2.2(a) shows the schema of a Turing transducer M that simulates P.

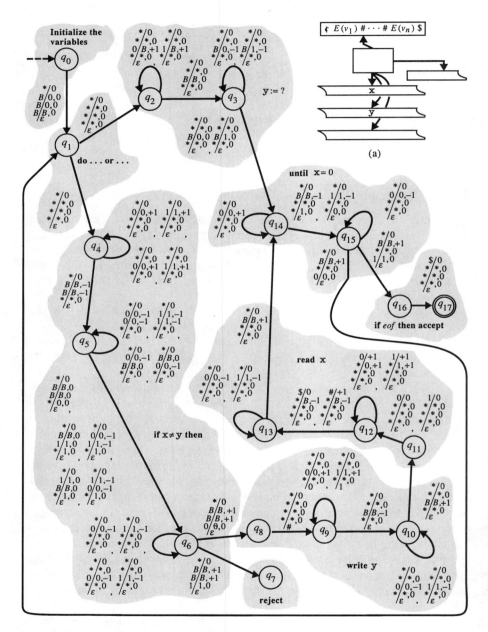

Figure 4.2.2 (a) A schema of a Turing transducer M that simulates the program of Figure 4.2.1. (b) A transition diagram for M. (The asterisk * stands for the current symbol under the corresponding head.)

The first auxiliary work tape of M is used for recording the values of x. The second is used for recording the values of y, and the third is used for recording the values of predicates (0 for *false* and 1 for *true*).

Figure 4.2.2(b) gives the transition diagram of M. Each of the components of M starts and ends each subcomputation with each of the heads of the auxiliary work tapes positioned at the leftmost, nonblank symbol of the corresponding tape.

The component "Initiate the variables" records the value 0 in the first and second auxiliary work tapes.

The component "**do** $\cdots$ **or** $\cdots$" nondeterministically chooses to proceed either to the component "$y := ?$" or to "**if** $x \neq y$ **then.**"

In state q_2 the component "$y := ?$" erases the value recorded in the second auxiliary work tape for y. Then the component enters state q_3 where it records a new value for y, which is found nondeterministically.

The component "**if** $x \neq y$ **then**" locates in state q_4 the rightmost digits in x and y. In state q_5 the component moves backward across the digits of x and y and determines whether the corresponding digits are equal. If so, the component stores the value 0 in the third auxiliary work tape. Otherwise, the component stores the value 1. In state q_6 the component locates the leftmost digits of x and y, and depending on the value stored on the third auxiliary work tape transfers the control either to the component "**reject**" or to "**write** y."

The component "**write** y" outputs the symbol $\#$ in state q_8, and the value of y in state q_9. Then it returns to the leftmost symbol of y.

The component "**read** x" verifies in state q_{11} that the input has a value to be read and reads it in state q_{12}. Then in state q_{13} the component locates the leftmost digit of x.

The component "**until** $x = 0$" checks whether x is 0 in state q_{14}. If so, the component stores 1 in the third auxiliary work tape. Otherwise, the component stores 0. In state q_{15} the component locates the leftmost digit of x, and then, depending on the value stored on the third auxiliary work tape, either moves to the component "**do** $\cdots$ **or** $\cdots$" or to "**if** *eof* **then accept.**"

The component "**if** *eof* **then accept**" moves from state q_{16} to the accepting state q_{17} if and only if the end of the input is reached. $\qquad\square$

From Turing Transducers to Programs

As a result of the previous discussion, we see that there is an algorithm that translates any given program to an equivalent Turing transducer. Conversely, there is also an algorithm that, for any given Turing transducer $M = <Q, \Sigma, \Gamma, \Delta, \delta, q_0, B, F>$, provides an equivalent program.

The program can be table-driven and of the form shown in Figure 4.2.3. The program simulates the Turing transducer in a manner like that of a finite-memory program in Section 2.2 simulating a finite-state transducer. It is also similar to a recursive finite-domain program in Section 3.2 simulating a pushdown transducer. The main difference is in the recording of the content of the tapes.

The variables of the program are assumed to have the domain of natural numbers. Intuitively, however, we consider the variables as having the domain $Q \cup$

/* Record the initial configuration $(uqv, u_1qv_1, \ldots, u_mqv_m, w)$
of M (see Figure 4.1.4).   */

```
state := q₀
u := ¢
v := get(input)
for j := 1 to m do
    begin
        uⱼ := B ··· B
        vⱼ := B ··· B
    end
w := ε
do
    /* Check for acceptance conditions. */
    if F(state) then
    begin
        write w
        if eof then accept
        reject
    end
    /* Determine the transition rule
        (state, a, b₁, ..., bₘ, next_state, d₀, c₁, d₁, ... cₘ, dₘ, ρ)
    to be used in the next simulated move.                    */
    a := top(v);  b₁ := top(v₁); ...; bₘ := top(vₘ)
    (next_state, d₀, c₁, d₁, ..., cₘ, dₘ, ρ) := δ(state, a, b₁, ..., bₘ)
    /* Record the changes in the input head position. */
    case
        d₀ = −1: a := top(u);  pop(u);  push(v, a)
        d₀ = +1: push(u, a);  pop(v)
    end
    /* Record the changes in the auxiliary work tapes and in their corre-
    sponding head positions.                                 */
    for j = 1 to m do
        case
            dⱼ = −1: pop(vⱼ);  push(vⱼ, cⱼ);  bⱼ := top(uⱼ);
                    pop(uⱼ);  push(vⱼ, bⱼ)
            dⱼ = 0: pop(vⱼ);  push(vⱼ, cⱼ)
            dⱼ = +1: push(uⱼ, cⱼ);  pop(vⱼ)
        end
    /* Record the output and modify the state. */
    w := append(w, ρ)
    state := next_state
until false
```

Figure 4.2.3 A table-driven program for simulating Turing transducers.

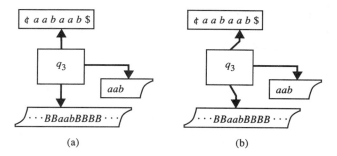

Figure 4.2.4 Configurations of a Turing transducer.

$(\{\mathnot{c}, \$\} \cup \Sigma)^* \cup \Gamma^* \cup \Delta^* \cup \{-1, 0, +1\}$.

For each of the nonoutput tapes of M the program has a pair of "pushdown" variables. One pushdown variable is used for holding the sequence of characters on the tape to the left of the corresponding head (at the given order). The other is used for holding the sequence of characters on the tape from the corresponding head position to its right (in reverse order). The pair of pushdown variables u and v is used for the input tape. The pair u_i and v_i is used for the ith auxiliary work tape. The variable w is used for recording the output, and the variable state is used for recording the state.

Example 4.2.2 The program records the configuration $(\mathnot{c}aabq_3aab\$, q_3aab, aab)$ in the following manner (see Figure 4.2.4(a)).

$$
\begin{aligned}
\text{state} &= q_3 \\
\text{u} &= \mathnot{c}aab \\
\text{v} &= \$baa \\
\text{u}_1 &= B \cdots B \\
\text{v}_1 &= B \cdots Bbaa \\
\text{w} &= aab
\end{aligned}
$$

Similarly, the program records the configuration $(\mathnot{c}aabaq_3ab\$, aq_3ab, aab)$ in the following manner (see Figure 4.2.4(b)).

$$
\begin{aligned}
\text{state} &= q_3 \\
\text{u} &= \mathnot{c}aaba \\
\text{v} &= \$ba \\
\text{u}_1 &= B \cdots Ba \\
\text{v}_1 &= B \cdots Bba \\
\text{w} &= aab
\end{aligned}
$$

$\square$

A simulation of a head movement to the right involves the pushing of a symbol to the first pushdown variable, and the popping of a symbol from the second. Similarly, a simulation of a head movement to the left involves the popping of a symbol from the first pushdown variable, and the pushing of a symbol to the second.

The program uses $top(\texttt{var})$ to determine the topmost symbol in $\texttt{var}$. The program uses $pop(\texttt{var})$ to remove the topmost symbol from $\texttt{var}$, and it uses $push(\texttt{var}, ch)$ and $append(\texttt{var}, \rho)$ to push ch and ρ, respectively, into $\texttt{var}$.

$v := get(\texttt{input})$ is assumed to be a code segment as shown in Figure 4.2.5(a). $F(\texttt{state})$ is assumed to be a table lookup function specifying whether $\texttt{state}$ holds an accepting state. $(\texttt{next\_state}, d_0, c_1, d_1, \ldots, c_m, d_m, \rho) := \delta(\texttt{state}, a, b_1, \ldots, b_m)$ is assumed to be a code segment as shown in Figure 4.2.5(b) for deterministic Turing transducers, and a code segment as shown in Figure 4.2.5(c) for nondeterministic Turing transducers. $\delta_{\text{state}}, \delta_{c_1}, \ldots, \delta_{c_m}, \delta_{d_0}, \ldots, \delta_{d_m}, \delta_\rho, \delta_{\text{tran}}$ are assumed to be table lookup functions specifying the desired information.

Example 4.2.3 For the deterministic Turing transducer M_1, whose transition diagram is given in Figure 4.1.6, the following equalities hold.

$$\begin{aligned}
\delta_{\text{state}}(q_0, a, B, B) &= q_1 \\
\delta_{c_1}(q_0, a, B, B) &= B \\
\delta_{c_2}(q_0, a, B, B) &= B \\
\delta_\rho(q_0, a, B, B) &= \epsilon \\
\delta_{d_0}(q_0, a, B, B) &= +1 \\
\delta_{d_1}(q_0, a, B, B) &= 0 \\
\delta_{d_2}(q_0, a, B, B) &= 0 \\
\delta_{\text{state}}(q_2, a, c, B) &= q_2 \\
\delta_{c_1}(q_2, a, c, B) &= a \\
\delta_{c_2}(q_2, a, c, B) &= B \\
\delta_\rho(q_2, a, c, B) &= \epsilon \\
\delta_{d_0}(q_2, a, c, B) &= -1 \\
\delta_{d_1}(q_2, a, c, B) &= -1 \\
\delta_{d_2}(q_2, a, c, B) &= 0
\end{aligned}$$

For the nondeterministic Turing transducer M_2, whose transition diagram is given in Figure 4.1.3, the following equalities hold.

$$\begin{aligned}
\delta_{\text{tran}}(q_0, a, B, q_1, +1, a, +1, a) &= true \\
\delta_{\text{tran}}(q_0, b, B, q_1, +1, b, +1, b) &= true \\
\delta_{\text{tran}}(q_0, \$, B, q_4, 0, B, 0, \epsilon) &= true \\
\delta_{\text{tran}}(q_0, a, b, q_2, 0, B, +1, \epsilon) &= false
\end{aligned}$$

For M_1 and M_2 the equalities $F(q_4) = true$, and $F(q_0) = F(q_1) = F(q_2) = F(q_3) = false$ hold. $\square$

```
read input
v := $
if not empty (input) then
    do
        char := top (input)
        if not input_symbol (char) then reject
        pop (input)
        push (v, char)
    until empty (input)
```

(a)

$$\text{next\_state} := \delta_{\text{state}}(\text{state}, a, b_1, \ldots, b_m)$$
$$c_1 := \delta_{c_1}(\text{state}, a, b_1, \ldots, b_m)$$
$$\vdots$$
$$c_m := \delta_{c_m}(\text{state}, a, b_1, \ldots, b_m)$$
$$d_1 := \delta_{d_1}(\text{state}, a, b_1, \ldots, b_m)$$
$$\vdots$$
$$d_m := \delta_{d_m}(\text{state}, a, b_1, \ldots, b_m)$$
$$\rho := \delta_\rho(\text{state}, a, b_1, \ldots, b_m)$$

(b)

```
next_state := ?
c₁ := ?
```
$$\vdots$$
```
cm := ?
d₀ := ?
```
$$\vdots$$
```
dm := ?
ρ  := ?
```
if not $\delta_{\text{tran}}(\text{state}, a, b_1, \ldots, b_m, \text{next\_state},$
$$d_0, c_1, d_1, \ldots, c_m, d_m, \rho) \text{ then reject}$$

(c)

Figure 4.2.5 (a) The code segment $v := get(\text{input})$. (b) The code segment
$(\text{next\_state}, d_0, c_1, d_1, \ldots, c_m, d_m, \rho) := \delta(\text{state}, a, b_1, \ldots, b_m)$
for a deterministic Turing transducer. (c) The code segment
$(\text{next\_state}, d_0, c_1, d_1, \ldots, c_m, d_m, \rho) := \delta(\text{state}, a, b_1, \ldots, b_m)$
for a nondeterministic Turing transducer.

The program represents each of the symbols in $Q \cup \Sigma \cup \Gamma \cup \Delta \cup \{\math025c, \$, -1, 0, +1\}$ by a distinct number between 0 and $k - 1$, where k denotes the cardinality of $Q \cup \Sigma \cup \Gamma \cup \Delta \cup \{\math025c, \$, -1, 0, +1\}$. In particular, the blank symbol B is assumed to correspond to 0. The variables are assumed to hold natural numbers that are interpreted as the strings corresponding to the representations of the numbers in base k.

top(var) returns the remainder of var divided by k. *push*(var, ch) assigns to var the value var $\times k + ch$. *pop*(var) assigns to var the integer value of var divided by k. *empty*(var) provides the value *true* if var $= 0$, and provides the value *false* otherwise. *input_symbol*(char) is assumed to provide the value *true* if char holds a symbol from Σ, and provides *false* otherwise. *append*(var, ρ) returns $k \times$ var $+ \rho$ if $\rho \neq 0$, and returns the value of var if $\rho = 0$.

Example 4.2.4 Let M be the deterministic Turing transducer whose transition diagram is given in Figure 4.1.6. For such an M the set $Q \cup \Sigma \cup \Gamma \cup \Delta \cup \{\math025c, \$, -1, 0, +1\}$ is equal to $\{B, a, b, c, \math025c, \$, -1, 0, +1, q_0, q_1, q_2, q_3, q_4\}$ and has cardinality $k = 14$. Under the given order for the elements of the set $Q \cup \Sigma \cup \Gamma \cup \Delta \cup \{\math025c, \$, -1, 0, +1\}$, the empty string ϵ, as well as any string $B \cdots B$ of blank symbols, is represented by 0. a is represented by 1, and b is represented by 2. On the other hand, the input string $abbab$ is represented by the natural number

$$
\begin{aligned}
44312 &= (((1 \cdot 14 + 2) \cdot 14 + 2) \cdot 14 + 1) \cdot 14 + 2 \\
&= 1 \cdot 14^4 + 2 \cdot 14^3 + 2 \cdot 14^2 + 1 \cdot 14^1 + 2 \cdot 14^0.
\end{aligned}
$$

$\square$

An obvious distinction between programs and Turing transducers is in the primitiveness and uniformity of the descriptions of the latter. These characteristics contribute to the importance of Turing transducers in the study of computation.

4.3 Nondeterminism versus Determinism

Nondeterministic finite-state transducers can compute some functions that no deterministic finite-state transducer can. Similarly, nondeterministic pushdown automata can accept some languages that no deterministic pushdown automaton can. However, every language that is accepted by a nondeterministic finite-state automaton is also accepted by a deterministic finite-state automaton.

From Nondeterminism to Determinism

The following theorem relates nondeterminism to determinism in Turing transducers.

Theorem 4.3.1 Every Turing transducer M_1 has a corresponding deterministic Turing transducer M_2 such that

    a. M_2 accepts the same inputs as M_1, that is, $L(M_2) = L(M_1)$.

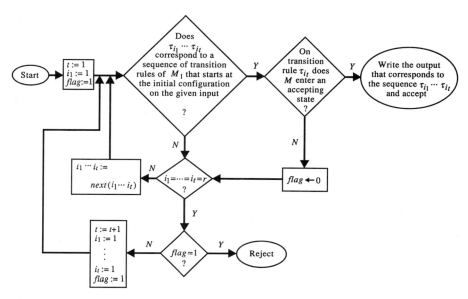

Figure 4.3.1 "Simulation" of a nondeterministic Turing transducer M_1 by a deterministic Turing transducer M_2.

b. M_2 halts on exactly the same inputs as M_1.

c. M_2 has an output y on a given input only if M_1 can output y on such an input, that is, $R(M_2) \subseteq R(M_1)$.

Proof Consider any m auxiliary-work-tape Turing transducer M_1 and any input x for M_1. Let $\tau_1, \ldots, \tau_r$ denote the transition rules of M_1. Let $C_{i_1 \ldots i_t}$ denote the configuration that M_1 reaches on input x from its initial configuration, through a sequence of moves that uses the sequence of transition rules $\tau_{i_1} \cdots \tau_{i_t}$. If no such sequence of moves is possible, then $C_{i_1 \ldots i_t}$ is assumed to denote an undefined configuration. The desired Turing transducer M_2 can be a deterministic $m + 1$ auxiliary-work-tape Turing transducer of the following form.

M_2 on the given input x searches along the sequence $C_\epsilon, C_1, C_2, \ldots, C_r,$ $C_{11}, C_{12}, \ldots, C_{rr}, C_{111}, C_{112}, \ldots, C_{rrr}, \ldots$ for an accepting configuration of M_1 on input x.

M_2 halts in an accepting configuration upon reaching an accepting configuration of M_1. M_2 halts in a rejecting configuration upon reaching a t, such that all the configurations $C_{i_1 \ldots i_t}$ of M_1 are undefined. In an accepting computation, M_2 provides the output associated with the accepting configuration of M_1.

A computation of M_2 on input x proceeds as follows. M_2 lists the strings $\alpha = i_1 \cdots i_t$ in $\{1, \ldots, r\}^*$ on its first auxiliary work tape, one at a time, in canonical order until either of the following two conditions holds (see the flowchart in Figure 4.3.1).

a. M_2 determines a string $\alpha = i_1 \cdots i_t$ in $\{1, \ldots, r\}^*$, such that $C_{i_1 \ldots i_t}$ is an accepting configuration of M_1 on input x. Such a configuration corresponds to the accepting computation $C_\epsilon \vdash C_{i_1} \vdash \cdots \vdash C_{i_1 \ldots i_t}$ of M_1 on input x. In such a case, M_2 has the same output as the accepting computation of M_1, and it halts in an accepting configuration.

M_2 finds out whether a given $C_{i_1 \ldots i_t}$ is a defined configuration by scanning over the string $i_1 \cdots i_t$ while trying to trace a sequence of moves $C_\epsilon \vdash C_{i_1} \vdash \cdots \vdash C_{i_1 \ldots i_t}$ of M_1 on input x. During the tracing M_2 ignores the output of M_1.

M_2 uses its input head to trace the input head movements of M_1. M_2 uses its finite-state control to record the states of M_1. M_2 uses m of its auxiliary work tapes to trace the changes in the corresponding auxiliary work tapes of M_1.

M_2 determines the output of M_1 that corresponds to a given string $i_1 \cdots i_t$ by scanning the string and extracting the output associated with the corresponding sequence of transition rules $\tau_{i_1} \cdots \tau_{i_t}$.

b. M_2 determines a t, such that $C_{i_1 \ldots i_t}$ is an undefined configuration for all the strings $\alpha = i_1 \cdots i_t$ in $\{1, \ldots, r\}^*$. In such a case, M_2 halts in a nonaccepting configuration.

M_2 determines that a given string $i_1 \cdots i_t$ corresponds to an undefined configuration $C_{i_1 \ldots i_t}$ by verifying that M_1 has no sequence of moves of the form $C_\epsilon \vdash C_{i_1} \vdash \cdots \vdash C_{i_1 \ldots i_t}$ on input x. The verification is made by a tracing similar to the one described in (a).

M_2 uses a flag in its finite-state control for determining the existence of a t, such that $C_{i_1 \ldots i_t}$ are undefined configurations for all $i_1 \cdots i_t$ in $\{1, \ldots, r\}^*$. M_2 sets the flag to 1 whenever t is increased by 1. M_2 sets the flag to 0 whenever a string $i_1 \cdots i_t$ is determined, such that $C_{i_1 \ldots i_t}$ is a defined configuration. M_2 determines that the property holds whenever t is to be increased on a flag that contains the value of 1.   □

Example 4.3.1 Let M_1 be the nondeterministic, one auxiliary-work-tape Turing transducer given in Figure 4.3.2(a). M_1 computes the relation $\{(ww^{\text{rev}}, w^{\text{rev}}) \mid w$ is in $\{a, b\}^+\}$. On input $abba$ the Turing transducer M_1 has an accepting computation $C_\epsilon \vdash C_1 \vdash C_{12} \vdash C_{124} \vdash C_{1246} \vdash C_{12465} \vdash C_{124657}$ that corresponds to the sequence of transition rules $\tau_1 \tau_2 \tau_4 \tau_6 \tau_5 \tau_7$.

Let M_2 be the deterministic Turing transducer in Figure 4.3.2(b). M_2 computes the same function as M_1 and is similar to the Turing transducer in the proof of Theorem 4.3.1. The main difference is that here M_2 halts only in its accepting computations.

On input $abba$ the Turing transducer M_2 lists the strings in $\{1, \ldots, 7\}^*$ on its first auxiliary work tape, one at a time, in canonical order. The Turing transducer M_2 checks whether each of those strings $\alpha = i_1 \cdots i_t$ defines an accepting computation $C_\epsilon \vdash C_{i_1} \vdash \cdots \vdash C_{i_1 \ldots i_t}$ of M_1.

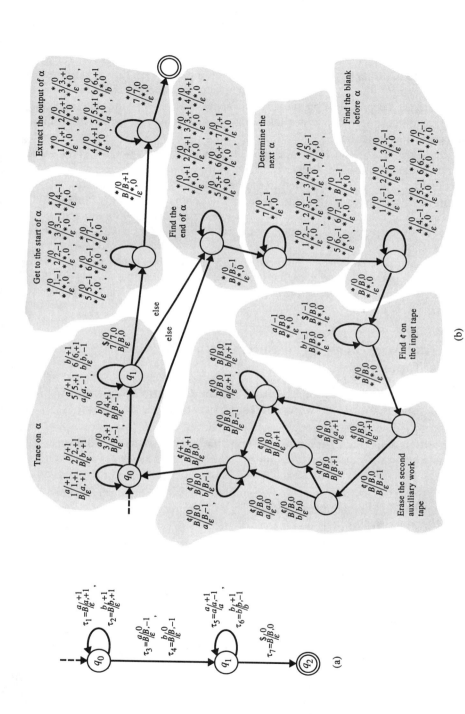

Figure 4.3.2 (a) A nondeterministic Turing transducer M. (b) A deterministic Turing transducer that computes the same function as M. (The asterisk * stands for the current symbol under the corresponding head.)

The Turing transducer M_2 detects that none of the strings " ", "1", ..., "7", "1 1", ..., "7 7", ..., "1 1 1 1 1 1", ..., "1 2 4 6 5 6", representing the sequences ϵ, $\tau_1, \ldots, \tau_7, \tau_1\tau_1, \ldots, \tau_7\tau_7, \ldots, \tau_1\tau_1\tau_1\tau_1\tau_1\tau_1, \ldots, \tau_1\tau_2\tau_4\tau_6\tau_5\tau_6$, respectively, corresponds to an accepting computation of M_1 on input $abba$. Then M_2 determines that the string "1 2 4 6 5 7", which represents the sequence $\tau_1\tau_2\tau_4\tau_6\tau_5\tau_7$, corresponds to an accepting computation of M_1 on input $abba$. With this determination, the Turing transducer M_2 writes the output of this computation, and halts in an accepting configuration.

M_2 uses the component "Trace on α" to check, by tracing on the given input, that there exists a sequence of moves of M_1 of the form $C_\epsilon \vdash C_{i_1} \vdash \cdots \vdash C_{i_1 \cdots i_t}$, for the $\alpha = i_1 \cdots i_t$ that is stored in the first auxiliary work tape of M_2. Such a sequence of moves corresponds to an accepting computation of M_1 if and only if $\tau_{i_t} = \tau_7$. The component "Trace on α" is essentially M_1 modified to follow the sequence of transition rules dictated by the content of the first auxiliary work tape of M_2.

M_2 uses the components "Find the end of α," "Determine the next α," "Find the blank before α," "Find c on the input tape," and "Erase the second auxiliary work tape" to prepare itself for the consideration of the next α from the canonically ordered set $\{1, \ldots, 7\}^*$. □

Deterministic Turing Transducers with Two Auxiliary Work Tapes

The following proposition implies that Theorem 4.3.1 also holds when M_2 is a deterministic, two auxiliary-work-tape Turing transducer.

Proposition 4.3.1 Each deterministic Turing transducer M_1 has an equivalent deterministic Turing transducer M_2 with two auxiliary work tapes.

Proof Consider any deterministic, m auxiliary-work-tape Turing transducer M_1. On a given input x, the Turing transducer M_2 simulates the computation $C_0 \vdash C_1 \vdash C_2 \vdash \cdots$ that M_1 has on input x.

M_2 starts by recording the initial configuration $C_0 = (\mathrm{c}q_0x\$, q_0, \ldots, q_0, \epsilon)$ of M_1 on input x. Then M_2 repeatedly replaces the recorded configuration C_i of M_1, with the next configuration C_{i+1} of the simulated computation.

M_2 halts upon reaching a halting configuration of M_1. M_2 halts in an accepting configuration if and only if it determines that M_1 does so.

M_2 records a configuration $C_i = (uqv, u_1qv_1, \ldots, u_mqv_m, w)$ of M_1 in the following manner. The state q is stored in the finite-state control of M_2. The input head location of M_1 is recorded by the location of the input head of M_2. The output w of M_1 is recorded on the output tape of M_2. The tuple $(u_1, v_1, \ldots, u_m, v_m)$ is stored as a string of the form $\#u_1\#v_1\# \cdots \#u_m\#v_m\#$ on an auxiliary work tape of M_2, where $\#$ is assumed to be a new symbol. The tuple is stored on the first auxiliary work tape of M_2 when i is even and on the second auxiliary work tape when i is odd.

The Turing transducer M_2 starts a computation by laying a string of $(2m + 1)$ symbols # in the first auxiliary work tape. Such a string represents the situation in which $u_1 = v_1 = \cdots = u_m = v_m = \epsilon$. M_2 determines the transition rule $(q, a, b_1, b_2, \ldots, b_m, p, d_0, c_1, d_1, c_2, d_2, \ldots, c_m, d_m, \rho)$ to be used in a given move by getting q from the finite-state control, a from the input tape, and $b_1, \ldots, b_m$ from the auxiliary work tape that records $\#u_1\#v_1\#\cdots\#u_m\#v_m\#$. $\qquad\square$

Example 4.3.2 Let M_1 be the Turing transducer whose transition diagram is given in Figure 4.3.3(a). The Turing transducer M_2 in the proof of Proposition 4.3.1 can use a segment D as in Figure 4.3.3(b) to determine the transition rule that M_1 uses on moving from state q_1.

D assumes that M_1 is in configuration $(uq_1v, u_1q_1v_1, \ldots, u_mq_1v_m, w)$, that M_2 is in state q_1, that $\#u_1\#v_1\#\cdots\#u_m\#v_m\#$ is stored on the first auxiliary work tape of M_2, and that the head of the first auxiliary work tape is placed on the first symbol of $\#u_1\#v_1\#\cdots\#u_m\#v_m\#$. $\qquad\square$

Since Turing transducers can compute relations that are not functions, it follows that nondeterministic Turing transducers have more definition power than deterministic Turing transducers. However, Theorem 4.3.1 implies that such is not the case for Turing machines. In fact, Theorem 4.3.1 together with Proposition 4.3.1 imply the following corollary.

Corollary 4.3.1 A function is computable (or, respectively, partially computable) by a Turing transducer if and only if it is computable (or, respectively, partially computable) by a deterministic, two auxiliary-work-tape Turing transducer.

4.4 Universal Turing Transducers

Programs are written to instruct computing machines on how to solve given problems. A program P is considered to be executable by a computing machine A if A can, when given P and any x for P, simulate any computation of P on input x.

In many cases, a single computing machine can execute more than one program, and thus can be programmed to compute different functions. However, it is not clear from the previous discussion just how general a computing machine can be. Theorem 4.4.1 below, together with Church's thesis, imply that there are machines that can be programmed to compute any computable function. One such example is the computing machine D, which consists of a "universal" Turing transducer U and of a translator T, which have the following characteristics (see Figure 4.4.1).

U is a deterministic Turing transducer that can execute any given deterministic Turing transducer M. That is, U on any given (M, x) simulates the computation of M on input x (see the proof of Theorem 4.4.1).

T is a deterministic Turing transducer whose inputs are pairs (P, x) of programs P written in some fixed programming language, and inputs x for P. T on a given input (P, x) outputs x together with a deterministic Turing transducer M that is equivalent to P. In particular, if P is a deterministic Turing transducer (i.e.,

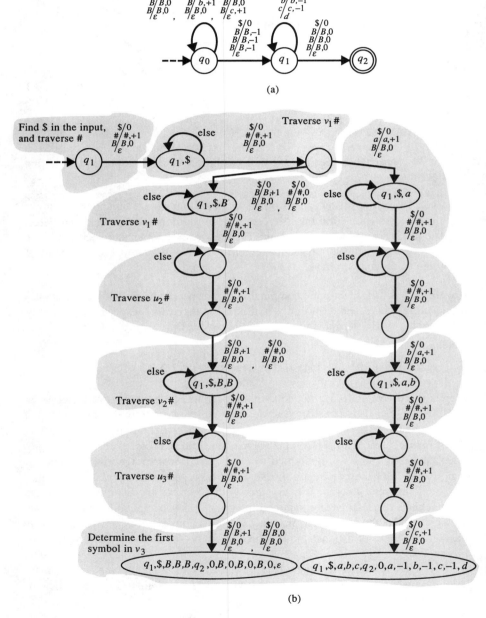

Figure 4.3.3 The segment of the Turing transducer in part (b) determines the transition rule used by the Turing transducer in part (a) from state q_1.

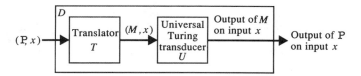

Figure 4.4.1 A programmable computing machine D.

a program written in the "machine" language), then T is a trivial translator that just outputs its input. On the other hand, if P is a program written in a higher level programming language, then T is a compiler that provides a deterministic Turing transducer M for simulating P.

When given an input (P, x), the computing machine D provides the pair to T, and then it feeds the output (M, x) of T to U, to obtain the desired output of P on input x.

Definitions A *universal Turing transducer* U is a deterministic Turing transducer that on any given pair (M, x), of a deterministic Turing transducer M and of an input x for M, simulates the behavior of M on x. Inputs that do not have the form (M, x) are rejected by U. *Universal Turing machines* are defined similarly.

It should be noted that a pair (M, x) is presented to a universal Turing transducer in encoded form, and that the output of the universal Turing transducer is the encoding of the output of M on input x. For convenience, the mentioning of the encoding is omitted when no confusion arises. Moreover, unless otherwise stated, a "standard" binary representation is implicitly assumed for the encodings.

A Representation for Turing Transducers

In what follows, a string is said to be a *standard binary representation* of a Turing transducer $M = <Q, \Sigma, \Gamma, \Delta, \delta, q_0, B, F>$ if it is equal to $E(M)$, where E is defined recursively in the following way.

a. $E(M) = E(F)01E(\delta)$.

b. $E(F) = E(p_1) \cdots E(p_k)$ for some ordering $\{p_1, \ldots, p_k\}$ of the states of F.

c. $E(B) = 0$ is the binary representation of the blank symbol.

d. $E(\delta) = E(\tau_1)01E(\tau_2)01 \cdots 01E(\tau_r)01$ for some ordering $\{\tau_1, \ldots, \tau_r\}$ of the transition rules of δ.

e. $E(\tau) = E(q)E(a)E(b_1) \cdots E(b_m)E(p)E(d_0)E(c_1)E(d_1) \cdots E(c_m)E(d_m)$
   $E(\rho)$ for each $\tau = (q, a, b_1, \ldots, b_m, p, d_0, c_1, d_1, \ldots, c_m, d_m, \rho)$ in δ.

f. $E(d) = 011$ for $d = -1$, $E(d) = 0111$ for $d = 0$, $E(d) = 01111$ for $d = +1$, and $E(\rho) = 0$ for an output $\rho = \epsilon$.

g. $E(q_i) = 01^{i+2}$ for each state q_i in Q, and some ordering $q_0, \ldots, q_s$ of the states of Q. Note that the order assumes the initial state q_0 to be the first.

h. $E(e_i) = 01^{i+1}$ for each symbol e_i in $(\Sigma \cup \Gamma \cup \Delta \cup \{\mathbb{c}, \$\}) - \{B\}$ and some order $\{e_1, \ldots, e_t\}$ in which $e_1 = \mathbb{c}$ and $e_2 = \$$.

Intuitively, we see that E provides a binary representation for the symbols in the alphabets of the Turing transducer, a binary representation for the states of the Turing transducer, and a binary representation for the possible heads movements. Then it provides a representation for a sequence of such entities, by concatenating the representations of the entities. The string 01 is used as separator for avoiding ambiguity.

By definition, a given Turing transducer can have some finite number of standard binary representations. Each of these representations depends on the order chosen for the states in Q, the order chosen for the symbols in $(\Sigma \cup \Gamma \cup \Delta \cup \{\mathbb{c}, \$\}) - \{B\}$, the order chosen for the states in F, and the order chosen for the transition rules in δ. On the other hand, different Turing transducers can have identical standard binary representations if they are *isomorphic*, that is, if they are equal except for the names of their states and the symbols in their alphabets.

Example 4.4.1 If M is the Turing transducer whose transition diagram is given in Figure 4.1.3, then $E(M)$ can be the standard binary representation

$$E(q_4)01E(q_0, a, B, q_1, +1, a, +1, a)01 \cdots 01E(q_3, \$, B, q_4, 0, B, 0, \epsilon)01 =$$
$$E(q_4)01E(q_0)E(a)E(B)E(q_1) \cdots E(q_3)E(\$)E(B)E(q_4)E(0)E(B)E(0)E(\epsilon)01$$

where $E(q_0) = 011$, $E(q_1) = 0111$, $E(q_2) = 01111$, $E(q_3) = 011111$, $E(q_4) = 0111111$, $E(B) = 0$, $E(\mathbb{c}) = 011$, $E(\$) = 0111$, $E(a) = 01111$, $\ldots$

0 and 00 are examples of binary strings that are not standard binary representations of any Turing transducer.

The string

$$\alpha = 01^40101^201^4001^201^401^401^401^60101^201^5001^301^30$$
$$01^200101^301^401^401^301^401^4001^200101^301^3001^401^4001^3001$$

represents a Turing transducer with one accepting state and four transition rules. Only the first transition rule has a nonempty output. The Turing transducer has one auxiliary work tape.   □

$E(M)01E(\mathbb{c}x\$)$ is assumed to be the standard binary representation of (M, x), with $E(\mathbb{c}x\$) = E(\mathbb{c})E(a_1) \cdots E(a_n)E(\$)$ when $x = a_1 \cdots a_n$.

A Universal Turing Transducer

The proof of the following result provides an example of a universal Turing transducer.

Theorem 4.4.1 There exists a universal Turing transducer U.

Proof *U* can be a two auxiliary-work-tape Turing transducer similar to M_2 in the proof of Proposition 4.3.1. Specifically, *U* starts each computation by checking that its input is a pair (M, x) of some deterministic Turing transducer $M = <Q, \Sigma, \Gamma, \Delta, \delta, q_0, B, F>$ and of some input *x* for *M* (given in standard binary representation). If the input is not of such a form, then *U* halts in a nonaccepting configuration. However, if the input is of such a form, *U* simulates a computation of *M* on *x*.

U, like M_2, uses two auxiliary work tapes for keeping track of the content of the auxiliary work tapes of *M*. However, *U* also uses the auxiliary work tapes for keeping track of the states and the input head locations of *M*. Specifically, the universal Turing transducer *U* records a configuration $(uqv, u_1qv_1, \ldots, u_mqv_m, w)$ of *M* by storing $\#E(q)\#|u|\#E(u_1)\#E(v_1)\# \cdots \#E(u_m)\#E(v_m)\#$ in an auxiliary work tape, and storing $E(w)$ in the output tape.

To determine the transition rule $(q, a, b_1, \ldots, b_m, p, d_0, c_1, d_1, \ldots, c_m, d_m, \rho)$ that *M* uses in a simulated move, *U* extracts the state $\dot{q}$ and the symbols *a*, $b_1, \ldots, b_m$. *U* records the string $E(q)E(a)E(b_1) \cdots E(b_m)$ in the auxiliary work tape that does not keep the configuration of *M* that is in effect. Then *U* determines $p, d_0, c_1, d_1, \ldots, c_m, d_m, \rho$ by searching $E(M)$ for the substring that follows a substring of the form $01E(q)E(a)E(b_1) \cdots E(b_m)$. $\square$

4.5 Undecidability

The finiteness of memory and the restricted access to it, respectively, constrain the capabilities of finite-state transducers and pushdown transducers. In the case of Turing transducers, however, none of the constraints made on memory is significant, because they can all be removed and still the transducers acquire no more definition power. Yet there are languages that Turing transducers cannot decide or even accept. The intuitive explanation for this phenomenon is that each Turing transducer is a description of a language (i.e., a set of strings), which itself has a description by a string. Consequently, there are more languages than Turing transducers.

Specifically, each language over an alphabet Σ is a subset of Σ^*. The set of all the languages over Σ is the power set 2^{Σ^*}, which is uncountably infinite. On the other hand, the number of Turing transducers that specify languages over Σ is countably infinite, because they are all representable by strings from Σ^*.

A Proof by a Generic Approach

The proof of the following theorem implicitly uses the previous observation. As with the limitations of the finite-memory programs in Section 2.4 and the limitations of the recursive finite-domain programs in Section 3.4, we here use a proof by reduction to contradiction. The variant of the technique used here is called a proof by diagonalization, owing to the employment of the diagonal of a table for choosing the language that provides the contradiction.

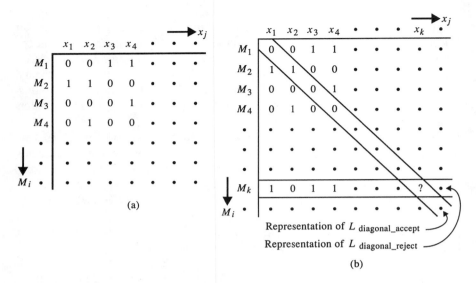

Figure 4.5.1 (a) Hypothetical table T_{accept} indicating acceptance of word x_j by Turing machine M_i. (b) Representations of $L_{\text{diagonal\_accept}}$ and $L_{\text{diagonal\_reject}}$ in T_{accept}.

Convention In this chapter x_i will denote the ith string in the canonically ordered set of binary strings. Similarly, M_i will denote the Turing machine that has a standard binary representation equal to the ith string, in the canonically ordered set of the standard binary representations of Turing machines. (With no loss of generality it is assumed that isomorphic Turing machines are equal.)

Theorem 4.5.1 There are nonrecursively enumerable languages, that is, languages that cannot be accepted by any Turing machine.

Proof Let L_{accept} be the language $\{ (M, x) \mid$ The turing machine M accepts the string $x \}$. The language L_{accept} has a table representation T_{accept} in which the rows are indexed by $M_1, M_2, M_3, \ldots$ the columns are indexed by $x_1, x_2, x_3, \ldots$ and each entry at row M_i and column x_j holds either 1 or 0, depending on whether M_i accepts x_j or not (see Figure 4.5.1(a)).

Each language L can be represented by a vector that holds 1 at its jth entry if x_j is in L, and holds 0 at its jth entry if x_j is not in L. In particular, the language $L(M_i)$ is represented by the ith row in T_{accept}.

The approach of the proof is to find a language that corresponds to no row in T_{accept}, and so cannot be accepted by any Turing machine. One such option is to construct the language from the diagonal of T_{accept}.

The diagonal of the table T_{accept} is a representation of $L_{\text{diagonal\_accept}} = \{ x \mid x = x_i$ and M_i accepts $x_i \}$. Let $L_{\text{diagonal\_reject}}$ denote the complementation $\{ x \mid x = x_i$ and M_i does not accept $x_i \}$ of $L_{\text{diagonal\_accept}}$. Each Turing machine that accepts $L_{\text{diagonal\_reject}}$ implies some row M_k in T_{accept} that holds values complementing those in the diagonal at similar locations (see Figure 4.5.1(b)). In particular, the kth digit in row M_k must be the complementation of the kth digit in the diagonal. However, the kth digit in row M_k is also the kth digit in the diagonal, consequently implying that no Turing machine can accept the language $L_{\text{diagonal\_reject}}$.

The discussion above can be formalized in the following way. For the sake of the proof assume that $L_{\text{diagonal\_reject}}$ is accepted by some Turing machine M. Then there exists an index k such that $M = M_k$. Now consider the string x_k. For x_k either of the following cases must hold.

Case 1 x_k is in $L_{\text{diagonal\_reject}}$. In Case 1, the assumption that the Turing machine M_k accepts the language $L_{\text{diagonal\_reject}}$ implies that M_k accepts the string x_k. Alternatively, the definition of $L_{\text{diagonal\_reject}}$ implies that M_k does not accept x_k. Thus Case 1 cannot hold.

Case 2 x_k is not in $L_{\text{diagonal\_reject}}$. Similarly, in Case 2, the assumption that M_k accepts $L_{\text{diagonal\_reject}}$ implies that M_k does not accept x_k. And alternatively, the definition of $L_{\text{diagonal\_reject}}$ implies that M_k accepts x_k. Hence, implying that Case 2 cannot hold either.

The result follows because for the assumption that there is a Turing machine M that accepts $L_{\text{diagonal\_reject}}$ to hold, either Case 1 or Case 2 must hold. ☐

By Church's thesis a decision problem is partially decidable if and only if there is a Turing machine that accepts exactly those instances of the problem that have the answer *yes*. Similarly, the problem is decidable if and only if there is a Turing machine that accepts exactly those instances that have the answer *yes* and that also halts on all instances of answer *no*.

The proof of Theorem 4.5.1 together with Church's thesis imply the following theorem. The importance of this theorem stems from its exhibiting the existence of an undecidable problem, and from its usefulness for showing the undecidability of other problems by means of reducibility.

Theorem 4.5.2 The membership problem is undecidable, and, in fact, not even partially decidable for $L_{\text{diagonal\_reject}}$.

Proofs by Reduction

A proof of the undecidability of a given problem by means of reducibility runs as follows (see Figure 4.5.2 and recall Section 1.5). For the purpose of the proof assume that the given problem K_A is decidable by some algorithm A. Find algorithms T_f and T_g that together with A provide an algorithm B, for solving a known undecidable problem K_B in the following manner. B, when given an instance I, uses T_f to obtain an instance I' of K_A, employs A on I' to obtain the output S' that A provides for I', and then introduces S' to T_g to obtain the output S of B. The undecidability of K_A then follows, because otherwise the decidability of a problem K_B that is known to be undecidable would have been implied.

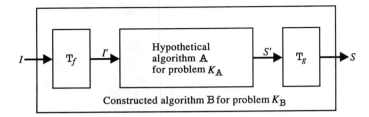

Figure 4.5.2 Reduction of K_B to K_A.

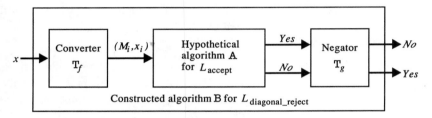

Figure 4.5.3 Reduction of the membership problem for $L_{\text{diagonal\_reject}}$ to the membership problem for L_{accept}.

The proof of the following theorem is an example of a proof that uses reduction between undecidable problems.

Theorem 4.5.3 The membership problem for Turing machines or, equivalently, for L_{accept} is undecidable.

Proof For the purpose of the proof assume that the given problem is decidable by a hypothetical algorithm A (see Figure 4.5.3). Then the membership problem for $L_{\text{diagonal\_reject}}$ can be decided by an algorithm B of the following form.

The algorithm B on a given input x uses a converter T_f to obtain a pair (M_i, x_i) such that $x = x_i$. T_f can find the index i for x by listing the binary strings ϵ, 0, $00, \ldots, x$ in canonical order, and determining the index of x in the list. T_f can find M_i by listing the binary strings ϵ, 0, 1, $00, \ldots$ in canonical order until the ith standard binary representation of a Turing machine is reached.

The output (M_i, x_i) of T_f is provided by B to A. Finally B employs T_g for determining that x is in $L_{\text{diagonal\_reject}}$ if A determines that x is not in L_{accept}, and that x is not in $L_{\text{diagonal\_reject}}$ if A determines that x is in L_{accept}.

The result follows from the undecidability of the membership problem for the language $L_{\text{diagonal\_reject}}$ (see Theorem 4.5.2).   □

The previous theorem and the next one imply that there are nonrecursive languages that are recursively enumerable.

Theorem 4.5.4 The membership problem for Turing machines or, equivalently, for L_{accept} is partially decidable.

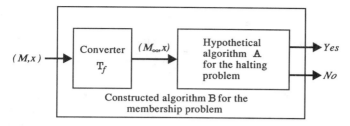

Figure 4.5.4 Reduction of the membership problem for Turing machines to the halting problem for Turing machines.

Proof L_{accept} is accepted by a nondeterministic Turing machine similar to the universal Turing machine M_2 in the proof of Theorem 4.4.1. $\quad\square$

Many problems, including the one in the following theorem, can be shown to be undecidable by reduction from the membership problem for Turing machines.

Theorem 4.5.5 The halting problem for Turing machines is undecidable.

Proof A Turing machine M does not halt on a given input x if and only if M does not accept x and on such an input M can have an infinite sequence of moves.

An answer *no* to the halting problem for an instance (M, x) implies the same answer to the membership problem for the instance (M, x). However, an answer *yes* to the halting problem for an instance (M, x) can correspond to either an answer *yes* or an answer *no* to the membership problem for the instance (M, x). The proof of the theorem relies on the observation that each Turing machine M can be modified to avoid the rejection of an input in a halting configuration. With such a modification, an answer *yes* to the halting problem at (M, x) also implies the same answer to the membership problem at (M, x).

For the purpose of the proof assume that the halting problem for Turing machines is decidable by a hypothetical algorithm A. Then an algorithm B, which decides the membership problem for Turing machines, can be constructed employing a translator T_f and the hypothetical algorithm A in the following manner (see Figure 4.5.4).

B provides any given instance (M, x) to T_f. T_f constructs from the given m auxiliary-work-tape Turing machine M an equivalent Turing machine M_∞, that halts on a given input if and only if M accepts the input. Specifically, M_∞ is just the Turing machine M with a "looping" transition rule of the form $(q, a, b_1, \ldots, b_m, q, 0, b_1, 0, \ldots, b_m, 0)$ added for each nonaccepting state q, each input symbol a, and each combination of auxiliary work-tape symbols $b_1, \ldots, b_m$ on which M has no next move. B feeds (M_∞, x) to A and assumes the output of A.

The result follows from Theorem 4.5.3, showing that the membership problem is undecidable for L_{accept}. $\quad\square$

Example 4.5.1 Let M be the Turing machine in Figure 4.5.5(a). Upon reaching state q_0 the Turing machine M enters a nonaccepting halting configuration

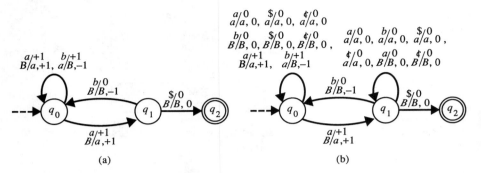

Figure 4.5.5 (a) A Turing machine M. (b) A Turing machine M_∞ that is equivalent to M.

if both the input head and the auxiliary work-tape head scan the symbol a. M can be modified to enter an infinite loop in such a configuration by forcing the Turing machine to make a move that does not change the configuration, that is, by introducing a transition rule of the form $(q_0, a, a, q_0, 0, a, 0)$.

Using the notations in the proof of Theorem 4.5.5, M_∞ is the Turing machine in Figure 4.5.5(b). $\qquad\square$

The next theorem provides another example of a proof of undecidability by means of reduction.

Theorem 4.5.6 The problem of deciding for any given Turing machine whether the machine accepts a regular language is undecidable.

Proof Consider any instance (M, x) of the membership problem for Turing machines. From (M, x) construct a Turing machine M_x that accepts $\{\, a^i b^i \mid i \geq 0 \,\}$ if M accepts x, and that accepts the empty set if M does not accept x.

Specifically, M_x on any given input w starts the computation by checking whether $w = a^i b^i$ for some $i \geq 0$. If the equality $w = a^i b^i$ holds for no $i \geq 0$, then M_x rejects w. Otherwise, M_x simulates the computation of M on input x. In the latter case, M_x accepts w if it determines that M accepts x, and M_x rejects w if it determines that M rejects x.

Consequently, M_x accepts a regular language (which is the empty set) if and only if M does not accept x. The result follows from the undecidability of the membership problem for Turing machines (see Theorem 4.5.3). $\qquad\square$

Example 4.5.2 Let M be the Turing machine given in Figure 4.5.6(a). Let $x = ababc$. Then M_x in the proof of Theorem 4.5.6 can be as in Figure 4.5.6(b). M_x has one more auxiliary work tape than M and consists of three subcomponents M_1, M_2, and M_3.

M_1 checks that the given input is of the form $a^i b^i$ for some $i \geq 0$. M_2 stores the string $\text{\textcent} x \text{\$}$ in the first auxiliary work tape. M_3 is just M modified to read its input from the first auxiliary work tape. $\text{\textcent}$ and $\text{\$}$ are the symbols used in the first auxiliary work tape representing the endmarkers $\text{\textcent}$ and $\$$, respectively. $\qquad\square$

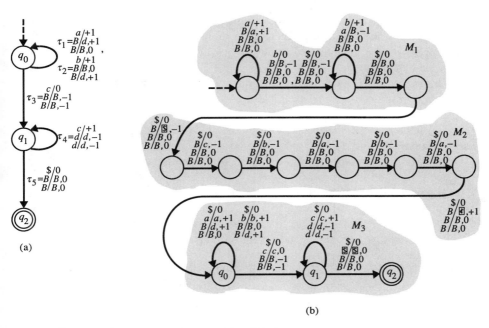

Figure 4.5.6 (a) A Turing machine M. (b) A corresponding Turing machine M_{ababc} that accepts $\{a^i b^i \mid i \geq 0\}$ if and only if M accepts $ababc$.

The universe of the undecidable problems includes numerous examples. For many of these problems the proof of undecidability is quite involved. The selection that has been made here should be appreciated at least for the simplification that it allows in introducing the concepts under consideration.

4.6 Turing Machines and Type 0 Languages

The classes of languages that are accepted by finite-state automata on the one hand and pushdown automata on the other hand were shown earlier to be the classes of Type 3 and Type 2 languages, respectively. The following two theorems show that the class of languages accepted by Turing machines is the class of Type 0 languages.

Theorem 4.6.1 Each Type 0 language is a recursively enumerable language.

Proof Consider any Type 0 grammar $G = <N, \Sigma, P, S>$. From G construct a two auxiliary-work-tape Turing machine M_G that on a given input x nondeterministically generates some string w in $L(G)$, and then accepts x if and only if $x = w$.

The Turing machine M_G generates the string w by tracing a derivation in G of w from S. M_G starts by placing the sentential form S in the first auxiliary work tape. Then M_G repeatedly replaces the sentential form stored on the first auxiliary work tape with the one that succeeds it in the derivation. The second auxiliary work tape is used as an intermediate memory, while deriving the successor of each of the sentential forms.

The successor of each sentential form γ is obtained by nondeterministically searching γ for a substring α, such that $\alpha \rightarrow \beta$ is a production rule in G, and then replacing α by β in γ.

M_G uses a subcomponent M_1 to copy the prefix of γ that precedes α onto the second auxiliary work tape.

M_G uses a subcomponent M_2 to read α from the first auxiliary work tape and replace it by β on the second.

M_G uses a subcomponent M_3 to copy the suffix of γ that succeeds α onto the second auxiliary work tape.

M_G uses a subcomponent M_4 to copy the sentential form created on the second auxiliary work tape onto the first. In addition, M_G uses M_4 to determine whether the new sentential form is a string in $L(G)$. If w is in $L(G)$, then the control is passed to a subcomponent M_5. Otherwise, the control is passed to M_1.

M_G uses the subcomponent M_5 to determine whether the input string x is equal to the string w stored on the first auxiliary work tape.   □

Example 4.6.1 Consider the grammar G which has the following production rules.

$$\begin{aligned} S &\rightarrow aSbS \\ Sb &\rightarrow \epsilon \end{aligned}$$

The language $L(G)$ is accepted by the Turing machine M_G, whose transition diagram is given in Figure 4.6.1.

The components M_1, M_2, and M_3 scan from left to right the sentential form stored on the first auxiliary work tape. As the components scan the tape they erase its content.

The component M_2 of M_G uses two different sequences of transition rules for the first and second production rules: $S \rightarrow aSbS$ and $Sb \rightarrow \epsilon$. The sequence of transition rules that corresponds to $S \rightarrow aSbS$ removes S from the first auxiliary work tape and stores $aSbS$ on the second. The sequence of transition rules that corresponds to $Sb \rightarrow \epsilon$ removes Sb from the first auxiliary work tape and stores nothing on the second.

The component M_4 scans from right to left the sentential form in the second auxiliary work tape, erasing the content of the tape during the scanning. M_4 starts scanning the sentential form in its first state, determining that the sentential form is a string of terminal symbols if it reaches the blank symbol B while in the first state. In such a case, M_4 transfers the control to M_5. M_4 determines that the sentential form is not a string of terminal symbols if it reaches a nonterminal symbol. In this case, M_4 switches from its first to its second state.   □

Theorem 4.6.2 Each recursively enumerable language is a Type 0 language.

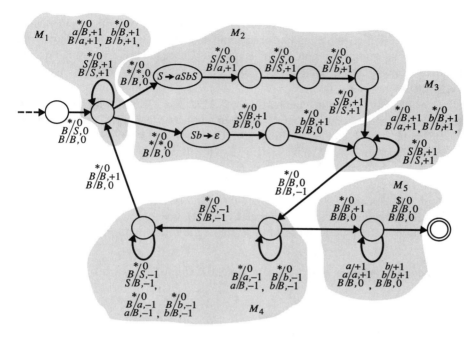

Figure 4.6.1 A Turing machine M_G for simulating the grammar G that has the production rules $S \to aSbS$ and $Sb \to \epsilon$.

Proof The proof consists of constructing from a given Turing machine M a grammar that can simulate the computations of M. The constructed grammar G consists of three groups of production rules.

The purpose of the first group is to determine the following three items.

a. An initial configuration of M on some input.

b. Some segment for each auxiliary work tape of M. Each segment must include the location under the head of the corresponding tape.

c. Some sequence of transition rules of M. The sequence of transition rules must start at the initial state, end at an accepting state, and be compatible in the transitions that it allows between the states.

The group of production rules can specify any initial configuration of M, any segment of an auxiliary work tape that satisfies the above conditions, and any sequence of transition rules that satisfies the above conditions.

The purpose of the second group of production rules is to simulate a computation of M. The simulation must start at the configuration determined by the first group. In addition, the simulation must be in accordance with the sequence of transition rules, and within the segments of the auxiliary work tapes determined by the first group.

The purpose of the third group of production rules is to extract the input whenever an accepting computation has been simulated, and to leave nonterminal symbols in the sentential form in the other cases. Consequently, the grammar can generate a given string if and only if the Turing machine M has an accepting computation on the string.

Consider any Turing machine $M = <Q, \Sigma, \Gamma, \delta, q_0, B, F>$. With no loss of generality it can be assumed that M is a two auxiliary-work-tape Turing machine (see Theorem 4.3.1 and Proposition 4.3.1), that no transition rule originates at an accepting state, and that $N = \Gamma \cup \{\tau \mid \tau$ is in $\delta\} \cup \{[q] \mid q$ is in $Q\}$ $\cup \{\cent, \$, \boxed{0}, \boxed{1}, \boxed{2}, \#, S, A, C, D, E, F, K\}$ is a multiset whose symbols are all distinct.

From M construct a grammar $G = <N, \Sigma, P, S>$ that generates $L(M)$, by tracing in its derivations the configurations that M goes through in its accepting computations. The production rules in P are of the following form.

a. Production rules for generating any sentential form that has the following pattern.

$$\cent \boxed{0} a_1 \cdots a_n \$ B \cdots B \boxed{1} B \cdots B \# B \cdots B \boxed{2} B \cdots B \# \tau_{i_1} \cdots \tau_{i_t}$$

Each such sentential form corresponds to an initial configuration $(\cent q_0 a_1 \cdots a_n \$, q_0, q_0)$ of M, and a sequence of transition rules $\tau_{i_1} \cdots \tau_{i_t}$. The transition rules define a sequence of compatible states that starts at the initial state and ends at an accepting state. $\boxed{0}$ represents the input head, $\boxed{1}$ represents the head of the first auxiliary work tape, and $\boxed{2}$ represents the head of the second auxiliary work tape. The string $B \cdots B \boxed{1} B \cdots B$ corresponds to a segment of the first auxiliary work tape, and the string $B \cdots B \boxed{2} B \cdots B$ to a segment of the second.

A string in the language is derivable from the sentential form if and only if the following three conditions hold.

1. The string is equal to $a_1 \cdots a_n$.

2. M accepts $a_1 \cdots a_n$ in a computation that uses the sequence of transition rules $\tau_{i_1} \cdots \tau_{i_t}$.

3. $B \cdots B \boxed{1} B \cdots B$ corresponds to a segment of the ith auxiliary work tape that is sufficiently large for the considered computation of M, $1 \le i \le 2$. The position of $\boxed{1}$ in the segment indicates the initial location of the corresponding auxiliary work-tape head in the segment.

The production rules are of the following form.

$$
\begin{aligned}
S &\rightarrow \mathcal{c}\boxed{0}A \\
A &\rightarrow aA \qquad\qquad \text{For each input symbol } a \text{ in } \Sigma. \\
&\rightarrow \$C \\
C &\rightarrow BC \\
&\rightarrow \boxed{1}D \\
D &\rightarrow BD \\
&\rightarrow \#E \\
E &\rightarrow BE \\
&\rightarrow \boxed{2}F \\
F &\rightarrow BF \\
&\rightarrow \#[q_0] \qquad\quad \text{For the initial state } q_0. \\
[q] &\rightarrow \tau[p] \qquad\quad\; \text{For each pair } q \text{ and } p \text{ of states, and for each} \\
&\qquad\qquad\qquad \text{transition rule } \tau, \text{ such that } \tau \text{ leaves state } q \\
&\qquad\qquad\qquad \text{and enters state } p. \\
[q_{\mathrm{f}}] &\rightarrow \epsilon \qquad\qquad\;\; \text{For each accepting state } q_{\mathrm{f}}.
\end{aligned}
$$

The production rules for the nonterminal symbols S and A can generate a string of the form $\mathcal{c}\boxed{0}a_1 \cdots a_n\$C$ for each possible input $a_1 \cdots a_n$ of M. The production rules for the nonterminal symbols C and D can generate a string of the form $B \cdots B\boxed{1}B \cdots B\#E$ for each possible segment $B \cdots B\boxed{1}B \cdots B$ of the first auxiliary work tape that contains the corresponding head location. The production rules for E and F can generate a string of the form $B \cdots B\boxed{2}B \cdots B\#[q_0]$ for each possible segment $B \cdots B\boxed{2}B \cdots B$ of the second tape that contains the corresponding head location. The production rules for the nonterminal symbols that correspond to the states of M can generate any sequence $\tau_{i_1} \cdots \tau_{i_t}$ of transition rules of M that starts at the initial state, ends at an accepting state, and is compatible in the transition between the states.

b. Production rules for deriving from a sentential form

$$
\tau_{i_1} \cdots \tau_{i_{j-1}} u\boxed{0}v\$B \cdots Bu_1\boxed{1}v_1 B \cdots B\#B \cdots Bu_2\boxed{2}v_2 B \cdots B\#\tau_{i_j} \cdots \tau_{i_t},
$$

which corresponds to configuration $\gamma = (uqv\$, u_1qv_1, u_2qv_2)$, a sentential form

$$
\tau_{i_1} \cdots \tau_{i_j} \hat{u}\boxed{0}\hat{v}\$B \cdots B\hat{u}_1\boxed{1}\hat{v}_1 B \cdots B\#B \cdots B\hat{u}_2\boxed{2}\hat{v}_2 B \cdots B\#\tau_{i_{j+1}} \cdots \tau_{i_t},
$$

which corresponds to configuration $\hat{\gamma} = (\hat{u}\hat{q}\hat{v}\$, \hat{u}_1\hat{q}\hat{v}_1, \hat{u}_2\hat{q}\hat{v}_2)$. γ and $\hat{\gamma}$ are assumed to be two configurations of M such that $\hat{\gamma}$ is reachable from γ by a move that uses the transition rule τ_{i_j}.

For each transition rule τ the set of production rules have

1. A production rule of the form $X\tau \rightarrow \tau X$ for each X in $\Sigma \cup \Gamma \cup \{\mathcal{c}, \$, \#\}$.

2. A production rule of the form $\boxed{0}\tau a \rightarrow \tau\boxed{0}a$, for each symbol a in $\Sigma \cup \{\mathfrak{c}, \$\}$ that satisfies the following condition: τ is a transition rule that scans the symbol a on the input tape without moving the input head.

3. A production rule of the form $\boxed{0}\tau a \rightarrow \tau a\boxed{0}$, for each symbol a in $\Sigma \cup \{\mathfrak{c}, \$\}$ that satisfies the following condition: τ is a transition rule that scans the symbol a in the input tape while moving the input head one position to the right.

4. A production rule of the form $a\boxed{0}\tau b \rightarrow \tau\boxed{0}ab$, for each pair of symbols a and b in $\Sigma \cup \{\mathfrak{c}, \$\}$ that satisfy the following condition: τ is a transition rule that scans the symbol b in the input tape while moving the input head one position to the left.

5. A production rule of the form $\boxed{i}\tau X \rightarrow \tau\boxed{i}Y$ for each $1 \leq i \leq 2$, and for each pair of symbols X and Y in Γ that satisfy the following condition: τ is a transition rule that replaces X with Y in the ith auxiliary work tape without changing the head position.

6. A production rule of the form $\boxed{i}\tau X \rightarrow \tau Y\boxed{i}$ for each $1 \leq i \leq 2$, and for each pair of symbols X and Y in Γ that satisfy the following condition: τ is a transition rule that replaces X with Y in the ith auxiliary work tape while moving the corresponding head one position to the right.

7. A production rule of the form $X\boxed{i}\tau Y \rightarrow \tau\boxed{i}XZ$ for each $1 \leq i \leq 2$, and for each triplet of symbols X, Y, and Z in Γ that satisfy the following condition: τ is a transition rule that replaces the symbol Y with Z in the ith auxiliary work tape while moving the corresponding head one position to the left.

The purpose of the production rules in (1) is to transport τ from right to left over the nonhead symbols in $\{\boxed{0}, \boxed{1}, \boxed{2}\}$, across a representation

$$u\boxed{0}v\$B \cdots Bu_1\boxed{1}v_1B \cdots B\#B \cdots Bu_2\boxed{2}v_2B \cdots B\#$$

of a configuration of M. τ gets across the head symbols $\boxed{0}$, $\boxed{1}$, and $\boxed{2}$ by using the production rules in (2) through (7). As τ gets across the head symbols, the production rules in (2) through (7) "simulate" the changes in the tapes of M, and the corresponding heads position, because of the transition rule τ.

c. Production rules for extracting from a sentential form

$$u\boxed{0}v\$B \cdots Bu_1\boxed{1}v_1B \cdots B\#B \cdots Bu_2\boxed{2}v_2B \cdots B\#,$$

which corresponds to an accepting configuration of M, the input that M accepts. The production rules are as follows.

$$\tau_f \mathord{\text{¢}} \;\rightarrow\; K \qquad \text{For each transition rule } \tau \text{ that enters an accepting}$$
state.

$$\tau K \;\rightarrow\; K \qquad \text{For each transition rule } \tau \text{ that does not enter an}$$
accepting state.

$$K a \;\rightarrow\; a K \qquad \text{For each input symbol } a \text{ in } \Sigma.$$

$$K X \;\rightarrow\; K \qquad \text{For each symbol } X \text{ in } \Gamma \cup \{\boxed{0}, \boxed{1}, \boxed{2}, \$, \# \}.$$

$$K \;\rightarrow\; \epsilon \qquad\qquad\qquad\qquad\qquad\qquad\qquad\quad \square$$

Example 4.6.2 Let M be the Turing machine whose transition diagram is given in Figure 4.5.6(a). $L(M)$ is generated by the grammar G that consists of the following production rules.

A. Production rules that find a sentential form that corresponds to the initial configuration of M, according to (a) in the proof of Theorem 4.6.2.

S	$\rightarrow$	$\text{¢}\boxed{0}A$	D	$\rightarrow$	BD	$[q_0]$	$\rightarrow$	$\tau_1[q_0]$
A	$\rightarrow$	aA		$\rightarrow$	$\#E$		$\rightarrow$	$\tau_2[q_0]$
	$\rightarrow$	bA	E	$\rightarrow$	BE		$\rightarrow$	$\tau_3[q_1]$
	$\rightarrow$	cA		$\rightarrow$	$\boxed{2}F$	$[q_1]$	$\rightarrow$	$\tau_4[q_1]$
	$\rightarrow$	$\$C$	F	$\rightarrow$	BF		$\rightarrow$	$\tau_5[q_2]$
C	$\rightarrow$	BC		$\rightarrow$	$\#[q_0]$	$[q_2]$	$\rightarrow$	ϵ
	$\rightarrow$	$\boxed{1}D$						

B. "Transporting" production rules that correspond to (b.1) in the proof of Theorem 4.6.2, $1 \le i \le 5$.

$a\tau_i$	$\rightarrow$	$\tau_i a$	$B\tau_i$	$\rightarrow$	$\tau_i B$
$b\tau_i$	$\rightarrow$	$\tau_i b$	$\text{¢}\tau_i$	$\rightarrow$	$\tau_i\text{¢}$
$c\tau_i$	$\rightarrow$	$\tau_i c$	$\$\tau_i$	$\rightarrow$	$\tau_i \$$
$d\tau_i$	$\rightarrow$	$\tau_i d$	$\#\tau_i$	$\rightarrow$	$\tau_i \#$

C. "Simulating" production rules that correspond to (b.2–b.4) in the proof of Theorem 4.6.2.

$\boxed{0}\tau_1 a$	$\rightarrow$	$\tau_1 a\boxed{0}$	$\boxed{0}\tau_2 b$	$\rightarrow$	$\tau_2 b\boxed{0}$	$\boxed{0}\tau_3 c$	$\rightarrow$	$\tau_3\boxed{0}c$
$\boxed{0}\tau_4 c$	$\rightarrow$	$\tau_4 c\boxed{0}$	$\boxed{0}\tau_5 \$$	$\rightarrow$	$\tau_5\boxed{0}\$$			

D. "Simulating" production rules that correspond to (b.5–b.7) in the proof of Theorem 4.6.2.

$\boxed{1}\tau_1 B$	$\rightarrow$	$\tau_1 d\boxed{1}$	$\boxed{1}\tau_2 B$	$\rightarrow$	$\tau_2\boxed{1}B$	$d\boxed{1}\tau_3 B$	$\rightarrow$	$\tau_3\boxed{1}dB$
$B\boxed{1}\tau_3 B$	$\rightarrow$	$\tau_3\boxed{1}BB$	$d\boxed{1}\tau_4 d$	$\rightarrow$	$\tau_4\boxed{1}dd$	$B\boxed{1}\tau_4 d$	$\rightarrow$	$\tau_4\boxed{1}Bd$
$\boxed{1}\tau_5 B$	$\rightarrow$	$\tau_5\boxed{1}B$						
$\boxed{2}\tau_1 B$	$\rightarrow$	$\tau_1\boxed{2}B$	$\boxed{2}\tau_2 B$	$\rightarrow$	$\tau_2 d\boxed{2}$	$d\boxed{2}\tau_3 B$	$\rightarrow$	$\tau_3\boxed{2}dB$
$B\boxed{2}\tau_3 B$	$\rightarrow$	$\tau_3\boxed{2}BB$	$d\boxed{2}\tau_4 d$	$\rightarrow$	$\tau_4\boxed{2}dd$	$B\boxed{2}\tau_4 d$	$\rightarrow$	$\tau_4\boxed{2}Bd$
$\boxed{2}\tau_5 B$	$\rightarrow$	$\tau_5\boxed{2}B$						

E. "Extracting" production rules that correspond to (c) in the proof of Theorem 4.6.2.

$$
\begin{aligned}
\tau_5 \mathrm{¢} &\rightarrow K \\
\tau_i K &\rightarrow K \qquad \text{For } i = 1, \ldots, 4. \\
K a &\rightarrow a K \\
K b &\rightarrow b K \\
K c &\rightarrow c K \\
K d &\rightarrow K \\
K B &\rightarrow K \\
K \boxed{i} &\rightarrow K \qquad \text{For } i = 0, 1, 2. \\
K \$ &\rightarrow K \\
K \# &\rightarrow K \\
K &\rightarrow \epsilon
\end{aligned}
$$

The string abc has a leftmost derivation of the following form in G.

$$
\begin{aligned}
S &\Rightarrow \mathrm{¢}\boxed{0}A \\
&\Rightarrow^* \mathrm{¢}\boxed{0}abc\$C \\
&\Rightarrow^* \mathrm{¢}\boxed{0}abc\$B\boxed{1}BB\#E \\
&\Rightarrow^* \mathrm{¢}\boxed{0}abc\$B\boxed{1}BB\#B\boxed{2}BB\#[q_0] \\
&\Rightarrow^* \mathrm{¢}\boxed{0}abc\$B\boxed{1}BB\#B\boxed{2}BB\#\tau_1\tau_2\tau_3\tau_4\tau_5 \qquad \text{The sentential forms} \\
&\Rightarrow^* \tau_1\mathrm{¢}a\boxed{0}bc\$Bd\boxed{1}B\#B\boxed{2}BB\#\tau_2\tau_3\tau_4\tau_5 \qquad \text{in the derivation,} \\
&\Rightarrow^* \tau_1\tau_2\mathrm{¢}ab\boxed{0}c\$Bd\boxed{1}B\#Bd\boxed{2}B\#\tau_3\tau_4\tau_5 \qquad \text{that correspond to} \\
&\Rightarrow^* \tau_1\tau_2\tau_3\mathrm{¢}ab\boxed{0}c\$B\boxed{1}dB\#B\boxed{2}dB\#\tau_4\tau_5 \qquad \text{the configurations} \\
&\Rightarrow^* \tau_1\tau_2\tau_3\tau_4\mathrm{¢}abc\boxed{0}\$\boxed{1}BdB\#\boxed{2}BdB\#\tau_5 \qquad \text{in the simulated} \\
&\Rightarrow^* \tau_1\tau_2\tau_3\tau_4\tau_5\mathrm{¢}abc\boxed{0}\$\boxed{1}BdB\#\boxed{2}BdB\# \qquad \text{computation of } M. \\
&\Rightarrow^* \tau_1\tau_2\tau_3\tau_4 K abc\boxed{0}\$\boxed{1}BdB\#\boxed{2}BdB\# \\
&\Rightarrow^* K abc\boxed{0}\$\boxed{1}BdB\#\boxed{2}BdB\# \\
&\Rightarrow^* abc K\boxed{1}BdB\#\boxed{2}BdB\# \\
&\Rightarrow^* abc K\boxed{2}BdB\# \\
&\Rightarrow^* abc K \\
&\Rightarrow abc \qquad\qquad\qquad\qquad\qquad\qquad\qquad\qquad\qquad\qquad\quad \Box
\end{aligned}
$$

Theorem 4.6.2, together with Theorem 4.5.3, implies the following result.

Corollary 4.6.1 The membership problem is undecidable for Type 0 grammars or, equivalently, for $\{ (G, x) \mid G \text{ is a Type 0 grammar, and } x \text{ is in } L(G) \}$.

A *context-sensitive grammar* is a Type 1 grammar in which each production rule has the form $\gamma_1 A \gamma_2 \rightarrow \gamma_1 \alpha \gamma_2$ for some nonterminal symbol A. Intuitively, a production rule of the form $\gamma_1 A \gamma_2 \rightarrow \gamma_1 \alpha \gamma_2$ indicates that $A \rightarrow \alpha$ can be used only if it is within the left context of γ_1 and the right context of γ_2. A language is said to be a *context-sensitive language*, if it can be generated by a context-sensitive grammar.

A language is context-sensitive if and only if it is a Type 1 language (Exercise 4.6.4), and if and only if it is accepted by a linear bounded automaton

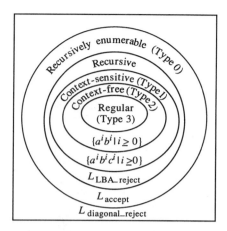

Figure 4.6.2 Hierarchy of some classes of languages. Each of the indicated languages belongs to the corresponding class but not to the class just below it in the hierarchy.

(Exercise 4.6.5). By definition and Theorem 3.3.1, each context-free language is also context-sensitive, but the converse is false because the non-context-free language $\{a^i b^i c^i \mid i \geq 0\}$ is context-sensitive. It can also be shown that each context-sensitive language is recursive (Exercise 1.4.4), and that the recursive language $L_{\text{LBA\_reject}} = \{x \mid x = x_i \text{ and } M_i \text{ does not have accepting computations on input } x_i \text{ in which at most } |x_i| \text{ locations are visited in each auxiliary work tape}\}$ is not context-sensitive (Exercise 4.5.6).

Figure 4.6.2 gives the hierarchy of some classes of languages. All the inclusions in the hierarchy are proper.

4.7 Post's Correspondence Problem

The *Post's Correspondence Problem*, or PCP for short, consists of the following domain and question.

   Domain: $\{<(x_1, y_1), \ldots, (x_k, y_k)> \mid k \geq 1 \text{ and } x_1, \ldots, x_k, y_1, \ldots, y_k \text{ are strings over some alphabet.}\}$

   Question: Are there an integer $n \geq 1$ and indices $i_1, \ldots, i_n$ for the given instance $<(x_1, y_1), \ldots, (x_k, y_k)>$ such that $x_{i_1} \cdots x_{i_n} = y_{i_1} \cdots y_{i_n}$? Each sequence $i_1, \ldots, i_n$ that provides a *yes* answer is said to be a *witness* for a positive solution to the given instance of PCP.

   The problem can be formulated also as a "domino" problem of the following form.

   Domain: $\left\{\left(\boxed{\begin{smallmatrix} x_1 \\ y_1 \end{smallmatrix}}, \ldots, \boxed{\begin{smallmatrix} x_k \\ y_k \end{smallmatrix}}\right) \mid k \geq 1, \text{ and each } \boxed{\begin{smallmatrix} x_i \\ y_i \end{smallmatrix}} \text{ is a domino card with the string } x_i \text{ on its top and the string } y_i \text{ on its bottom}, 1 \leq i \leq k.\right\}$

Question: Given $k \geq 1$ piles of cards

$$\boxed{\begin{array}{c} x_1 \\ y_1 \end{array}}, \ldots, \boxed{\begin{array}{c} x_k \\ y_k \end{array}}$$

with infinitely many cards in each pile, can one draw a sequence of $n \geq 1$ cards

$$\boxed{\begin{array}{c} x_{i_1} \\ y_{i_1} \end{array}}, \ldots, \boxed{\begin{array}{c} x_{i_n} \\ y_{i_n} \end{array}}$$

from these piles, so that the string $x_{i_1} \cdots x_{i_n}$ formed on the top of the cards will equal the string $y_{i_1} \cdots y_{i_n}$ formed on the bottom?

Example 4.7.1 PCP has the solution of *yes* for the instance $<(01,0), (110010,0), (1,1111), (11,01)>$ or, equivalently, for the following instance in the case of the domino problem.

$$\left(\boxed{\begin{array}{c} 01 \\ 0 \end{array}}, \boxed{\begin{array}{c} 110010 \\ 0 \end{array}}, \boxed{\begin{array}{c} 1 \\ 1111 \end{array}}, \boxed{\begin{array}{c} 11 \\ 01 \end{array}} \right)$$

The tuple $(i_1, i_2, i_3, i_4, i_5, i_6) = (1, 3, 2, 4, 4, 3)$ is a witness for a positive solution because $x_1 x_3 x_2 x_4 x_4 x_3 = y_1 y_3 y_2 y_4 y_4 y_3 = 01111001011111$. The positive solution has also the witnesses $(1, 3, 2, 4, 4, 3, 1, 3, 2, 4, 4, 3)$, $(1, 3, 2, 4, 4, 3, 1, 3, 2, 4, 4, 3)$, etc. On the other hand, the PCP has the solution *no* for $<(0,10), (01,1)>$. □

The Undecidability of Post's Correspondence Problem

Post's correspondence problem is very useful for showing the undecidability of many other problems by means of reducibility. Its undecidability follows from its capacity for simulating the computations of Turing machines, as exhibited indirectly in the following proof through derivations in Type 0 grammars.

Theorem 4.7.1 The PCP is an undecidable problem.

Proof By Corollary 4.6.1 the membership problem is undecidable for Type 0 grammars. Thus, it is sufficient to show how from each instance (G, w) of the membership problem for Type 0 grammars, an instance I can be constructed, such that the PCP has a positive solution at I if and only if w is in $L(G)$.

For the purpose of the proof consider any Type 0 grammar $G = <N, \Sigma, P, S>$ and any string w in Σ^*. With no loss of generality assume that $\#$, $\math"cent"$, and $\$$ are new symbols not in $N \cup \Sigma$. Then let the corresponding instance $I = <(x_1, y_1), \ldots, (x_k, y_k)>$ of PCP be of the following form.

PCP has a positive solution at I if and only if I can trace a derivation that starts at S and ends at w.

For each derivation in G of the form $S \Rightarrow \gamma_1 \Rightarrow \cdots \Rightarrow \gamma_m \Rightarrow w$, the instance I has a witness $(i_1, \ldots, i_n)$ of a positive solution such that either

$$x_{i_1} \cdots x_{i_n} = y_{i_1} \cdots y_{i_n} = \math"cent" S \underline{\#} \gamma_1 \# \gamma_2 \underline{\# \gamma_3} \# \gamma_4 \cdots \gamma_m \underline{\#} w \$$$

or

$$x_{i_1} \cdots x_{i_n} = y_{i_1} \cdots y_{i_n} = \math"cent" S \underline{\#} \underline{S} \# \gamma_1 \# \underline{\gamma_2} \# \gamma_3 \underline{\# \gamma_4} \cdots \gamma_m \underline{\#} w \$,$$

depending on whether m is even or odd, respectively.

On the other hand, each witness $(i_1, \ldots, i_n)$ of a positive solution for PCP at I has a smallest integer $t \geq 1$ such that $x_{i_1} \cdots x_{i_t} = y_{i_1} \cdots y_{i_t}$. In such a case, $x_{i_1} \cdots x_{i_t} = y_{i_1} \cdots y_{i_t} = \textit{¢}S\#\gamma_1\#\gamma_2\#\gamma_3\#\gamma_4 \cdots \gamma_m\#w$ for some derivation $S \Rightarrow^* \gamma_1 \Rightarrow^* \gamma_2 \Rightarrow^* \cdots \Rightarrow^* \gamma_m \Rightarrow^* w$.

The instance I consists of pairs of the following form

a. A pair of the form $(\textit{¢}S\#, \textit{¢})$.

b. A pair of the form $(\$, \#w\$)$.

c. A pair of the form $(X, \underline{X})$, and a pair of the form $(\underline{X}, X)$, for each symbol X in $\Sigma \cup N \cup \{\#\}$.

d. A pair of the form $(\beta, \underline{\alpha})$, and a pair of the form $(\underline{\beta}, \alpha)$, for each production rule $\alpha \rightarrow \beta$ in G that satisfies $\beta \neq \epsilon$.

e. A pair of the form $(X, \underline{X\alpha})$, and a pair of the form $(\underline{X}, X\alpha)$, for each production rule $\alpha \rightarrow \epsilon$ in G and for each X in $\Sigma \cup N \cup \{\#\}$.

The underlined symbols are introduced to allow only $(\textit{¢}S\#, \textit{¢})$ as a first pair, and $(\$, \#w\$)$ as a last pair, for each witness of a positive solution. The pair $(\textit{¢}S\#, \textit{¢})$ in (a) is used to start the tracing of a derivation at S. The pair $(\$, \#w\$)$ in (b) is used to end the tracing of a derivation at w.

The other pairs are used to force the tracing to go from each given sentential form γ to a sentential form γ', such that $\gamma \Rightarrow^* \gamma'$. The tracing is possible because each of the pairs (x_i, y_i) is defined so that y_i provides a "window" into γ, whereas x_i provides an appropriate replacement for y_i in γ'.

The pairs of the form $(X, \underline{X})$ and $(\underline{X}, X)$ in (c) are used for copying substrings from γ to γ'. The pairs of the form $(\beta, \underline{\alpha})$ and $(\underline{\beta}, \alpha)$, $\beta \neq \epsilon$, in (d) are used for replacing substrings α in γ by substrings β in γ'. The pairs of the form $(X, \underline{X\alpha})$ and $(\underline{X}, X\alpha)$ in (e) are used for replacing substrings α in γ by the empty string ϵ in γ'.

The window is provided because for each $1 \leq i_1, \ldots, i_j \leq k$, the strings $x = x_{i_1} \cdots x_{i_j}$ and $y = y_{i_1} \cdots y_{i_j}$ satisfy the following properties.

a. If x is a prefix of y, then $x = y$. Otherwise there would have been a least l such that $x_{i_1} \cdots x_{i_l}$ is a proper prefix of $y_{i_1} \cdots y_{i_l}$. In which case (x_{i_l}, y_{i_l}) would be equal to (v, uvv') for some nonempty strings v and v'. However, by definition, no pair of such a form exists in I.

b. If y is a proper prefix of x, then the sum of the number of appearances of the symbols $\#$ and $\underline{\#}$ in x is equal to one plus the sum of the number of appearances of $\#$ and $\underline{\#}$ in y. Otherwise, there would be a least $l > 1$ for which $x_{i_1} \cdots x_{i_l}$ and $y_{i_1} \cdots y_{i_l}$ do not satisfy the property. In such a case, because of the minimality of l, x_{i_l} and y_{i_l} would have to differ in the number of $\#$ and $\underline{\#}$ they contain. That is, by definition of I, (x_{i_l}, y_{i_l}) would have to equal either $(\$, \#w\$)$ or $(\textit{¢}S\#, \textit{¢})$. However, $(\$, \#w)$ is an impossible choice because it implies that $x_{i_1} \cdots x_{i_l} = y_{i_1} \cdots y_{i_l}$, and $(\textit{¢}S\#, \textit{¢})$ is an

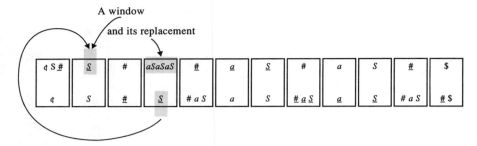

Figure 4.7.1 An arrangement of PCP cards for describing a derivation for ϵ, in the grammar that consists of the production rules $S \rightarrow aSaSaS$ and $aS \rightarrow \epsilon$.

impossible choice because it implies that $x_{i_1} \cdots x_{i_{l-1}} = y_{i_1} \cdots y_{i_{l-1}}$ (and hence that the property holds).

The correctness of the construction can be shown by induction on the number of production rules used in the derivation under consideration or, equivalently, on the number of pairs of type (d) and (e) used in the given witness for a positive solution.   □

Example 4.7.2 If G is a grammar whose set of production rules is $\{S \rightarrow aSaSaS,$ $aS \rightarrow \epsilon\}$, then the instance of the PCP that corresponds to (G, ϵ) as determined by the proof of Theorem 4.7.1, is $<(\mathfrak{c}S\#, \mathfrak{c}), (\underline{aSaSaS}, S), (aSaSaS, \underline{S}), (\#, \#aS),$ $(\#, \underline{\#aS}), (a, aaS), (a, \underline{aaS}), (\underline{S}, SaS), (S, \underline{SaS}), (\#, \#), (\underline{\#}, \#), (a, \underline{a}), (\underline{a}, a),$ $(S, \underline{S}), (\underline{S}, S), (\$, \#\$)>$.

The instance has a positive solution with a witness that corresponds to the arrangement in Figure 4.7.1. The witness also corresponds to the derivation $S \Rightarrow^*$ $S \Rightarrow aSaSaS \Rightarrow aSaS \Rightarrow aS \Rightarrow \epsilon$ in G.   □

Applications of Post's Correspondence Problem

The following corollary exhibits how Post's correspondence problem can be used to show the undecidability of some other problems by means of reducibility.

Corollary 4.7.1 The equivalence problem is undecidable for finite-state transducers.

Proof Consider any instance $<(x_1, y_1), \ldots, (x_k, y_k)>$ of PCP. Let Δ be the minimal alphabet such that $x_1, \ldots, x_k, y_1, \ldots, y_k$ are all in Δ^*. With no loss of generality assume that $\Sigma = \{1, \ldots, k\}$ is an alphabet.

Let $M_1 = <Q_1, \Sigma, \Delta, \delta_1, q_0, F_1>$ be a finite-state transducer that computes the relation $\Sigma^* \times \Delta^*$, that is, a finite-state transducer that accepts all inputs over Σ, and on each such input can output any string over Δ.

Let $M_2 = <Q_2, \Sigma, \Delta, \delta_2, q_0, F_2>$ be a finite-state transducer that on input $i_1 \cdots i_n$ outputs some w such that either $w \neq x_{i_1} \cdots x_{i_n}$ or $w \neq y_{i_1} \cdots y_{i_n}$. Thus,

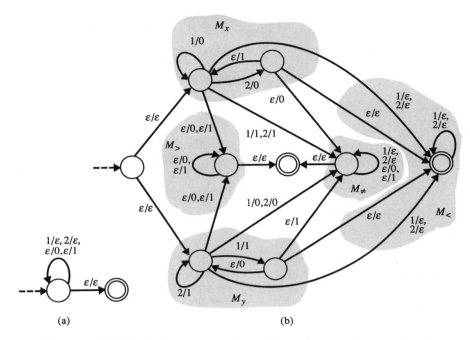

Figure 4.7.2 The finite-state transducer in (a) is equivalent to the finite-state transducer in (b) if and only if the PCP has a positive solution at $<(0, 10), (01, 1)>$.

M_2 on input $i_1 \cdots i_n$ can output any string in Δ^* if $x_{i_1} \cdots x_{i_n} \neq y_{i_1} \cdots y_{i_n}$. On the other hand, if $x_{i_1} \cdots x_{i_n} = y_{i_1} \cdots y_{i_n}$, then M_2 on such an input $i_1 \cdots i_n$ can output any string in Δ^*, except for $x_{i_1} \cdots x_{i_n}$.

It follows that M_1 is equivalent to M_2 if and only if the PCP has a negative answer at the given instance $<(x_1, y_1), \ldots, (x_k, y_k)>$. $\square$

Example 4.7.3 Consider the instance $<(x_1, y_1), (x_2, y_2)> = <(0, 10), (01, 1)>$ of PCP. Using the terminology in the proof of Corollary 4.7.1, $\Delta = \{0, 1\}$ and $\Sigma = \{1, 2\}$. The finite-state transducer M_1 can be as in Figure 4.7.2(a), and the finite-state transducer M_2 can be as in Figure 4.7.2(b).

M_2 on a given input $i_1 \cdots i_n$ nondeterministically chooses between its components M_x and M_y. In M_x it outputs a prefix of $x_{i_1} \cdots x_{i_n}$, and in M_y it outputs a prefix of $y_{i_1} \cdots y_{i_n}$. Then M_2 nondeterministically switches to $M_>$, $M_<$, or $M_{\neq}$.

M_2 switches from M_x to $M_>$ to obtain an output that has $x_{i_1} \cdots x_{i_n}$ as a proper prefix. M_2 switches from M_x to $M_<$ to obtain an output that is proper prefix of $x_{i_1} \cdots x_{i_n}$. M_2 switches from M_x to $M_{\neq}$ to obtain an output that differs from $x_{i_1} \cdots x_{i_n}$ within the first $|x_{i_1} \cdots x_{i_n}|$ symbols.

M_2 switches from M_y to $M_>$, $M_<$, $M_{\neq}$ for similar reasons, respectively. $\square$

The following corollary has a proof similar to that given for the previous one.

Corollary 4.7.2 The equivalence problem is undecidable for pushdown automata.

Proof Consider any instance $<(x_1, y_1), \ldots, (x_k, y_k)>$ of PCP. Let Σ_1 be the minimal alphabet such that $x_1, \ldots, x_k, y_1, \ldots, y_k$ are all in Σ_1^*. With no loss of generality assume that $\Sigma_2 = \{1, \ldots, k\}$ is an alphabet, that Σ_1 and Σ_2 are mutually disjoint, and that Z_0 is a new symbol not in Σ_1.

Let $M_1 = <Q_1, \Sigma_1 \cup \Sigma_2, \Sigma_1 \cup Z_0, \delta_1, q_0, Z_0, F_1>$ be a pushdown automaton that accepts all the strings in $(\Sigma_1 \cup \Sigma_2)^*$. (In fact, M_1 can also be a finite-state automaton.)

Let $M_2 = <Q_2, \Sigma_1 \cup \Sigma_2, \Sigma_1 \cup Z_0, \delta_2, q_0, Z_0, F_2>$ be a pushdown automaton that accepts an input w if and only if it is of the form $i_n \cdots i_1 u$, for some $i_1 \cdots i_n$ in Σ_1^* and some u in Σ_2^*, such that either $u \neq x_{i_1} \cdots x_{i_n}$ or $u \neq y_{i_1} \cdots y_{i_n}$.

It follows that M_1 and M_2 are equivalent if and only if the PCP has a negative answer at the given instance.   □

The pushdown automaton M_2 in the proof of Corollary 4.7.2 can be constructed to halt on a given input if and only if it accepts the input. The constructed pushdown automaton halts on all inputs if and only if the PCP has a negative solution at the given instance. Hence, the following corollary is also implied from the undecidability of PCP.

Corollary 4.7.3 The uniform halting problem is undecidable for pushdown automata.

PCP is a partially decidable problem because given an instance $<(x_1, y_1), \ldots, (x_k, y_k)>$ of the problem one can search exhaustively for a witness of a positive solution, for example, in $\{1, \ldots, k\}^*$ in canonical order. With such an algorithm a witness will eventually be found if the instance has a positive solution. Alternatively, if the instance has a negative solution, then the search will never terminate.

Exercises

4.1.1 Let M be the Turing transducer whose transition diagram is given in Figure 4.1.3. Give the sequence of moves between configurations that M has on input *baba*.

4.1.2 For each of the following relations construct a Turing transducer that computes the relation.

    a. $\{(a^i b^i c^i, d^i) \mid i \geq 0\}$

    b. $\{(x, d^i) \mid x$ is in $\{a, b, c\}^*$ and $i = $ (the number of a's in x) = (the number of b's in x) = (the number of c's in x)$\}$

    c. $\{(x, d^i) \mid x$ is in $\{a, b, c\}^*$ and $i = min$(number of a's in x, number of b's in x, number of c's in x)$\}$

d. $\{ (xx^{\mathrm{rev}}y, a^i) \mid x$ and y are in $\{a, b\}^*$, and $i =$ (number of a's in $x) =$ (number of a's in $y) \}$

e. $\{ (a^i, b^j) \mid j \geq i^2 \}$

4.1.3 For each of the following languages construct a Turing machine that recognizes the language.

a. $\{ xyx \mid x$ and y are in $\{a, b\}^*$ and $|x| \geq 1 \}$

b. $\{ xy \mid xy$ is in $\{a, b, c\}^*$, $|x| = |y|$, and (the number of a's in $x) =$ (the number of a's in $y) \}$

c. $\{ xy \mid xy$ is in $\{a, b, c\}^*$, $|x| = |y|$, and (the number of a's in $x) \neq$ (the number of a's in $y) \}$

d. $\{ a^i x b^i \mid x$ is in $\{a, b\}^*$, and $i =$ (the number of a's in $x) =$ (the number of b's in $x) \}$

e. $\{ a^i b^i c^j d^j \mid i \neq j \}$

f. $\{ aba^2b^2a^3b^3 \cdots a^nb^n \mid n \geq 0 \}$

4.1.4 Show that the relations computable by Turing transducers are closed under the following operations .

a. Union.

b. Intersection.

c. Reversal, that is, the operation that for a given relation R provides the relation $\{ (x^{\mathrm{rev}}, y^{\mathrm{rev}}) \mid (x, y)$ is in $R \}$.

4.1.5 Show that recursive languages are closed under complementation. (The result does not carry over to recursively enumerable languages because the language $L_{\mathrm{diagonal\_reject}}$, as defined in Section 4.5, is not a recursively enumerable language, whereas its complementation is.)

4.1.6 Show that each linear bounded automaton has an equivalent linear bounded automaton that halts on all inputs.

4.1.7 Show that each Turing transducer has an equivalent three-states Turing transducer.

4.2.1 Redo Example 4.2.1 for the case that P has the instructions of Figure 4.E.1.

4.2.2 Find the values of $\delta_{\mathrm{state}}(q_2, \textcent, B, B)$, $\delta_{c_1}(q_2, \textcent, B, B)$, $\delta_{c_2}(q_2, \textcent, B, B)$, $\delta_{d_0}(q_2, \textcent, B, B)$, $\delta_{d_1}(q_2, \textcent, B, B)$, $\delta_{d_2}(q_2, \textcent, B, B)$, and $\delta_\rho(q_2, \textcent, B, B)$ in Figure 4.2.5(b) for the case that M is the deterministic Turing transducer in Figure 4.1.6.

4.2.3 Find the values of $\delta_{\mathrm{tran}}(q_2, a, B, q_2, 0, B, +1, \epsilon)$ and $\delta_{\mathrm{tran}}(q_3, a, b, q_3, +1, a, +1, \epsilon)$ in Figure 4.2.5(c) for the case that M is the nondeterministic Turing transducer in Figure 4.1.3.

> **do**
> > $y := y + 1$
> **or**
> > **if** $x = y$ **then**
> > > **if** *eof* **then accept**
> > > **read** x
> > > **write** x
> > **until** *false*

Figure 4.E.1

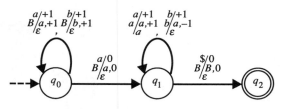

Figure 4.E.2

4.2.4 For each of the following cases determine the value of the corresponding item according to Example 4.2.4.

> a. The natural number that represents the string $BBBccc$.
>
> b. The string represented by the natural number 21344.

4.3.1 Find the transition diagram of M_2 in Example 4.3.1 for the case that M_1 is the Turing transducer of Figure 4.E.2.

4.3.2 Show that each deterministic, two auxiliary-work-tape Turing transducer M_1 has an equivalent deterministic, one auxiliary-work-tape Turing transducer M_2.

4.4.1 Find a standard binary representation for the Turing transducer whose transition diagram is given in Figure 4.E.2.

4.4.2 Let M be a Turing transducer whose standard binary representation is the string $01^40101^201^4001^201^401^401^400101^201^5001^301^4001^200101^301^401^401^301^401^4$ $01^200101^301^301^401^401^3001^301^401$.

> a. How many accepting states does M have?
>
> b. How many transition rules does M have?
>
> c. How many transition rules of M provide a nonempty output?
>
> d. How many auxiliary work tapes does M have?

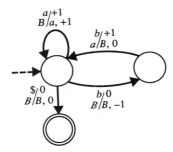

Figure 4.E.3

4.4.3 For each of the following strings either give a Turing transducer whose standard binary representation is equal to the string, or justify why the string is not a standard binary representation of any Turing transducer.

    a. 011010110001101111101101111

    b. $01^40101^201^4001^201^401^401^401^40101^201^5001^301^3001^200101^301^501^401^201^4001^3$
    $00101^201^3001^401^3001^3001$

    c. $01^40101^201^4001^201^401^401^401^40101^201^5001^301^3001^200101^301^501^301^201^4001^3$
    $00101^201^3001^401^301^3001$

4.5.1 Discuss the appropriateness of the following languages as a replacement for the language $L_{\text{diagonal\_reject}}$ in the proof of Theorem 4.5.1.

    a. $\{\, x \mid x = x_i, \text{ and } M_{i+2} \text{ does not accept } x_i \,\}$.

    b. $\{\, x \mid x = x_i, \text{ and } M_{\lceil i/2 \rceil} \text{ does not accept } x_i \,\}$.

    c. $\{\, x \mid x = x_i, \text{ and either } M_{2i-1} \text{ does not accept } x_i \text{ or } M_{2i} \text{ does not accept } x_i \,\}$.

4.5.2 The proof of Theorem 4.5.1 uses the diagonal of the table T_{accept} to find the language $L_{\text{diagonal\_reject}}$ that is accepted by no Turing machine. Show that besides the diagonal, there are infinitely many other ways to derive a language from T_{accept} that is accepted by no Turing machine.

4.5.3 Use a proof by diagonalization to show that there is an undecidable membership problem for a unary language.

4.5.4 What is M_∞ in the proof of Theorem 4.5.5 if M is the Turing machine given in Figure 4.E.3?

4.5.5 Find a Turing machine M_x that satisfies the conditions in the proof of Theorem 4.5.6 if M is the Turing machine in Figure 4.E.3 and $x = abb$.

4.5.6 Show that no linear bounded automaton can accept $L_{\text{LBA\_reject}} = \{\, x \mid x = x_i \text{ and } M_i \text{ does not have an accepting computation on input } x_i \text{ in which at most } |x_i| \text{ locations are visited in each auxiliary work tape} \,\}$.

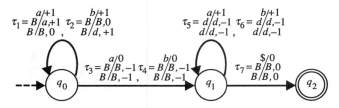

Figure 4.E.4

4.5.7 Use the undecidability of the membership problem for Turing machines to show the undecidability of the following problems for Turing machines.

    a. The problem defined by the following domain and question.

        Domain: $\{(M, x, p) \mid M$ is a Turing machine, p is a state of M, and x is an input for $M\}$.

        Question: Does M reach state p on input x, for the given instance (M, x, p)?

    b. Empty-word membership problem.

    c. Uniform halting problem.

    d. Emptiness problem.

    e. Equivalence problem.

If the Turing machine M is as in Figure 4.5.6(a) and $x = ababc$, then what is the corresponding instance implied by your reduction for each of the problems in (a) through (e)?

4.5.8 Show that the nonacceptance problem for Turing machines is not partially decidable.

4.6.1 Let G be the grammar whose production rules are listed below.

$$
\begin{aligned}
S &\rightarrow aSSb \\
&\rightarrow \epsilon \\
abS &\rightarrow bSaS
\end{aligned}
$$

Find a Turing machine M_G, in accordance with the proof of Theorem 4.6.1, that accepts $L(G)$.

4.6.2 Let M be the Turing machine whose transition diagram is given in Figure 4.E.4. Use the construction in the proof of Theorem 4.6.2 to obtain a grammar that generates $L(M)$.

4.6.3 For each of the following languages find a context-sensitive grammar that generates the language.

    a. $\{a^i b^i c^i \mid i \geq 0\}$

    b. $\{\, a^i b^j c^j d^j \mid i \neq j \,\}$

    c. $\{\, xx \mid x \text{ is in } \{a, b\}^* \,\}$

4.6.4 Show that a language is Type 1 if and only if it is a context-sensitive language.

4.6.5 Show, by refining the proofs of Theorem 4.6.1 and Theorem 4.6.2, that a language is Type 1 if and only if it is accepted by a linear bounded automaton.

4.7.1 Solve the PCP problem for each of the following instances (and justify your solutions).

    a. $<(1^{15}, 1^3), (1^{17}, 1^8), (1^{12}, 1^{29})>$

    b. $<(1, 10), (10, 01), (0, 011), (100, 01)>$

    c. $<(0100, 01), (10, 0), (1, 10)>$

4.7.2 Show that PCP is decidable when the strings are over a unary alphabet.

4.7.3 Let G be the grammar whose production rules are

$$
\begin{aligned}
S &\rightarrow aSSa \\
&\rightarrow Sb \\
&\rightarrow \epsilon
\end{aligned}
$$

Find the instance of PCP that corresponds to the instance (G, aba), as determined by the proof of Theorem 4.7.1.

4.7.4 Find the finite-state transducers M_1 and M_2 in the proof of Corollary 4.7.1 for the instance $<(ab, a), (a, ba)>$ of PCP.

4.7.5 Find the pushdown automata M_1 and M_2 in the proof of Corollary 4.7.2 for the instance $<(ab, a), (a, ba)>$ of PCP.

4.7.6 Show, by reduction from PCP, that the ambiguity problem is undecidable for finite-state transducers and for pushdown automata.

Bibliographic Notes

Deterministic Turing machines with a single read-write tape, and universal Turing machines were introduced by Turing (1936) for modeling the concept of effective procedures. Church's thesis was proposed independently by Church (1936) and Turing (1936).

    The equivalence of nondeterministic and deterministic Turing machines was noticed in Evey (1963). The undecidability of the membership problem for Turing machines is due to Turing (1936). Chomsky (1959) showed that the class of languages that Turing machines accept is the Type 0 languages.

Myhill (1960) identified the deterministic linear bounded automata. Chomsky (1959) introduced the context-sensitive grammars. Kuroda (1964) introduced the Type 1 grammars and the nondeterministic linear bounded automata, and showed their equivalency to the class of context-sensitive grammars. Landweber (1963) showed that there are languages that cannot be accepted by any deterministic linear bounded automaton but that can be accepted by a linear bounded automaton.

Post (1946) showed that PCP is an undecidable problem. The undecidability of the equivalence problem for finite-state transducers is due to Griffiths (1968). The undecidability of the equivalence problem for context-free languages, and the undecidability of the problem of determining for any given context-free language whether it is regular, are due to Bar-Hillel, Perles, and Shamir (1961). The undecidability of the ambiguity problem for context-free languages is due to Chomsky and Schutzenberger (1963).

Further coverage for the above topics can be found in Hopcroft and Ullman (1979).

Chapter 5

RESOURCE-BOUNDED COMPUTATION

So far, when considering programs and problems, we assumed there was no bound to the amount of resources (such as time and space) allowed during computations. This assumption enabled us to examine some useful questions about programs and problems. For instance, we discussed problems that cannot be solved by any program, regardless of the amount of resources available. Moreover, we explored the development of approaches for identifying unsolvable problems. However, our study provided no hint about the feasibility of solving those problems that are solvable.

A natural outgrowth of the study of unrestricted computations is the examination of resource-bounded computations. This chapter aims at such a study, and in many cases it turns out to be simply a refinement of the study conducted in Chapter 4.

The first section of this chapter introduces the models of random access machines as abstractions for computers. It also introduces the notions of time and space for random access machines and Turing transducers, and relates the resource requirements of these different models. The second section shows the existence of a hierarchy of problems; as established by the time required for their solutions. In addition, Section 2 argues about the feasibility of "polynomial time" computations, the infeasibility of "exponential time" computations, and the importance of the "easiest" hard problems. The third and fourth sections consider the place of "nondeterministic polynomial" time in the hierarchy, and propose some "easiest" hard problems. The fifth section considers space-bounded computations. And the sixth section deals with the hardest problems among those problems that can be solved in polynomial time.

5.1   Time and Space

The time and space requirements of a given program depend on the program itself and on the agent executing it.

Each agent has its own sets of primitive data items and primitive operations. Each primitive data item of a given agent requires some fixed amount of memory space. Similarly, each primitive operation requires some fixed amount of execution time.

Moreover, each pair of agents that execute the same program are relatively primitive. That is, each primitive data item of one agent can be represented by some fixed number of primitive data items of the other agent. Similarly, each primitive operation of one agent can be simulated by some fixed number of primitive operations of the other agent.

When executing a given program, an agent represents the elements the program processes with its own primitive data items. Similarly, the agent simulates with its own primitive operations the instructions the program uses.

As a result, each computation of a given program requires some $c_1 s$ space and some $c_2 t$ time, where s and t depend only on the program and c_1 and c_2 depend only on the agent. c_1 represents the packing power of the agent; c_2 represents the speed of the agent and the simulation power of its operations.

Since different agents differ in their implied constants c_1 and c_2, and since the study of computation aims at the development of a general theory, then one can, with no loss of generality, restrict the study of time and space to behavioral analyses. That is, to analyses in which the required accuracy is only up to some linear factor from the time and memory requirements of the actual agents. Such analyses can be carried out by employing models of computing machines, such as the random access machines and Turing transducers used here.

Random Access Machines

In general, programs are written for execution on computers. Consequently, abstractions of computers are of central interest when considering the resources that programs require. A conventional computer can be viewed as having an input tape, an output tape, a fixed program, and a memory (see Figure 5.1.1).

The input and output tapes are one-way sequential tapes used for holding the input values and the output values, respectively. The memory consists of cells that can be accessed in any order. Each cell can hold values from a domain that has a binary representation. The number of cells can be assumed to be unbounded, because of the availability of giant memories for computers. Similarly, because of the large variety of values that can be stored in each cell, the size of each cell can be assumed to be unbounded. The fixed program can consist of any "standard" kind of deterministic instructions (e.g., read, write, add, subtract, goto).

Such abstract computers are called *random access machines*, or simply RAM's. In what follows, RAM's will be identified with deterministic programs of similar characteristics. In particular, the programs will be assumed to have domains of variables that are equal to the set of natural numbers, and variables that can be

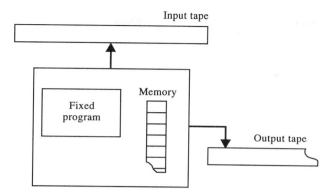

Figure 5.1.1 The structure of a computer.

```
read K
for i := 1 up to K do read A(i)
for i := 2 up to K do
  for j := i down to 2 do
    if A(j) < A(j − 1) then A(j) ↔ A(j − 1)
for i := 1 up to K do write A(i)
```

Figure 5.1.2 A RAM that sorts any given set of numbers.

viewed as one-dimensional arrays. Each entry $A(l)$ of an array A will be assumed to be accessed through an indexing operator whose parameters are A and l.

Example 5.1.1 The RAM in Figure 5.1.2 sorts any given set of natural numbers. It is represented by a deterministic program of free format and employs the variables i, j, K, and A.

The RAM reads into K the cardinality N of the set to be sorted, and into $A(1), \ldots, A(N)$ the N elements to be sorted. Then the RAM sorts the set incrementally, starting with the trivially sorted subset that consists only of the element in $A(1)$. At each stage the element in the next entry $A(l)$ of A is added to the sorted subset and placed in its appropriate position.   □

In the case of RAM's there are two common kinds of cost criteria for the space and time analyses: the logarithmic and the uniform cost criteria.

Under the *logarithmic cost criterion* the following assumptions are made. The primitive data items are the bits in the binary representations of the natural numbers being used. The primitive operations are the bit operations needed for executing the instructions of the RAM's. The memory needed in a computation of a given RAM is equal to that required by the entries of the variables. The memory required by a given entry of a variable, in turn, is equal to the length of the binary representation of the largest value v being stored in it, that is, to $\lceil log(v + 1) \rceil$ if

$v \neq 0$ and to 1 if $v = 0$. The time needed by the computation is equal to the number of bit operations needed for executing the instructions.

The *uniform cost criterion* is a degeneration of the logarithmic cost criterion in which the following assumptions are made. Each value is a primitive data item, the memory required by a given variable is equal to the number of entries in the array that it represents, the memory required by a RAM is equal to the total memory required by its variables, and the time required by a RAM is equal to the number of instructions being executed.

Example 5.1.2 Consider the RAM of Example 5.1.1 (see Figure 5.1.2). On input $N, v_1, \ldots, v_N$ the RAM requires 1 unit of space for K, one unit for i, one for j, and N units for A, under the uniform cost criterion. On the other hand, under the logarithmic cost criterion, the RAM requires $\lceil log\, N \rceil$ units of space for K, $\lceil log\, N \rceil$ units for i, $\lceil log\, N \rceil$ for j, and $N max(\lceil log\, v_1 \rceil, \ldots, \lceil log\, v_N \rceil)$ units of space for A. (In this example $\lceil log\, \alpha \rceil$ is assumed to equal $\lceil log\, (\alpha + 1) \rceil$ if $\alpha \neq 0$ and to equal 1 if $\alpha = 0$.)

The **read** K instruction takes one unit of time under the uniform cost criterion, and $\lceil log\, N \rceil$ units under the logarithmic cost criterion.

If i holds the value l then the instruction **read** A(i) takes 2 units of time under the uniform cost criterion: one unit for accessing the value l of i, and one unit for accessing the value of A(l). Under the logarithmic cost criterion the instruction requires $\lceil log\, l \rceil + \lceil log\, v_l \rceil$ units of time. Similarly, in such a case the instruction **write** A(i) takes 2 units of time under the uniform cost criterion, and $\lceil log\, l \rceil + \lceil log\, (\text{the } l\text{th smallest value in } \{v_1, \ldots, v_N\}) \rceil$ units under the logarithmic cost criterion.

The code segments **for** i := 1 **up to** K **do read** A(i) and **for** i := 1 **up to** K **do write** A(i) take time that is linear in N under the uniform cost criterion, and that is linear in $(1 + log\, v_1) + (log\, 2 + log\, v_2) + \cdots + (log\, N + log\, v_N) \leq N log\, N + log\, (v_1 \cdots v_N)$ under the logarithmic cost criterion.

The RAM requires space that is linear in N under the uniform cost criterion, and linear in $N log\, m$ under the logarithmic cost criterion. m denotes the largest value in the input. The RAM requires time that is linear in N^2 under the uniform cost criterion, and linear in $N^2 log\, m$ under the logarithmic cost criterion. $\square$

In general, both the time and the space required for finding a solution to a problem at a given instance increase with the length of the representation of the instance. Consequently, the time and space requirements of computing machines are specified by functions of the length of the inputs.

In what follows, n will be used for denoting the length of the instances in question.

Example 5.1.3 A natural number greater than 1 and divisible only by 1 and itself, is called a *prime number*. The *primality problem* asks for any given positive integer number m whether it is prime. The RAM in Figure 5.1.3, represented by a deterministic program in free format, solves the primality problem using a brute-force approach.

```
read x
if x < 2 then halt with answer no
if x = 2 then halt with answer yes
y := ⌈√x⌉
do
    if x is divisible by y then halt with answer no
    y := y − 1
until y = 1
halt with answer yes
```

Figure 5.1.3 A RAM that solves the primality problem.

An input m can be given to the RAM in a unary or binary representation, whereas the variables can hold their values only in binary. A unary representation for m has length $n = m$, and a binary representation for m has length $n = \lceil \log (m + 1) \rceil$ if $m \neq 0$ and length $n = 1$ if $m = 0$.

With a unary representation for a given instance m of the problem, under the uniform cost criterion, the RAM requires a constant space, and time linear in n. On the other hand, under the logarithmic cost criterion, the RAM requires space linear in $\log n$ and time linear in $n(\log n)^k$ for some $k > 0$. A linear time in n is required for reading the input m and storing it in binary (see Exercise 5.1.2), and a polynomial time in $\log n$ is required for checking the divisibility of m by an integer i, where $2 \leq i \leq \sqrt{m}$.

With a binary representation for a given instance m of the problem, the RAM requires a constant space under the uniform cost criterion, and space linear in n under the logarithmic cost criterion. But the algorithm requires time polynomial in m, or in 2^n, under both the uniform and logarithmic cost criteria. $\square$

Time and Space on Turing Transducers

In the case of Turing transducers we assume the following. The transition rules are the primitive operations, and the characters of the alphabets are the primitive data items. Each move takes one unit of time, and the time a computation takes is equal to the number of moves made during the computation. The space that a computation requires is equal to the number of locations visited in the auxiliary work tape, which has the maximal such number. (A possible alternative for the space measurement could be the sum of the number of locations visited over all the auxiliary work tapes. However, since the number of auxiliary work tapes is fixed for a given Turing transducer, and since constant factors are ignored in the analyses performed here, we use the traditional definition.)

A Turing transducer M is said to be a $T(n)$ *time-bounded Turing transducer*, or of *time complexity* $T(n)$, if all the possible computations of M on each input x of length n take no more than $T(n)$ time. M is said to be *polynomially time-bounded*, or of *polynomial time complexity*, if $T(n)$ is a polynomial in n. The Turing transducer M is said to be an $S(n)$ *space-bounded Turing transducer*, or of *space complexity* $S(n)$, if all the possible computations of M on each input x of length n take no more than $S(n)$ space. M is said to be *polynomially space-bounded*, or of *polynomial space complexity*, if $S(n)$ is a polynomial in n. M is said to be *logspace-bounded*, or of *logspace complexity*, if $S(n) = c \log n$ for some constant c. Similar definitions also hold for Turing machines, RAM's, and other classes of computing machines.

The following statement adds a refinement to Church's thesis. As in the case of the original thesis, the refinement cannot be proved to be correct. However, here too one can intuitively be convinced of the correctness of the statement, by showing the existence of translations between the different classes of models of computation under which the result is invariant. The translations between RAM's and deterministic Turing transducers can be similar to those exhibited in Section 4.2.

The Sequential Computation Thesis   A function is computable (or, respectively, partially computable) by an algorithm A only if it is computable (or, respectively, partially computable) by a deterministic Turing transducer that satisfies the following conditions: A on a given input has a computation that takes $T(n)$ time and $S(n)$ space only if on such an input the Turing transducer has a computation that takes $p(T(n))$ time and $p(S(n))$ space, where $p()$ is some fixed polynomial not dependent on the input.

Complexity of Problems

With no loss of generality, in what follows it is assumed that a time-bound $T(n)$ is equal to $max(n, \lceil T(n) \rceil)$, that is, is equal to at least the time needed to read all the input. In addition, a space-bound $S(n)$ is assumed to equal $max(1, \lceil S(n) \rceil)$. $\log 0$ is assumed to equal 1. $f(n)$ is assumed to equal $\lceil f(n) \rceil$ for all the other functions $f(n)$.

The *big O notation* $f(n) = O(g(n))$ will be used for specifying that there exist a constant $c > 0$ and n_0 such that $f(n) \leq cg(n)$ for all $n \geq n_0$. In such a case, $f(n)$ will be said to be *of order* $g(n)$.

A problem will be said to be of *time complexity* $T(n)$ if it is solvable by a $T(n)$ time-bounded, deterministic Turing transducer. The problem will be said to be of *nondeterministic time complexity* $T(n)$ if it is solvable by a $T(n)$ time-bounded Turing transducer. The problem will be said to be of *space complexity* $S(n)$ if it is solvable by an $S(n)$ space-bounded, deterministic Turing transducer. The problem will be said to be of *nondeterministic space complexity* $S(n)$ if it is solvable by an $S(n)$ space-bounded Turing transducer.

Similarly, a language will be said to be of *time complexity* $T(n)$ if it is accepted by a $T(n)$ time-bounded, deterministic Turing machine. The language will be said to be of *nondeterministic time complexity* $T(n)$ if it is accepted by a $T(n)$ time-bounded, nondeterministic Turing machine. The language will be said to be of *space complexity* $S(n)$ if it is accepted by an $S(n)$ space-bounded, deterministic Turing machine. The language will be said to be of *nondeterministic space* complexity $S(n)$ if it is accepted by an $S(n)$ space-bounded, nondeterministic Turing machine.

Complexity Classes

The following classes are important to our study of time and space.

$DTIME\,(T(n))$ — the class of languages that have time complexity $O(T(n))$.

$NTIME\,(T(n))$ — the class of languages that have nondeterministic time complexity $O(T(n))$.

$DSPACE\,(S(n))$ — the class of languages that have deterministic space complexity $O(S(n))$.

$NSPACE\,(S(n))$ — the class of languages that have nondeterministic space complexity $O(S(n))$.

P — the class of membership problems for the languages in

$$\bigcup_{p(n)} DTIME\,(p(n))$$

($p(n)$ stands for a polynomial in n.)

NP — the class of membership problems for the languages in

$$\bigcup_{p(n)} NTIME\,(p(n)).$$

$EXPTIME$ — the class of membership problems for the languages in

$$\bigcup_{p(n)} DTIME\,(2^{p(n)}).$$

$PSPACE$ — the class of membership problems for the languages in

$$\bigcup_{p(n)} DSPACE\,(p(n)).$$

$NLOG$ — the class of membership problems for the languages in $NSPACE\,(log\,n)$.

$DLOG$ — the class of membership problems for the languages in $DSPACE\,(log\,n)$.

So that our analyses of the complexity of problems will be meaningful, only "natural" representations are assumed for their instances. The "naturalness" is considered with respect to the resources being analyzed.

Example 5.1.4 The primality problem can be solved by a deterministic Turing transducer in polynomial time if the instances are given in unary representations, and in exponential time if the instances are given in nonunary representations (see Example 5.1.3). However, for a given instance m both approaches require time that is polynomial in m.

When considering the complexity of the primality problem, a nonunary representation for the instances is considered natural and a unary representation for the instances is considered unnatural. The specific choice of the cardinality d of a nonunary representation is of no importance, because the lengths of such different representations of a number m are equal up to a constant factor. Specifically, a length $log_{d_1} m$ and a length $log_{d_2} m$, for a pair of representations of m, satisfy the relation $log_{d_1} m = (log_{d_1} d_2) log_{d_2} m$ when d_1 and d_2 are greater than 1.

Consequently, the RAM in Figure 5.1.3 and the sequential computation thesis imply that the primality problem is of exponential time complexity.   □

Time and Space on Universal Turing Transducers

An analysis of the proof of Theorem 4.4.1 provides the following lemma.

Lemma 5.1.1 The universal Turing transducer U of Theorem 4.4.1 on a given input (M, x), of a deterministic Turing transducer M and an input x for M,

    a. Halts within $c_M t^2$ moves, if M halts within t moves on input x and $t \geq |x|$.

    b. Visits at most $c_M s$ locations in each of the auxiliary work tapes, if M visits no more than s locations in each of its auxiliary work tapes and $s \geq log |x|$.

c_M is assumed to be some polynomial in the length of the representation of M. (The polynomial does not depend on M.)

Proof   Assume the notations in the proof of Theorem 4.4.1. The number of moves that U needs to check for proper input (M, x) is at most some constant times $|x|$, where the constant depends only on the length of the representation of M.

Specifically, U needs $|E(M)| + 3$ moves for finding $E(M)$. $|E(M)|$ moves for scanning $E(M)$, and 3 moves for determining the 01 that follows the suffix 01 of $E(M)$.

Checking for a proper representation $E(M)$ of a Turing transducer M takes a number of moves, which is linear in $|E(M)|$, that is,

    a. $|E(M)|$ moves for determining the number m of auxiliary work tapes of M, and for verifying that each transition rule $\tau = (q, a, b_1, \ldots, b_m, p, d_0, c_1, d_1, \ldots, c_m, d_m, \rho)$ of M contains $3m + 5$ entries. Each transition rule τ is represented in $E(M)$ by a substring $E(\tau)$ that is enclosed between two separators of the form 01. The substring $E(\tau)$ must contain exactly $3m + 5$ 0's.

    b. $|E(M)|$ moves for determining that the head movements d_i in the transition rules are represented by binary strings of the form $E(-1) = 011$, $E(0) = 0111$, and $E(+1) = 01111$.

c. $|E(M)|$ moves for determining that the transition rules refer to the blank symbol B of M only in the auxiliary work tapes, and to the left endmarker ¢ and the right endmarker \$ only in the input tape.

d. $|E(M)|$ moves for determining that none of the states of M is represented by the binary string 0.

Checking that M is deterministic takes a number of moves that is linear in $|E(M)|^2$. The checking can be done by copying $E(M)$ to an auxiliary work tape of U, and then comparing each transition rule τ in the auxiliary work tape of U against each of the transition rules that follows τ in the input tape of U.

Checking for a proper input x for the Turing transducer M requires time that is linear in $|E(M)|(|E(M)| + |x|)$. Specifically, U in time that is linear in $|E(M)|^2$ determines the input symbols of M and stores them in an auxiliary work tape. Then U in $|E(M)| \cdot |x|$ time checks that only symbols from the auxiliary work tape are in x.

U requires $log\,|x| + |E(M)|(ms + 1) + 2m + 3 \le \tilde{c}s$ locations in the auxiliary work tapes for recording the strings $\#E(q)\#|u|\#E(u_1)\#E(v_1)\# \cdots \#E(u_m)\# E(v_m)\#$ which represent the configurations $(uqv, u_1qv_1, \ldots, u_mqv_m, w)$ of M, where $\tilde{c} = 8|E(M)|m$. U requires $log\,|x|$ locations for $|u|$, $|E(M)|$ locations for q, $|E(M)|$ locations for each symbol in each u_i, $|E(M)|$ locations for each symbol in each v_i, and $2m + 3$ locations for the symbols $\#$.

Given a string $\#E(q)\#|u|\#E(u_1)\#E(v_1)\# \cdots \#E(u_m)\#E(v_m)\#$, the universal Turing transducer U can determine in at most $\hat{c}(s + |x|) \le \hat{c}t$ moves the first $m + 2$ elements q, a, b_1, $\ldots$, b_m of the transition rule $\tau = (q, a, b_1, \ldots, b_m, p, d_0, c_1, d_1, \ldots, c_m, d_m, \rho)$ to be used in the next simulated move of M, where $\hat{c}$ is some constant whose magnitude is linear in $|E(M)|$ and b_i denotes the first symbol in $v_i B$. The transducer takes at most $\hat{c}s$ moves for extracting $|u|$, $E(q)$, $E(b_1)$, $\ldots$, $E(b_m)$ from $\#E(q)\#|u|\#E(u_1)\#E(v_1)\# \cdots \#E(u_m)\#E(v_m)\#$. In particular, $6|u|$ moves are needed over the string representing $|u|$ for counting down from $|u|$ to 0 (see Exercise 5.1.2), and $|E(M)| + |01| + |E(u)|$ moves are needed for extracting the symbol a from the input tape.

Given the first $m+2$ elements $(q, a, b_1, \ldots, b_m)$ in τ, the universal Turing transducer U can determine the tuple $(p, d_0, c_1, d_1, \ldots, c_m, d_m, \rho)$ in a single sweep over the input tape. Having such a tuple, U can also modify the recorded configuration of M in a single sweep.

Consequently, the total number of moves that U needs for simulating the moves of M is no greater than ct^2. c is some polynomial (independent of M) in the length of the standard binary representation of M. ☐

5.2 A Time Hierarchy

Intuitively, it seems obvious that some problems require more time to solve than others. The following result confirms this intuitive assessment while implying the existence of a time hierarchy for the class of language recognition problems.

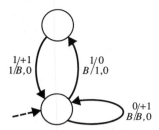

Figure 5.2.1 A $T(n) = 2n$ time-bounded, deterministic Turing machine.

Definitions A function $T(n)$ is said to be *time-constructible* if there exists a $T(n)$ time-bounded, deterministic Turing machine that for each n has an input of length n on which it makes exactly $T(n)$ moves. The function is said to be *fully time-constructible* if there exists a deterministic Turing machine that makes exactly $T(n)$ moves on each input of length n. A function $S(n)$ is said to be *space-constructible* if there exists an $S(n)$ space-bounded, deterministic Turing machine that for each n has an input of length n on which it requires exactly $S(n)$ space. The function is said to be *fully space-constructible* if there exists a deterministic Turing machine that requires exactly $S(n)$ space on each input of length n.

Example 5.2.1 The deterministic Turing machine M in Figure 5.2.1 makes exactly $t(x) = |x| +$ (number of 1's in x) moves on a given input x. $t(x) = 2|x|$ when x contains no 0's, and $t(x) < 2|x|$ when x contains 0's.

The existence of M implies that $T(n) = 2n$ is a time-constructible function, because

    a. M is $2n$ time-bounded, and

    b. For each n there exists the input 1^n of length n on which M makes exactly $2n$ moves.

The existence of the deterministic Turing machine M does not imply that $2n$ is fully time-constructible, because M does not make exactly $2n$ moves on each input of length n. However, M can be modified to show that $2n$ is a fully time-constructible function. ☐

Convention In this section M_x denotes a Turing machine that is represented by the string x of the following form. If $x = 1^j x_0$ for some $j \geq 0$ and for some standard binary representation x_0 of a deterministic Turing machine M, then M_x denotes M. Otherwise, M_x denotes a deterministic Turing machine that accepts no input. The string x is said to be a *padded binary representation* of M_x.

Theorem 5.2.1 Consider any function $T_1(n)$ and any fully time-constructible function $T_2(n)$, that for each $c > 0$ have an n_c such that $T_2(n) \geq c(T_1(n))^2$ for all $n \geq n_c$. Then there is a language which is in *DTIME* $(T_2(n))$ but not in *DTIME* $(T_1(n))$.

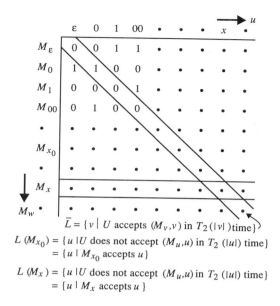

$$\overline{L} = \{\, v \mid U \text{ accepts } (M_v, v) \text{ in } T_2(|v|) \text{time}\,\}$$

$$L(M_{x_0}) = \{\, u \mid U \text{ does not accept } (M_u, u) \text{ in } T_2(|u|) \text{ time}\,\}$$
$$\qquad\;\; = \{\, u \mid M_{x_0} \text{ accepts } u \,\}$$

$$L(M_x) = \{\, u \mid U \text{ does not accept } (M_u, u) \text{ in } T_2(|u|) \text{ time}\,\}$$
$$\qquad\; = \{\, u \mid M_x \text{ accepts } u \,\}$$

Figure 5.2.2 Hypothetical table $T_{\text{universal}}$ indicating membership in the language $\{\, (M_w, u) \mid U \text{ accepts } (M_w, u) \text{ in } T_2(|u|) \text{ time} \,\}$.

Proof Let $T_1(n)$ and $T_2(n)$ be as in the statement of the theorem. Let U be a universal Turing machine similar to the universal Turing transducer in the proof of Lemma 5.1.1. The main difference is that here U assumes an input (M, x) in which M is represented by a padded binary representation instead of a standard binary representation. U starts each computation by going over the "padding" 1^j until it reaches the first 0 in the input. Then U continues with its computation in the usual manner while ignoring the padding. U uses a third auxiliary work tape for keeping track of the distance of its input head from the end of the padding. The result is shown by diagonalization over the language $L = \{\, v \mid v \text{ is in } \{0, 1\}^*,$ and U does not accept (M_v, v) in $T_2(|v|)$ time $\}$.

L is obtained from the diagonal of the table $T_{\text{universal}}$ (see Figure 5.2.2). In the table $T_{\text{universal}}$ the entry at row M_w and column u is equal to 1 if U accepts (M_w, u) in $T_2(|u|)$ time, and it is equal to 0 if U does not. The proof relies on the observation that each $O(T_1(n))$ time-bounded, deterministic Turing machine M_{x_0} that accepts L has also a padded representation x for which U can simulate the whole computation of M_x on x in $T_2(|x|)$ time. Consequently, M_x accepts x if and only if U does not accept (M_x, x) or, equivalently, if and only if M_x does not accept x.

Specifically, for the purpose of showing that L is not in $DTIME(T_1(n))$, assume to the contrary that L is in the class. Under this assumption, there is a $dT_1(n)$ time-bounded, deterministic Turing machine M that accepts L, for some constant d. Let x_0 be a standard binary representation of M, and c be the corresponding constant c_M implied by Lemma 5.1.1 for the representation x_0 of M.

Let $x = 1^j x_0$ for some j that satisfies $j + c(dT_1(j + |x_0|))^2 \leq T_2(j + |x_0|)$, that is, $x = 1^j x_0$ for a large enough j to allow U sufficient time $T_2(|x|)$ for simulating the whole computation of M_x on input x. Such a value j exists because for big enough j the following inequalities hold.

$$
\begin{aligned}
j + c\left(dT_1(j + |x_0|)\right)^2 &\leq (j + |x_0|) + c\left(dT_1(j + |x_0|)\right)^2 \\
&\leq T_1(j + |x_0|) + c\left(dT_1(j + |x_0|)\right)^2 \\
&\leq (1 + cd^2)\left(T_1(j + |x_0|)\right)^2 \\
&\leq T_2(j + |x_0|)
\end{aligned}
$$

Consider the string $x = 1^j x_0$. By definition, $|x| = j + |x_0|$ and so $j + c(dT_1(|x|))^2 \leq T_2(|x|)$. Moreover, x is a padded binary representation of M. For the string x one of the following two cases must hold. However, neither of them can hold, so implying the desired contradiction to the assumption that L is in $DTIME(T_1(n))$.

Case 1 x is in L. The assumption together with $L = L(M_x)$ imply that M_x accepts x in $dT_1(|x|)$ time. In such a case, by Lemma 5.1.1 U accepts (M_x, x) in $j + c(dT_1(|x|))^2 \leq T_2(|x|)$ time. On the other hand, x in L together with the definition of L imply that U does not accept x in $T_2(|x|)$ time. The contradiction implies that this case cannot hold.

Case 2 x is not in L. The assumption together with $L = L(M_x)$ imply that M_x does not accept x. In such a case, U does not accept (M_x, x) either. On the other hand, x not in L together with the definition of L imply that U accepts (M_x, x). The contradiction implies that this case cannot hold either.

To show that L is in $DTIME(T_2(n))$ consider the deterministic four auxiliary-work-tape Turing machine M that on input x proceeds according to the following algorithm.

Step 1 M stores (M_x, x) in its first auxiliary work tape. That is, M stores the string x, followed by the separator 01, followed by the representation 011 of the left endmarker ¢, followed by x, followed by the representation 0111 of the right endmarker \$. In addition, M encloses the sequence of strings above between the "left endmarker" ⓒ and the "right endmarker" Ⓢ, respectively.

Step 2 M computes the value of $T_2(|x|)$ and stores it in the second auxiliary work tape.

Step 3 M follows the moves of U on the content of its first auxiliary work tape, that is, on (M_x, x). M uses its third and fourth auxiliary work tapes for recording the content of the two auxiliary work tapes of U. During the simulation M interprets ⓒ as the left endmarker ¢, and Ⓢ as the right endmarker \$. M halts in an accepting configuration if it determines that U does not reach an accepting state in $T_2(|x|)$ moves. Otherwise, M halts in a nonaccepting configuration.

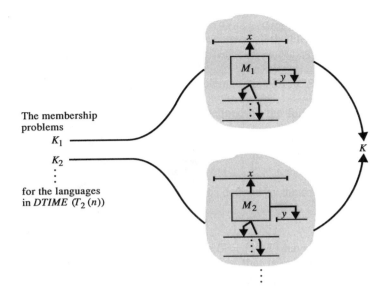

Figure 5.2.3 A set of Turing transducers M_1, M_2, ... for reducing the problems K_1, K_2, ... in $DTIME(T_2(n))$ to a given language recognition problem K. Each M_i on instance x of K_i provides an instance y of K, where K has the answer *yes* for y if and only if K_i has the answer *yes* for x.

By construction, the Turing machine M is of $O(T_2(|x|))$ time complexity. The fully time-constructibility of $T_2(n)$ is required for Step 2. □

Example 5.2.2 Let $T_1(n) = n^k$ and $T_2(n) = 2^n$. $T_1(n)$ and $T_2(n)$ satisfy the conditions of Theorem 5.2.1. Therefore the class $DTIME(2^n)$ properly contains the class $DTIME(n^k)$. □

Lower Bounds on Time Complexity

In addition to implying the existence of a time hierarchy for the language recognition problems, Theorem 5.2.1 can be used to show lower bounds on the time complexity of some problems. Specifically, consider any two functions $T_1(n)$ and $T_2(n)$ that satisfy the conditions of Theorem 5.2.1. Assume that each membership problem K_i for a language in $DTIME(T_2(n))$ can be reduced by a $T_3(n)$ time-bounded, deterministic Turing transducer M_i to some fixed problem K (see Figure 5.2.3). In addition, assume that each such M_i on input x of length n provides an output y of length $f(n)$ at most. Then the membership problems for the languages in $DTIME(T_2(n))$ are decidable in $T_3(n) + T(f(n))$ time if K can be solved in $T(n)$ time. In such a case, a lower bound for the time complexity $T(n)$ of K is implied, since by Theorem 5.2.1 the class $DTIME(T_2(n))$ contains a problem that requires more than $cT_1(n)$ time for each constant c, that

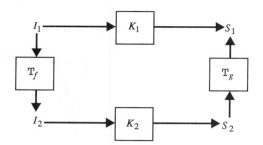

Figure 5.2.4 Reduction by polynomially time-bounded, deterministic Turing transducers T_f and T_g.

is, the inequality $T_3(n) + T(f(n)) > cT_1(n)$ must hold for infinitely many n's. The lower bound is obtained by substituting m for $f(n)$ to obtain the inequality $T(m) > cT_1(f^{-1}(m)) - T_3(f^{-1}(m))$ or, equivalently, the inequality $T(n) > cT_1(f^{-1}(n)) - T_3(f^{-1}(n))$.

Example 5.2.3 Consider the time bounds $T_1(n) = 2^{an}$, $T_2(n) = 2^{bn}$ for $b > 2a$, and $T_3(n) = f(n) = n\,log\,n$. For such a choice, $T_3(n) + T(f(n)) > cT_1(n)$ implies that $n\,log\,n + T(n\,log\,n) > c2^{an}$. By substituting m for $n\,log\,n$ it follows that $T(m) > c2^{an} - m = c2^{am/log\,n} - m \geq c2^{am/log\,m} - m \geq 2^{dm/log\,m}$ or, equivalently, that $T(n) > 2^{dn/log\,n}$ for some constant d. $\qquad\qquad\square$

The approach above for deriving lower bounds is of special interest in the identification of intractable problems, that is, problems that require impractical amounts of resources to solve. Such an identification can save considerable effort that might otherwise be wasted in trying to solve intractable problems.

Tractability and Intractability

In general, a problem is considered to be tractable if it is of polynomial time complexity. This is because its time requirements grow slowly with input length. Conversely, problems of exponential time complexity are considered to be intractable, because their time requirements grow rapidly with input length and so can be practically solved only for small inputs. For instance, an increase by a factor of 2 in n, increases the value of a polynomial $p(n)$ of degree k by at most a factor of 2^k. On the other hand, such an increase at least squares the value of $2^{p(n)}$.

The application of the approach above in the identification of intractable problems employs polynomially time-bounded reductions.

A problem K_1 is said to be *polynomially time reducible* to a problem K_2 if there exist polynomially time-bounded, deterministic Turing transducers T_f and T_g that for each instance I_1 of K_1 satisfy the following conditions (see Figure 5.2.4).

   a. T_f on input I_1 gives an instance I_2 of K_2.

b. K_1 has a solution S_1 at I_1 if and only if K_2 has a solution S_2 at I_2, where S_1 is the output of T_g on input S_2.

In the case that K_1 and K_2 are decision problems, with no loss of generality it can be assumed that T_g computes the identity function $g(S) = S$, that is, that T_g on input S_2 outputs $S_1 = S_2$.

A given complexity class C of problems can be used to show the intractability of a problem K by showing that the following two conditions hold.

a. C contains some intractable problems.

b. Each problem in C is polynomially time reducible to K, that is, K is at least as hard to solve as any problem in C.

Once a problem K is determined to be intractable, it then might be used to show the intractability of some other problems $\hat{K}$ by showing that K is polynomially time reducible to $\hat{K}$. In such a case, the easier K is the easier the reductions are, and the larger the class of such applicable problems $\hat{K}$ is.

The observation above sparks our interest in the "easiest" intractable problems K, and in the complexity classes C whose intractable problems are all "easiest" intractable problems.

In what follows, a problem K is said to be a *C-hard problem with respect to polynomial time reductions*, or just a *C-hard problem* when the polynomial time reductions are understood, if every problem in the class C is polynomially time reducible to the problem K. The problem K is said to be *C-complete* if it is a C-hard problem in C.

Our interest here is in the cases that $C = NP$ and $C = PSPACE$.

5.3 Nondeterministic Polynomial Time

The subclass NP, of the class of problems that can be solved nondeterministically in polynomial time, seems to play a central role in the investigation of intractability. By definition, NP contains the class P of those problems that can be decided deterministically in polynomial time, and by Corollary 5.3.1 the class NP is contained in the class $EXPTIME$ of those problems that can be decided deterministically in exponential time. Moreover, by Theorem 5.2.1, P is properly contained in $EXPTIME$ (see Figure 5.3.1). However, it is not known whether P is properly contained in NP and whether NP is properly contained in $EXPTIME$. Consequently, the importance of NP arises from the refinement that it may offer to the boundary between the tractability and intractability of problems.

In particular, if it is discovered that NP is not equal to P, as is widely being conjectured, then NP is likely to provide some of the easiest problems (namely, the NP-complete problems) for proving the intractability of new problems by means of reducibility. On the other hand, if NP is discovered to equal P, then many important problems, worked on without success for several decades, will turn out to be solvable in polynomial time.

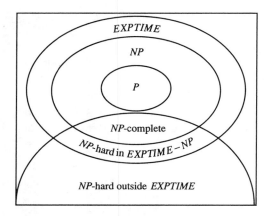

Figure 5.3.1 A classification of the decidable problems.

From Nondeterministic to Deterministic Time

An analysis of the proof of Theorem 2.3.1 implies an exponential increase in
the number of states a deterministic finite-state automaton needs for simulating a
nondeterministic finite-state automaton. The following corollary implies a similar
exponential increase in the number of moves that a deterministic Turing machine
requires for simulating a nondeterministic Turing machine.

Corollary 5.3.1 For each nondeterministic Turing transducer M_1 there exists an
equivalent deterministic Turing transducer M_2 with the following characteristics.
If M_1 halts on a given input x in t moves, then M_2 on such an input halts within
2^{ct} moves, where c is some constant that depends only on M_1. Moreover, in such
a case M_2 visits at most $2t$ locations on each of its auxiliary work tapes.

Proof Let M_1 and M_2 be the Turing Transducers M_1 and M_2 of Theorem 4.3.1.
Assume that M_1 halts on input x in t steps. Then M_2 needs to consider only the
strings α in $\{1, \ldots, r\}^*$ whose lengths are no greater than t or $t + 1$, depending
on whether M_1 accepts or rejects x, respectively. The number of such strings α
is no greater than $(r + 1)^{t+1}$.

For each string $\alpha = i_1 \cdots i_j$ in $\{1, \ldots, r\}^*$ the Turing transducer M_2 uses
some number of moves linear in j to derive α and to try simulating a sequence
of moves of the form $C_\epsilon \vdash \cdots \vdash C_\alpha$. Consequently, M_2 needs some number of
moves linear in $(r + 1)^{t+1}t$. 2^{ct} is therefore a bound on the number of moves,
because $v = 2^{\log v}$ for every positive integer value v.

Similarly, for each string $\alpha = i_1 \cdots i_j$ the Turing transducer M_2 needs j locations in the first auxiliary work tape for storing α, and at most j locations in each
of the other auxiliary work tapes for recording the content of the corresponding
tapes of M_1. By setting the heads of the auxiliary work tapes at their initial positions before starting the simulation of M_1 on α, it is assured that the heads do not
depart more than t locations from their initial positions. $\square$

The Satisfiability Problem

The following theorem shows the existence of *NP*-complete problems through example.

Definitions A *Boolean expression* is an expression defined inductively in the following way.

 a. The constants 0 (*false*) and 1 (*true*) are Boolean expressions.

 b. Each variable x is a Boolean expression.

 c. If E_1 and E_2 are Boolean expressions, then so are the negation $\neg E_1$, the conjunction $E_1 \wedge E_2$, the disjunction $E_1 \vee E_2$, and the parenthesizing (E_1).

Each assignment of 0's and 1's to the variables of a Boolean expression provides a value to the expression. If E is a Boolean expression, then (E) has the same value as E. $\neg E$ has the value 0 if E has the value 1, and $\neg E$ has the value 1 if E has the value 0. If E_1 and E_2 are Boolean expressions, then $E_1 \vee E_2$ has the value 1 whenever E_1 or E_2 has the value 1. $E_1 \vee E_2$ has the value 0 whenever both E_1 and E_2 have the value 0. The value of $E_1 \wedge E_2$ is 1 if both E_1 and E_2 have the value 1, otherwise $E_1 \wedge E_2$ has the value 0. It is assumed that among the Boolean operations of $\neg$, $\wedge$, and $\vee$, the operation $\neg$ has the highest precedence, followed by $\wedge$, and then $\vee$.

A Boolean expression is said to be *satisfiable* if its variables can be assigned 0's and 1's so as to provide the value 1 to the expression. The *satisfiability problem* asks for any given Boolean expression whether it is satisfiable, that is, whether the instance is in the set $L_{\text{sat}} = \{ E \mid E$ is a satisfiable Boolean expression $\}$.

Example 5.3.1 The Boolean expression $E = x_2 \wedge x_3 \vee (\neg x_1 \wedge x_2)$ is satisfiable by each assignment in which $x_2 = 1$ and $x_3 = 1$, as well as by each assignment in which $x_1 = 0$ and $x_2 = 1$. All the other assignments provide a 0 value to E. $(x_2 \wedge x_3) \vee ((\neg x_1) \wedge x_2)$ is a fully parenthesized version of E.

$x \wedge \neg x$ is an example of an unsatisfiable Boolean expression. □

The proof of the following theorem uses a generic approach.

Theorem 5.3.1 The satisfiability problem is *NP*-complete.

Proof The satisfiability of any Boolean expression can be checked in polynomial time by nondeterministically assigning some values to the variables of the given expression and then evaluating the expression for such an assignment. Consequently, the problem is in *NP*.

To show that the satisfiability problem is *NP*-hard, it is sufficient to demonstrate that each problem K in *NP* has a polynomially time-bounded, deterministic Turing transducer T_K, such that T_K reduces K to the satisfiability problem. For the purpose of the proof consider any problem K in *NP*. Assume that $M = <Q, \Sigma, \Gamma, \delta, q_0, B, F>$ is a nondeterministic Turing machine with $Q \cap (\Sigma \cup \Gamma \cup \{\mathrm{c}, \$\}) = \emptyset$ that decides K in $T(n) = O(n^k)$ time. Let m denote the number of auxiliary work tapes of M; then T_K can be a Turing transducer that on input x outputs a Boolean expression E_x of the following form.

The Structure of E_x

The Boolean expression E_x describes how an accepting computation of M on input x should look. E_x is satisfiable by a given assignment if and only if the assignment corresponds to an accepting computation $C_0 \vdash C_1 \vdash \cdots \vdash C_{T(|x|)}$ of M on input x. The expression has the following structure, where $t = T(|x|)$.

$$E_{\text{conf}_0} \wedge \cdots \wedge E_{\text{conf}_t} \wedge E_{\text{init}} \wedge E_{\text{rule}_1} \wedge \cdots \wedge E_{\text{rule}_t} \wedge E_{\text{accept}} \wedge E_{\text{follow}_1} \wedge \cdots \wedge E_{\text{follow}_t}$$

$E_{\text{conf}_0} \wedge \cdots \wedge E_{\text{conf}_t}$ states that an accepting computation consists of a sequence $C_0, \ldots, C_t$ of $t + 1$ configurations. E_{init} states that C_0 is an initial configuration.

$E_{\text{rule}_1} \wedge \cdots \wedge E_{\text{rule}_t}$ states that an accepting computation uses a sequence Ψ of t transition rules. E_{accept} states that the last transition rule in Ψ enters an accepting state. With no loss of generality it is assumed that a transition rule can also be "null", that is, a transition rule on which M can have a move without a change in its configuration. Such an assumption allows us to restrict the consideration only to computations that consist of exactly $T(|x|)$ moves.

E_{follow_i} states that M by using the ith transition rule in Ψ reaches configuration C_i from configuration C_{i-1}, $1 \leq i \leq t$.

The Variables of E_x

The Boolean expression E_x uses variables of the form $w_{i,r,j,X}$ and variables of the form $w_{i,\tau}$. Each variable provides a statement about a possible property of an accepting computation. An assignment that satisfies E_x provides the value 1 to those variables whose statements hold for the computation in question, and provides the value 0 to those variables whose statements do not hold for that computation.

$w_{i,r,j,X}$ states that X is the jth character of the rth tape in the ith configuration, $0 \leq r \leq m$. $r = 0$ refers to the input tape, and $1 \leq r \leq m$ refers to the rth auxiliary work tape.

$w_{i,\tau}$ states that τ is the transition rule in the ith move of the computation.

The Structure of E_{conf_i}

The expression E_{conf_i} is the conjunction of the following Boolean expressions.

    a. $\vee \{ w_{i,0,j,X} \mid X \text{ is in } \Sigma \cup \{\mathfrak{c}, \$\} \cup Q \}$ for $1 \leq j \leq |x| + 3$.

    This expression states that a configuration has an input segment with $|x| + 3$ entries, with each entry having at least one symbol from $\Sigma \cup \{\mathfrak{c}, \$\} \cup Q$.

    b. $\wedge \{ \neg(w_{i,0,j,X} \wedge w_{i,0,j,Y}) \mid X \text{ and } Y \text{ are in } \Sigma \cup \{\mathfrak{c}, \$\} \cup Q \text{ and } X \neq Y \}$ for $1 \leq j \leq |x| + 3$.

    This expression states that each entry in the input segment has at most one symbol.

    c. $\vee \{ w_{i,r,j,X} \mid X \text{ is in } \Gamma \cup Q \}$ for $1 \leq r \leq m$ and $1 \leq j \leq t + 1$.

    This expression states that a configuration has m auxiliary work-tape segments, each segment having $t + 1$ entries, and each entry having at least one symbol from $\Gamma \cup Q$.

d. $\wedge \{ \neg(w_{i,r,j,X} \wedge w_{i,r,j,Y}) \mid X$ and Y are in $\Gamma \cup Q$ and $X \neq Y \}$ for $1 \leq r \leq m$ and $1 \leq j \leq t+1$.

This expression states that each entry in an auxiliary work-tape segment has at most one symbol.

Each assignment that satisfies the expressions in parts (a) and (b) above implies a string of length $|x| + 3$. The string corresponds to the input tape of M, and consists of input symbols, endmarker symbols $\cent$ and \$, and state symbols. In particular, the symbol X is at location j in the string if and only if $w_{i,0,j,X}$ is assigned the value 1.

Similarly, each assignment that satisfies the expressions in parts (c) and (d) above for a specific value r, provides a string of length $t + 1$ that corresponds to the rth auxiliary work tape of M. The string consists of auxiliary work tape symbols and state symbols. In particular, the string consists of the symbol X at location j if and only if $w_{i,r,j,X}$ is assigned the value 1.

The Structure of E_{init}

The expression E_{init} is the conjunction of the following three Boolean expressions.

a. $w_{0,0,1,\cent} \wedge w_{0,0,2,q_0} \wedge \{ w_{0,0,j+2,a_j} \mid 1 \leq j \leq |x| \} \wedge w_{0,0,|x|+3,\$}$.

This expression states that in the initial configuration the input segment consists of the string $\cent q_0 a_1 \cdots a_n \$$, where a_j denotes the jth input symbol in x.

b. $\vee \{ w_{0,r,j,q_0} \mid 1 \leq j \leq t+1 \}$ for $1 \leq r \leq m$.

This expression states that in the initial configuration each auxiliary work-tape segment contains the initial state q_0.

c. $w_{0,r,j,B} \vee w_{0,r,j,q_0} \wedge \{ w_{0,r,s,B} \mid 1 \leq s \leq t+1$ and $s \neq j \}$ for $1 \leq j \leq t+1$ and $1 \leq r \leq m$.

This expression states that in the initial configuration each auxiliary work-tape segment consists of blank symbols B and at most one appearance of q_0.

Each assignment that satisfies E_{init} corresponds to an initial configuration of M on input x. Moreover, each also satisfies E_{conf_0}.

The Structure of E_{rule_i} and E_{accept}

The expression E_{rule_i} is the conjunction of the following two Boolean expressions.

a. $\vee \{ w_{i,\tau} \mid \tau$ is in $\delta \}$

b. $\wedge \{ \neg(w_{i,\tau_1} \wedge w_{i,\tau_2}) \mid \tau_1, \tau_2$ are in δ and $\tau_1 \neq \tau_2 \}$.

The expression in part (a) implies, that for each assignment that satisfies E_{rule_i}, at least one of the variables $w_{i,\tau}$ has the value 1. The expression in part (b) implies, that for each assignment that satisfies E_{rule_i}, at most one of the variables $w_{i,\tau}$ has a value 1. Hence, each assignment that satisfies E_{rule_i} assigns the value 1

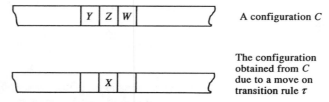

Figure 5.3.2 The value X of $f_\tau(Y, Z, W, \tau)$.

to exactly one of the variables $w_{i,\tau}$, namely, to the variable that corresponds to the transition rule τ used in the ith move of the computation in question.

The expression E_{accept} is of the form $\vee \{ w_{t,\tau} \mid \tau \text{ takes } M \text{ into an accepting state} \}$.

The Structure of E_{follow_i}

The expression E_{follow_i} is the conjunction of the following Boolean expressions.

a. $\vee \{ (w_{i,0,j,X} \wedge w_{i-1,0,j-1,Y} \wedge w_{i-1,0,j,Z} \wedge w_{i-1,0,j+1,W} \wedge w_{i,\tau}) \mid X, Y, Z,$
   $W,$ and τ such that $X = f_0(Y, Z, W, \tau) \}$ for $1 \le j \le |x| + 3$.

b. $\vee \{ (w_{i,r,j,X} \wedge w_{i-1,r,j-1,Y} \wedge w_{i-1,r,j,Z} \wedge w_{i-1,r,j+1,W} \wedge w_{i,\tau}) \mid X, Y, Z, W,$
   and τ such that $X = f_r(Y, Z, W, \tau) \}$ for $1 \le r \le m$ and $1 \le j \le t + 1$.

where

$f_r(Y, Z, W, \tau)$ is a function that determines the replacement X for a symbol Z in a configuration, resulting from the application of the transition rule τ (see Figure 5.3.2). Z is assumed to be enclosed between Y on its left and W on its right.

$w_{i-1,0,0,Y}, \ldots, w_{i-1,m,0,Y}, w_{i-1,0,|x|+4,W}, w_{i-1,1,t+2,W}, \ldots, w_{i-1,m,t+2,W}$ are new variables. They are introduced to handle the boundary cases in which the symbol Z in $f_r(Y, Z, W, \tau)$ corresponds to an extreme (i.e., leftmost or rightmost) symbol for a tape.

If $\tau = (q, a, b_1, \ldots, b_m, p, d_0, c_1, d_1, \ldots, c_m, d_m)$, then the value X of the function $f_r(Y, Z, W, \tau)$ satisfies $X = p$ whenever one of the following cases holds.

a. $Z = q$ and $d_r = 0$.

b. $Y = q$ and $d_r = +1$.

c. $W = q$ and $d_r = -1$.

Similarly, $X = c_r$ whenever one of the following cases holds, $1 \le r \le m$.

a. $Z = q$, $W = b_r$, and $d_r = +1$.

b. $Y = q$, $Z = b_r$, and $d_r = 0$.

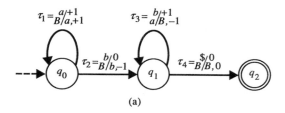

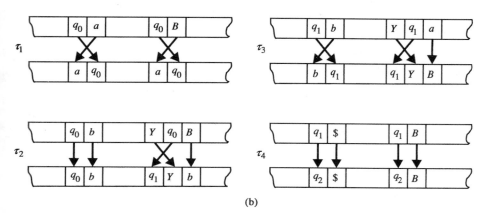

(b)

Figure 5.3.3 (a) A Turing machine M. (b) The effect that τ_1, τ_2, τ_3, and τ_4 have on the configurations of M.

   c. $Y = q$, $Z = b_r$, and $d_r = -1$.

On the other hand,

   a. $X = W$ whenever $Z = q$, $r = 0$, and $d_0 = +1$.

   b. $X = Y$ whenever $Z = q$ and $d_r = -1$.

In all the other cases $X = Z$ because the head of the rth tape is "too far" from Z.

   The result now follows because T_K on input x can compute $t = T(|x|)$ in polynomial time and then output (the string that represents) E_x.   □

Example 5.3.2 Let M be the Turing machine in Figure 5.3.3(a). The time complexity of M is $T(n) = n + 2$. On input $x = ab$ the Turing machine has an accepting computation $C_0 \vdash C_1 \vdash C_2 \vdash C_3 \vdash C_4$ of $t = 4$ moves, where each C_i is a configuration $(uqv, u'qv')$ that satisfies $uv = \text{¢}ab\$$ and $|u'v'| \leq t$.

   Using the notation in the proof of Theorem 5.3.1, the following equalities hold for the M and x above.

$$E_{\text{init}} \;=\; w_{0,0,1,\text{¢}} \wedge w_{0,0,2,q_0} \wedge w_{0,0,3,a} \wedge w_{0,0,4,b} \wedge w_{0,0,5,\$}$$

$$\wedge \; (w_{0,1,1,q_0} \vee w_{0,1,2,q_0} \vee w_{0,1,3,q_0} \vee w_{0,1,4,q_0} \vee w_{0,1,5,q_0})$$
$$\wedge \; (w_{0,1,1,B} \vee w_{0,1,1,q_0} \wedge w_{0,1,2,B} \wedge w_{0,1,3,B} \wedge w_{0,1,4,B} \wedge w_{0,1,5,B})$$
$$\wedge \; (w_{0,1,2,B} \vee w_{0,1,2,q_0} \wedge w_{0,1,1,B} \wedge w_{0,1,3,B} \wedge w_{0,1,4,B} \wedge w_{0,1,5,B})$$
$$\wedge \; (w_{0,1,3,B} \vee w_{0,1,3,q_0} \wedge w_{0,1,1,B} \wedge w_{0,1,2,B} \wedge w_{0,1,4,B} \wedge w_{0,1,5,B})$$
$$\wedge \; (w_{0,1,4,B} \vee w_{0,1,4,q_0} \wedge w_{0,1,1,B} \wedge w_{0,1,2,B} \wedge w_{0,1,3,B} \wedge w_{0,1,5,B})$$
$$\wedge \; (w_{0,1,5,B} \vee w_{0,1,5,q_0} \wedge w_{0,1,1,B} \wedge w_{0,1,2,B} \wedge w_{0,1,3,B} \wedge w_{0,1,4,B})$$

$$
\begin{aligned}
E_{\text{rule}_i} \; = \; & (w_{i,\tau_1} \vee w_{i,\tau_2} \vee w_{i,\tau_3} \vee w_{i,\tau_4}) \\
& \wedge \neg(w_{i,\tau_1} \wedge w_{i,\tau_2}) \\
& \wedge \neg(w_{i,\tau_1} \wedge w_{i,\tau_3}) \\
& \wedge \neg(w_{i,\tau_1} \wedge w_{i,\tau_4}) \\
& \wedge \neg(w_{i,\tau_2} \wedge w_{i,\tau_3}) \\
& \wedge \neg(w_{i,\tau_2} \wedge w_{i,\tau_4}) \\
& \wedge \neg(w_{i,\tau_3} \wedge w_{i,\tau_4})
\end{aligned}
$$

$$E_{\text{accept}} \; = \; w_{4,\tau_4}$$

$$
\left.
\begin{aligned}
f_0(q_1, b\,, W, \tau_3) &= q_1 \\
f_0(Y, q_1, b\,, \tau_3) &= b \\
f_0(Y, Z, q_1, \tau_3) &= Z \\
f_0(Y, Z, W, \tau_3) &= Z \\
f_1(q_1, a\,, W, \tau_3) &= B \\
f_1(Y, q_1, a\,, \tau_3) &= Y \\
f_1(Y, Z, q_1, \tau_3) &= q_1 \\
f_1(Y, Z, W, \tau_3) &= Z
\end{aligned}
\right\}
\quad
\begin{aligned}
&\text{For all } Y,\, Z,\, W \text{ in } \{a, b, B, \mathfrak{c}, \$\} \\
&\text{(see Figure 5.3.3(b)-}\tau_3\text{).}
\end{aligned}
$$

Figure 5.3.3(b) illustrates the changes in the configurations of M due to the transition rules τ_1, τ_2, τ_3, and τ_4.   ☐

The 3-Satisfiability Problem

A slight modification to the the previous proof implies the *NP*-completeness of the following restricted version of the satisfiability problem.

Definitions A Boolean expression is said to be a *literal* if it is a variable or a negation of a variable. A Boolean expression is said to be a *clause* if it is a disjunction of literals. A Boolean expression is said to be in *conjunctive normal form* if it is a conjunction of clauses. A Boolean expression is said to be in *k-conjunctive normal form* if it is in conjunctive normal form and each of its clauses consists of exactly k literals. The *k-satisfiability problem* asks for any given Boolean expression in k-conjunctive normal form whether the expression is satisfiable.

With no loss of generality, in what follows it is assumed that no variable can appear more than once in any given clause.

Theorem 5.3.2 The 3-satisfiability problem is *NP*-complete.

Proof The expression E_x in the proof of Theorem 5.3.1 needs only slight modifications to have a 3-conjunctive normal form.

   a. Except for the expressions E_{follow_i} and part (c) of E_{init}, all the other expressions can be modified to be in conjunctive normal form by using the equivalence $\neg(w_1 \wedge w_2) \equiv (\neg w_1) \vee (\neg w_2)$.

   b. Each expression in E_{follow_i} and part (c) of E_{init} can be modified to be in conjunctive normal form by using the equivalence $w_1 \vee (w_2 \wedge w_3) \equiv (w_1 \vee w_2) \wedge (w_1 \vee w_3)$.

   c. Each disjunction $w_1 \vee \cdots \vee w_s$ with $s > 3$ clauses can be modified to be in 3-conjunctive normal form by repeatedly replacing subexpressions of the form $w_1 \vee \cdots \vee w_s$ with subexpressions of the form $(w_1 \vee w_2 \vee w) \wedge (\neg w \vee w_3 \vee \cdots \vee w_s)$, where the w's are new variables. $\qquad\square$

The *NP*-completeness result for the satisfiability problem is of importance in the study of problems for two reasons. First, it exhibits the existence of an *NP*-complete problem. And, second, it is useful in showing the *NP*-hardness of some other problems.

5.4   More *NP*-Complete Problems

The *NP*-hardness of the satisfiability problem was demonstrated by exhibiting the existence of a polynomial time reduction, from each problem in *NP* to the satisfiability problem. A similar approach was used for showing the *NP*-hardness of the 3-satisfiability problem. However, in general the proof of the *NP*-hardness of a given problem need not be generic in nature, but can be accomplished by polynomial time reduction from another *NP*-hard problem.

A proof by reduction is possible because the composition of polynomial time reductions is also a polynomial time reduction. That is, if a problem K_a is reducible to a problem K_b in $T_1(n)$ time, and K_b is reducible to a problem K_c in $T_2(n)$ time, then K_a is reducible to K_c in $T_2(T_1(n))$ time. Moreover, $T_2(T_1(n))$ is polynomial if $T_1(n)$ and $T_2(n)$ are so.

The $0 - 1$ Knapsack Problem

The proofs of the following two theorems exhibit the *NP*-hardness of the problems in question by means of reduction.

Theorem 5.4.1 The problem defined by the following pair, called the $0 - 1$ *knapsack problem*, is an *NP*-complete problem.

Domain: $\{(a_1, \ldots, a_N, b) \mid N \geq 1, \text{ and } a_1, \ldots, a_N, b \text{ are natural numbers}\}$.

Question: Are there $v_1, \ldots, v_N$ in $\{0, 1\}$ such that $a_1 v_1 + \cdots + a_N v_N = b$ for the given instance $(a_1, \ldots, a_N, b)$?

Proof Consider a Turing machine M that on any given instance $(a_1, \ldots, a_N, b)$ of the problem nondeterministically assigns values from $\{0, 1\}$ to $v_1, \ldots, v_N$, checks whether $a_1 v_1 + \cdots + a_N v_N = b$, and accepts the input if and only if the equality holds. M can be of polynomial time complexity. Therefore the $0 - 1$ knapsack problem is in *NP*.

To show that the $0 - 1$ knapsack problem is *NP*-hard consider any instance E of the 3-satisfiability problem. Let $x_1, \ldots, x_m$ denote the variables in the Boolean expression E. E is a conjunction $c_1 \wedge \cdots \wedge c_k$ of some clauses $c_1, \ldots, c_k$. Each C_i is a disjunction $c_{i1} \vee c_{i2} \vee c_{i3}$ of some literals c_{i1}, c_{i2}, c_{i3}. Each c_{ij} is a variable x_t, or a negation $\neg x_t$ of a variable x_t, for some $1 \leq t \leq m$.

From Boolean Expression to a System of Linear Equations

From the Boolean expression E a system S of linear equations of the following form can be constructed.

$$
\begin{aligned}
x_1 + \bar{x}_1 &= 1 \\
&\vdots \\
x_m + \bar{x}_m &= 1 \\
c_{11} + c_{12} + c_{13} + y_{11} + y_{12} &= 3 \\
&\vdots \\
c_{k1} + c_{k2} + c_{k3} + y_{k1} + y_{k2} &= 3
\end{aligned}
$$

The system S has the variables $x_1, \ldots, x_m, \bar{x}_1, \ldots, \bar{x}_m, y_{11}, \ldots, y_{k2}$. The variable x_t in S corresponds to the literal x_t in E. The variable $\bar{x}_t$ in S corresponds to the literal $\neg x_t$ in E. c_{ij} stands for the variable x_t in S, if x_t is the jth literal in C_i. c_{ij} stands for the variable $\bar{x}_t$ in S, if $\neg x_t$ is the jth literal in C_i.

Each equation of the form $x_i + \bar{x}_i = 1$ has a solution over $\{0, 1\}$ if and only if either $x_i = 1$ and $\bar{x}_i = 0$, or $x_i = 0$ and $\bar{x}_i = 1$. Each equation of the form $c_{i1} + c_{i2} + c_{i3} + y_{i1} + y_{i2} = 3$ has a solution over $\{0, 1\}$ if and only if at least one of the equalities $c_{i1} = 1$, $c_{i2} = 1$, and $c_{i3} = 1$ holds. It follows that the system S has a solution over $\{0, 1\}$ if and only if the Boolean expression E is satisfiable.

From a System of Linear Equations to an Instance of the $0 - 1$ Knapsack Problem

The system S can be represented in a vector form as follows.

$$
\begin{pmatrix} a_{11} \\ \vdots \\ a_{m+k\,1} \end{pmatrix} z_1 + \cdots + \begin{pmatrix} a_{1\,2m+2k} \\ \vdots \\ a_{m+k\,2m+2k} \end{pmatrix} z_{2m+2k} = \begin{pmatrix} b_1 \\ \vdots \\ b_{m+k} \end{pmatrix}
$$

The variables $z_1, \ldots, z_{2m+2k}$ in the vector form stand for the variables $x_1, \ldots, x_m$, $\overline{x}_1, \ldots, \overline{x}_m$, $y_{1\,1}, \ldots, y_{k\,2}$ of S, respectively. a_{ij} is assumed to be the coefficient of z_j in the ith equation of S. b_i is assumed to be the constant in the right-hand side of the ith equation in S.

Similarly, the system S can also be represented by the equation H of the following form.

$$a_1 z_1 + \cdots + a_{2m+2k} z_{2m+2k} = b$$

In H, each a_j stands for the integer whose decimal representation is $a_{1\,j} \cdots a_{m+k\,j}$. Similarly, b stands for the integer whose decimal representation is $b_1 \cdots b_{m+k}$. The representation is possible because the sum $a_{i\,1} + \cdots + a_{i\,2m+2k}$ is either equal to 2 or to 5 for each $1 \leq i \leq m+k$. That is, the ith digit in the sum $c = a_1 + \cdots + a_{2m+2k}$ depends only on the ith digits of $a_1, \ldots, a_{2m+2k}$. It follows that S is satisfiable over $\{0, 1\}$ if and only if H is satisfiable over $\{0, 1\}$.

As a result, the instance E of the 3-satisfiability problem is satisfiable if and only if the instance $(a_1, \ldots, a_{2m+2k}, b)$ of the $0 - 1$ knapsack problem has a positive solution. Moreover, a polynomially time-bounded, deterministic Turing transducer can similarly construct corresponding instance of the $0 - 1$ knapsack problem, from each instance E of the 3-satisfiability problem. Consequently, the *NP*-hardness of the $0 - 1$ knapsack problem follows from the *NP*-hardness of the 3-satisfiability problem. $\qquad\square$

Example 5.4.1 Consider the Boolean expression E of the form $(x_1 \vee x_2 \vee \neg x_3) \wedge (\neg x_2 \vee x_3 \vee \neg x_4) \wedge (x_1 \vee x_3 \vee x_4) \wedge (\neg x_1 \vee x_2 \vee x_4)$. E is an instance of the 3-satisfiability problem. The Boolean expression is satisfiable if and only if the following system S of linear equations has a solution over $\{0, 1\}$.

$$
\begin{bmatrix}1\\0\\0\\0\\1\\0\\1\\0\end{bmatrix}x_1 +
\begin{bmatrix}0\\1\\0\\0\\1\\0\\0\\1\end{bmatrix}x_2 +
\begin{bmatrix}0\\0\\1\\0\\0\\1\\1\\0\end{bmatrix}x_3 +
\begin{bmatrix}0\\0\\0\\1\\0\\1\\0\\1\end{bmatrix}x_4 +
\begin{bmatrix}1\\0\\0\\0\\0\\0\\0\\1\end{bmatrix}\overline{x}_1 +
\begin{bmatrix}0\\1\\0\\0\\0\\1\\0\\0\end{bmatrix}\overline{x}_2 +
\begin{bmatrix}0\\0\\1\\0\\1\\0\\0\\0\end{bmatrix}\overline{x}_3 +
\begin{bmatrix}0\\0\\0\\1\\1\\0\\0\\0\end{bmatrix}\overline{x}_4 +
$$

$$
\begin{bmatrix}0\\0\\0\\0\\1\\0\\1\\0\end{bmatrix}y_{1\,1} +
\begin{bmatrix}0\\0\\0\\0\\1\\0\\0\\0\end{bmatrix}y_{1\,2} +
\begin{bmatrix}0\\0\\0\\0\\0\\1\\0\\0\end{bmatrix}y_{2\,1} +
\begin{bmatrix}0\\0\\0\\0\\0\\1\\0\\0\end{bmatrix}y_{2\,2} +
\begin{bmatrix}0\\0\\0\\0\\0\\0\\1\\0\end{bmatrix}y_{3\,1} +
\begin{bmatrix}0\\0\\0\\0\\0\\0\\1\\0\end{bmatrix}y_{3\,2} +
\begin{bmatrix}0\\0\\0\\0\\0\\0\\0\\1\end{bmatrix}y_{4\,1} +
\begin{bmatrix}0\\0\\0\\0\\0\\0\\0\\1\end{bmatrix}y_{4\,2} =
\begin{bmatrix}1\\1\\1\\1\\3\\3\\3\\3\end{bmatrix}
$$

On the other hand, the system S has a solution over $\{0, 1\}$ if and only if the equation H of the following form has a solution over $\{0, 1\}$. The leading zeros are ignored in the constants of H.

$$
\begin{aligned}
& 10001010\, x_1 + 1001001\, x_2 + 100110\, x_3 + 10011\, x_4 \\
+\ & 10000001\, \bar{x}_1 + 1000100\, \bar{x}_2 + 101000\, \bar{x}_3 + 10100\, \bar{x}_4 \\
+\ & \quad\ 1000\, y_{1\,1} + \quad\ 1000\, y_{1\,2} \\
+\ & \quad\ \ 100\, y_{2\,1} + \quad\ \ 100\, y_{2\,2} \\
+\ & \quad\ \ \ 10\, y_{3\,1} + \quad\ \ \ 10\, y_{3\,2} \\
+\ & \qquad\ \ y_{4\,1} + \qquad\quad y_{4\,2} \qquad\qquad\qquad = 11113333
\end{aligned}
$$

The expression E is satisfiable if and only if the instance (10001010, 1001001, 100110, 10011, 10000001, 1000100, 101000, 10100, 1000, 1000, 100, 100, 10, 10, 1, 1, 11113333) of the $0-1$ knapsack problem has a positive solution. □

The Clique Problem

The previous examples of *NP*-complete problems deal with Boolean expressions and linear equations. The following example deals with graphs.

Theorem 5.4.2 The problem defined by the following pair, called the *clique problem*, is an *NP*-complete problem.

Domain: $\{(G, k) \mid G$ is a graph and k is a natural number $\}$.

Question: Does G has a clique of size k for the given instance (G, k)?
(A *clique* is a subgraph with an edge between each pair of nodes. The number of nodes in a clique is called the *size of the clique*.)

Proof Consider a Turing machine M that on a given instance (G, k) of the clique problem proceeds as follows. M starts by nondeterministically choosing k nodes in G. Then it determines whether there is an edge in G between each pair of the k chosen nodes. If so, then M accepts the input; otherwise it rejects the input. M is of polynomial time complexity. Consequently the clique problem is in *NP*.

To show the *NP*-hardnes of the clique problem consider any instance E of the 3-satisfiability problem. As in the proof of the previous result, let $x_1, \ldots, x_m$ denote the variables in the Boolean expression E. E is a conjunction $c_1 \wedge \cdots \wedge c_k$ of some clauses $c_1, \ldots, c_k$. Each C_i is a disjunction $c_{i\,1} \vee c_{i\,2} \vee c_{i\,3}$ of some literals $c_{i\,1}, c_{i\,2}, c_{i\,3}$. Each $c_{i\,j}$ is a variable x_t, or a negation $\neg x_t$ of a variable x_t, for some $1 \leq t \leq m$. From the Boolean expression E a graph G of the following form can be constructed.

The graph G has a node corresponding to each pair $(c_i, (d_1, d_2, d_3))$ of an assignment (d_1, d_2, d_3) that satisfies a clause C_i. The node that corresponds to a pair $(c_i, (d_1, d_2, d_3))$ is labeled by the set $\{x_{i\,1} = d_1, x_{i\,2} = d_2, x_{i\,3} = d_3\}$, where $x_{i\,1}, x_{i\,2}, x_{i\,3}$ are assumed to be the variables used in $c_{i\,1}, c_{i\,2}, c_{i\,3}$, respectively. It follows that for each C_i, the graph G has seven associated nodes.

The graph G has an edge between a node labeled by a set $\{x_{i\,1} = d_1, x_{i\,2} = d_2, x_{i\,3} = d_3\}$ and a node labeled by a set $\{x_{j\,1} = d'_1, x_{j\,2} = d'_2, x_{j\,3} = d'_3\}$ if and only if no variable x_t has conflicting assignments in the two sets, $1 \leq t \leq m$.

By construction, no pair of nodes associated with the same clause C_i have an edge between them. On the other hand, the edges between the nodes that correspond to each pair of clauses, relate exactly those assignments to the variables that satisfy both clauses simultaneously. Consequently, the Boolean expression E is satisfiable if and only if G has a clique of size k.

A polynomially time-bounded, deterministic Turing transducer can in a similar way determine a corresponding instance (G, k) of the clique problem for each instance E of the 3-satisfiability problem. Therefore, implying the NP-hardness of the clique problem.   □

Example 5.4.2 Let E be the Boolean expression $(x_1 \lor x_2 \lor \neg x_3) \land (\neg x_2 \lor x_3 \lor \neg x_4) \land (x_1 \lor x_3 \lor x_4) \land (\neg x_1 \lor x_2 \lor x_4)$. Let G be the graph in Figure 5.4.1. Then by the proof of the last theorem, E is satisfiable if and only if $(G, 4)$ is satisfiable. The assignment $(x_1, x_2, x_3, x_4) = (1, 0, 0, 1)$ that satisfies E corresponds to the clique in G whose nodes are shaded.   □

From the definition of NP-completeness, it follows that P is equal to NP if and only if there is an NP-complete problem in P.

It should be noticed that all the known algorithms, for the NP-complete problems, are in essence based on exhaustive search over some domain. For instance, in the case of the satisfiability problem, an exhaustive search is made for an assignment to the variables that satisfies the given expression. In the case of the $0 - 1$ knapsack problem, the exhaustive search is made for a subset of a given multiset $\{a_1, \ldots, a_N\}$, whose values sum up to some given value b. In the case of the clique problem, the exhaustive search is made for a clique of the desired size. In all of these cases the search is over a domain of exponential size, and so far it seems this is the best possible for the NP-complete problems.

5.5 Polynomial Space

By Corollary 5.3.1 $NTIME(T(n)) \subseteq DSPACE(T(n))$ and so $PSPACE$ contains NP. Moreover, by Theorem 5.5.1 $PSPACE$ is contained in $EXPTIME$. These containments suggest that $PSPACE$ be studied similarly to NP. Specifically, such a study will be important in the remote possibility that NP turns out to be equal to P — the same reason the study was important for NP in the first place. However, if NP turns out to be different from P, then the study of $PSPACE$ might provide some insight into the factors that increase the complexity of problems.

Lemma 5.5.1 An $S(n) \geq \log n$ space-bounded Turing machine M can reach at most $2^{dS(n)}$ configurations on a given input of length n. d is assumed to be some constant dependent only on M.

Proof Consider any Turing machine $M = <Q, \Sigma, \Gamma, \delta, q_0, B, F>$ of space complexity $S(n) \geq \log n$. For input x of length n the Turing machine M can have at most $|Q| (n+2) (S(n)|\Gamma|^{S(n)})^m$ different configurations. $|Q|$ denotes the number of states of M, m denotes the number of auxiliary work tapes of M, and $|\Gamma|$ denotes the size of the auxiliary work-tape alphabet Γ of M.

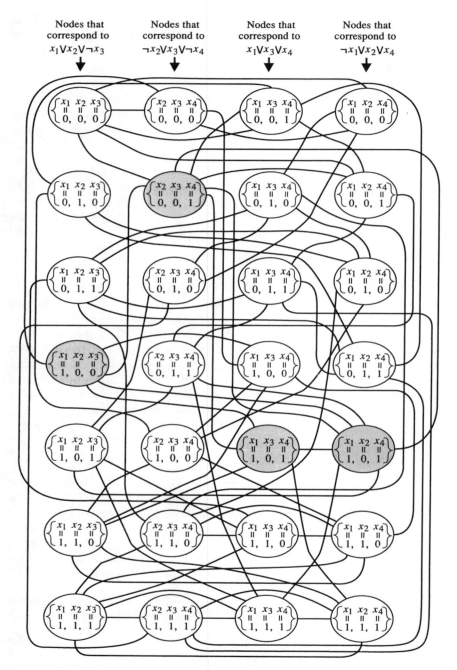

Figure 5.4.1 A graph G which relates the assignments that satisfy the clauses of the Boolean expression

$$(x_1 \lor x_2 \lor \neg x_3) \land (\neg x_2 \lor x_3 \lor \neg x_4) \land (x_1 \lor x_3 \lor x_4) \land (\neg x_1 \lor x_2 \lor x_4).$$

The factor of $|Q|$ arises because in the configurations $(uqv, u_1qv_1, \ldots, u_mqv_m)$ which satisfy $uv = \mathdollar x\mathdollar$ the state q comes from a set Q of cardinality $|Q|$. The factor $n + 2$ arises because the input head position $|u|$ can be in $n + 2$ locations. $S(n)$ represents the number of possible locations for the head of an auxiliary work tape, and $|\Gamma|^{S(n)}$ represents the number of different strings that can be stored on an auxiliary work tape.

The expression $|Q|\, (n + 2)\, (S(n)|\Gamma|^{S(n)})^m$ has a constant d such that

$$\begin{aligned}
|Q|\, (n + 2)\, (S(n)|\Gamma|^{S(n)})^m &= 2^{\log|Q|} 2^{\log(n+2)} (2^{\log S(n)} 2^{S(n)\log|\Gamma|})^m \\
&\leq 2^{dS(n)}
\end{aligned}$$

for all n if $S(n) \geq \log n$. □

From Nondeterministic Space to Deterministic Time

By Corollary 5.3.1 nondeterministic and deterministic time satisfy the relation $NTIME\,(T(n)) \subseteq \bigcup_{c>0} DTIME\,(2^{cT(n)})$. The following theorem provides a refinement to this result because $NTIME\,(T(n)) \subseteq NSPACE(T(n))$.

Definition The *configurations tree* of a Turing machine M on input x is a possibly infinite tree Ω defined in the following manner. The root of Ω is a node labeled by the initial configuration of M on input x. A node in Ω, which is labeled by a configuration C_1, has an immediate successor that is labeled by configuration C_2 if and only if $C_1 \vdash C_2$.

Theorem 5.5.1 If $S(n) \geq \log n$ then

$$NSPACE\,(S(n)) \quad \subseteq \quad \bigcup_{c>0} DTIME\,(2^{cS(n)})$$

Proof Consider any $S(n)$ space-bounded Turing machine $M_1 = <Q, \Sigma, \Gamma, \delta, q_0, B, F>$. A deterministic Turing machine M_2 can determine if M_1 accepts a given input x by determining whether the configurations tree Ω, of M_1 on input x, contains an accepting configuration. M_2 can do so by finding the set A of all the configurations in Ω, and then checking whether the set contains an accepting configuration. The set A can be generated by following the algorithm.

Step 1 Initiate A to contain only the initial configuration of M_1 on input x.

Step 2 For each configuration C in A that has not been considered yet determine all the configurations that M_1 can reach from C in a single move, and insert them to A.

Step 3 Repeat Step 2 as long as more configurations can be added to A.

By Lemma 5.5.1 the Turing machine M_1 on input x of length n has at most $2^{dS(n)}$ different configurations, for some constant that depends only on M_1. Each of the configurations $(uqv, y_1qz_1, \ldots, y_mqz_m)$ of M_1 on input x can be represented by M_2 in $\log n + m(S(n)+1)$ space. The set A can be explicitly represented

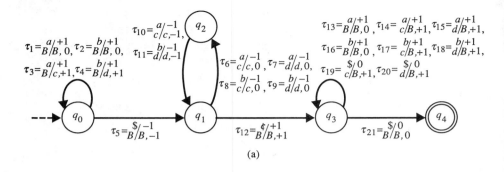

(a)

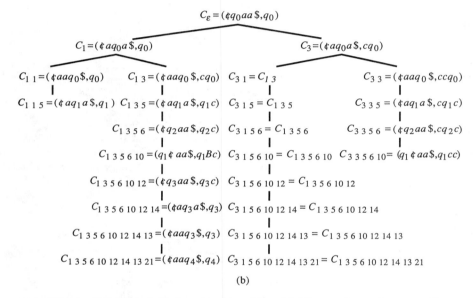

(b)

Figure 5.5.1 (a) A Turing machine M_1. (b) The configurations tree Ω of M_1 on input aa.

in $(\log n + m(S(n) + 1))2^{dS(n)} \leq 2^{eS(n)}$ space, where e is some constant. The number of times that A is accessed is bounded above by the number of elements that it contains. Consequently, the result follows. $\square$

Example 5.5.1 Let M_1 be the Turing machine in Figure 5.5.1(a). The configurations tree Ω of M_1 on input aa is given in Figure 5.5.1(b). For a given input x of M_1 let $C_{i_1 \dots i_t}$ denote the configuration that M_1 reaches from its initial configuration through a sequence of moves using the transition rules $\tau_{i_1}, \dots, \tau_{i_t}$. If no such sequence of moves is possible, then $C_{i_1 \dots i_t}$ is assumed to be an undefined configuration.

The algorithm in the proof of Theorem 5.5.1 inserts C_ϵ to A in Step 1. The first iteration of Step 2 determines the immediate successors C_1 and C_3 of C_ϵ, and

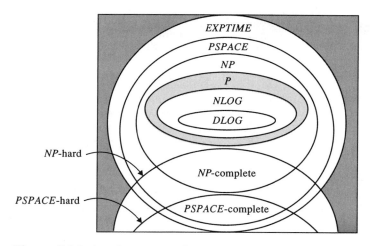

Figure 5.5.2 A refinement to the classification in Figure 5.3.1.

inserts them into A. The second iteration considers either the configuration C_1 or the configuration C_3.

If C_1 is considered before C_3, then C_{11} and C_{13} are the configurations contributed by C_1 to A. In such a case, C_3 contributes C_{33} to A.

Upon completion A contains the configurations $C_\epsilon, C_1, C_3, C_{11}, C_{13}\,(= C_{31})$, $C_{33}, C_{115}, C_{135}\,(= C_{315}), C_{335}, \ldots, C_{3\,15\,6\,10\,12\,14\,13\,21}$. $\qquad\qquad\square$

From Nondeterministic to Deterministic Space

The previous theorem, together with Corollary 5.3.1, imply the hierarchy $DLOG \subseteq NLOG \subseteq P \subseteq NP \subseteq PSPACE \subseteq EXPTIME$ (see Figure 5.5.2). By the following theorem, nondeterministic Turing machines of polynomial space complexity can be simulated by deterministic Turing machines of similar complexity. However, from Exercise 5.2.6 $NLOG$ is properly included in $PSPACE$. Besides this proper inclusion, and the proper inclusion of P in $EXPTIME$, it is not known whether any of the other inclusions in the above hierarchy is proper.

The following theorem provides an approach more economical in space, than that of the proof of the previous theorem. However, the improvement in the space requirements is achieved at the cost of slower simulations.

Theorem 5.5.2 If $S(n)$ is a fully space-constructible function and $S(n) \geq \log n$ then

$$NSPACE\,(S(n)) \quad \subseteq \quad DSPACE\,((S(n))^2)$$

Proof Consider any $cS(n)$ space-bounded Turing machine M_1, where $S(n) \geq \log n$ is fully space-constructible. With no loss of generality it can be assumed that on entering into an accepting configuration the auxiliary work tapes of M_1 are all blank, and the input head of M_1 is on the right endmarker \$. In addition, it can be

$C_0 :=$ the initial configuration of M_1 on input x
$C_f :=$ the accepting configuration of M_1 on input x
if $R(C_0, C_f, 2^{dS(|x|)})$ **then accept**
reject
function $R(C_1, C_2, t)$
  if $t \le 1$ **then**
    if M_1 can in t steps reach configuration C_2
        from configuration C_1 **then return** (*true*)
  else for each configuration C of M_1 on input x
        of length $\le d's(|x|)$ **do**
    if $R(C_1, C, \lceil t/2 \rceil)$ **and**
      $R(C, C_2, \lfloor t/2 \rfloor)$ **then return** (*true*)
  return (*false*)
end

Figure 5.5.3 A deterministic simulation of a nondeterministic Turing machine M_1.

assumed that M_1 has exactly one accepting state q_f. Consequently, an accepting computation of M_1 on a given input x must end at the accepting configuration $(\updownarrow x q_f \$, q_f, \ldots, q_f)$.

By definition, M_1 accepts a given input x if and only if M_1 on input x has a sequence of moves, starting at the initial configuration C_0 of M_1 on input x and ending at the accepting configuration C_f of M_1 on input x. By Lemma 5.5.1 the Turing machine M_1 can reach at most $2^{dS(n)}$ different configurations on an input of length n. By Theorem 5.5.1 each configuration requires at most $d's(n)$ space when the input string is excluded. Consequently, M_1 accepts x if and only if it has a sequence of at most $2^{dS(|x|)}$ moves that starts at C_0 and ends at C_f.

A deterministic Turing machine M_2 can determine whether M_1 accepts an input x by the algorithm in Figure 5.5.3.

The algorithm uses a recursive function $R(C_1, C_2, t)$ whose task is to determine whether M_1 on input x has a sequence of at most t moves, starting at C_1 and ending at C_2. The property is checked directly when $t \le 1$. Otherwise, it is checked recursively by exhaustively searching for a configuration C of M_1, such that both $R(C_1, C, \lceil t/2 \rceil)$ and $R(C, C_2, \lfloor t/2 \rfloor)$ hold.

The algorithm uses $O(S(n))$ levels of recursion in $R(C_1, C_2, t)$. Each level of recursion requires space $O(S(n))$. Consequently M_2 uses $O((S(n))^2)$ space.

When it derives the configurations of M_1, M_2 relies on the property that $S(n)$ is space-constructible. $\qquad\qquad\qquad\qquad\qquad\qquad\qquad\qquad\qquad\qquad\qquad\square$

PSPACE-Complete Problems

Approaches similar to those used for showing the *NP*-hardness of some given problems, can also be used for showing *PSPACE*-hardness. The following theorem is an example of a *PSPACE*-complete problem whose *PSPACE*-hardness is shown by a generic transformation.

Theorem 5.5.3 The membership problem for linear bounded automata or, equivalently, for $L = \{(M, x) \mid M$ is a linear bounded automaton that accepts $x\}$ is a *PSPACE*-complete problem.

Proof The language L is accepted by a nondeterministic Turing machine M_U similar to the universal Turing machine in the proof of Theorem 4.4.1. M_U on input (M, x) nondeterministically finds a sequence of moves of M on x. M_U accepts the input if and only if the sequence of moves starts at the initial configuration of M on input x, and ends at an accepting configuration. The computation of M_U proceeds in the following manner.

M_U starts by constructing the initial configuration C_0 of M on input x. Then it repeatedly and nondeterministically finds a configuration C that M can reach in one step from the last configuration that has been determined for M by M_U. M_U accepts (M, x) if and when it reaches an accepting configuration of M.

By construction, M_U requires a space no greater than the amount of memory required for recording a single configuration of M. A single configuration $(uqv, u_1qv_1, \ldots, u_mqv_m)$ of M requires space equal to the amount of memory needed for recording a single symbol times the number of symbols in the configuration, that is,

$$O(|M|((1 + |uv|) + (1 + |u_1v_1|) + \cdots + (1 + |u_mv_m|))) =$$
$$O(|M|(m + 1)(1 + |x|)) = O(|M|^2|x|)$$

where $|M|$ stands for the length of the representation of M. Consequently, M_U requires a space which is polynomial in the size of its input (M, x). It follows from Theorem 5.5.2 that the language L is in *PSPACE*.

To show that the membership problem for L is *PSPACE*-hard, consider any problem K in *PSPACE*. Assume that A is a deterministic Turing machine of space complexity $S(n) = O(n^k)$ that decides K. From $(A, S(n))$ a polynomially time-bounded, deterministic Turing transducer T_K can be constructed to output the pair (M, y) on input x.

y is assumed to be the string $\#^j x$, where $j = S(|x|)$ and $\#$ is a new symbol. M is assumed to be a linear bounded automaton, which on input $\#^j x$ simulates the computation of A on x with j space. That is, M accepts y if and only if A accepts x within j space.   □

Example 5.5.2 Let A be the Turing machine in Figure 5.3.3. Using the terminology in the proof of Theorem 5.5.3, the corresponding linear bounded automaton M can be the one given in Figure 5.5.4.

M starts each computation by copying the leading symbols $\#$, from the input to its auxiliary work tape. Then M nondeterministically locates its auxiliary work-tape head over one of the symbols $\#$. Finally, M follows a computation similar to A's on the remainder of the input. The main difference is that M expects the symbol $\#$ whenever A scans the left endmarker $\mathcal{c}$ or a blank symbol B.   □

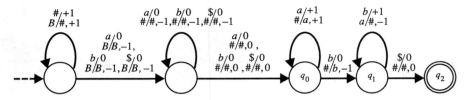

Figure 5.5.4 A linear bounded automaton corresponding to the Turing machine of Figure 5.3.3.

The following theorem is an example of a problem whose *PSPACE*-hardness is shown by reduction from another *PSPACE*-hard problem.

Theorem 5.5.4 The inequivalence problem for finite-state automata is *PSPACE*-complete.

Proof Let (M_1, M_2) be any given pair of finite-state automata. A Turing machine M can determine the inequivalency of M_1 and M_2 by finding nondeterministically an input $a_1 \cdots a_N$ that is accepted by exactly one of the finite-state automata M_1 and M_2.

M starts its computation by determining the set S_0 of all the states that M_1 and M_2 can reach on empty input. With no loss of generality it is assumed that M_1 and M_2 have disjoint sets of states. Then M determines, one at a time, the symbols in $a_1 \cdots a_N$. For each symbol a_i that M determines, M also finds the set S_i (from those states that are in S_{i-1}) that M_1 and M_2 can reach by consuming a_i.

M halts in an accepting configuration upon, and only upon, finding an S_N that satisfies either of the following conditions.

a. S_N contains an accepting state of M_1 and no accepting state of M_2.

b. S_N contains an accepting state of M_2 and no accepting state of M_1.

At each instance of the computation, M needs to record only the last symbol a_i and the associated sets S_{i-1} and S_i, that M determines. That is, M on input (M_1, M_2) uses space linear in $|M_1| + |M_2|$. As a result, M is of nondeterministically polynomial space complexity. From Theorem 5.5.2 it follows that the inequivalence problem for finite-state automata is in *PSPACE*.

To show that the inequivalence problem for finite-state automata is a *PSPACE*-hard problem, it is sufficient to demonstrate the existence of a polynomially time-bounded, deterministic Turing transducer T that has the following property: T on input (M, x), of a linear bounded automaton M and of an input x for M, outputs a pair (M_1, M_2) of finite-state automata M_1 and M_2. Moreover, M_1 and M_2 are inequivalent if and only if M accepts x.

M_1 can be a finite-state automaton that accepts a given input if and only if the input is not of the form $\#C_0\#C_1\# \cdots \#C_f\#$. C_0 is assumed to be the initial configuration of M on input x. C_f is assumed to be an accepting configuration of M on input x. C_i is assumed to be a configuration that M can reach in one move from C_{i-1}, $i = 1,\ldots,\mathrm{f}$. The length of each C_i is assumed to equal $(n+3) + m(S(n)+1)$, m is assumed to be the number of auxiliary work tapes of M, $S(n)$ is assumed to be the space complexity of M, and $\#$ is assumed to be a new symbol.

M_1 can determine that an input is not of such a form, by nondeterministically choosing to check for one of the following conditions.

a. The first symbol in the input is not $\#$.

b. The last symbol in the input is not $\#$.

c. C_0 is not an initial configuration of M on input x.

d. C_f does not contain an accepting state of M.

e. C_i is not consistent with C_{i-1} for some i (chosen nondeterministically). M_1 can check for this condition by nondeterministically finding a j such that the jth symbol in C_i is not consistent with the jth symbol in C_{i-1} and its two neighbors.

M_1 can check for each of these conditions by using a polynomial number of states in the length of x.

By construction, M_1 accepts all inputs if and only if M does not accept x. The result then follows immediately if M_2 is taken to accept all the strings over the input alphabet of M_1. □

Example 5.5.3 The Turing machine M in Figure 5.5.1(a) has space complexity of $S(n) = n + 2$. For the string $x = aa$ the Turing machine M in the proof of Theorem 5.5.4 has the corresponding finite-state automaton M_1 of Figure 5.5.5. Each configuration (uqv, u_1qv_1) of M on input aa is assumed to be represented in M_1 by a string $uqvu_1qv_1$ of length $(n+3) + (S(n)+1) = 2n + 6$.

On a given input M_1 nondeterministically chooses to execute one of the subcomponents A_1, A_2, A_3, A_4, or A_5.

A_1 checks that the input does not start with the symbol $\#$. A_2 checks that the input does not end with the symbol $\#$. A_3 checks that the string between the first two $\#$ symbols is not the initial configuration of M on input aa. A_4 checks that the accepting state q_4 does not appear in the last configuration C_f.

A_5 checks for inconsistency between consecutive configurations. Its specification is omitted here. □

Closure Properties

The classes $NTIME(T(n))$ and $NSPACE(S(n))$ are closed under union and intersection (see Exercise 5.1.3(a)), but it is not known whether they are closed under complementation. However, the following theorem holds for $NSPACE(S(n))$.

Theorem 5.5.5 The class $NSPACE(S(n))$ is closed under complementation for $S(n) \geq \log n$.

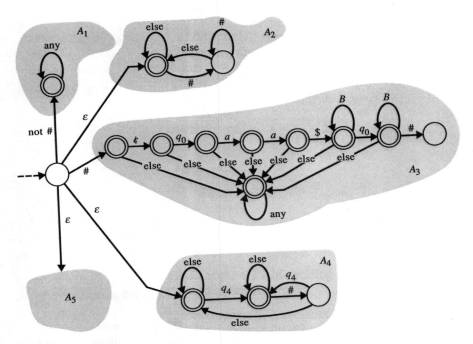

Figure 5.5.5 A finite-state automaton that accepts all inputs if and only if the Turing machine in Figure 5.5.1(a) does not accept aa.

Proof Consider any $S(n)$ space-bounded, nondeterministic Turing machine M_1. From M_1 an $S(n)$ space-bounded, nondeterministic Turing machine M_2 can be constructed to accept the complementation of $L(M_1)$.

Specifically, on a given input x the Turing machine M_2 determines whether the configurations tree Ω of M_1 on x contains an accepting configuration. If so, then M_2 rejects x. Otherwise, M_2 accepts x.

M_2 traverses Ω by stages, according to the algorithm in Figure 5.5.6(a). At the ith stage M_2 determines the configurations C at the ith level of Ω, that is, the configurations in the set $\Omega_i = \{ C \mid M_1 \text{ has a sequence } C_0 \vdash^* C \text{ of exactly } i \text{ moves that starts at the initial configuration } C_0 \text{ of } M_1 \text{ on input } x \}$.

M_2 halts during the ith stage in a nonaccepting configuration if it determines an accepting configuration in Ω_i. However, it halts at the end of the ith stage in an accepting configuration if it determines that Ω_i cannot contain new configurations (i.e., by determining that i is greater than the number of configurations M_1 can reach on input x).

The configurations C that are in Ω_i are found nondeterministically from i and the number N of configurations in Ω_i. In particular, M_2 simulates the instructions of the form **"for** each configuration C in Ω_i **do** α" in accordance with the algorithm in Figure 5.5.6(b). The nondeterminism is required for simulating the sequences of moves $C_0 \vdash^* C$.

```
i := 0
l := length of the initial configuration C₀ of M₁ on input x
N := 1
repeat
    for each configuration C in Ωᵢ do
        if C is an accepting configuration then reject
    l := max(1, length of longest configuration in Ωᵢ₊₁)
    N := number of configurations in Ωᵢ₊₁
    i := i + 1
until i > (the number of configurations, of M₁ on input x,
          of length l)
accept
```

$$i := 0$$
$$\texttt{l} := \text{length of the initial configuration } C_0 \text{ of } M_1 \text{ on input } x$$
$$N := 1$$

(a)

```
count := 0
for each configuration C, of M₁ on
        input x, of length l at most     do
    if C₀ ⊢* C in exactly i moves then
    begin count := count + 1
        α
    end
if count ≠ N then reject
```

(b)

```
nextN := 0
for each configuration C', of
        M₁ on input x, of length l do
    begin countup := false
        for each configuration C in Ωᵢ do
            if C ⊢ C' then countup := true
        if countup then nextN := nextN + 1
    end
N := nextN
```

(c)

Figure 5.5.6 (a) A breadth-first search algorithm for accepting the complementation of $L(M_1)$. (b) Simulation of "**for** each configuration C in Ω_i **do** α". (c) Evaluation of the number of configurations in Ω_{i+1}.

M_2 determines the number N of configurations in Ω_{i+1} by determining which configuration can be directly reached from those that are in Ω_i. The algorithm is given in Figure 5.5.6(c).

The result now follows because by Lemma 5.5.1, the Turing machine M_1 can reach at most $2^{O(S(n))}$ different configurations on inputs of length n, that is, M_2 considers only $i \leq 2^{O(S(n))}$ levels of Ω. $\square$

The class $DTIME(T(n))$ is closed under union, intersection, and complementation (see Exercise 5.1.3(b)). The closure of $DSPACE(S(n))$ under union, intersection, and complementation can be easily shown by direct simulations. For the last operation, however, the following theorem is required.

Definitions An s *space-bounded configuration* is a configuration that requires at most s space in each auxiliary work tape. An s *space-bounded, backward-moving-configurations tree* of a Turing machine M is a tree Ω, defined in the following manner. The root of Ω is labeled by an s space-bounded configuration of M. A node in Ω, labeled by a configuration C_2, has an immediate successor labeled by configuration C_1 if and only if C_1 is an s space-bounded configuration of M such that $C_1 \vdash C_2$.

Theorem 5.5.6 Each $S(n)$ space-bounded, deterministic Turing machine M_1 has an equivalent $S(n)$ space-bounded, deterministic Turing machine M_2 that halts on all inputs.

Proof Consider any $S(n)$ space-bounded, deterministic Turing machine $M_1 = <Q, \Sigma, \Gamma, \delta, q_0, B, F>$. M_2 can be of the following form. M_2 on a given input x determines the space s_x that M_1 uses on input x. Then M_2 checks whether M_1 has an accepting computation on input x. If so, then M_2 halts in an accepting configuration. Otherwise M_2 halts in a rejecting one.

To determine the value of s_x the Turing machine M_2 initializes s_x to equal 1. Then M_2 increases s_x by 1 as long as it finds an s_x space-bounded configuration C_1, and an $(s_x + 1)$ space-bounded configuration C_2, such that the following conditions hold.

   a. $C_1 \vdash C_2$.

   b. M_1 has an s_x space-bounded, backward-moving-configurations tree Ω, the root of which is C_1 and which contains the initial configuration of M_1 on x.

M_2 searches for an s_x space-bounded configuration C_1 that satisfies the above conditions by generating all the s_x space-bounded configurations in canonical order, and checking each of them for the conditions.

To check whether M_1 has an accepting computation on input x the Turing machine M_2 searches for an s_x space-bounded, backward-moving-configurations tree that satisfies the following conditions.

   a. The root of Ω is an accepting configuration of M_1 on input x.

   b. Ω contains the initial configuration of M_1 on input x.

$C := C_{\text{root}}$
do
    if C is an initial configuration **then**
      begin
        while C has a predecessor in Ω_s **do**
          $C :=$ predecessor of C in Ω_s
        return (*true*)
      end
    if C is not a terminal node in Ω_s **then**
      $C :=$ the leftmost successor of C in Ω_s
    else if C has a right neighbor in Ω_s **then**
      $C :=$ the right neighbor C in Ω_s
    else if C has a predecessor in Ω_s **then**
      $C :=$ the predecessor of C in Ω_s
    else return (*false*)
until *false*

Figure 5.5.7 Depth-first search for an initial configuration in Ω_s.

M_2 follows the algorithm in Figure 5.5.7 for determining whether M_1 on input x has an s space-bounded, backward-moving-configurations tree Ω_s, the root of which is C_{root} and which contains a node that corresponds to an initial configuration. Upon halting, the algorithm is at configuration $C = C_{\text{root}}$.

The algorithm is used only on configurations C_{root}, such that if $C_{\text{root}} \vdash C'$ then C' is not an s space-bounded configuration. This property is used by the algorithm to determine the root of Ω_s upon backtracking.

The algorithm relies on the observation that the determinism of M_1 implies the following properties for each s space-bounded, backward-moving-configurations tree Ω_s.

a. The tree Ω_s is finite because no configuration can be repeated in a path that starts at the root.

b. The predecessors, successors, and siblings of each node can be determined simply from the configuration assigned to the node. □

5.6 *P*-Complete Problems

In some cases it is of interest to study the limitations of some subclasses of P. The motivation might be theoretical, as in the case of the subclass *NLOG* of P, or practical, as in the case of the subclass *U_NC* of the problems in P that can be solved by efficient parallel programs (see Section 7.5). In such cases the notion of the "hardest" problems in P is significant.

Specifically, a problem K_1 is said to be *logspace reducible* to a problem K_2 if there exist logspace-bounded, deterministic Turing transducers T_f and T_g that for each instance I_1 of K_1 satisfy the following conditions.

a. T_f on input I_1 gives an instance I_2 of K_2.

b. K_1 has a solution S_1 at I_1 if and only if K_2 has a solution S_2 at I_2, where S_1 is the output of T_g on input S_2.

A problem K is said to be a *P-hard problem* if every problem in P is logspace reducible to K. The problem is said to be *P-complete* if it is a P-hard problem in P.

By the definitions above, the P-complete problems are the hardest problems in P, and by Section 7.5 $NLOG \subseteq U\_NC \subseteq P$. Consequently, $NLOG$ contains a P-complete problem if and only if $P = NLOG$, and U_NC contains a P-complete problem if and only if $P = U\_NC$. It is an open problem whether P equals $NLOG$ or U_NC.

Theorem 5.6.1 The emptiness problem for context-free grammars is P-complete.

Proof Consider any context-free grammar $G = < N, \Sigma, R, S >$. The emptiness of $L(G)$ can be determined by the following algorithm.

Step 1 Mark each of the terminal symbols in Σ.

Step 2 Search R for a production rule $A \rightarrow \alpha$, in which α consists only of marked symbols and A is unmarked. If such a production rule $A \rightarrow \alpha$ exists, then mark A and repeat the process.

Step 3 If the start symbol S is unmarked, then declare $L(G)$ to be empty. Otherwise, declare $L(G)$ to be nonempty.

The number of iterations of Step 2 is bounded above by the number of non-terminal symbols in N. Consequently, the algorithm requires polynomial time and the problem is in P.

To show that the emptiness problem for context-free grammars is P-hard, consider any problem K in P. Assume that $M = <Q, \Sigma, \Gamma, \delta, q_0, B, F>$ is a deterministic Turing machine that decides K in $T(n) = O(n^k)$ time and that $Q \cap (\Sigma \cup \Gamma \cup \{\mathfrak{c}, \$\}) = \emptyset$. Let m denote the number of auxiliary work tapes of M, and let r denote the cardinality of δ. Then K can be reduced to the emptiness problem for context-free grammars by a logspace-bounded, deterministic Turing transducer T_K of the following form.

T_K on input x outputs a context-free grammar G_x such that

a. $L(G_x) = \emptyset$ if K has answer *yes* at x.

b. $L(G_x) = \{\epsilon\}$ if K has answer *no* at x.

T_K constructs the grammar G_x to describe the computation of M on input x.

The Nonterminal Symbols of G_x

The nonterminal symbols of G_x represent the possible characteristics of the computation of M on input x. Specifically, G_x has the following nonterminal symbols (t is assumed to denote the value $T(|x|)$).

a. The start symbol S. S represents the possibility of having a nonaccepting computation of M on input x.

b. A nonterminal symbol $A_{i,\tau}$ for each transition rule τ of M and each $1 \leq i \leq t$. $A_{i,\tau}$ represents the possibility that the ith move of M on input x uses the transition rule τ.

c. A nonterminal symbol $A_{i,0,j,X}$ for each $0 \leq i \leq t$, $1 \leq j \leq |x| + 3$, and X in $\{\mathbf{c}, \$\} \cup \Sigma \cup Q$. $A_{i,0,j,X}$ represents the possibility of having X in the ith configuration of the computation at the jth location of the input description.

d. A nonterminal symbol $A_{i,r,j,X}$ for each $0 \leq i \leq t$, $1 \leq r \leq m$, $1 \leq j \leq 2t + 1$, and X in $\Gamma \cup Q$. $A_{i,r,j,X}$ represents the possibility of having X in the ith configuration of the computation at the jth location of the rth auxiliary work tape description.

e. A nonterminal $B_{i,r,q,X}$ for each $0 \leq i \leq t$, $0 \leq r \leq m$, q in Q, and X in $\Sigma \cup \Gamma \cup \{\mathbf{c}, \$\}$. $B_{i,r,q,X}$ represents the possibility that in the ith configuration the state is q and the symbol under the head of the rth tape is X.

The Production Rules of G_x

The production rules of G_x describe how the characteristics of the computation of M on input x are determined. Specifically, the characteristic that is represented by a nonterminal symbol A holds for the computation if and only if $A \Rightarrow^* \epsilon$ in G_x. The production rules of G_x are as follows.

a. Production rules that determine the input segment in the initial configuration.

$$
\begin{aligned}
A_{0,0,1,\mathbf{c}} &\rightarrow \epsilon \\
A_{0,0,2,q_0} &\rightarrow \epsilon \\
A_{0,0,i+2,i\text{th symbol in } x} &\rightarrow \epsilon \qquad \text{for } 1 \leq i \leq |x| \\
A_{0,0,|x|+3,\$} &\rightarrow \epsilon
\end{aligned}
$$

b. Production rules that determine the segment of the rth auxiliary work tape in the initial configuration, $1 \leq r \leq m$.

$$
\begin{aligned}
A_{0,r,j,B} &\rightarrow \epsilon \qquad \text{for } 1 \leq j \leq t \text{ and } t + 2 \leq j \leq 2t + 1 \\
A_{0,r,t+1,q_0} &\rightarrow \epsilon
\end{aligned}
$$

c. Production rules that determine the jth symbol for the rth tape in the ith configuration of the computation.

$$
A_{i,r,j,X} \rightarrow A_{i-1,r,j-1,Y}\, A_{i-1,r,j,Z}\, A_{i-1,r,j+1,W}\, A_{i,\tau}
$$

for each X, Y, Z, W, τ, such that $f_r(Y, Z, W, \tau) = X$. $f_r(Y, Z, W, \tau)$ is assumed to be a function that determines the replacement X of Z for the rth tape when Y is to the left of Z, W is to the right of Z, and τ is the transition rule in use. The left "boundary symbols" $A_{i-1,0,-1,Y}, \ldots, A_{i-1,m,-1,Y},$ $A_{i-1,0,|x|+4,W}$ and the right ones $A_{i-1,1,2t+2,W}, \ldots, A_{i-1,m,2t+2,W}$ are assumed to equal the empty string ϵ.

   d. Production rules that determine whether the computation is nonaccepting.

$$S \quad \to \quad B_{i,0,q,a} B_{i,1,q,b_1} \cdots B_{i,m,q,b_m}$$

for each $0 \leq i \leq t$, a nonaccepting state q, and a, b_1, $\ldots$, b_m such that $\delta(q, a, b_1, \ldots, b_m) = \emptyset$ (i.e., M has no next move).

   e. Production rules that determine the transition rule to be used in the ith move of the computation, $1 \leq i \leq t$.

$$A_{i,\tau} \quad \to \quad B_{i-1,0,q,a} B_{i-1,1,q,b_1} \cdots B_{i-1,m,q,b_m}$$

for each transition rule $\tau = (q, a, b_1, \ldots, b_m, p, d_o, c_1, d_1, \ldots, c_m, d_m)$ of the Turing machine M.

Since M is deterministic, for a given i there exists at most one τ such that $A_{i,\tau} \Rightarrow^* \epsilon$.

   f. Production rules that are used for determining the state of M and the symbols scanned by the heads of M in the ith configuration, $0 \leq i \leq t$.

$$
\begin{aligned}
B_{i,0,q,a} &\quad \to \quad A_{i,0,j_0,q} A_{i,0,j_0+1,a} \\
B_{i,1,q,b_1} &\quad \to \quad A_{i,1,j_1,q} A_{i,1,j_1+1,b_1} \\
&\quad\vdots \\
B_{i,m,q,b_m} &\quad \to \quad A_{i,m,j_m,q} A_{i,m,j_m+1,b_m}
\end{aligned}
$$

for each $1 \leq j_0 \leq |x| + 2$, and $1 \leq j_r \leq 2t$ with $1 \leq r \leq m$. $\qquad \square$

Example 5.6.1 Let M be the deterministic Turing machine of Figure 5.3.3(a), $x = ab$, and assume the notations in Theorem 5.6.1.

    The following production rules of G_x determine the input segment in the initial configuration of M on x.

$$
\begin{aligned}
A_{0,0,1,\mathfrak{c}} &\quad \to \quad \epsilon \\
A_{0,0,2,q_0} &\quad \to \quad \epsilon \\
A_{0,0,3,a} &\quad \to \quad \epsilon \\
A_{0,0,4,b} &\quad \to \quad \epsilon \\
A_{0,0,5,\$} &\quad \to \quad \epsilon
\end{aligned}
$$

    The production rules that determine the segment of the auxiliary work tape in the initial configuration have the following form.

$$B_{0,0,j,B} \quad \rightarrow \quad \epsilon \quad\quad 1 \le j \le 4 \ \text{ and } \ 6 \le j \le 9$$
$$B_{0,0,5,q_0} \quad \rightarrow \quad \epsilon$$

The following production rules determine the second configuration from the first.

$$
\begin{aligned}
A_{1,0,1,\mathfrak{c}} \quad &\rightarrow \quad\quad\quad A_{0,0,1,\mathfrak{c}} \ A_{0,0,2,q_0} \ A_{1,\tau_1}\\
A_{1,0,2,a} \quad &\rightarrow \quad A_{0,0,1,\mathfrak{c}} \ A_{0,0,2,q_0} \ A_{0,0,3,a} \ A_{1,\tau_1}\\
A_{1,0,3,q_0} \quad &\rightarrow \quad A_{0,0,2,q_0} \ A_{0,0,3,a} \ A_{0,0,4,b} \ A_{1,\tau_1}\\
A_{1,0,4,b} \quad &\rightarrow \quad A_{0,0,3,a} \ A_{0,0,4,b} \ A_{0,0,5,\$} \ A_{1,\tau_1}\\
A_{1,0,5,\$} \quad &\rightarrow \quad A_{0,0,4,b} \ A_{0,0,5,\$} \quad\quad\quad A_{1,\tau_1}\\
A_{1,1,1,B} \quad &\rightarrow \quad\quad\quad A_{0,1,1,B} \ A_{0,1,2,B} \ A_{1,\tau_1}\\
A_{1,1,2,B} \quad &\rightarrow \quad A_{0,1,1,B} \ A_{0,1,2,B} \ A_{0,1,3,B} \ A_{1,\tau_1}\\
A_{1,1,3,B} \quad &\rightarrow \quad A_{0,1,2,B} \ A_{0,1,3,B} \ A_{0,1,4,B} \ A_{1,\tau_1}\\
A_{1,1,4,B} \quad &\rightarrow \quad A_{0,1,3,B} \ A_{0,1,4,B} \ A_{0,1,5,q_0} \ A_{1,\tau_1}\\
A_{1,1,5,a} \quad &\rightarrow \quad A_{0,1,4,B} \ A_{0,1,5,q_0} \ A_{0,1,6,B} \ A_{1,\tau_1}\\
A_{1,1,6,q_0} \quad &\rightarrow \quad A_{0,1,5,q_0} \ A_{0,1,6,B} \ A_{0,1,7,B} \ A_{1,\tau_1}\\
A_{1,1,7,B} \quad &\rightarrow \quad A_{0,1,6,B} \ A_{0,1,7,B} \ A_{0,1,8,B} \ A_{1,\tau_1}\\
A_{1,1,8,B} \quad &\rightarrow \quad A_{0,1,7,B} \ A_{0,1,8,B} \ A_{0,1,9,B} \ A_{1,\tau_1}\\
A_{1,1,9,B} \quad &\rightarrow \quad A_{0,1,8,B} \ A_{0,1,9,B} \quad\quad\quad A_{1,\tau_1}
\end{aligned}
$$

The production rule $A_{1,\tau_1} \rightarrow B_{0,0,q_0,a} B_{0,1,q_0,B}$ determines the transition rule used in the first move.

The following production rules determine the state of M and the symbols scanned by the heads of M, in the first configuration.

$$B_{0,0,q_0,a} \quad \rightarrow \quad A_{0,0,2,q_0} A_{0,0,3,a}$$
$$B_{0,1,q_0,B} \quad \rightarrow \quad A_{0,1,5,q_0} A_{0,1,6,B} \quad\quad\quad \square$$

Exercises

5.1.1 The RAM represented by the program of Figure 5.E.1 is based on Euclid's algorithm and determines the greatest common divisor of any given pair of positive integers. Find the time and space complexity of the RAM.

    a. Under the uniform cost criterion.

    b. Under the logarithmic cost criterion.

5.1.2 Show that a RAM can compute the relation $\{ (1^n, y) \mid n \ge 0, \text{ and } y \text{ is the}$ binary representation of $n \}$ in time linear in n.

    Hint: Note that $(1/2^1) + (2/2^2) + (3/2^3) + \cdots < 3$.

5.1.3 Show that each of the following classes is closed under the given operations.

    a. *NTIME*$(T(n))$ and *NSPACE*$(S(n))$ under the operations of union and intersection.

```
read x
read y
if x < y then
    do
        t := x
        x := y
        y := t
    until true
do
    t := x mod y
    x := y
    y := t
until t = 0
write x
if eof then accept
```

Figure 5.E.1

b. $DTIME\,(T(n))$ under the operations of union, intersection, and complementation.

5.1.4 Consider any two functions $T_1(n)$ and $T_2(n)$. Assume that for each constant c, there is a constant n_c such that $T_2(n) \geq cT_1(n)$ for all $n \geq n_c$. Show that $DTIME\,(T_1(n)) \subseteq DTIME\,(T_2(n))$.

5.1.5 *(Tape Compression Theorem)* Let c be any constant greater than 0. Show that each $S(n)$ space-bounded, m auxiliary-work-tape Turing machine M has an equivalent $cS(n)$ space-bounded, m auxiliary-work-tape Turing machine M_c.

5.1.6 Show that each of the following problems is in *NP*.

a. The *nonprimality problem* defined by the following pair.

Domain: $\{\,m \mid m$ is a natural number$\,\}$.

Question: Is the given instance m a nonprime number?

b. The *traveling-salesperson problem* defined by the following pair.

Domain: $\{\,(G, d, b) \mid G$ is a graph, d is a "distance" function that assigns a natural number to each edge of G, and b is a natural number$\,\}$.

Question: Does the given instance (G, d, b) have a cycle that contains all the nodes of G and is of length no greater than b?

c. The *partition problem* defined by the following pair.

Domain: $\{\,(a_1, \ldots, a_N) \mid N > 0$ and $a_1, \ldots, a_N$ are natural numbers$\,\}$.

Question: Is there a subset S of $\{a_1, \ldots, a_N\}$ for the given instance $(a_1, \ldots, a_N)$ such that (the sum of all the elements in S) = (the sum of all the elements in $\{a_1, \ldots, a_N\} - S$)?

5.1.7 Show that each of the following problems is in *NSPACE* $(\log n)$.

a. The *graph accessibility problem* defined by the following pair.

Domain: $\{(G, u, v) \mid G$ is a graph, and u and v are nodes of $G\}$.

Question: Is there a path from u to v in G for the given instance (G, u, v)?

b. The *c-bandwidth problem* for graphs defined by the following pair, where c is a natural number.

Domain: $\{G \mid G$ is a graph $\}$.

Question: Does the given graph $G = (V, E)$ have a linear ordering on V with bandwidth c or less, that is, a one-to-one function $f : V \to \{1, \ldots, |V|\}$ such that $|f(u) - f(v)| \leq c$ for all (u, v) in E?

5.1.8 Show that the following problems are solvable by logspace-bounded Turing transducers.

a. Sorting sequences of integers.

b. Addition of integers.

c. Multiplication of integers.

d. Multiplication of matrices of integers.

5.2.1 Show that each of the following functions is a fully time-constructible function.

a. n^k for $k \geq 1$.

b. 2^n.

5.2.2 Show that each of the following functions is a fully space-constructible function.

a. $\log n$.

b. $\sqrt{n}$.

5.2.3 Show that each space-constructible function $S(n) \geq n$ is also a fully space-constructible function.

5.2.4 Show that there are infinitely many functions $T_1(n)$ and $T_2(n)$ such that the containments $DTIME\,(T_1(n)) \subseteq DTIME\,(T_2(n)) \subseteq NP$ are proper.

5.2.5 Show that for each $T(n) > n$, the language $\{\, x \mid x = x_i$ and M_i is a deterministic Turing machine that does not accept x_i in $T(|x_i|)$ time $\}$ is not in $DTIME\,(T(n))$.

Hint: Use the following result.

Linear Speed-Up Theorem A $T(n)$ time-bounded Turing machine M_1 has an equivalent $cT(n)$ time-bounded Turing machine M_2 if $T(n) > n$ and $c > 0$. Moreover, M_2 is deterministic if M_1 is so.

5.2.6 *(Space Hierarchy Theorem)* Consider any function $S_1(n) \geq \log n$ and any fully space-constructible function $S_2(n)$. Assume that for each $c > 0$ there exists an n_c, such that $cS_1(n) < S_2(n)$ for all $n \geq n_c$. Show that there is a language in $DSPACE\,(S_2(n))$ that is not in $DSPACE\,(S_1(n))$.

5.3.1 What will be the value of

5.3.2 What will be the value of

     a. E_{init}

     b. E_{accept}

     c. $f_0(q_0, a, W, \tau_1)$

     d. $f_0(Y, q_0, a, \tau_1)$

     e. $f_0(Y, Z, q_0, \tau_1)$

     f. $f_0(Y, Z, W, \tau_1)$

     g. $f_1(q_0, B, W, \tau_1)$

     h. $f_1(Y, q_0, B, \tau_1)$

     i. $f_1(Y, Z, q_0, \tau_1)$

     j. $f_1(Y, Z, W, \tau_1)$

in Example 5.3.2 if $x = abb$?

5.3.3 Show that the proof of Theorem 5.3.1 implies a Boolean expression E_x of size $O((T(|x|)^2 \log T(|x|))$.

5.3.4 Show that the problem $\hat{K}$ concerning the solvability of systems of linear Diophantine equations over $\{0, 1\}$ is an *NP*-complete problem. Use a generic proof, in which each problem in *NP* is shown to be directly reducible to $\hat{K}$, to show the *NP*-hardness of the problem.

5.4.1 What is the instance of the $0 - 1$ knapsack problem that corresponds to the instance $(x_1 \lor \neg x_2 \lor x_4) \land (\neg x_1 \lor x_2 \lor x_3) \land (\neg x_2 \lor \neg x_3 \lor \neg x_4)$ of the 3-satisfiability problem, according to the proof of Theorem 5.4.1?

5.4.2 Modify the proof of Theorem 5.4.1 to show that the problem defined by the following pair, called the *integer knapsack problem*, is an *NP*-complete problem.

> *Domain:* $\{(a_1, \ldots, a_N, b) \mid N \geq 1,$ and $a_1, \ldots, a_N, b$ are natural numbers $\}$.

> *Question:* Are there natural numbers $v_1, \ldots, v_N$ such that $a_1 v_1 + \cdots + a_N v_N = b$ for the given instance $(a_1, \ldots, a_N, b)$?

Hint: Construct the system E so that its ith equation from the start equals the ith equation from the end.

5.4.3 Show, by reduction from the $0 - 1$ knapsack problem, that the partition problem is an *NP*-hard problem.

5.4.4 What is the instance of the clique problem that corresponds to the instance $(x_1 \vee \neg x_2 \vee x_4) \wedge (\neg x_1 \vee x_2 \vee x_3) \wedge (\neg x_2 \vee \neg x_3 \vee \neg x_4)$ of the 3 satisfiability problem, according to the proof of Theorem 5.4.2?

5.4.5 A *LOOP*(1) program is a *LOOP* program in which no nesting of **do**'s is allowed. Show that the inequivalence problem for *LOOP*(1) programs is an *NP*-hard problem.

5.5.1 Modify Example 5.5.1 for the case that M is the Turing machine in Figure 5.5.1(a) and $x = aba$.

5.5.2 The proof of Theorem 5.5.2 shows that

$$NSPACE\,(S_1(n)) \quad \subseteq \quad DSPACE\,(S_2(n))$$

for $S_2(n) = (S_1(n))^2$ if the following two conditions hold.

1. $S_1(n) \geq \log n$.
2. $S_1(n)$ is fully space-constructible.

   a. What is the bound that the proof implies for $S_2(n)$ if condition (1) is revised to have the form $S_1(n) < \log n$?
   b. Determine the time complexity of M_2 in the proof of Theorem 5.5.2.
   c. Show that condition (2) can be removed.

5.5.3 Modify Example 5.5.2 for the case that A is the Turing machine in Figure 5.5.1(a).

5.5.4 A *two-way finite-state automaton* is an 0 auxiliary-work-tape Turing machine. Show that the nonemptiness problem for two-way deterministic finite-state automata is *PSPACE*-complete.

5.5.5 Show that each $S(n) \geq \log n$ space-bounded Turing transducer M_1 has an equivalent $S(n)$ space-bounded Turing transducer M_2 that halts on all inputs.

5.6.1 Show that logspace reductions are closed under composition, that is, if problem K_a is logspace reducible to problem K_b and K_b is logspace reducible to problem K_c then K_a is logspace reducible to K_c.

5.6.2 Let G_x be the grammar of Example 5.6.1. List all the production rules $A \rightarrow \alpha$ of G_x that satisfy $\alpha \Rightarrow^* \epsilon$ but are not listed in the example.

5.6.3 The *circuit-valued problem*, or *CVP*, is defined by the following pair.

> *Domain*: $\{ (I_1, \ldots, I_m) \mid m \geq 0$, and each I_i is an instruction of any of the following forms.
>
> > a. $x_i := 0$.
> >
> > b. $x_i := 1$.
> >
> > c. $x_i := x_j \odot x_k$ for some $j < i$, $k < i$, and some function $\odot : \{0, 1\}^2 \rightarrow \{0, 1\}$.   }
>
> *Question*: Does $x_m = 1$ for the given instance $(I_1, \ldots, I_m)$?

Show that *CVP* is a *P*-complete problem.

Bibliographic Notes

The intensive interest in time and space complexity was spurted by Hartmanis and Stearns (1965). The relationship between RAM's and Turing transducers was considered in Cook and Reckhov (1973). The time hierarchy result in Theorem 5.2.1 and the Linear Speed-Up Theorem in Exercise 5.2.5 are from Hartmanis and Stearns (1965). Exercise 5.1.5 and Exercise 5.2.6 are from Stearns, Hartmanis, and Lewis (1965).

The polynomial time complexity of several problems was noticed by Cobham (1964). Edmonds (1965a) identified tractability with polynomial time, and informally defined the class *NP*. In addition, Edmonds (1965b) conjectured that the traveling-salesperson problem is in $NP - P$. Karp (1972) showed that the problem is *NP*-complete.

Cook (1971) laid the foundations for the theory of *NP*-completeness, by formally treating the $P = NP$ question and exhibiting the existence of *NP*-complete problems. The importance of the theory was demonstrated by Karp (1972) by exhibiting the *NP*-completeness of a large number of classical problems. Similar investigation was carried out independently by Levin (1973).

The *NP*-completeness of the satisfiability problem was shown in Cook (1971). Karp (1972) showed the *NP*-completeness of the clique problem, the partition problem, and the $0 - 1$ knapsack problem. The *NP*-completeness of the integer knapsack problem was shown by Lueker (1975). The *NP*-completeness of the inequivalence problem for $LOOP(1)$ programs was shown by Hunt, Constable, and Sahni (1980).

The quadratic relationship between deterministic and nondeterministic space in Theorem 5.5.2 is due to Savitch (1970). The *PSPACE*-completeness of the membership problem for linear bounded automata in Theorem 5.5.3 is due to Karp (1972). The *PSPACE*-completeness of the inequivalence problem for finite-state automata in Theorem 5.5.4 is implied from Kleene (1956). The *PSPACE*-completeness of the emptiness problem for two-way deterministic finite-state automata in Exercise 5.5.4 is due to Hunt (1973). The closure in Theorem 5.5.5

of $NSPACE(S(n))$ under complementation was independently obtained by Immerman (1987) and Szelepcsenyi (1987). Theorem 5.5.6 is due to Sipser (1978). Exercise 5.5.5 is due to Hopcroft and Ullman (1969).

The P-completeness in Theorem 5.6.1 of the emptiness problem for context-free grammars is due to Jones and Laaser (1976). The P-completeness in Exercise 5.6.3 of CVP is due to Ladner (1975).

Additional insight into the topic of resource-bounded computation is offered in Hopcroft and Ullman (1979), Garey and Johnson (1979), and Stockmeyer (1985).

Chapter 6

PROBABILISTIC COMPUTATION

So far, in analyzing programs for their time requirements, we have considered worst cases. Programs whose worst cases are good, are obviously the most desirable ones for solving given problems. However, in many circumstances we might also be satisfied with programs that generally behave well for each input, where no better program available. In fact, one might be satisfied with such programs, even when they contain a small probability of providing wrong answers. Programs of this nature are created by allowing instructions to make random choices. These types of programs are referred to as probabilistic.

The first section of this chapter introduces probabilistic instructions into programs. And the second section considers the usefulness of such programs that might err. The third section introduces the notion of probabilistic Turing transducers for modeling the computations of probabilistic programs. The chapter concludes with a consideration of some probabilistic polynomial time classes of problems.

6.1 Error-Free Probabilistic Programs

Randomization is an important programming tool. Intuitively, its power stems from choice. The ability to make "random choices" can be viewed as a derivation of the ability to make "nondeterministic choices."

In the nondeterministic case, each execution of an instruction must choose between a number of options. Some of the options might be "good", and others "bad." The choice must be for a good option, whenever it exists. The problem is that it does not generally seem possible to make nondeterministic choices in an efficient manner.

The options in the case for random choices are similar to those for the nondeterministic case, however, no restriction is made on the nature of the option to be chosen. Instead, each of the good and bad options is assumed to have an equal

```
call SELECT(k, S)
procedure SELECT(k,S)
    x  := first element in S
    S₁ := { y | y is in S, and y < x }
    n₁ := cardinality of the set stored in S₁
    S₂ := { y | y is in S, and y > x }
    n₂ := cardinality of the set stored in S₂
    n₃ := (cardinality of the set stored in S) − n₂
    case
            k ≤ n₁: SELECT(k, S₁)
            n₃ < k : SELECT(k − n₃, S₂)
        n₁ < k ≤ n₃: x holds the desired element
    end
end
```

Figure 6.1.1 A program that selects the kth smallest element in S.

probability of being chosen. Consequently, the lack of bias among the different options enables the efficient execution of choices. The burden of increasing the probability of obtaining good choices is placed on the programmer.

Here random choices are introduced to programs through *random assignment instructions* of the form $x := random(S)$, where S can be any finite set. An execution of a random assignment instruction $x := random(S)$ assigns to x an element from S, where each of the elements in S is assumed to have an equal probability of being chosen. Programs with random assignment instructions, and no nondeterministic instructions, are called *probabilistic programs*.

Each execution sequence of a probabilistic program is assumed to be a *computation*. On a given input a probabilistic program might have both accepting and nonaccepting computations.

The execution of a random assignment instruction $x := random(S)$ is assumed to take one unit of time under the uniform cost criteria, and $|v| + log|S|$ time under the logarithmic cost criteria. $|v|$ is assumed to be the length of the representation of the value v chosen from S, and $|S|$ is assumed to denote the cardinality of S.

A probabilistic program P is said to have an *expected time complexity* $\bar{t}(x)$ *on input* x if $\bar{t}(x)$ is equal to $p_0(x) \cdot 0 + p_1(x) \cdot 1 + p_2(x) \cdot 2 + \cdots$. The function $p_i(x)$ is assumed to be the probability for the program P to have on input x a computation that takes exactly i units of time.

The program P is said to have an *expected time complexity* $\overline{T}(n)$ if $\overline{T}(|x|) \geq \bar{t}(x)$ for each x.

The following example shows how probabilism can be used to guarantee an improved behavior (on average) for each input.

Example 6.1.1 Consider the deterministic program in Figure 6.1.1 (given in a free format using recursion). The program selects the kth smallest element in any given set S of finite cardinality.

Let $T(n)$ denote the time (under the uniform cost criteria) that the program takes to select an element from a set of cardinality n. $T(n)$ satisfies, for some constant c and some integer $m < n$, the following inequalities.

$$T(n) \leq \begin{cases} T(m) + cn & \text{if } n > 1 \\ \\ c & \text{if } n \leq 1 \end{cases}$$

From the inequalities above

$$
\begin{aligned}
T(n) &\leq T(n-1) + cn \\
&\leq T(n-2) + c\left(n + (n-1)\right) \\
&\leq T(n-3) + c\left(n + (n-1) + (n-2)\right) \\
&\leq \cdots \\
&\leq T(1) + c\left(n + (n-1) + \cdots + 2\right) \\
&\leq cn^2.
\end{aligned}
$$

That is, the program is of time complexity $O(n^2)$.

The time requirement of the program is sensitive to the ordering of the elements in the sets in question. For instance, when searching for the smallest element, $O(n)$ time is sufficient if the elements of the set are given in nondecreasing order. Alternatively, the program uses $O(n^2)$ time when the elements are given in nonincreasing order.

This sensitivity to the order of the elements can be eliminated by assigning a random element from S to x, instead of the first element of S. In such a case, the expected time complexity $\overline{T}(n)$ of the program satisfies the following inequalities, for some constant c.

$$\overline{T}(n) \leq \begin{cases} \frac{1}{n}\left(\overline{T}(0) + \overline{T}(1) + \cdots + \overline{T}(n-1)\right) + cn & \text{if } n > 1 \\ \\ c & \text{if } n \leq 1 \end{cases}$$

From the inequalities above

$$
\begin{aligned}
\overline{T}(n) &\leq \tfrac{1}{n}\left(\overline{T}(0) + \cdots + \overline{T}(n-1)\right) + cn \\
&\leq \tfrac{1}{n}\left(\overline{T}(0) + \cdots + \overline{T}(n-2)\right) \\
&\quad + \tfrac{1}{n}\left(\tfrac{1}{n-1}\left(\overline{T}(0) + \cdots + \overline{T}(n-2)\right)\right) + \tfrac{1}{n}\left(c(n-1)\right) + cn \\
&\leq \tfrac{1}{n}\left(1 + \tfrac{1}{n-1}\right)\left(\overline{T}(0) + \cdots + \overline{T}(n-2)\right) + c\left(1 - \tfrac{1}{n}\right) + cn \\
&\leq \tfrac{1}{n-1}\left(\overline{T}(0) + \cdots + \overline{T}(n-2)\right) + c + cn \\
&\leq \tfrac{1}{n-1}\left(\overline{T}(0) + \cdots + \overline{T}(n-3)\right) \\
&\quad + \tfrac{1}{n-1}\left(\tfrac{1}{n-2}\left(\overline{T}(0) + \cdots + \overline{T}(n-3)\right)\right) \\
&\quad + \tfrac{1}{n-1}\left(c(n-2)\right) + c + cn
\end{aligned}
$$

```
read x
y := random({2, ..., √x̄})
if x is divisible by y then
    answer := yes        /* not a prime number */
else answer := no
```

Figure 6.2.1 An undesirable probabilistic program for the nonprimality problem.

$$\leq \frac{1}{n-1}\left(1 + \frac{1}{n-2}\right)\left(\overline{T}(0) + \cdots + \overline{T}(n-3)\right) + 2c + cn$$
$$\leq \frac{1}{n-2}\left(\overline{T}(0) + \cdots + \overline{T}(n-3)\right) + 2c + cn$$
$$\leq \frac{1}{n-3}\left(\overline{T}(0) + \cdots + \overline{T}(n-4)\right) + 3c + cn$$
$$\leq \cdots$$
$$\leq \overline{T}(1) + (n-1)c + cn$$
$$\leq 2cn.$$

That is, the modified program is probabilistic and its expected time complexity is $O(n)$. For every given input (k, S) with S of cardinality $|S|$, the probabilistic program is guaranteed to find the kth smallest element in S within $O(|S|^2)$ time. However, on average it requires $O(|S|)$ time for a given input. □

6.2 Probabilistic Programs That Might Err

For many practical reasons programs might be allowed a small probability of erring on some inputs.

Example 6.2.1 A brute-force algorithm for solving the nonprimality problem takes exponential time (see Example 5.1.3). The program in Figure 6.2.1 is an example of a probabilistic program that determines the nonprimality of numbers in polynomial expected time.

The program has zero probability for an error on inputs that are prime numbers. However, for infinitely many nonprime numbers the program has a high probability of giving a wrong answer. Specifically, the probability for an error on a nonprime number m is $1 - s/(\sqrt{m} - 1)$, where s is assumed to be the number of distinct divisors of m in $\{2, ..., \sqrt{m}\}$. In particular, the probability for an error reaches the value of $1 - 1/(\sqrt{m} - 1)$ for those numbers m that are a square of a prime number.

The probability of getting a wrong answer for a given number m can be reduced by executing the program k times. In such a case, the number m is declared to be nonprime with full confidence, if in any of k executions the answer *yes* is obtained. Otherwise, m is determined to be prime with probability of at most $(1 - 1/(\sqrt{m} - 1))^k$ for an error. With $k = c(\sqrt{m} - 1)$ this probability approaches the value of $(1/\varrho)^c < 0.37^c$ as m increases, where ϱ is the constant $2.71828\ldots$

```
read x
y := random{2, ..., x − 1}
if Wₓ(y) then answer := yes
else answer := no
```

Figure 6.2.2 A good probabilistic program for the nonprimality problem.

However, such a value for k is forbidingly high, because it is exponential in the length of the representation of m, that is, in $\log m$.

An improved probabilistic program can be obtained by using the following known result.

Result Let $W_m(b)$ be a predicate that is *true* if and only if either of the following two conditions holds.

  a. $(b^{m-1} - 1) \bmod m \neq 0$.

  b. $1 < gcd(b^t - 1, m) < m$ for some t and i such that $m - 1 = t \cdot 2^i$.

Then for each integer $m \geq 2$ the conditions below hold.

  a. m is a prime number if and only if $W_m(b)$ is *false* for all b such that $2 \leq b < m$.

  b. If m is not prime, then the set $\{ b \mid 2 \leq b < m,$ and $W_m(b)$ holds $\}$ is of cardinality $(3/4)(m - 1)$ at least.

The result implies the probabilistic program in Figure 6.2.2. For prime numbers m the program always provides the right answers. On the other hand, for nonprime numbers m, the program provides the right answer with probability of at most $1 - (3/4)(m - 1)/(m - 2) \leq 1/4$ for an error.

The probability for a wrong answer can be reduced to any desired constant ϵ by executing the program for $k \geq \log_{1/4} \epsilon$ times. That is, the number of times k that the program has to be executed is independent of the input m.

Checking for the condition $(b^{m-1} - 1) \bmod m \neq 0$ can be done in polynomial time by using the relation $(a + b) \bmod m = ((a \bmod m) + (b \bmod m)) \bmod m$ and the relation $(ab) \bmod m = ((a \bmod m)(b \bmod m)) \bmod m$. Checking for the condition $gcd(b^t - 1, m)$ can be done in polynomial time by using Euclid's algorithm (see Exercise 5.1.1). Consequently, the program in Figure 6.2.2 is of polynomial time complexity. □

Example 6.2.2 Consider the problem of deciding for any given matrices A, B, and C whether $AB \neq C$. A brute-force algorithm to decide the problem can compute $D = AB$, and $E = D - C$, and check whether

$$
E \neq \begin{pmatrix} 0 & \cdots & 0 \\ \vdots & \ddots & \vdots \\ 0 & \cdots & 0 \end{pmatrix}
$$

A brute-force multiplication of A and B requires $O(N^3)$ time (under the uniform cost criteria), if A and B are of dimension $N \times N$. Therefore, the brute-force algorithm for deciding whether $AB \neq C$ also takes $O(N^3)$ time.

The inequality $AB \neq C$ holds if and only if the inequality

$$
(AB - C) \begin{pmatrix} \hat{x}_1 \\ \vdots \\ \hat{x}_N \end{pmatrix} \neq \begin{pmatrix} 0 \\ \vdots \\ 0 \end{pmatrix}
$$

holds for some vector

$$
\hat{x} = \begin{pmatrix} \hat{x}_1 \\ \vdots \\ \hat{x}_N \end{pmatrix}
$$

Consequently, the inequality $AB \neq C$ can be determined by a probabilistic program that determines

a. A column vector

$$
\hat{x} = \begin{pmatrix} \hat{x}_1 \\ \vdots \\ \hat{x}_N \end{pmatrix}
$$

of random numbers from $\{-1, 1\}$.

b. The value of the vector $\hat{y} = B\hat{x}$.

c. The value of the vector $\hat{z} = A\hat{y}$.

d. The value of the vector $\hat{u} = C\hat{x}$.

e. The value of the vector

$$
\begin{aligned}
\hat{v} &= \hat{z} - \hat{u} \\
&= A\hat{y} - C\hat{x} \\
&= AB\hat{x} - C\hat{x} \\
&= (AB - C)\hat{x} \\
&= \begin{pmatrix} d_{11} & \cdots & d_{1N} \\ \vdots & \ddots & \vdots \\ d_{N1} & \cdots & d_{NN} \end{pmatrix} \begin{pmatrix} \hat{x}_1 \\ \vdots \\ \hat{x}_N \end{pmatrix} \\
&= \begin{pmatrix} d_{11}\hat{x}_1 + \cdots + d_{1N}\hat{x}_N \\ \vdots \\ d_{N1}\hat{x}_1 + \cdots + d_{NN}\hat{x}_N \end{pmatrix}
\end{aligned}
$$

If some of the entries in the vector

$$
\hat{v} = \begin{pmatrix} d_{11}\hat{x}_1 + \cdots + d_{1N}\hat{x}_N \\ \vdots \\ d_{N1}\hat{x}_1 + \cdots + d_{NN}\hat{x}_N \end{pmatrix}
$$

are nonzeros, then the probabilistic program reports that the inequality $AB \neq C$ must hold. Otherwise, the program reports that $AB = C$ with probability of at most $1/2$ for an error. The program takes $O(N^2)$ time.

The analysis of the program for its error probability relies on the following result.

Result Let $d_1 x_1 + \cdots + d_N x_N = 0$ be a linear equation with coefficients that satisfy the inequality $(d_1, \ldots, d_N) \neq (0, \ldots, 0)$. Then the linear equation has at most 2^{N-1} solutions $(\hat{x}_1, \ldots, \hat{x}_N)$ over $\{-1, 1\}$.

Proof Consider any linear equation $d_1 x_1 + \cdots + d_N x_N = 0$. With no loss of generality assume that $d_1 > 0$.

If $(\hat{x}_1, \ldots, \hat{x}_N)$ is a solution to the linear equation over $\{-1, 1\}$ then $(-\hat{x}_1, \hat{x}_2, \ldots, \hat{x}_N)$ does not solve the equation. On the other hand, if both $(\hat{x}_1, \ldots, \hat{x}_N)$ and $(\tilde{x}_1, \ldots, \tilde{x}_N)$ solve the equation over $\{-1, 1\}$, then the inequality $(-\hat{x}_1, \hat{x}_2, \ldots, \hat{x}_N) \neq (-\tilde{x}_1, \tilde{x}_2, \ldots, \tilde{x}_N)$ holds whenever $(\hat{x}_1, \ldots, \hat{x}_N) \neq (\tilde{x}_1, \ldots, \tilde{x}_N)$.

As a result, each solution to the equation has an associated assignment that does not solve the equation. That is, at most half of the possible assignments over $\{-1, 1\}$ to $(x_1, \ldots, x_N)$ can serve as solutions to the equation. □

The probabilistic program can be executed k times on any given triplet A, B, and C. In such a case, if any of the executions results in a nonzero vector $\hat{v}$ then $AB \neq C$ must hold. Otherwise, $AB = C$ with probability of at most $(1/2)^k$ for an error. That is, by repeatedly executing the probabilistic program, one can reduce the error probability to any desired magnitude. Moreover, the resulting error probability of $(1/2)^k$ is guaranteed for all the possible choices of matrices A, B, and C. □

Error Probability of Repeatedly Executed Probabilistic Programs

The probabilistic programs in the previous two examples exhibit the property of one-sided error probability. Specifically, their *yes* answers are always correct. On the other hand, their *no* answers might sometimes be correct and sometimes wrong. In general, however, probabilistic programs might err on more than one kind of an answer. In such a case, the answer can be arrived at by taking the majority of answers obtained in repeated computations on the given instance.

The following lemma analyzes the probability of error in repeated computations to establish an answer by absolute majority.

Lemma 6.2.1 Consider any probabilistic program P. Assume that P has probability e of providing an output that differs from y on input x. Then P has probability

$$\Phi(N, e) = \sum_{k=0}^{N} \binom{2N+1}{k} e^{2N+1-k} (1-e)^k$$

of having at least $N + 1$ computations with outputs that differ from y in any
sequence of $2N + 1$ computations of P on input x.

Proof Let P, x, y, and e be as in the statement of the lemma. Let $\varphi(N, e, k)$
denote the probability that, in a sequence of $2N + 1$ computations on input x, P
will have exactly k computations with an output that is equal to y. Let $\Phi(N, e)$
denote the probability that, in a sequence of $2N + 1$ computations on input x, P
will have at least $N + 1$ computations with outputs that differ from y.

By definition,

$$
\begin{aligned}
\Phi(N, e) \quad = \quad & \text{(Probability that in exactly } 2N + 1 \text{ computations the} \\
& \text{output will not equal } y) \\
& + \text{ (Probability that in exactly } 2N \text{ computations the} \\
& \quad\ \text{output will not equal } y) \\
& \ \ \vdots \\
& + \text{ (Probability that in exactly } N+1 \text{ computations the} \\
& \quad\ \text{output will not equal } y) \\
= \quad & \text{(Probability that in exactly } 0 \text{ computations the output} \\
& \text{will equal } y) \\
& + \text{ (Probability that in exactly } 1 \text{ computation the out-} \\
& \quad\ \text{put will equal } y) \\
& \ \ \vdots \\
& + \text{ (Probability that in exactly } N \text{ computations the out-} \\
& \quad\ \text{put will equal } y) \\
= \quad & \sum_{k=0}^{N} \varphi(N, e, k).
\end{aligned}
$$

The probability of having the answer y at and only at the i_1 st, $\ldots$, i_k th computations, in a sequence of $2N + 1$ computations of P on input x, is equal to

$$
e^{i_1 - 1}(1 - e)e^{i_2 - i_1 - 1}(1 - e)e^{i_3 - i_2 - 1}(1 - e) \cdots e^{i_k - i_{k-1} - 1}(1 - e)e^{2N+1-i_k}
$$
$$
= \quad (1 - e)^k e^{2N+1-k}
$$

$i_1, \ldots, i_k$ are assumed to satisfy $1 \le i_1 < i_2 < \cdots < i_k \le 2N + 1$.

Each collection $\{C_1, \ldots, C_{2N+1}\}$ of $2N + 1$ computations of P has

$$
(2N + 1)(2N)(2N - 1) \cdots (2N + 1 - k + 1) \quad = \quad \frac{(2N+1)!}{(2N+1-k)!}
$$

possible arrangements $C_{i_1} \cdots C_{i_k}$ of k computations. In these arrangements only

$$
\frac{(2N+1)!}{k!\,(2N+1-k)!} \quad = \quad \binom{2N+1}{k}
$$

satisfy the condition $i_1 < \cdots < i_k$. Consequently, in each sequence of $2N + 1$
computations of P there are $\binom{2N+1}{k}$ possible ways to obtain the output y for exactly
k times.

The result follows because $\varphi(N, e, k) =$ (the number of possible sequences of
$2N + 1$ computations in which exactly k computations have the output y) times
(the probability of having a sequence of $2N + 1$ computations with exactly k
outputs of y).   □

In general, we are interested only in probabilistic programs which run in polynomial time, and which have error probability that can be reduced to a desired constant by executing the program for some polynomial number of times. The following theorem considers the usefulness of probabilistic programs that might err.

Theorem 6.2.1 Let $\Phi(N, e)$ be as in the statement of Lemma 6.2.1. Then $\Phi(N, e)$ has the following properties.

    a. $\Phi(N, \frac{1}{2}) = 1/2$ for all N.

    b. $\Phi(N, e)$ approaches 0 for each constant $e < 1/2$, when N approaches ∞.

    c. $\Phi(N, \frac{1}{2} - \frac{1}{N})$ approaches a constant that is greater than $1/(2\varrho^6)$, when N approaches ∞.

Proof   a. The equality $\Phi(N, \frac{1}{2}) = 1/2$ for all N is implied from the following relations.

$$
\begin{aligned}
2\Phi(N, \tfrac{1}{2}) &= 2 \sum_{k=0}^{N} \binom{2N+1}{k} \left(\tfrac{1}{2}\right)^{2N+1-k} \left(1 - \tfrac{1}{2}\right)^{k} \\
&= \sum_{k=0}^{N} \binom{2N+1}{k} \left(\tfrac{1}{2}\right)^{2N+1-k} \left(1 - \tfrac{1}{2}\right)^{k} \\
&\quad + \sum_{k=N+1}^{2N+1} \binom{2N+1}{k} \left(\tfrac{1}{2}\right)^{2N+1-k} \left(1 - \tfrac{1}{2}\right)^{k} \\
&= \left(\tfrac{1}{2} + \left(1 - \tfrac{1}{2}\right)\right)^{2N+1} \\
&= 1
\end{aligned}
$$

b. The equality

$$
\sum_{k=0}^{2N+1} \binom{2N+1}{k} = 2^{2N+1}
$$

implies the following inequality for $0 \le k \le 2N + 1$.

$$
\binom{2N+1}{k} \le 2^{2N+1}
$$

Consequently, the result is implied from the following relations that hold for $e = 1/2 - \delta$.

$$
\begin{aligned}
\Phi(N, e) &= \sum_{k=0}^{N} \binom{2N+1}{k} e^{2N+1-k} (1 - e)^{k} \\
&\le (N + 1) \binom{2N+1}{N} e^{N+1} (1 - e)^{N}
\end{aligned}
$$

$$\leq \;\; (N+1)2^{2N+1}e^{N+1}(1-e)^N$$
$$= \;\; (N+1)2^{2N+1}\left(\tfrac{1}{2}-\delta\right)^{N+1}\left(\tfrac{1}{2}+\delta\right)^N$$
$$= \;\; 2\left(\tfrac{1}{2}-\delta\right)(N+1)(1-2\delta)^N(1+2\delta)^N$$
$$= \;\; 2e(N+1)(1-4\delta^2)^N$$

c. The result follows from the following relations because $(1-2/N)^{N/2}$ approaches $1/\varrho$ with N.

$$\Phi\left(N,\tfrac{1}{2}-\tfrac{1}{N}\right) \;=\; \sum_{k=0}^{N}\binom{2N+1}{k}\left(\tfrac{1}{2}-\tfrac{1}{N}\right)^{2N+1-k}\left(1-\left(\tfrac{1}{2}-\tfrac{1}{N}\right)\right)^{k}$$

$$=\; \sum_{k=0}^{N}\binom{2N+1}{k}\left(\tfrac{1}{2}-\tfrac{1}{N}\right)^{2N+1-k}\left(\tfrac{1}{2}+\tfrac{1}{N}\right)^{k}$$

$$=\; \left(\tfrac{1}{2}-\tfrac{1}{N}\right)^{2N+1}\sum_{k=0}^{N}\binom{2N+1}{k}\left(\frac{1/2+1/N}{1/2-1/N}\right)^{k}$$

$$>\; \left(\tfrac{1}{2}-\tfrac{1}{N}\right)^{2N+1}\sum_{k=0}^{N}\binom{2N+1}{k}$$

$$=\; \tfrac{1}{2}\left(\tfrac{1}{2}-\tfrac{1}{N}\right)^{2N+1}\sum_{k=0}^{2N+1}\binom{2N+1}{k}$$

$$=\; \tfrac{1}{2}\left(\tfrac{1}{2}-\tfrac{1}{N}\right)^{2N+1}(1+1)^{2N+1}$$

$$=\; \tfrac{1}{2}\left(1-\tfrac{2}{N}\right)^{2N+1}$$

$$=\; \tfrac{1}{2}\left(\left(1-\tfrac{2}{N}\right)^{N/2}\right)^{(4+2/N)}$$

$$\geq\; \tfrac{1}{2}\left(\left(1-\tfrac{2}{N}\right)^{N/2}\right)^{6}$$

$\square$

According to Theorem 6.2.1(a), a probabilistic program must have an error probability $e(x)$ smaller than $1/2$, in order to reduce in the probability of obtaining a wrong solution through repeatedly running the program. According to Theorem 6.2.1(b), error probability $e(x)$ smaller than some constant $\epsilon < 1/2$ allows a reduction to a desired magnitude in speed that is independent from the given input x. On the other hand, by Theorem 6.2.1(c) the required speed of reduction is bounded below by $f(x) = 1/((1/2)-e(x))$, because the probability $\Phi(f(x),e(x))$ of obtaining a wrong solution through repeatedly running the program for $f(x)$ times is greater than $1/(2\varrho^6)$. In particular, when $f(x)$ is more than a polynomial in $|x|$, then the required speed of reduction is similarly greater.

Outputs of Probabilistic Programs

The previous theorems motivate the following definitions.

A probabilistic program P is said to have an *output* y on input x, if the probability of P having a computation with output y on input x is greater than $1/2$. If no such y exists, then the output of P on input x is undefined.

A probabilistic program P is said to *compute a function* $f(x)$ if P on each input x has probability $1 - e(x)$ for an accepting computation with output $f(x)$, where

a. $e(x) < 1/2$ whenever $f(x)$ is defined.

b. $e(x)$ is undefined whenever $f(x)$ is undefined.

$e(x)$ is said to be the *error probability* of P. The error probability $e(x)$ is said to be a *bounded-error probability* if there exists a constant $\epsilon < 1/2$ such that $e(x) \le \epsilon$ for all x on which $e(x)$ is defined. P is said to be a *bounded-error probabilistic program* if it has a bounded-error probability.

By the previous discussion it follows that the probabilistic programs, which have both polynomial time complexity and bounded-error probability, are "good" programs.

6.3   Probabilistic Turing Transducers

The study of nonprobabilistic computations employed the abstract models of deterministic and nondeterministic Turing transducers. For the study of probabilistic computations we will use similar abstract models, called probabilistic Turing transducers.

Informally, a probabilistic Turing transducer is a Turing transducer that views nondeterminism as randomness. Formally, a *probabilistic Turing transducer* is a Turing transducer $M = <Q, \Sigma, \Gamma, \Delta, \delta, q_0, B, F>$ whose computations are defined in the following manner.

A sequence C of the moves of M is said to be a *computation* if the two conditions below hold.

a. C starts at an initial configuration.

b. Whenever C is finite, it ends either at an accepting configuration or a nonaccepting configuration from which no move is possible.

A computation of M is said to be an *accepting computation* if it ends at an accepting configuration. Otherwise, the computation is said to be a *nonaccepting*, or a *rejecting, computation*.

By definition, a probabilistic Turing transducer might have both accepting computations and nonaccepting computations on a given input.

Each computation of a probabilistic Turing transducer is similar to that of a nondeterministic Turing transducer, the only exception arising upon reaching a configuration from which more than one move is possible. In such a case, the

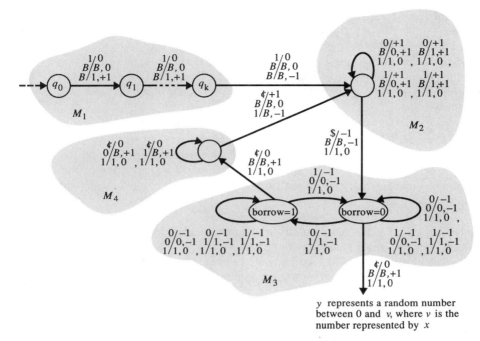

Figure 6.3.1 A segment of a probabilistic Turing machine that generates a random number.

choice between the possible moves is made randomly, with an equal probability of each move occurring.

The function that a probabilistic Turing transducer computes and its error probability are defined similarly to probabilistic programs. *Probabilistic Turing machines* are defined similarly to probabilistic Turing transducers.

A probabilistic Turing machine M is said to *accept a language L* if

a. On input x from L, M has probability $1 - e(x) > 1/2$ for an accepting computation.

b. On input x not from L, M has probability $1 - e(x) > 1/2$ for a nonaccepting computation.

$e(x)$ is said to be the *error probability* of M. The error probability is said to be *bounded* if there exists a constant $\epsilon < 1/2$ such that $e(x) \leq \epsilon$ for all x. M is said to be a *bounded-error probabilistic Turing machine* if it has bounded-error probability.

Example 6.3.1 Figure 6.3.1 gives the transition diagram of a segment M of a probabilistic Turing machine. On input x, M finds a random number between 0 and v, with probability $1 - (1/2)^k$. x is assumed to be a string in $\{0,1\}^*$ that starts with 1, and v is assumed to be the natural number represented by x. The binary representation of the random number is stored in the first auxiliary work tape.

M starts each computation by employing M_1 for recording the value of k. Then M repeatedly employs M_2, M_3, and M_4 for generating a random string y of length $|x|$, and checking whether y represents an integer no greater than v. M terminates its subcomputation successfully if and only if it finds such a string y within k tries.

M_1 records the value of k in unary in the second auxiliary work tape of M. In the first auxiliary work tape of M, M_2 generates a random string y of length $|x|$ over $\{0, 1\}$. M_3 checks whether x represents a number greater than the one y represents. M_3 performs the checking by simulating a subtraction of the corresponding numbers. M_4 erases the string y that is stored on the first auxiliary work tape.

The number of executed cycles M_2, M_3, M_4 is controlled by the length k of the string $1 \cdots 1$ that is stored on the second auxiliary work tape. At the end of each cycle the string shrinks by one symbol.

The probability that M_2 will generate a string that represents a number between 0 and v is $(v+1)/2^{|x|} \geq 1/2$. The probability that such a string will be generated in k cycles is

> (Probability of generating the string in the first cycle)
> $+$ (Probability of generating the string in the second cycle, but not in the first cycle)
> $\vdots$
> $+$ (Probability of generating the string in the kth cycle, but not in the first $k-1$ cycles).

The sum of these probabilities is equal to

$$
\begin{aligned}
&\tfrac{v+1}{2^{-|x|}} \left(1 + \left(1 - \tfrac{v+1}{2^{-|x|}}\right) + \left(1 - \tfrac{v+1}{2^{-|x|}}\right)^2 + \cdots + \left(1 - \tfrac{v+1}{2^{-|x|}}\right)^{k-1}\right) \\
&= \tfrac{v+1}{2^{-|x|}} \left(\left(1 - \tfrac{v+1}{2^{-|x|}}\right)^k - 1\right) \left(\left(1 - \tfrac{v+1}{2^{-|x|}}\right) - 1\right)^{-1} \\
&= 1 - \left(1 - \tfrac{v+1}{2^{-|x|}}\right)^k \\
&\geq 1 - (1/2)^k. \qquad\qquad\qquad\qquad\qquad\qquad\qquad\qquad\qquad \Box
\end{aligned}
$$

The probabilistic Turing machine in the following example is, in essence, a probabilistic pushdown automaton that accepts a non-context-free language. This automaton can be modified to make exactly $n+2$ moves on each input of length n, whereas each one auxiliary-work-tape, nonprobabilistic Turing machine seems to require more than $n+2$ time to recognize the language.

Example 6.3.2 The one auxiliary-work-tape, probabilistic Turing machine M of Figure 6.3.2 accepts the language $L = \{\, w \mid w \text{ is in } \{a_1, b_1, \ldots, a_k, b_k\}^*, \text{ and } w$ has the same number of a_i's as b_i's for each $1 \leq i \leq k \,\}$.

M on any given input w starts its computation by choosing randomly some number r between 1 and $2k$. It does so by moving from the initial state q_0 to the

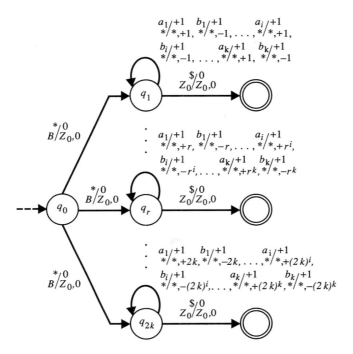

Figure 6.3.2 A one auxiliary-work-tape, probabilistic Turing machine M that accepts the language $L = \{ w \mid w$ is in $\{a_1, b_1, \ldots, a_k, b_k\}^*$, and w has the same number of a_i's as b_i's for each $1 \leq i \leq k \}$. ($^{c}_{*}/^{+1}_{*,j}$ stands for a sequence of j transition rules that move the head of the auxiliary work tape, j positions to the right. The sequence does not change the content of the tape.)

corresponding state q_r. In addition, M writes Z_0 on its auxiliary work tape. Then M moves its auxiliary work-tape head r^i positions to the right for each symbol a_i that it reads, and r^i positions to the left for each symbol b_i that it reads.

At the end of each computation, the auxiliary work-tape head is located $(n(a_1) - n(b_1))r + (n(a_2) - n(b_2))r^2 + \cdots + (n(a_k) - n(b_k))r^k$ positions to the right of Z_0, where $n(c)$ denotes the number of times the symbol c appears in w. If the head is located on Z_0, then the input is accepted. Otherwise, the input is rejected.

By construction, M accepts each input w from the language L. Alternatively, M might also accept some strings not in L with probability $e(x) = \epsilon < 1/2$, where $\epsilon = (k - 1)/(2k)$.

The equality $\epsilon = (k - 1)/(2k)$ holds because if w is not in L then $n(a_i) - n(b_i) \neq 0$ for at least one i. In such a case, the equation $(n(a_1) - n(b_1))r + \cdots + (n(a_k) - n(b_k))r^k = 0$ can be satisfied by at most $k - 1$ nonzero values of r. However, there are $2k$ possible assignments for r. As a result the probability that r will get a value that satisfies the equation is no greater than $\epsilon = (k - 1)/(2k)$.

The bound ϵ on the error probability $e(x)$ can be reduced to any desirable value, by allowing r to be randomly assigned with a value from $\{1, \ldots, \lceil k/\epsilon \rceil\}$.

M takes no more than $T(n) = (2k)^k n + 2$ moves on input of length n. M can be modified to make exactly $T(n) = n + 2$ moves by recording values modulo $(2k)^k$ in the auxiliary work tape. In such a case, smaller intermediate values are stored in the finite-state control of M. $\square$

6.4   Probabilistic Polynomial Time

As in the case of deterministic and nondeterministic Turing transducers, each move of a probabilistic Turing transducer is assumed to take one unit of time. The *time* that a computation takes is assumed to be equal to the number of moves made during the computation. The *space* the computation takes is assumed to equal the number of locations visited in the auxiliary work tape, which has the maximal such number.

Probabilistic Time Complexity

A probabilistic Turing transducer M is said to be $T(n)$ *time-bounded*, or of *time complexity* $T(n)$, if M halts within $T(n)$ time in each computation on each input of length n. If $T(n)$ is a polynomial, then M is also said to be *polynomially time-bounded*, or to have *polynomial time complexity*.

M is said to be $T(n)$ *expected time-bounded*, or of *expected time complexity* $T(n)$, if for each input x of M the function $T(n)$ satisfies

$$T(|x|) \geq \sum_{j=0}^{\infty} \left(\begin{array}{c} \text{Probability that } M \text{ on input } x \text{ will have} \\ \text{a computation that takes exactly j moves} \end{array} \right) \cdot j$$

If $T(n)$ is a polynomial, then M is said to be *polynomially expected time-bounded*, or of *polynomially expected time complexity*.

Arguments similar to those given for Church's Thesis in Section 4.1, and for the sequential computation thesis in Section 5.1, also apply for the following thesis.

The Probabilistic Computation Thesis   A function that is computable mechanically with the aid of probabilistic choices can also be computed by a probabilistic Turing transducer of polynomially related time complexity and polynomially related, expected time complexity.

Probabilistic Complexity Classes

The tractability of problems with respect to probabilistic time is determined by the existence of bounded-error probabilistic Turing transducers of polynomial time complexity for solving the problems. In light of this observation, the following classes of language recognition problems are of interest here.

> *BPP* — the class of membership problems for the languages in
>
>> $\{\, L \mid L$ is a language accepted by a bounded-error probabilistic Turing machine of polynomial time complexity $\}$.

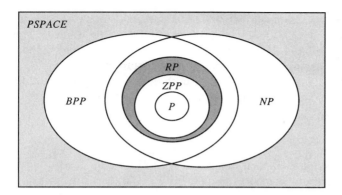

Figure 6.4.1 A hierarchy of some classes of problems.

RP — the class of membership problems for the languages in

{ L | L is a language accepted by a polynomially time-bounded, probabilistic Turing machine M, which satisfies the following two conditions for some constant $\epsilon < 1$.

    a. On input x from L, M has an accepting computation with probability $1 - e(x) \geq 1 - \epsilon$.

    b. On input x not from L, M has only nonaccepting computations.   }

ZPP — the class of membership problems for the languages in

{ L | L is a language accepted by a probabilistic Turing machine, which has zero error probability and polynomially expected time complexity. }

Relationships between Probabilistic and Nonprobabilistic Complexity Classes

The relationship between the different classes of problems, as well as their relationship to the classes studied in Chapter 5, is illustrated in Figure 6.4.1. None of the inclusions is known to be proper. The relationship is proved below.

Theorem 6.4.1 *BPP* is included in *PSPACE*.

Proof Consider any problem K in *BPP*. Let L denote the language that K induces. By the definition of *BPP* there exists a bounded-error, polynomially time-bounded, probabilistic Turing machine M_1 that accepts L. Let $\epsilon < 1/2$ be a constant that bounds the error probability of M_1, and let $p(n)$ be the time complexity of M_1.

With no loss of generality it is assumed that M_1 has a constant k, such that in each probabilistic move, M_1 has exactly k options. (Any probabilistic Turing machine can be modified to have such a property, with k being the least common multiple of the number of options in the different moves of the Turing machine.)

In addition, it is assumed that M_1 has some polynomial $q(n)$, such that in each computation on each input x it makes exactly $q(|x|)$ probabilistic moves. Consequently, M_1 on each input x has exactly $k^{q(|x|)}$ possible computations, with each computation having an equal probability of occurring.

From M_1, a deterministic Turing machine M_2 can be constructed to accept the language L. M_2 relies on the following two properties of M_1.

   a. If x is in L, then M_1 has at least probability $1 - \epsilon > 1/2$ of having an accepting computation on input x.

   b. If x is not in L, then M_1 has at least probability $1 - \epsilon > 1/2$ of having a nonaccepting computation on input x.

On a given input x, M_2 determines which of the above properties holds, and accordingly decides whether to accept or reject the input.

Given an input x, the Turing machine M_2 starts its computation by computing $p(|x|)$. Then one at a time, M_2 lists all the sequences of transition rules of M_1 whose lengths are at most $p(|x|)$. For each such sequence, M_2 checks whether the sequence corresponds to a computation of M_1. M_2 determines whether each computation of M_1 is accepting or rejecting. In addition, M_2 counts the number m_a of accepting computations, and the number m_r of nonaccepting computations.

M_2 accepts the input x if it determines that the probability $m_a/(m_a + m_r)$ of M_1 accepting x is greater than $1/2$, that is, if $m_a > m_r$. M_2 rejects x if it determines that the probability $m_r/(m_a + m_r)$ of M_1 rejecting x is greater than $1/2$, that is, if $m_r > m_a$.   □

The nonprimality problem is an example of a problem in the class RP (see Example 6.2.1). For RP the following result holds.

Theorem 6.4.2 RP is in $BPP \cap NP$.

Proof Consider any problem K in RP. Let L be the language that K induces. By the definition of RP, it follows that there exist a constant $\epsilon < 1$, and a polynomially time-bounded Turing machine M_1, that satisfy the following conditions.

   a. If x is in L, then M_1 has a probability $1 - \epsilon > 0$ of having an accepting computation on x.

   b. If x is not in L, then M_1 has only nonaccepting computations on x.

L is accepted by a nondeterministic Turing machine M_2 similar to M_1 and of identical time complexity. The only difference is that M_2 considers each probabilistic move of M_1 as nondeterministic. Consequently, RP is in NP.

M_1 can also be simulated by a bounded-error probabilistic Turing machine M_3 of similar time complexity. Specifically, let k be any constant such that $\epsilon^k < 1/2$. Then M_3 simulates k computations of M_1 on a given input x. M_3 accepts x if M_1 accepts x in any of the simulated computations. Otherwise, M_3 rejects x. It follows that RP is also in BPP.   □

Finally, for *ZPP* the following result is shown.

Theorem 6.4.3 *ZPP* is contained in *RP*.

Proof Consider any probabilistic Turing machine M_1 that has 0 error probability. Let $\overline{T}(n)$ denote the expected time complexity of M_1. Assume that $\overline{T}(n)$ is some polynomial in n.

From M_1, a probabilistic Turing machine M_2 of the following form can be constructed. Given an input x, the probabilistic Turing machine M_2 starts its computation by evaluating $\overline{T}(|x|)$. Then M_2 simulates $c\overline{T}(|x|)$ moves of M_1 on input x for some constant $c > 1$. M_2 halts in an accepting state if during the simulation it reaches an accepting state of M_1. Otherwise, M_2 halts in a nonaccepting state.

By construction M_2 has no accepting computation on input x if x is not in $L(M_1)$. On the other hand, if x is in $L(M_1)$, then M_2 halts in a nonaccepting state, with probability equal to that of M_1 having an accepting computation that requires more than $c\overline{T}(|x|)$ moves. That is, the error probability $e(x)$ is equal to $\sum_{i=c\overline{T}(|x|)+1}^{\infty} p_i$, where p_i denotes the probability that, on x, M_1 will have a computation that takes exactly i steps.

Now

$$\overline{T}(|x|) \geq \overline{t}(x)$$
$$= p_0 \cdot 0 + p_1 \cdot 1 + \cdots + p_{c\overline{T}(|x|)} \cdot c\overline{T}(|x|) + \cdots$$
$$\geq p_0 \cdot 0 + p_1 \cdot 1 + \cdots + p_{c\overline{T}(|x|)} \cdot c\overline{T}(|x|) + (c\overline{T}(|x|) + 1) \cdot \sum_{i=c\overline{T}(|x|)+1}^{\infty} p_i$$
$$= p_0 \cdot 0 + p_1 \cdot 1 + \cdots + p_{c\overline{T}(|x|)} \cdot c\overline{T}(|x|) + (c\overline{T}(|x|) + 1)e(x)$$
$$= (c\overline{T}(|x|) + 1) e(x) + \cdots$$

Consequently, M_2 accepts x with probability

$$1 - e(x) \geq 1 - \frac{\overline{T}(|x|)}{c\overline{T}(|x|) + 1}$$
$$\geq 1 - 1/c \qquad \square$$

Exercises

6.1.1 The recursive program in Figure 6.E.1 sorts any given sequence A of natural numbers. The program requires time $T(n) = T(m - 1) + T(n - m) + O(n)$ under the uniform cost criteria for some $1 \leq m \leq n$. The recurrence equation in $T(n)$ implies that $T(n) \leq O(n^2)$. That is, the program is of $O(n^2)$ time complexity.

Find a probabilistic variation of the program that has $O(n \log n)$ expected time complexity.

```
call QuickSort(A)
procedure QuickSort(A)
   if A has cardinality 1 then return
   A₁ := elements in A that are smaller than A(1)
   A₂ := elements in A that are greater than A(1)
   call QuickSort(A₁)
   call QuickSort(A₂)
   A := concatenation of (A₁, A − A₁ − A₂, A₂)
   return
end
```

Figure 6.E.1

Hint: A proof by induction can be used to show that $T(n) = O(n \log n)$ if $T(n) \leq cn + 2/n \sum_{i=0}^{n-1} T(i)$.

6.2.1 Let K be the problem in Example 6.2.2 of deciding the inequality $AB \neq C$ for matrices. Consider the following algorithm.

Step 1 Randomly choose an entry (i, j) in matrix C for the given instance (A, B, C) of K, and let d_1 denote the element at this entry.

Step 2 Use the ith row of A and the jth column of B to compute the value d_2 at entry (i, j) of AB.

Step 3 Declare that the inequality $AB \neq C$ holds if $d_1 \neq d_2$. Otherwise, declare that $AB = C$.

What are the time complexity and the error probability of the algorithm?

6.2.2 A univariate polynomial $s(x)$ in variable x of degree N has the form $a_0 x^N + a_1 x^{N-1} + \cdots + a_{N-1} x + a_N$. A brute-force algorithm for deciding the equality $p(x) \cdot q(x) = t(x)$ takes $O(N^2)$ time under the uniform cost criteria, if $p(x)$, $q(x)$, and $t(x)$ are univariate polynomials of degree N, at most, and the coefficients are natural numbers. Show that a probabilistic program can decide the problem in $O(N)$ time, with an error probability smaller than some constant $\epsilon < 1/2$.

Hint: Note that a univariate polynomial $s(x)$ of degree N has at most N roots, that is, N values x_0 such that $s(x_0) = 0$.

6.2.3 Let K be the problem defined by the following pair. (See page 45 for the definitions of polynomial expressions and Diophantine polynomials.)

Domain: $\{ E(x_1, \ldots, x_m) \mid E(x_1, \ldots, x_m)$ is a polynomial expression with variables $x_1, \ldots, x_n \}$.

Question: Does the given instance represent a Diophantine polynomial that is identically equal to zero?

Show that K is solvable

    a. Deterministically in exponential time.

    b. Probabilistically in polynomial time.

Hint: Show that each Diophantine polynomial $E(x_1, \ldots, x_m)$ of degree d that is not identically equal to 0 has at most N^m/c roots $(\hat{x}_1, \ldots, \hat{x}_m)$ that satisfy $1 \leq \hat{x}_1, \ldots, \hat{x}_m \leq N$, if $N \geq cd$ and $c \geq 1$.

6.3.1 Let M_1 be a probabilistic Turing machine with error probability $e(x) < 1/3$. Find a probabilistic Turing machine M_2 that accepts $L(M_1)$ with error probability $e(x) < 7/27$.

6.3.2 Show that an error-bounded probabilistic pushdown automaton can accept the language $\{a^i b^i c^i \mid i \geq 0\}$.

6.3.3 a. Show that if $(v_1, \ldots, v_m)$ is a nonzero vector of integers and $d_1, \ldots, d_m$ are chosen randomly from $\{1, \ldots, r\}$ then $d_1 v_1 + \cdots + d_m v_m = 0$ with probability no greater than $1/r$.

    b. Show that $L = \{a^1 b^m a^2 b^{m-1} \cdots a^m b^1 \mid m \geq 0\}$ is accepted by a bounded-error probabilistic pushdown automaton.

    Hint: Use part (a) of the problem to check that the inputs have the form $a^{i_1} b^{j_1} a^{i_2} b^{j_2} \cdots a^{i_m} b^{j_m}$ with $i_2 - i_1 - 1 = 0$, $i_3 - i_2 - 1 = 0$, $\ldots$ and $j_1 - j_2 - 1 = 0$, $j_2 - j_3 - 1 = 0$, $\ldots$

6.3.4 Show that a language accepted by an n-states, nondeterministic finite-state automaton M_1 is also accepted by an $(n+d)$-states, bounded-error, two-way, probabilistic finite-state automaton M_2, that is, an $(n+d)$-states, bounded-error, 0 auxiliary-work-tape, probabilistic Turing machine M_2. d is assumed to be a constant independent of M_1.

Hint: Allow M_2 to halt in a rejecting configuration with probability $(1/2)^n$ and to start a new simulation of M_1 with probability $1 - (1/2)^n$, after simulating a nonaccepting computation of M_1.

6.4.1 Show that *ZPP* and *BPP* are each closed under union.

6.4.2 Show that each function computable by a bounded-error probabilistic Turing transducer with polynomially time-bounded complexity, is also computable by a polynomially space-bounded, deterministic Turing transducer.

Bibliographic Notes

Probabilistic choices have been used for a long time in algorithms. The surge of interest in probabilistic computations is motivated by the work of Rabin (1976), Solovay and Strassen (1977), and Gill (1977).

    The probabilistic algorithm in Example 6.1.1, for finding the kth smallest integer, is after Aho, Hopcroft, and Ullman (1974). The probabilistic algorithm in Example 6.2.1 for checking nonprimality is due to Rabin (1976). A similar algorithm was discovered independently by Solovay and Strassen (1977). Example 6.2.2 and Exercise 6.2.2 are from Freivalds (1979). Exercise 6.2.3 is from Schwartz (1980).

Probabilistic Turing machines were introduced by DeLeeuw, Moore, Shannon, and Shapiro (1956). Example 6.3.2 and Exercise 6.3.3 are from Freivalds (1979). Exercise 6.3.4, the results in Section 6.4, and Exercise 6.4.1, are due to Gill (1977).

Johnson (1984), Maffioli, Speranza, and Vercellis (1985) and Welsh (1983) provide surveys and bibliographies for the field.

Chapter 7

PARALLEL COMPUTATION

The previous chapter studied the applicability of randomness to speeding up sequential computations. This chapter considers how parallelism achieves a similar objective. The first section introduces the notion of parallelism in programs. A generalization of RAM's, called parallel random access machines, or PRAM's, that allows a high-level abstraction for parallel computations is taken up in Section 2. The third section introduces families of Boolean circuits, with the goal of providing a hardware-level abstraction for parallel computations. The problems involved in adapting the general class of families of Boolean circuits as a low-level abstraction is discussed in Section 4, and a restricted class is proposed for such a purpose. The families in this restricted class are called uniform families of circuits. The fifth section relates the uniform families of circuits to sequential computations. In particular, it shows that parallelism does not increase the class of tractable problems. In addition, it discusses the applicability of parallelism in significantly increasing the speed of feasible computations. In Section 6 the chapter concludes by relating PRAM's and uniform families of circuits.

7.1 Parallel Programs

A parallel program $\hat{P}$ is a system $<P, X, Y>$ of infinitely many deterministic sequential programs $P_1, P_2, \ldots$, infinitely many input variables $X(1), X(2), \ldots$, and infinitely many output variables $Y(1), Y(2), \ldots$ The sequential programs $P_1, P_2, \ldots$ are assumed to be identical, except for the ability of each P_i to refer to its own index i. That is, for each pair of indices i and j the sequential program P_j can be obtained from the sequential program P_i by replacing each reference to i in P_i with a reference to j.

At the start of a computation, the input of $\hat{P}$ is stored in its input variables. An input that consists of N values is stored in $X(1), \ldots, X(N)$, where each of the variables holds one of the input values. During the computation, $\hat{P}$ employs $P_1, \ldots, P_m$ for some m dependent on the input. Each P_i is assumed to know the value of N and the value of m. Upon halting, the output of $\hat{P}$ is assumed to be in its output variables. An output that consists of K values is assumed to be in $Y(1), \ldots, Y(K)$, where each of the variables holds one output value.

Each step in a computation of $\hat{P}$ consists of four phases as follows.

    a. Each P_i reads an input value from one of the input variables $X(1), \ldots, X(N)$.

    b. Each P_i performs some internal computation.

    c. Each P_i may write into one of the output variables $Y(1), Y(2), \ldots$

    d. $P_1, \ldots, P_m$ communicate any desirable information among themselves.

Each of the phases is synchronized to be carried in parallel by all the sequential programs $P_1, \ldots, P_m$.

Although two or more sequential programs may read simultaneously from the same input variable, at no step may they write into the same output variable.

The *depth of a computation* of a parallel program $\hat{P} = <P, X, Y>$ is the number of steps executed during the computation. The parallel program is said to have *depth complexity* $D(N)$ if for each N all its computations, over the inputs that consist of N values, have at most depth $D(N)$. The parallel program $\hat{P}$ is said to have *size complexity* $Z(N)$ if it employs no sequential programs other than $P_1, \ldots, P_{Z(N)}$ on each input that consists of N values.

The time required by a computation of a parallel program and that program's time complexity can be defined in a similar way. However, such notions are unmeasurable here because we have not yet specified how sequential programs communicate.

Example 7.1.1 Consider the problem Q of selecting the smallest value in a given set S. Restrict your attention to parallel programs that in each step allow each sequential program to receive information from no more than one sequential program.

The problem is solvable by a parallel program $\hat{P}_1 = <P, X, Y>$ of size complexity $Z(N) \geq N(N - 1)/2$ and a constant depth complexity, where N denotes the cardinality of the given set S. The parallel program can use a brute-force approach for such a purpose.

Specifically, let each pair (i_1, i_2), such that $1 \leq i_1 < i_2 \leq N$, correspond to a different i, such that $1 \leq i \leq N(N - 1)/2$. For instance, the correspondence can be of the form $i = 1 + 2 + \cdots + (i_2 - 2) + i_1 = (i_2 - 2)(i_2 - 1)/2 + i_1$ (see Figure 7.1.1). Let $P_{(i_1, i_2)}$ denote the sequential program P_i, where (i_1, i_2) is the pair that corresponds to i.

Each computation of $\hat{P}$ starts with a step in which each P_i derives the pair (i_1, i_2) that corresponds to i, $1 \leq i \leq N(N - 1)/2$. The computation continues with two steps in which each $P_{(i_1, i_2)}$ reads the elements of S that are stored in $X(i_1)$ and $X(i_2)$. In addition, in the third step each $P_{(i_1, i_2)}$ compares the values read from $X(i_1)$ and $X(i_2)$, and communicates a "negative" outcome to P_{i_1} or P_{i_2}. This outcome is communicated to P_{i_1} if $X(i_1) \geq X(i_2)$. Otherwise, the outcome is communicated to P_{i_2}. During the fourth step, the only active sequential program is P_j, $1 \leq j \leq N$, which did not receive a negative outcome. During that step P_j

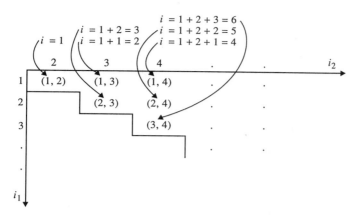

Figure 7.1.1 An ordering i on the pairs (i_1, i_2), such that $1 \le i_1 < i_2$.

reads the value of $X(j)$ and writes it out into $Y(1)$. The computation terminates after the fourth step.

The problem Q can be solved also by a parallel program $\hat{P}_2 = <\text{P}, \text{X}, \text{Y}>$ of size complexity $Z(N) = \lceil N/2 \rceil$ and depth complexity $D(N) = O(\log N)$. In this case the program simply repeatedly eliminates about half of the elements from S, until S is left with a single element.

At the first stage of each computation each P_i, $1 \le i \le \lceil N/2 \rceil$, reads the values stored in $X(2i - 1)$ and $X(2i)$. In addition, each P_i compares the values that it read. If $X(2i - 1) < X(2i)$, then P_i communicates to $\text{P}_{\lceil i/2 \rceil}$ the value of $X(2i - 1)$. Otherwise, P_i communicates to $\text{P}_{\lceil i/2 \rceil}$ the value of $X(2i)$. At the end of the first stage $\text{P}_1, \ldots, \text{P}_{\lceil \lceil n/2 \rceil/2 \rceil}$ hold the elements of S that have not been eliminated yet.

At the start of each consecutive stage of the computation, a sequential program P_i determines itself active if and only if it has been communicated some values of S in the previous stage. During a given stage, each active P_i compares the values a_1 and a_2 that were communicated to it in the previous stage. If the values satisfy the relation $a_1 < a_2$, then P_i communicates a_1 to $\text{P}_{\lceil i/2 \rceil}$. Otherwise, P_i communicates a_2 to $\text{P}_{\lceil i/2 \rceil}$.

After $O(\log N)$ stages only P_1 is active, and it holds a single value of S. Then P_1 writes the value into $Y(1)$ and the computation terminates.

Figure 7.1.2 illustrates the flow of information in $\hat{P}_2$ during a computation of the parallel program.

Similarly, the problem Q can be solved by a parallel program $\hat{P}_3 = <\text{P}, \text{X}, \text{Y}>$ of size complexity $Z(N) < \lceil N/2 \rceil$ and depth complexity $O(N/Z(N) + \log Z(N))$. At the start of each computation each P_i computes $m = Z(N)$ and finds independently in $O(N/m)$ steps the smallest value in $X(\lceil \frac{N}{m} \rceil (i - 1) + 1), \ldots, X(\lceil \frac{N}{m} \rceil i)$. Then, as in the previous case of $\hat{P}_2$, $\text{P}_1, \ldots, \text{P}_m$ proceed in parallel to determine in $O(\log m)$ steps the smallest value among the m values that they hold.   □

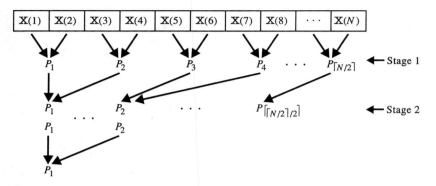

Figure 7.1.2 Flow of information.

7.2 Parallel Random Access Machines

The study of sequential computations has been conducted through abstract models, namely RAM's and Turing transducers. RAM's turned out to be useful for designing such computations, and Turing transducers were helpful in analyzing them. Viewing parallel computations as generalizations of sequential ones, calls for similar generalizations to the associated models. A generalization along such lines to RAM's is introduced below.

A *parallel random access machine*, or *PRAM*, $\hat{M}$ is a system $<M, X, Y, A>$, of infinitely many RAM's $M_1, M_2, \ldots$, infinitely many input cells $X(1), X(2), \ldots$, infinitely many output cells $Y(1), Y(2), \ldots$, and infinitely many shared memory cells $A(1), A(2), \ldots$ Each M_i is called a *processor* of $\hat{M}$. All the processors $M_1, M_2, \ldots$ are assumed to be identical, except for the ability of each M_i to recognize its own index i.

At the start of a computation, $\hat{M}$ is presented with some N input values that are stored in $X(1), \ldots, X(N)$, respectively. At the end of the computation the output values are stored in $Y(1), \ldots, Y(K)$, $K \geq 0$. During the computation $\hat{M}$ uses m processors $M_1, \ldots, M_m$, where m depends only on the input. It is assumed that each of the processors is aware of the number N of the given input values and of the number m of processors.

Each step in a computation consists of the five following phases, carried in parallel by all the processors.

a. Each processor reads a value from one of the input cells $X(1), \ldots, X(N)$.

b. Each processor reads one of the shared memory cells $A(1), A(2), \ldots$

c. Each processor performs some internal computation.

d. Each processor may write into one of the output cells $Y(1), Y(2), \ldots$

e. Each processor may write into one of the shared memory cells $A(1), A(2), \ldots$

Two or more processors may read simultaneously from the same cell. However, a *write conflict* occurs when two or more processors try to write simultaneously into the same cell. Write conflicts are treated according to the variant of PRAM in use. The following are three such possible variants.

a. CREW (Concurrent Read — Exclusive Write). In this variant no write conflicts are allowed.

b. COMMON. In this variant all the processors that simultaneously write to the same memory cell must write the same value.

c. PRIORITY. In this variant the write conflicts are resolved in favor of the processor M_i that has the least index i among those processors involved in the conflict.

The *length n of an input* $(v_1, \ldots, v_N)$ of a PRAM $\hat{M}$ is assumed to equal the length of the representation of the instance.

The *depth of a computation* of a PRAM, and its *depth* and *size complexity* are defined with respect to the length n of the inputs in a similar way to that for parallel programs. The *time requirement of a computation* of a PRAM and its *time complexity*, under the uniform and logarithmic cost criteria, are defined in the obvious way.

When no confusion arises, because of the obvious relationship between the number N of values in the input and the length n of the input, N and n are used interchangeably.

Example 7.2.1 COMMON and PRIORITY PRAM's, $\hat{M} = <M, X, Y, A>$ similar to the parallel programs $\hat{P}_i = <P, X, Y>$ of Example 7.1.1, can be used to solve the problem Q of selecting the smallest element in a given set S of cardinality N. The communication between the processors can be carried indirectly through the shared memory cells $A(1)$, $A(2)$, $\ldots$

Specifically, each message to M_i is stored in $A(i)$. Where the PRAM's are similar to $\hat{P}_1$, no problem arises because all the messages are identical. Alternatively, where the PRAM's are similar to $\hat{P}_2$ or $\hat{P}_3$, no problem arises because no write conflicts occur. □

By definition, each CREW PRAM is also a COMMON PRAM, and each COMMON PRAM is also a PRIORITY PRAM. The following result shows that each PRIORITY PRAM can be simulated by a CREW PRAM.

Theorem 7.2.1 Each PRIORITY PRAM $\hat{M}$ of size complexity $Z(n)$ and depth complexity $D(n)$ has an equivalent CREW PRAM $\hat{M}'$ of size complexity $Z^2(n)$ and depth complexity $D(n) \log Z(n)$.

Proof Consider any PRIORITY PRAM $\hat{M} = <M, X, Y, A>$. $\hat{M}' = <M', X, Y, A>$ can be a CREW PRAM of the following form, whose processors are denoted $M_{1\,1}, \ldots, M_{1\,m}, M_{2\,1}, \ldots, M_{2\,m}, \ldots, M_{m\,1}, \ldots, M_{m\,m}$.

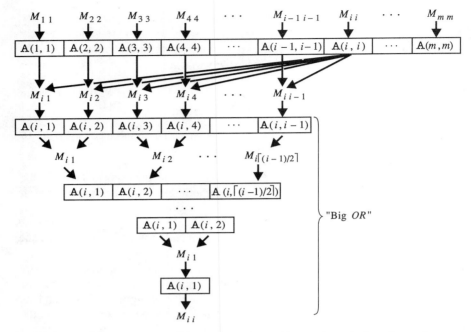

Figure 7.2.1 Flow of information for determining the priority of M_{ii} in writing.

On a given input, $\hat{M}'$ simulates the computation of $\hat{M}$. $\hat{M}'$ uses the processors M_{11}, M_{22}, ..., M_{mm} for simulating the respective processors M_1, M_2, ..., M_m of $\hat{M}$. Similarly, $\hat{M}'$ records in the shared memory cell $A(m^2 + i)$ the values that $\hat{M}$ records in the shared memory cell $A(i)$, $i \geq 1$. The main difference arises when a write is to be simulated.

In such a case, each M_{jj} communicates to each M_{ii} the address of the cell where M_j wants to write. Each M_{ii} then determines from those addresses, if it has the highest priority of writing into its designated cell, and accordingly decides whether to perform the write operation. M_{ii} employs the processors $M_{i1}, \ldots, M_{i\,i-1}$ and the shared memory cells $A(i, 1), \ldots, A(i, i-1)$ for such a purpose, where $A(i_1, i_2)$ stands for $A((i_1 - 1)m + i_2)$.

To resolve the write conflicts each M_{jj} stores into $A(j, j)$ the address where M_j wants to write (see Figure 7.2.1). Then M_{ii} determines in the following manner whether the shared memory cell $A(i, i)$ holds an address that differs from those stored in $A(1, 1), \ldots, A(i - 1, i - 1)$.

Each processor M_{ir}, $1 \leq r < i$, starts by reading the addresses stored in $A(r, r)$ and in $A(i, i)$, and storing 1 in $A(i, r)$ if and only if $A(r, r) = A(i, i)$. Then the processors $M_{i1}, \ldots, M_{i\lceil(i-1)/2\rceil}$ are employed in parallel to determine in $O(\log i)$ steps whether the value 1 appears in any of the shared memory cells $A(i, 1), \ldots, A(i, i-1)$. At each step the number of "active" processors and the number of the active shared memory cells is reduced by half. At any given step each of the active processors M_{ir} stores the value 1 in $A(i, r)$ if and only if either $A(i, 2r - 1)$ or $A(i, 2r)$ holds that value.

M_{ii} determines that $A(i, i)$ holds an address that differs from those stored in $A(1, 1), \ldots, A(i - 1, i - 1)$ by determining that $A(i, 1)$ holds a value that differs from 1. In such a case, M_{ii} determines that M_i has the highest priority for writing in its designated cell. Otherwise, M_{ii} determines that M_i does not have the highest priority. □

7.3 Circuits

Many abstract models of parallel machines have been offered in the literature, besides those of PRAM's. However, unlike the case for the abstract models of sequential machines, there is no obvious way for relating the different abstract models of parallel machines. Therefore, the lowest common denominator of such models, that is, their hardware representations, seems a natural choice for analyzing the models for the resources that they require.

Here the representations are considered in terms of undirected acyclic graphs, called *combinatorial Boolean circuits* or simply *circuits*. Each node in a circuit is assumed to have an indegree no greater than 2, and an outdegree of unbounded value. Each node of indegree 0 is labeled either with a variable name, with the constant 0, or with the constant 1. Each node of indegree 1 is labeled with the Boolean function ¬. Each node of indegree 2 is labeled either with the Boolean functions ∧ or ∨.

Each node of indegree greater than 0 is called a *gate*. A gate is said to be a *NOT gate* if it is labeled with ¬, an *AND gate* if labeled with ∧, and an *OR gate* if labeled with ∨. Nodes labeled with variable names are called *input nodes*. Nodes of outdegree 0 are called *output nodes*. A node labeled with 0 is called a *constant node 0*. A node labeled with 1 is called a *constant node 1*.

A circuit c that has n input nodes and m output nodes *computes a function* $f: \{0, 1\}^n \rightarrow \{0, 1\}^m$ in the obvious way.

Example 7.3.1 The circuit in Figure 7.3.1 has $7 \times 4 + 8 + 1 = 37$ nodes, of which 8 are input nodes and 1 is an output node.

The circuit computes the parity function for $n = 8$ input values. The circuit provides the output of 0 for the case where $a_1 \cdots a_8$ has an odd number of 1's. The circuit provides the output of 1 for the case where $a_1 \cdots a_8$ has an even number of 1's.

The circuit's strategy relies on the following two observations.

a. The parity function does not change its value when a 0 is removed from its input string.

b. The parity function does not change its value if a pair of 1's is replaced with a 0 in its input string.

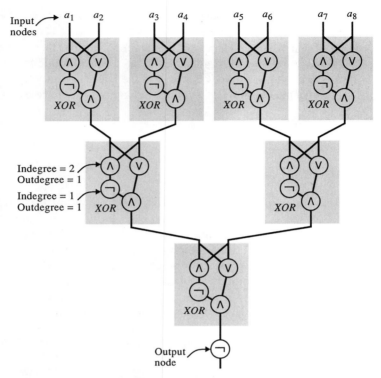

Figure 7.3.1 Parity checker.

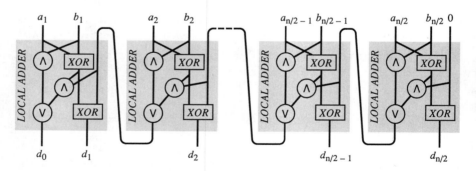

Figure 7.3.2 Adder.

Each group *XOR* of gates outputs 1 if its input values are not equal, and 0 if its input values are equal. Each level of *XOR*'s in the circuit reduces the size of the given input by half.   ☐

Example 7.3.2 The circuit in Figure 7.3.2 is an adder that computes the sum $d = a + b$. $d_0 \cdots d_{n/2}, a_1 \cdots a_{n/2}$, and $b_1 \cdots b_{n/2}$ are assumed to be the binary representations of d, a, and b, respectively. Each *LOCAL ADDER* in the circuit has an input that consists of two corresponding bits of a and b, as well as a carry from the previous *LOCAL ADDER*. The output of each *LOCAL ADDER* is the corresponding bit in d, as well as a new carry to be passed on to the next *LOCAL ADDER*. □

The *size* of a circuit is the number of gates in it. The *depth* of a circuit is the number of gates in the longest path from an input node to an output node.

Example 7.3.3 In the circuit of Figure 7.3.1 each *XOR* has size 4 and depth 3. The whole circuit has size 29 and depth 10.

In the circuit of Figure 7.3.2 each *LOCAL ADDER* has size 11 and depth 6. The whole circuit has size $11n/2$ and depth $5 + 2(n/2 - 2) + 3 = n + 4$. □

Families of Circuits

$C = (c_0, c_1, c_2, \ldots)$ is said to be a *family of circuits* if c_n is a circuit with n input nodes for each $n \geq 0$. A family $C = (c_0, c_1, c_2, \ldots)$ of circuits is said to have *size complexity* $Z(n)$ if $Z(n) \geq$ (size of c_n) for all $n \geq 0$. The family is said to have *depth complexity* $D(n)$ if $D(n) \geq$ (depth of c_n) for all $n \geq 0$.

A family $C = (c_0, c_1, c_2, \ldots)$ of circuits is said to *compute* a given function $f: \{0, 1\}^* \to \{0, 1\}^*$ if for each $n \geq 0$ the circuit c_n computes the function $f_n: \{0, 1\}^n \to \{0, 1\}^k$ for some $k \geq 0$ that depends on n. f_n is assumed to be a function that satisfies $f_n(x) = f(x)$ for each x in $\{0, 1\}^n$.

A function f is said to be of *size complexity* $Z(n)$ if it is computable by a family of circuits of size complexity $Z(n)$. The function f is said to have *depth complexity* $D(n)$ if it is computable by a family of circuits with depth complexity $D(n)$.

A family $C = (c_0, c_1, c_2, \ldots)$ of circuits is said to *decide a language* L in $\{0, 1\}^*$ if the characteristic function of L is computable by C. (f is the characteristic function of L if $f(x) = 1$ for each x in L, and $f(x) = 0$ for each x not in L.) The size and depth complexities of a language are the size and depth complexities of its characteristic function.

Example 7.3.4 The language $\{ a_1 \cdots a_n \mid a_1, \ldots, a_n$ are in $\{0, 1\}$, and $a_1 \cdots a_n$ has an even number of 1's $\}$ is decidable by a family of circuits similar to the circuit in Figure 7.3.1. The language has depth complexity $O(\log n)$, and size complexity $O(n/2 + n/4 + \cdots + 1) = O(n)$. □

Representation of Circuits

In what follows, we will assume that each circuit c has a representation of the following form. Associate the number 0 with each constant node 0 in c, the number 1 with each constant node 1 in c, and the numbers $2, \ldots, n + 1$ with the n input nodes of c. Associate consecutive numbers starting at $n+2$, with each of c's gates. Then a representation of c is a string of the form $E(u_1) \cdots E(u_m) F(v_1) \cdots F(v_k)$.

$u_1, \ldots, u_m$ are the gates of c, and $v_1, \ldots, v_k$ are the output nodes. $E(u)$ is equal to (g, t, g_L, g_R), where g is the number assigned to gate u, t is the type of

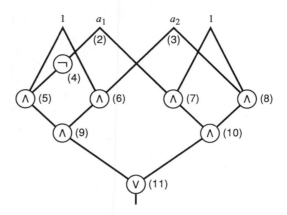

Figure 7.3.3 A circuit with enumerated nodes.

u in $\{\neg, \vee, \wedge\}$, and g_L and g_R are the numbers assigned to the immediate prede-cessors of u. In particular, $g_L = g_R$ when $t = \neg$. $F(v)$ is equal to (g), where g is the number assigned to gate v.

Example 7.3.5 Figure 7.3.3 provides a circuit whose nodes are enumerated. The circuit has the following representation.

$(4, \neg, 2, 2)(5, \wedge, 1, 4)(6, \wedge, 1, 3)(7, \wedge, 2, 1)(8, \wedge, 3, 1)(9, \wedge, 5, 6)(10, \wedge, 7, 8)(11, \vee, 9, 10)(11)$ $\square$

7.4   Uniform Families of Circuits

"Table Look-Up" Circuits

Families of circuits were introduced to help characterize the resources that prob-lems require from parallel machines. The following theorem implies that the fam-ilies cannot serve such a purpose in their general form, because they can recognize languages that are not recursively enumerable.

Theorem 7.4.1 Each language L in $\{0, 1\}^*$ is decidable by a family of circuits.

Proof Consider any language L in $\{0, 1\}^*$, and any natural number n. Let L_n denote the set $L \cap \{0, 1\}^n$. That is, L_n denotes the set of all the binary strings of length n in L.

For any given string w in L_n, a subcircuit c_w with n input nodes can be constructed that accepts a given input if and only if the input is equal to w. The language L_n is finite. As a result, the subcircuits c_w that correspond to the strings w in L_n can be merged, by letting them share the input nodes and by OR ing their outputs. The obtained circuit c_n determines the membership in L_n by a table look-up technique.

Consequently, L is decidable by the family $(c_0, c_1, c_2, \ldots)$ of circuits. $\square$

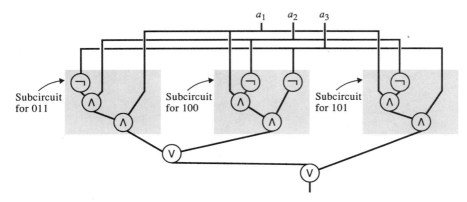

Figure 7.4.1 A "table look-up" circuit for the language $L_3 = \{011, 100, 101\}$.

Example 7.4.1 The circuit c_3 in Figure 7.4.1 decides the language $L_3 = \{011, 100, 101\}$ by a table look-up approach. For each string w in L_3, the circuit has a corresponding subcircuit c_w that decides just the membership of the string. ☐

The families of table look-up circuits in the proof of Theorem 7.4.1 have size complexity $2^{O(n)}$ and depth complexity $O(n)$. These families do not reflect the complexity of deciding the languages, because they assume the knowledge of which strings are in a given language and which are not. That is, the complexity involved in deciding the languages is shifted into the complexity of constructing the corresponding families of circuits.

"Unrolled Hardware" Circuits

A circuit can be obtained to characterize a halting computation of a parallel machine $\hat{M}$ by laying down the portion of the hardware of $\hat{M}$ that is involved in the computation. During the laying down of the hardware, cycles can be avoided by unrolling the hardware. The depth of such a circuit provides a measurement for the time that the computation requires, and the circuits size provides an upper bound on the space the computation requires.

Example 7.4.2 The circuit in Figure 7.4.2(b) computes the function that the hardware of Figure 7.4.2(a) computes in three units of time. It is assumed that initially each input to a gate is either an input value or the constant 0. ☐

In a similar way, one can also obtain a circuit c_n that corresponds to all the halting computations of $\hat{M}$ on instances of length n, $n \geq 0$. (The outputs for the inputs of a given length n are assumed to be appended by a string of the form $10 \cdots 0$ to let them all have identical lengths.) Consequently, the approach implies a family $C = (c_0, c_1, c_2, \ldots)$ of circuits for each parallel machine $\hat{M}$ that halts on all inputs. Moreover, the families of circuits faithfully reflect the complexity of the parallel computations and can be effectively obtained from each such parallel machine $\hat{M}$.

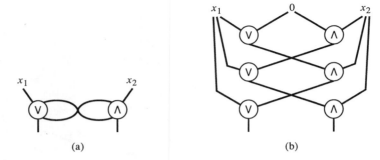

Figure 7.4.2 (a) "Hardware." (b) Corresponding "unrolled hardware."

Uniform Families of Circuits

By the previous discussion, from each parallel machine $\hat{M}$ that halts on all inputs, a circuits constructor can be obtained to compute $\{(1^n, c_n) \mid n \geq 0\}$, where $C = (c_0, c_1, c_2, \ldots)$ is a family of circuits that computes the same function as $\hat{M}$. The circuits constructor can be one that provides families of table look-up, unrolled hardware, or other types of circuits.

The interest here is in circuits constructors that preserve, in the families of circuits that they construct, the complexity of the given parallel machines. Such constructors do not allow the shift of complexity from the constructed families of circuits to the constructors. Moreover, they also do not allow an unrealistic increase in the complexity of the constructed families of circuits. Circuits constructors with such characteristics are said to be uniform circuits constructors. A family $C = (c_0, c_1, c_2, \ldots)$ of circuits is said to be uniform if a uniform circuits constructor can compute the function $\{(1^n, c_n) \mid n \geq 0\}$.

Many characterizations have been offered for the uniform circuits constructors. The characterization used here, which has been widely accepted, defines these conditions in terms of a class of deterministic Turing transducers.

Definition A Turing transducer is said to be a *uniform circuits constructor* if it is an $O(\log Z(n))$ space-bounded, deterministic Turing transducer that computes $\{(1^n, c_n) \mid n \geq 0\}$, where $C = (c_0, c_1, c_2, \ldots)$ is a family of circuits of size complexity $Z(n)$. A family $C = (c_0, c_1, c_2, \ldots)$ of circuits of size complexity $Z(n)$ is said to be a *uniform family of circuits* if an $O(\log Z(n))$ space-bounded, deterministic Turing transducer can compute $\{(1^n, c_n) \mid n \geq 0\}$.

The characterization of uniform families of circuits is motivated by the unrolled hardware approach. With such an approach the circuits constructor needs $O(\log H(n) + \log T(n)) = O(\log(H(n)T(n)))$ space, if the parallel machine has size complexity $H(n)$ and time complexity $T(n)$. $O(\log H(n))$ space is used for tracing through the hardware, and $O(\log T(n))$ space is used for tracing through time. $H(n)T(n)$ is of a similar order of magnitude to the size $Z(n)$ of the circuits.

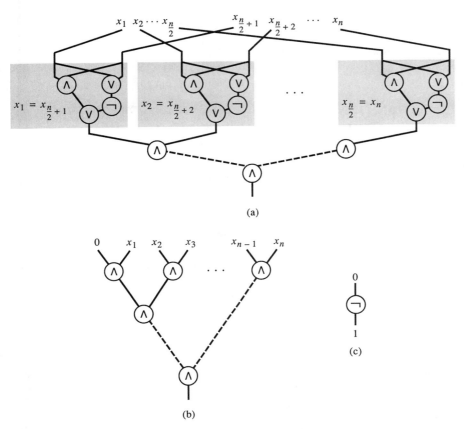

Figure 7.4.3 A circuit c_n that, according to the case, checks whether an input of length n is of the form uu. (a) $n \neq 0$, and n is even. (b) n is odd. (c) $n = 0$.

Example 7.4.3 Consider the language $L = \{ uu \mid u \text{ is in } \{0, 1\}^* \}$. Let $L_n = L \cap \{0, 1\}^n$ for $n \geq 0$, that is, L_n denotes the set of all the binary strings of length n in L. The language L_n is decided by the circuit c_n in Figure 7.4.3(a) if n is a nonzero even integer, by the circuit c_n in Figure 7.4.3(b) if n is an odd integer, and by the circuit c_n in Figure 7.4.3(c) if $n = 0$.

The family $(c_0, c_1, c_2, \dots)$ of circuits is of depth complexity $D(n) = O(\log n)$ and size complexity $Z(n) = O(n/2 + n/4 + \cdots + 1) = O(n)$. The family is uniform because the function $\{ (1^n, c_n) \mid n \geq 0 \}$ is computable by a $\log Z(n) = O(\log n)$ space-bounded, deterministic Turing transducer. $\qquad \square$

The following thesis for parallel computations is stated in terms of uniform families of circuits. As in the previous theses for sequential and probabilistic computations, only supportive evidences can be provided to exhibit the correctness of the thesis.

The Parallel Computation Thesis A function can be mechanically computed by a parallel machine of size complexity $H(n)$ and time complexity $T(n)$ only if it has a uniform family of circuits of size complexity $p(H(n)T(n))$ and depth complexity $p(T(n))$, for some polynomial $p(\cdot)$.

7.5   Uniform Families of Circuits and Sequential Computations

The size of circuits is a major resource for parallel computations, as is time for sequential computations. The following theorem shows that these two types of resources are polynomially related.

Notation In what follows $DTIME\_F\,(T(n))$ will denote the class of functions computable by $O(T(n))$ time-bounded, deterministic Turing transducers. The class of functions with size complexity $SIZE\_F\,(Z(n))$ will be denoted $O(Z(n))$. The class of languages whose characteristic functions are in $SIZE\_F\,(Z(n))$ will be denoted $SIZE\,(Z(n))$. $U\_SIZE\_F\,(Z(n))$ will denote the class of functions computable by uniform families of circuits of size complexity $O(Z(n))$. The class of languages whose characteristic functions are in $U\_SIZE\_F\,(Z(n))$ will be denoted $U\_SIZE\,(Z(n))$. $U\_DEPTH\_F\,(D(n))$ will denote the class of functions computable by uniform families of circuits of depth complexity $O(D(n))$, and the class of languages whose characteristic functions are in $U\_DEPTH\_F\,(D(n))$ will be denoted $U\_DEPTH\,(D(n))$. $U\_SIZE\_DEPTH\_F\,(Z(n), D(n))$ will denote the class of functions computable by uniform families of circuits with simultaneous size complexity $Z(n)$ and depth complexity $D(n)$.

Theorem 7.5.1 If $log\,T(n)$ is fully space-constructible, then

$$\bigcup_{d \geq 0} DTIME\_F\,(T^d(n)) \quad = \quad \bigcup_{d \geq 0} U\_SIZE\_F\,(T^d(n))$$

The proof of the theorem is implied from the two lemmas below.

From Sequential Time to Circuit Size

The proof of the first lemma consists of unrolling the hardware of deterministic Turing transducers.

Lemma 7.5.1 If $log\,T(n)$ is fully space-constructible, then

$$DTIME\_F\,(T(n)) \quad \subseteq \quad U\_SIZE\_F\,(T^2(n)).$$

Proof Consider any $T(n)$ time-bounded, deterministic Turing transducer $M = <Q, \Sigma, \Gamma, \Delta, \delta, q_0, B, F>$, where $log\,T(n)$ is fully space-constructible. With no loss of generality assume that $\Sigma = \{0, 1\}$. Let m denote the number of auxiliary work tapes of M.

A Modified Version of M

Assume that Δ does not contain the symbols a and b. Modify M in the following way.

    a. Modify each transition rule that provides no output to a rule that provides the output b.

    b. Remove the transition rules that originate at the accepting states, convert the accepting states into nonaccepting states, add a new nonaccepting state, and add new transition rules that force M to go from the old accepting states to the new state while writing the symbol a. Call the new state an a state.

    c. For each state q, input symbol c, and auxiliary work-tape symbols $b_1, \ldots, b_m$ on which $\delta(q, c, b_1, \ldots, b_m)$ is undefined, add the transition rule $(q, c, b_1, \ldots, b_m, q, 0, b_1, 0, \ldots, b_m, 0, \alpha)$ to δ. α is assumed to equal a if q is the a state, and α is assumed to equal b if q is not the a state.

The modified M is a deterministic Turing transducer, which on each input has a computation of an unbounded number of moves. On an input on which the original M has i moves, the modified M enters an infinite loop in the $i + 1$st move. In each move the modified M writes one symbol onto the output tape. The output of the modified M in the $i + 1$st, $i + 2$nd, $\ldots$ moves is a if and only if the input is accepted by the original M. Moreover, the output of the original M can be obtained from the string that the modified M writes on the output tape, by removing all the symbols a and all the symbols b.

A Circuit c_n for Simulating M

A circuit c_n of the following form can simulate the original M on inputs of length n, by simulating the first $t = 2^{\lceil \log(T(n)+1) \rceil}$ moves of the modified M on the given input.

The simulation of exactly $t = 2^{\lceil \log(T(n)+1) \rceil}$ moves of (the modified) M, allows c_n to generate outputs of identical length t for all the inputs of length n. Such a uniformity in the length of the outputs is needed because of the circuits' rigidity in the length of their outputs.

The choice of $t = 2^{\lceil \log(T(n)+1) \rceil}$ instead of $T(n) + 1$ for the number of moves of M, is made to allow the value to be calculated just by marking a space of size $O(\log T(n))$.

c_n assumes some fixed binary representation for the set $\Sigma \cup \Gamma \cup \Delta \cup \{a, b, \mathfrak{c},$ $\$, -1, 0, +1, \boxed{0}, \ldots, \boxed{m}\} \cup Q$. The elements of the set can be represented by binary strings of identical length k. $\boxed{0}, \ldots, \boxed{m}$ are assumed to be new symbols corresponding to the heads of M.

c_n consists of $t + 2$ subcircuits, referred to as IN, $MOVE_1, \ldots, MOVE_t$, and OUT, respectively (see Figure 7.5.1).

IN is a subcircuit which derives the initial (i.e., 0th) configuration

$$(\mathfrak{c}q_0 a_1 \cdots a_n \$, B^t q_0 B^t, \ldots, B^t q_0 B^t, \epsilon)$$

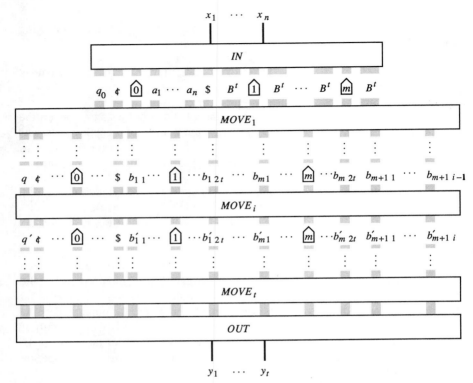

Figure 7.5.1 A circuit c_n that computes the function computable by a deterministic Turing transducer M on instances of length n.

of M on the given input $a_1 \cdots a_n$. *IN* uses the values $a_1, \ldots, a_n$ of the input nodes $x_1, \ldots, x_n$; the values of some constant nodes 0; and the values of some constant nodes 1 for obtaining the desired (representation of the) configuration.

The subcircuit $MOVE_i$, $1 \le i \le t$, derives the ith configuration

$$(\text{¢}a_1 \cdots q' \cdots a_n \$, b'_{1\,1} \cdots q' \cdots b'_{1\,2t}, \ldots, b'_{m\,1} \cdots q' \cdots b'_{m\,2t}, b'_{m+1\,1} \cdots b'_{m+1\,i})$$

of M from the $i - 1$st configuration

$$(\text{¢}a_1 \cdots q \cdots a_n \$, b_{1\,1} \cdots q \cdots b_{1\,2t}, \ldots, b_{m\,1} \cdots q \cdots b_{m\,2t}, b_{m+1\,1} \cdots b_{m+1\,i-1})$$

of M.

OUT is a subcircuit that extracts the (encoding of the) output $b_1 \cdots b_t$ that M has in the tth configuration. *OUT* does so by eliminating the symbols that are not in $\Delta \cup \{a, b\}$, for example, by using *AND* gates.

The Subcircuit MOVE$_i$

$MOVE_i$ uses components *PREFIX_FINDER* and *SUFFIX_FINDER* for determining the transition rule $(q, a, b_1, \ldots, b_m, p, d_0, c_1, d_1, \ldots, c_m, d_m, \rho)$ that M uses in its ith

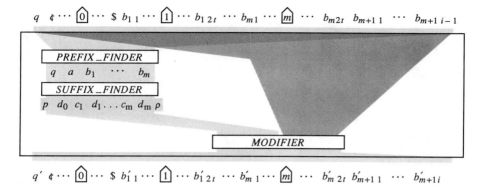

Figure 7.5.2 Subcircuit $MOVE_i$ for simulating a transition of a deterministic Turing transducer between two configurations.

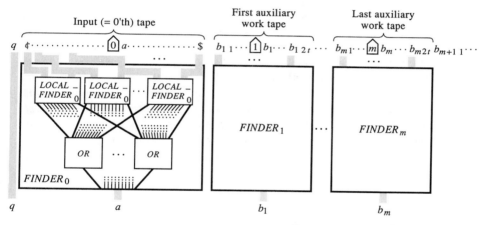

Figure 7.5.3 A subcircuit $PREFIX\_FINDER$ for determining a transition rule of a Turing transducer.

move (see Figure 7.5.2). $PREFIX\_FINDER$ determines the prefix $(q, a, b_1, \ldots, b_m)$ of the transition rule from the $i - 1$st configuration of M. $SUFFIX\_FINDER$ determines the suffix $(p, d_0, c_1, d_1, \ldots, c_m, d_m, \rho)$ of the transition rule from $(q, a, b_1, \ldots, b_m)$. $MOVE_i$ uses a component $MODIFIER$ for carrying out the necessary modifications to the $i - 1$st configuration of M.

$PREFIX\_FINDER$ has a component $FINDER_i$, $0 \le i \le m$, corresponding to each of the nonoutput tapes of M (see Figure 7.5.3). $FINDER_i$ determines the symbol that is under the head of the ith tape of M. $FINDER_i$ employs a subcircuit $LOCAL\_FINDER_i$ for each pair of consecutive symbols in the portion of the configuration that corresponds to the ith tape of M. $LOCAL\_FINDER_i$ outputs (the representation of) the symbol α if its input corresponds to a pair of the form $\boxed{i}\alpha$. Otherwise, the

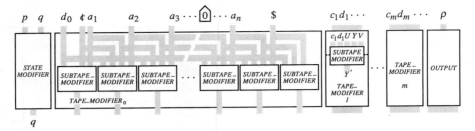

Figure 7.5.4 A subcircuit *MODIFIER* for modifying a configuration of a Turing transducer.

subcircuit $LOCAL\_FINDER_i$ outputs just 0's. The output of each $LOCAL\_FINDER_i$ is determined by a table look-up circuit. The outputs of all the $LOCAL\_FINDER_i$'s are *OR*ed to obtain the desired output of $FINDER_i$.

$SUFFIX\_FINDER$ on input $(q, a, b_1, \ldots, b_m)$ employs a table look-up approach to find $(p, d_0, c_1, d_1, \ldots, c_m, d_m, \rho)$.

MODIFIER contains one component $TAPE\_MODIFIER_i$ for each of the nonoutput tapes i of the Turing transducer M, $0 \le i \le m$ (see Figure 7.5.4). $TAPE\_MODIFIER_i$ contains one subcircuit $SUBTAPE\_MODIFIER$ for each location in the constructed configuration of the Turing transducer M. A $SUBTAPE\_MODIFIER$ that corresponds to location j receives the three symbols U, Y, and V as inputs at locations $j-1$, j, and $j+1$ in the configuration of M that is being modified. (The only exception occurs when the jth location is a boundary location. In such a case the $SUBTAPE\_MODIFIER$ receives only two input values.) In addition, the $SUBTAPE\_MODIFIER$ gets as input the modifications (c_i and d_i) that are to be made in the ith tape of M. The $SUBTAPE\_MODIFIER$ outputs the symbol Y' for the jth location in the constructed configuration of M.

A Uniform Circuits Constructor

IN has size 0. Each $FINDER_i$ contains $O(T(n))$ subcircuits $LOCAL\_FINDER_i$, and a constant number of subcircuits *OR*. Each $LOCAL\_FINDER_i$ has constant size. Each subcircuit *OR* has size $O(T(n))$. Hence, $PREFIX\_FINDER$ has size $O(T(n))$. $SUFFIX\_FINDER$ has constant size, and $TAPE\_MODIFIER$ has size $O(T(n))$. Consequently, c_n has size $O(T^2(n))$.

An $O(\log T(n))$ space-bounded, deterministic Turing transducer X can be constructed, to compute $\{ (1^n, c_n) \mid n \ge 0 \}$ in a brute-force manner. $\qquad\square$

Example 7.5.1 Let M be the one auxiliary-work-tape deterministic Turing transducer in Figure 7.5.5(a). M has time complexity $T(n) = n + 1$. For the purpose of the example take M as it is, without modifications. Using the terminology in the proof of Lemma 7.5.1, $Q = \{q_0, q_1, \ldots, q_4\}$, $\Sigma = \Delta = \{0, 1\}$, $\Gamma = \{0, 1, B\}$, $m = 1$, and $k = 4$. Choose the following binary representation E: $E(0) = 0000$, $E(1) = 0001$, $E(\mathcal{c}) = 0010$, $E(\$) = 0011$, $E(B) = 0100$, $E(a) = 0101$, $E(b) = 0110$, $E(\boxed{0}) = 0111$, $E(\boxed{1}) = 1000$, $E(q_0) = 1001$, $E(q_1) = 1010$, $E(q_2) = 1011$, $E(q_3) = 1100$, $E(q_4) = 1101$, $E(-1) = 1110$,

$E(+1) = 1111$. Choose $n = 3$.

In such a case, $t = 4$. The subcircuit *IN* is given in Figure 7.5.5(b), the subcircuit *PREFIX_FINDER* is given in Figure 7.5.5(c), and the subcircuit *SUFFIX_FINDER* is given in Figure 7.5.5(d). ☐

From Circuits Size to Sequential Time

The previous lemma deals with applying parallelism for simulating sequential computations. The following lemma deals with the simulation of parallel computations by sequential computations.

Lemma 7.5.2 $U\_SIZE\_F(Z(n)) \subseteq \bigcup_{d \geq 0} DTIME\_F(Z^d(n))$.

Proof Consider any function $Z(n)$, and any uniform family $C = (c_0, c_1, c_2, \ldots)$ of circuits of size complexity $Z(n)$. Let X be an $O(log\, Z(n))$ space-bounded, deterministic Turing transducer that computes the function $\{(1^n, c_n) \mid n \geq 0\}$. A deterministic Turing transducer M can compute the same function as C in the following manner.

Given an input $a_1 \cdots a_n$, M employs X to determine the representation of the circuit c_n. The representation can be found in $2^{O(log\, Z(n))} = Z^{O(1)}(n)$ time because X is $O(log\, Z(n))$ space-bounded (see Theorem 5.5.1). Moreover, the representation has length $O(Z(n)log\, Z(n))$ because c_n has at most $Z(n)$ gates, and each gate (g, t, g_L, g_R) has a representation of length $O(log\, Z(n))$.

Having the representation of c_n, the Turing transducer M evaluates the output of each node in c_n. M does so by repeatedly scanning the representation of c_n for quadruples (g, t, g_L, g_R), that correspond to nodes g_L and g_R, whose output values are already known. Having found such a quadruple (g, t, g_L, g_R), the Turing transducer M evaluates and also records the output value of g. After at most $Z(n)$ iterations, M determines the output values of all the nodes in c_n.

Finally, M determines which nodes of c_n are the output nodes, and writes out their values. ☐

By Theorem 7.5.1, the time of sequential computations and the size of uniform families of circuits are polynomially related.

Corollary 7.5.1 A problem is solvable in polynomial time if and only if it is solvable by a uniform family of circuits of polynomial size complexity.

U_FNC, U_NC, and NC

Sequential computations are considered feasible only if they are polynomially time-bounded. Similarly, families of circuits are considered feasible only if they are polynomially size-bounded. As a result, parallelism does not seem to have major influence on problems that are not solvable in polynomial time. On the other hand, for those problems that are solvable in polynomial time, parallelism is of central importance when it can significantly increase computing speed. One such

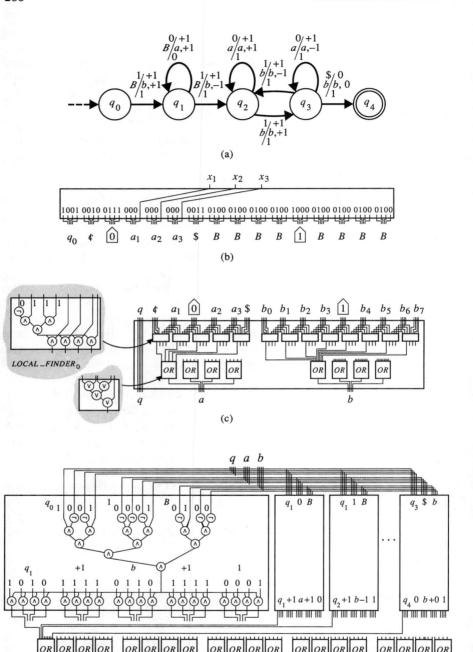

Figure 7.5.5 (a) A Turing transducer. (b) Corresponding subcircuit *IN*. (c) Corresponding subcircuit *PREFIX_FINDER*. (d) Corresponding subcircuit *SUFFIX_FINDER*.

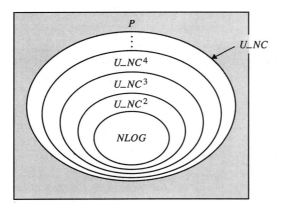

Figure 7.5.6 A hierarchy of decision problems between $NLOG$ and P.

class of problems is that which can be solved by uniform families of circuits, simultaneously having polynomial size complexity and *polylog* (i.e., $O(log^i n)$ for some $i \geq 0$) depth complexity. This class of problems is denoted U_FNC.

The subclass of U_FNC, which is obtained by restricting the depth complexity of the families of circuits to $O(log^i n)$, is denoted U_FNC^i. The subclass of decision problems in U_FNC is denoted U_NC. The subclass of decision problems in U_FNC^i is denoted U_NC^i.

FNC denotes the class of problems solvable by (not necessarily uniform) families of circuits that simultaneously, have polynomial size complexity and polylog depth complexity. The subclass of decision problems in FNC is denoted NC. The subclass of FNC, obtained by restricting the families of circuits to depth complexity $O(log^i n)$, is denoted FNC^i. NC^i denotes the class of decision problems in FNC^i.

For nonuniform families of circuits the following contrasting theorem holds.

Theorem 7.5.2 NC^1 contains undecidable problems.

Proof Every unary language L over the alphabet $\{1\}$ can be decided by a family $C = (c_0, c_1, c_2, \dots)$ of circuits of simultaneous polynomial size complexity and logarithmic depth complexity. Specifically, each c_n in C is a table look-up circuit that outputs 1 on a given input $a_1 \cdots a_n$ if and only if $a_1 \cdots a_n = 1^n$ and 1^n is in L.

However, a proof by diagonalization implies that the membership problem is undecidable for the unary language $\{ 1^i \mid$ The Turing machine M_i does not accept the string $1^i \}$. $\qquad \square$

Sequential Space and Parallel Time

By Corollary 7.5.1, the definitions above, and the following lemma, the hierarchy shown in Figure 7.5.6 holds.

Lemma 7.5.3 $NLOG \subseteq U\_NC^2$.

Proof Consider any $S(n) = O(\log n)$ space-bounded, nondeterministic Turing machine $M = <Q, \Sigma, \Gamma, \delta, q_0, B, F>$ with m auxiliary work tapes. With no loss of generality assume that $\Sigma = \{0, 1\}$. Let a tuple $w = (q, i, a, u_1, v_1, \ldots, u_m, v_m)$ be called a partial configuration of M on input $a_1 \cdots a_n$, if M has a configuration $(\alpha q a \beta, u_1 q v_1, \ldots, u_m q v_m)$ with $\alpha a \beta = \mathcal{c} a_1 \cdots a_n \$$ and $|\alpha| = i$. Let a partial configuration be called an initial partial configuration if it corresponds to an initial configuration. Let a partial configuration be called an accepting partial configuration if it corresponds to an accepting configuration.

Each partial configuration of M requires $O(\log n)$ space. The number k of partial configurations $w_1, \ldots, w_k$ that M has on the set of inputs of length n satisfies $k = 2^{O(\log n)} = n^{O(1)}$.

Say that M can directly reach partial configuration w' from partial configuration w if w and w' correspond to some configurations Ω_w and $\Omega_{w'}$ of M, respectively, such that $\Omega_w \vdash \Omega_{w'}$. Say that M can reach partial configuration w' from partial configuration w if w and w' correspond to some configurations Ω_w and $\Omega_{w'}$ of M, respectively, such that $\Omega_w \vdash^* \Omega_{w'}$.

For the given n, the language $L(M) \cap \{0, 1\}^n$ is decidable by a circuit c_n that consists of $\lceil \log k \rceil + 2$ subcircuits, namely, *DIRECT*, *FINAL*, and $\lceil \log k \rceil$ copies of *INDIRECT* (Figure 7.5.7). The structure of c_n relies on the observation that the Turing machine M accepts a given input $a_1 \cdots a_n$ if and only if M has partial configurations $w_0, \ldots, w_t$ on input $a_1 \cdots a_n$, such that w_0 is an initial partial configuration, w_t is an accepting partial configuration, and M can directly reach w_i from w_{i-1} for $1 \leq i \leq t$.

DIRECT has a component $CHECK_{ij}$ for each possible pair (w_i, w_j) of distinct partial configurations of M on the inputs of length n. $CHECK_{ij}$ has the output 1 on a given input $a_1 \cdots a_n$ if w_i as well as w_j are partial configurations of M on input $a_1 \cdots a_n$, and M can directly reach w_j from w_i. Otherwise, $CHECK_{ij}$ has the output 0.

The component $CHECK_{ij}$ is a table look-up circuit. Specifically, assume that $CHECK_{ij}$ corresponds to the partial configurations $w_i = (q, l, a, u_1, v_1, \ldots, u_m, v_m)$ and $w_j = (\hat{q}, \hat{l}, \hat{a}, \hat{u}_1, \hat{v}_1, \ldots, \hat{u}_m, \hat{v}_m)$. In such a case, $CHECK_{ij}$ is the constant node 0 when M cannot directly reach w_j from w_i. On the other hand, when M can directly reach w_j from w_i, then $CHECK_{ij}$ is a circuit that has the output 1 on input $a_1 \cdots a_n$ if and only if the $l + 1$st symbol in $\mathcal{c} a_1 \cdots a_n \$$ is a and the $\hat{l} + 1$st symbol in $\mathcal{c} a_1 \cdots a_n \$$ is $\hat{a}$.

Each copy of the subcircuit *INDIRECT* modifies the values of the "variables" $x_{12}, x_{13}, \ldots, x_{n\,n-1}$ in parallel, where the value of x_{ij} is modified by a component called $UPDATE_{ij}$. Upon reaching the rth *INDIRECT* the variable x_{ij} holds 1 if and only if M can reach w_j from w_i in at most 2^r moves (through partial configurations of M on the given input), $1 \leq r \leq \lceil \log k \rceil$. Upon leaving the rth *INDIRECT* the variable x_{ij} holds 1 if and only if M can reach w_j from w_i in at most 2^{r+1} moves. In particular, upon reaching the first *INDIRECT*, x_{ij} holds the output of $CHECK_{ij}$. However, upon leaving the last *INDIRECT*, x_{ij} holds 1 if and only if M can reach w_j from w_i.

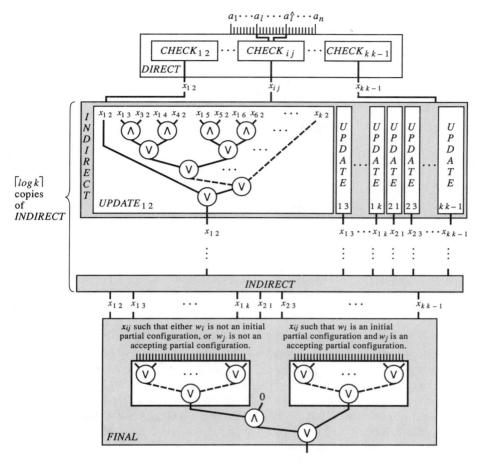

Figure 7.5.7 A circuit c_n that corresponds to an $O(\log n)$ space-bounded, nondeterministic Turing machine.

FINAL determines whether M can reach an accepting partial configuration from an initial partial configuration on the given input $a_1 \cdots a_n$, that is, whether x_{ij} is equal to 1 for some initial partial configuration w_i and some accepting partial configuration w_j.

The subcircuit *DIRECT* has size $O(k^2) = n^{O(1)}$ and constant depth. Each of the subcircuits *FINAL* and *INDIRECT* has size no greater than $O(k^2) = n^{O(1)}$ and depth no greater than $O(\log k) = O(\log n)$. As a result, the circuit c_n has size of at most $O(k^2(\lceil \log k \rceil + 2)) = n^{O(1)}$, and depth of at most $O((\lceil \log k \rceil + 2)\log k) = O(\log^2 n)$. $\qquad\Box$

The containment of *DLOG* in *U_NC* and the conjecture that *U_NC* is properly contained in *P*, suggest that the *P*-complete problems can not be solved efficiently by parallel programs. The following theorem provides a tool for detecting problems that can be solved efficiently by parallel programs (e.g., the problems in

Exercise 5.1.8). Moreover, the proof of the theorem implies an approach for mechanically obtaining the parallel programs from corresponding nondeterministic sequential programs that solve the problems.

Notation   In what follows, $NSPACE\_F(S(n))$ denotes the set of functions computable by $O(S(n))$ space-bounded, nondeterministic Turing transducers.

Theorem 7.5.3 $NSPACE\_F(\log n) \subseteq U\_FNC^2$.

Proof   Consider any Turing transducer $M = <Q, \Sigma, \Gamma, \Delta, \delta, q_0, B, F>$ of space complexity $S(n) = O(\log n)$. Assume that M computes some function f. In addition, with no loss of generality assume that $\Sigma = \Delta = \{0, 1\}$. From M, for each symbol a in Σ, a Turing machine $M_a = <Q_a, \Sigma, \Gamma, \delta_a, q_{0a}, B, F_a>$ can be constructed to accept the language $\{1^i0x \mid$ The ith output symbol of M on input x is $a\}$.

Specifically, on a given input 1^i0x, M_a records the value of i in binary on an auxiliary work tape. Then M_a follows the computation of M on input x. During the simulated computation, M_a uses the stored value of i to find the ith symbol in the output of M, while ignoring the output itself. M_a accepts 1^i0x if and only if M has an accepting computation on input x with a as the ith symbol in the output.

The function f is computable by a family $C = (c_0, c_1, c_2, \ldots)$ of circuits of the following form. Each c_n provides an output $y_1 \cdots y_{2S(n)+1}$ of length $2 \cdot 2^{S(n)}$ on input $x_1 \cdots x_n$. Each substring $y_{2j-1}y_{2j}$ of the output is equal to 00, 11, or 10, depending on whether the jth symbol in the output of M is 0, 1, or undefined, respectively. y_{2j-1} is obtained by negating the output of a circuit that simulates M_a for $a = 0$ on input $1^j0x_1 \cdots x_n$. y_{2j} is obtained by a circuit that simulates M_a for $a = 1$ on input $1^j0x_1 \cdots x_n$.

The result then follows from Lemma 7.5.3 because M_a is a logspace-bounded, Turing machine for $a = 0$ and for $a = 1$. $\square$

A proof similar to the one provided for the previous theorem can be used to show that $NSPACE\_F(S(n)) \subseteq \cup_{d>0} U\_SIZE\_DEPTH\_F(2^{dS(n)}, S^2(n))$ for each fully space-constructible function $S(n) \geq \log n$. By this containment and a proof similar to that of Exercise 7.5.3, the space requirements of sequential computations and the time requirements of parallel computations are polynomially related.

7.6   Uniform Families of Circuits and PRAM's

This section shows that uniform families of circuits and PRAM's are polynomially related in the resources they require. As a corollary, U_FNC is exactly the class of problems that can be solved by the PRAM's that have polynomial space complexity and polylog time complexity.

Notation   In what follows, $PROCESSORS\_TIME\_F(Z(n), T(n))$ denotes the set of functions that can be computed by the PRAM's having both $O(Z(n))$ size complexity and $O(T(n))$ time complexity (under the logarithmic cost criterion).

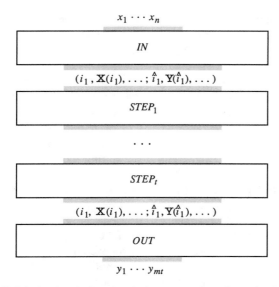

Figure 7.6.1 A circuit for simulating a computation of a PRAM.

From PRAM's to Uniform Families of Circuits

The proof of the following theorem consists of showing how the hardware of any given PRAM can be unrolled to obtain a corresponding uniform family of circuits. The degenerated case in which PRAM's are restricted to being RAM's has been considered in Lemma 7.5.1.

Theorem 7.6.1 If $\log T(n)$ and $\log Z(n)$ are fully space-constructible, $\log Z(n) \leq T(n)$, and $n \leq O\left(Z(n)T(n)\right)$, then

$$PROCESSORS\_TIME\_F\left(Z(n), T(n)\right) \subseteq$$
$$\bigcup_{d \geq 0} U\_SIZE\_DEPTH\_F\left((Z(n)T(n))^d, T^d(n)\right).$$

Proof Consider any PRAM $\hat{\text{M}} = <\text{M}, \text{X}, \text{Y}, \text{A}>$ of size complexity $Z(n)$ and time complexity $T(n)$. By Theorem 7.2.1 it can be assumed that $\hat{\text{M}}$ is a CREW PRAM. Consider any n and let $m = Z(n)$ and $t = T(n)$. The computations of $\hat{\text{M}}$ on inputs of length n can be simulated by the circuit c_n of Figure 7.6.1.

The Structure of c_n

The circuit c_n has an underlying structure similar to the circuit c_n in the proof of Lemma 7.5.1 (see Figure 7.5.1). It consists of $t + 2$ subcircuits, namely, *IN*, *STEP*$_1$, ..., *STEP*$_t$, and *OUT*. *IN* considers a given input of length n as an encoding of some input $(v_1, \ldots, v_N)$ of $\hat{\text{M}}$, and determines the initial configuration of $\hat{\text{M}}$. *STEP*$_i$ determines the configuration that $\hat{\text{M}}$ reaches after its ith step. *OUT* extracts the output of $\hat{\text{M}}$ from the output of *STEP*$_t$.

Each configuration of $\hat{M}$ is assumed to have the form $(i_1, X(i_1), i_2, X(i_2), \ldots ; \hat{i}_1, Y(\hat{i}_1), \hat{i}_2, Y(\hat{i}_2), \ldots ; \hat{i}_1, A(\hat{i}_1), \hat{i}_2, A(\hat{i}_2), \ldots ; \hat{i}_1, V_1(\hat{i}_1), \hat{i}_2, V_1(\hat{i}_2), \ldots ; \ldots ; \hat{i}_1, V_m(\hat{i}_1), \hat{i}_2, V_m(\hat{i}_2), \ldots)$, where $V_i(j)$ is assumed to be the value of the jth local variable of processor M_i.

$STEP_i$ consists of three layers, namely, *READ*, *SIMULATE*, and *WRITE*. The *READ* layer simulates the reading, from the input cells and shared memory cells, that takes place during the ith step of the simulated computation. The *SIMULATE* layer simulates the internal computation that takes place during the ith step by the processors $M_1, \ldots, M_m$. The *WRITE* layer simulates the writing, to the output cells and shared memory cells, that takes place during the ith step of the simulated computation.

With no loss of generality, it is assumed that in each step processor M_i reads from the input cell $X(V_i(1))$ into $V_i(1)$, and from the shared memory cell $A(V_i(2))$ into $V_i(2)$. Similarly, it is assumed that in each step M_i writes the value of $V_i(3)$ into the output cell $Y(V_i(4))$, and the value of $V_i(5)$ into $A(V_i(6))$.

SIMULATE contains a subcircuit *SIM_RAM* for each of the processors $M_1, \ldots, M_m$. The internal computation of processor M_j is simulated by a *SIM_RAM* whose input is $(i_1, V_j(i_1), i_2, V_j(i_2), \ldots)$. With no loss of generality it is assumed that the index j of M_j is stored in $V_j(7)$.

The Complexity of c_n

The circuits *IN*, *READ*, *WRITE*, and *OUT* can each simulate an $O(log\,(nZ(n)T(n)))$ space-bounded, deterministic Turing transducer that carries out the desired task. The simulations can be as in the proof of Lemma 7.5.3. Hence, each of these circuits has size no greater than $(nZ(n)T(n))^{O(1)} \leq (Z(n)T(n))^{O(1)}$ and depth no greater than $(log\,(nZ(n)T(n)))^{O(1)} \leq T^{O(1)}(n)$. *SIM_RAM* can simulate a processor M_i indirectly as in the proof of Lemma 7.5.1, through a deterministic Turing transducer equivalent to M_i. Hence, each *SIM_RAM* has size no greater than $T^{O(1)}(n)$. $\square$

From Uniform Families of Circuits to PRAM's

The previous theorem considered the simulation of PRAM's by uniform families of circuits. The next theorem considers simulations in the other direction.

Theorem 7.6.2

$$U\_SIZE\_DEPTH\_F\,(Z(n), D(n)) \subseteq \bigcup_{d>0} PROCESSORS\_TIME\_F\,(Z^d(n), D(n)log^{\,d}Z(n)).$$

Proof Consider any uniform family $C = (c_0, c_1, c_2, \ldots)$ of circuits with size complexity $Z(N)$ and depth complexity $D(n)$. Let $T = <Q, \Sigma, \Gamma, \delta, q_0, B, F>$ be an $S(n) = O(log\,Z(n))$ space-bounded, deterministic Turing transducer that computes $\{\,(1^n, c_n) \mid n \geq 0\,\}$. From T a CREW PRAM $\hat{M} = <M, X, Y, A>$ of size complexity $Z^{O(1)}(n)$ and time complexity $D(n)log^{\,O(1)}Z(n)$ can be constructed to simulate the computations of C in a straightforward manner.

The Simulation of Gate g_i by Processor M$_i$

Specifically, for each gate g_i in c_n, the PRAM $\hat{M}$ employs a corresponding processor M$_i$ and a corresponding shared memory cell A(i). The processor M$_i$ is used for simulating the operation of g_i, and the cell A(i) is used for recording the outcome of the simulation.

At the start of each simulation, M$_i$ initializes the value of A(i) to 2, as an indication that the output of g_i is not available yet. Then M$_i$ waits until its operands become available, that is, until its operands reach values that differ from 2. M$_i$ has the input cell X(j) as an operand if g_i gets an input from the jth input node x_j. M$_i$ has the shared memory cell A(j) as an operand if g_i gets an input from the jth gate g_j. When its operands become available, M$_i$ performs on them the same operation as does g_i. M$_i$ stores the result in Y(j), if g_i is the jth output node of c_n. Otherwise, M$_i$ stores the result in A(i).

The Identification of Gate g_i by processor M$_i$

Before the start of a simulation of c_n the PRAM $\hat{M}$ determines for each gate g_i in c_i, what the type t is in $\{\neg, \vee, \wedge\}$ of g_i, and which are the predecessors g_L and g_R of g_i. $\hat{M}$ does so by determining in parallel the output of T on input 1^n, and communicating each substring of the form (g_i) and each substring of the form (g_i, t, g_L, g_R) in the output to the corresponding processor M$_i$.

$\hat{M}$ determines the output of T by employing a group B$_1$, $\ldots$, B$_{O(Z(n)\log Z(n))}$ of processors. The task of processor B$_j$ is to determine the jth symbol in the output of T.

B$_j$, in turn, employs a processor B$_{ja}$ for each symbol a in the output alphabet Δ of T. The task of B$_{ja}$ is to notify B$_j$ whether the jth symbol in the output of T is the symbol a. B$_{ja}$ does so by simulating a $\log Z(n)$ space-bounded Turing machine M_T that accepts the language $\{\, 1^n \mid a \text{ is the } j\text{th symbol in the output of } T\,\}$. The simulation is performed in parallel by a group of processors that uses an approach similar to that described in the proof of Lemma 7.5.3.

Once the output of T is determined, each processor B$_j$ that holds the symbol "(" communicates the string "$(g_i \cdots)$" that is held by B$_j$, $\ldots$, B$_{j+|(g_i\cdots)|-1}$ to the corresponding processor M$_i$ of $\hat{M}$.

Finally, each processor M$_i$ that has been communicated to with a string of the form (g_i, t, g_L, g_R) communicates with its predecessors to determine the input nodes of c_n. $\square$

Exercises

7.1.1 Let Q be the problem of determining the number of times the value 0 appears in any given sequence. Describe a parallel program $\hat{P} = <P, X, Y>$ of depth complexity $D(N) = O(\log N)$ that solves Q. The parallel program should allow each sequential program P$_i$ to communicate with at most one other sequential program P$_j$ in each step.

7.2.1 Show that a CREW PRAM of linear size complexity and $O(\log n)$ depth complexity, can output the sum of its input values.

7.2.2 Show that a COMMON PRAM of linear size complexity, under the uniform cost criterion, can determine in $O(1)$ time whether an input consists only of values that are equal to 1.

7.2.3 Show that for each of the following statements there is a PRIORITY PRAM which can, under the uniform cost criterion, determine in $O(1)$ time whether the statement holds.

   a. The number of distinct values in the input is greater than two.

   b. The input values can be sorted into a sequence of consecutive numbers starting at 1.

7.2.4 Show that one step of a PRIORITY PRAM can be simulated in constant depth by a COMMON PRAM.

7.2.5 A TOLERANT PRAM is a PRAM that resolves the write conflicts in favor of no processor, that is, it leaves unchanged the content of the memory cells being involved in the conflicts. Show that each TOLERANT PRAM of size complexity $Z(n)$ and depth complexity $D(n)$ can be simulated by a PRIORITY PRAM of size complexity $Z(n)$ and depth complexity $O(D(n))$.

7.3.1 Show that $\{\, x \mid x$ is in $\{0,1\}^*$, and 1 appears exactly once in $x \,\}$ is decidable by a family of circuits of size complexity $O(n)$ and depth complexity $O(\log n)$.

7.3.2 Show that each circuit of size $Z(n)$ and depth $D(n)$ has an equivalent circuit, of size at most $Z^2(n)$ and depth at most $D(n)\log Z(n)$, whose gates all have outdegree of at most 2.

7.4.1 Provide a table look-up circuit that accepts the language $L = \{1011, 0100, 1101, 1001\}$.

7.4.2 Show that each of the following languages is decidable by a uniform family of circuits of linear size complexity and $O(\log n)$ depth complexity.

   a. $\{\, 0^i 1^i 0^i \mid i \geq 1 \,\}$.
   b. $\{\, 0^i 1^j \mid i \leq j \,\}$.

A gate g' is said to be the predecessor of a gate g in a circuit c_n with respect to a path π if any of the following cases holds.

   a. $\pi = \epsilon$ and $g' = g$.

   b. π is in $\{L, R\}$, and (g, t, g_L, g_R) is in c_n for $g_\pi = g''$.

   c. $\pi = \pi_1 \pi_2$ for some g'' such that g'' is the predecessor of g in c_n with respect to π_1, and g' is the predecessor of g'' in c_n with respect to π_2.

The *connection language* L_C for a family $C = (c_0, c_1, c_2, \ldots)$ of circuits is the language $\{ (g, g', \pi, \tau, n) \mid \pi$ is in $\{L, R\}^*$. $|\pi| \leq O(log (\text{size of } c_n)).$ g' is the predecessor of g in c_n with respect to π. If g' is a gate of type t in $\{\neg, \vee, \wedge\}$ or a constant node t in $\{0, 1\}$, then $\tau = t$, otherwise $\tau = \Lambda \}$.

Example Consider the circuit c_2 of the following form.

$(4, \neg, 2, 2)(5, \wedge, 1, 4)(6, \wedge, 1, 3)(7, \wedge, 2, 1)(8, \wedge, 3, 1)(9, \wedge, 5, 6)(10, \wedge, 7, 8)(11, \vee, 9, 10)(11)$

The gate $g' = 9$ of c_2 is the predecessor of the gate $g = 11$ with respect to $\pi = L$, and $g' = 2$ is the predecessor of $g = 9$ with respect to $\pi = LRR$ (see Example 7.3.5 and Figure 7.3.3).

For a family of circuits C that contains the circuit c_2, both $(11, 9, L, \wedge, 2)$ and $(9, 2, LRR, \Lambda, 2)$ are in L_C. $\qquad\qquad\qquad\qquad\qquad\qquad\qquad\qquad\qquad\qquad\square$

A family $C = (c_0, c_1, c_2, \ldots)$ of circuits is said to be *uniform$_E$* if there exists a deterministic Turing machine that accepts the language L_C, and on any given input (g, g', π, τ, n) the Turing machine halts in $O(log (\text{ size of } c_n))$ time.

7.4.3 Show that every uniform$_E$ family of circuits is also a uniform family of circuits.

7.5.1 Find *SUBTAPE_MODIFIER* for Example 7.5.1.

7.5.2 Analyze the depth of c_n in the proof of Lemma 7.5.1.

7.5.3 Show that the containment $U\_DEPTH (D(n)) \subseteq DSPACE (D(n))$ holds for fully space-constructible functions $D(n)$.

> *Hint*: A circuit that recognizes a language has the following properties.
>
> a. The depth d of the circuit provides the upper bound of 2^d on the size of the circuit.
>
> b. Each node in the circuit can be represented by a path, given in reverse, from the node in question to the output node.

7.5.4 Show that U_NC^1 contains $NSPACE(1)$, that is, the class of regular languages.

7.5.5 Show that for each $k \geq 0$ there are languages that are not in $SIZE (n^k)$.

7.5.6 Show that $RP \subseteq \cup_{k \geq 0} SIZE (n^k)$.

Bibliographic Notes

The applicability of parallel programs in general, and to the problem of finding the minimum element in a set in particular (see Example 7.1.1), is considered in Batcher (1968). The trade off between the size and depth complexities of parallel programs is considered in Valiant (1975). Applications of parallel programs to the design of sequential programs are exhibited in Megiddo (1981). Exercise 7.1.1(b) is from Muller and Preparata (1975).

Fortune and Wyllie (1978) introduced the CREW PRAM's, Kučera (1982) introduced the COMMON PRAM's, and Goldschlager (1982) introduced the PRI-ORITY PRAM's. Shiloach and Vishkin (1981) adapted the trade-off results of Valiant (1975) for COMMON PRAM's. Exercise 7.2.3 and Exercise 7.2.5 are from Grolmusz and Ragde (1987). Exercise 7.2.4 is from Kučera (1982).

Complexity of circuits were studied since Shannon (1949). Uniform families of circuits were introduced in Borodin (1977). Ruzzo (1981) and Allender (1986) discuss some variations of uniform families of circuits. Exercise 7.4.3 is from Ruzzo (1981). The class *FNC* was introduced in Pippenger (1979).

The results in Section 7.5 and in Exercise 7.5.5, relating uniform families of circuits with sequential computations, are from Borodin (1977). Exercise 7.5.5 is from Kannan (1982), and Exercise 7.5.6 is from Adleman (1978). Chandra, Stockmeyer, and Vishkin (1984) consider the relationship in Section 7.6 between uniform families of circuits and PRAM's. Exercise 7.5.6 is from Adleman (1978). Hong (1985) discusses farther the relations between complexity classes.

Cook (1983), Cook (1981), Kindervater and Lenstra (1985), and Johnson (1983) offer reviews of the subject.

Appendix A

MATHEMATICAL NOTIONS

This appendix briefly reviews some basic concepts that are prerequisites for understanding the text.

A.1   Sets, Relations, and Functions

Sets

A *set* is a collection of elements. The order or repetition of the elements are immaterial. Notation of the form $\{\, x \mid x$ satisfies the property $Q \,\}$ is used for specifying the set of all elements x that satisfy property Q. Finite sets are also specified by explicitly listing their members between braces.

The number of elements in a set A, denoted $|A|$, is called the *cardinality* of the set. A set with no elements (i.e., cardinality equals 0) is called the *empty* set and is denoted by $\emptyset$.

Two sets A and B are said to be *equal*, denoted $A = B$, if they have precisely the same members. A is said to be a *subset* of B, denoted $A \subseteq B$, if every element of A is also an element of B. A is said to be a *proper subset* of B, denoted $A \subset B$, if A is a subset of B and A is not equal to B.

The relationship between sets is sometimes illustrated by *Venn diagrams*. In a Venn diagram each of the elements of the given sets is represented by a point in the plan, and each set is represented by a geometrical shape enclosing only those points that represent the elements of the set (see Figure A.1.1).

The *power set* of a set A, denoted 2^A, is the set of all subsets of A, that is, the set $\{\, S \mid S$ is a subset of $A \,\}$.

A *multiset* is a collection of elements in which repetition of elements is counted. The set of *natural numbers* is the set of all the nonnegative integers.

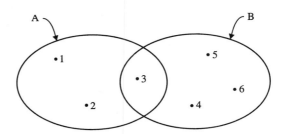

Figure A.1.1 Venn diagram for the sets $A = \{1, 2, 3\}$ and $B = \{3, 4, 5, 6\}$.

Set Operations

The *union* of A and B, denoted $A \cup B$, is the set $\{ x \mid x$ is either in A or in $B \}$. The *intersection* of A and B, denoted $A \cap B$, is the set $\{ x \mid x$ is both in A and in $B \}$. A and B are said to be *disjoint* if they have no element in common, that is, if $A \cap B = \emptyset$.

The *difference* between A and B, denoted $A - B$, is the set $\{ x \mid x$ is in A but not in $B \}$. If B is a subset of A, then $A - B$ is said to be the *complementation of B with respect to A*. When A is understood, $A - B$ is simply said to be the *complementation* of B, denoted $\overline{B}$. In such a case A is called the *universe*.

The *Cartesian product* of two sets A_1 and A_2, denoted $A_1 \times A_2$, is the set $\{ (a_1, a_2) \mid a_1$ is in A_1, and a_2 is in $A_2 \}$. A Cartesian product of the form $((\cdots((A_1 \times A_2) \times A_3) \cdots) \times A_k)$ is also denoted $A_1 \times A_2 \times \cdots \times A_k$. Similarly, a $((\cdots((a_1, a_2), a_3) \cdots), a_k)$ in $A_1 \times A_2 \times \cdots \times A_k$ is also denoted $(a_1, \ldots, a_k)$.

Relations

A *relation* R from A to B is a subset of the cartesian product $A \times B$. If $A = B$, then R is said to be a *relation on* A.

The *domain* of R is the set $\{ x \mid (x, y)$ is in R for some y in $B \}$. If the domain of R is the set A, then R is said to be *total*. Otherwise, R is said to be *partial*.

The *range* of R is the set $\{ y \mid (x, y)$ is in R for some x in $A \}$. The *range of R at x*, denoted $R(x)$, is the set $\{ y \mid (x, y)$ is in $R \}$.

Functions

A *function* f from A to B, denoted $f \colon A \to B$, is a relation from A to B, whose range $f(x)$ at each x in A has cardinality 0 or 1. $f(x)$ is said to be *defined* if it has cardinality 1, that is, if $f(x) = \{y\}$ for some y. In such a case, $f(x)$ is said to have the value of y, written $f(x) = y$. Otherwise, $f(x)$ is said to be *undefined*.

f is said to be *one-to-one* if $f(x) = f(y)$ implies $x = y$ for all x and y in A. f is said to be *onto* if B is the range of f. f is said to be a *predicate*, or an *assertion*, if $B = \{false, true\}$.

$\lceil x \rceil$ denotes the smallest integer that is not smaller than x. $mod\,(x, y)$ denotes the remainder of an integer division of x by y. $min(S)$ denotes the smallest value in S. $max(S)$ denotes the biggest value in S. $gcd\,(x, y)$ denotes the greatest common divisor of x and y.

Countability

A set A is said to be *countable* if there exists an onto function f from the set of natural numbers to A. The set is said to be *countably infinite* if there exists a one-to-one onto function f from the set of natural numbers to A. A set that is not countable is said to be *uncountable*.

A.2   Graphs and Trees

Graphs

A *directed graph* G is a pair (V, E), where V is a finite set and E is a relation on V. The elements of V are called *nodes* or *vertices*. The elements of E are called *edges* or *arcs*.

u is a *predecessor* of v, and v is *successor* of u, in G if (u, v) is an edge of G. The graph is said to be *ordered* if some ordering is assumed on the predecessors of each node, and on the successors of each node.

A *path* in G is a sequence $v_1, \ldots, v_n$ of nodes such that v_i is a successor of v_{i-1} for $i = 2, \ldots, n$. The *length* of the path is $n - 1$. The path is a *cycle* if $n > 1$ and $v_n = v_1$.

A graph $G_1 = (V_1, E_1)$ is said to be a *subgraph* of a graph $G_2 = (V_2, E_2)$, if $V_1 \subseteq V_2$ and $E_1 \subseteq E_2$.

Each graph $G = (V, E)$ can be represented by a diagram of the following form. For each node v in V the graph has a corresponding geometric shape (e.g. period, circle). For each edge (u, v) in E the graph has an arrow from the geometric shape corresponding to u to the geometric shape corresponding to v. Whenever the graphs are ordered, the predecessors and successors of each node are drawn from left to right in their given orders.

Rooted Acyclic Graphs

A directed graph is said to be *acyclic* if it contains no cycles. An acyclic graph is said to be *rooted* if exactly one of its nodes, called the *root*, has no predecessors. A node in a graph with no successors is called a *leaf*. A rooted, acyclic, directed graph is called a *tree* if each of its nodes, excluding the root, has exactly one predecessor.

In general, a rooted acyclic graph is drawn with the root on top and the arcs pointing downward. The directions on the arrows are omitted.

Appendix B

BIBLIOGRAPHY

Adleman, L. (1978). "Two theorems on random polynomial time," *Proceedings of the 19th IEEE Symposium on Foundations of Computer Science*, 75–83.

Aho, A., Hopcroft, J., and Ullman, J. (1974). *The Design and Analysis of Computer Algorithms*, Reading, MA: Addison-Wesley.

Aho, A., Sethi, R., and Ullman, J. (1986). *Compilers: Principles, Techniques, and Tools*, Reading, MA: Addison-Wesley.

Allender, E. (1986). "Characterizations of PUNC and precomputation," *International Colloquium on Automata, Languages and Programming*, Lecture Notes in Computer Science 226, Berlin: Springer-Verlag, 1–10.

Bar-Hillel, Y., Perles, M., and Shamir, E. (1961). "On formal properties of simple phrase structure grammars," *Zeitschrift für Phonetik Sprachwissenschaft und Kommunikations-forschung 14*, 143–172.

Batcher, K. (1968). "Sorting networks and their applications," *Proceedings of the 32nd AFIPS Spring Joint Computer Conference*, 307–314.

Bird, M. (1973). "The equivalence problem for deterministic two-tape automata," *Journal of Computer and Systems Sciences 7*, 218–236.

Borodin, A. (1977). "On relating time and space to size and depth," *SIAM Journal on Computing 6*, 733–744.

Büchi, J. (1960). "Weak second-order arithmetic and finite automata," *Zeitschrift für Math. Logik und Grundlagen d. Math. 6*, 66–92.

Chandra, A., Stockmeyer, L., and Vishkin, U. (1984). "Constant depth reducibilities," *SIAM Journal on Computing 13*, 423–439.

Chomsky, N. (1959). "On certain formal properties of grammars," *Information and Control 2*, 137–167.

Chomsky, N. (1962). "Context-free grammars and pushdown storage," *Quarterly Progress Report 65*, MIT Research Laboratories of Electronics, 187–194.

Chomsky, N., and Miller, G. (1958). "Finite-state languages," *Information and Control 1*, 91–112.

Chomsky, N., and Schutzenberger, M. (1963). "The algebraic theory of context-free languages," *Computer Programming and Formal Systems*, 118–161.

Church, A. (1936). "An unsolvable problem of elementary number theory," *American Journal of Mathematics* 58, 345–363.

Cobham, A. (1964). "The intrinsic computational difficulty of functions," *Proceedings of the 1964 Congress for Logic, Mathematics, and the Philosophy of Science*, Amsterdam: North Holland, 24–30.

Cook, S. (1971). "The complexity of theorem-proving procedures," *Proceedings of the 3rd Annual ACM Symposium on Theory of Computing*, 151–158.

Cook, S. (1981). "Towards a complexity theory of synchronous parallel computations," *L'Enseignement Mathematique* 27, 99–124.

Cook, S. (1983). "The classification of problems which have fast parallel algorithms," *Proceedings of the 4th International Foundations of Computer Science Conference*, Lecture Notes in Computer Science 158, Berlin: Springer-Verlag, 78–93.

Cook, S., and Reckhov, R. (1973). "Time bounded random access machines," *Journal of Computer and Systems Sciences* 7, 354–375.

Danthine, A. (1980). "Protocol representation with finite state models," *IEEE Transactions on Communications 4*, 632–643.

DeLeeuw, K., Moore, E., Shannon, C., and Shapiro, N. (1956). "Computability by probabilistic machines," *Automata Studies*, Princeton, NJ: Princeton University Press, 183–212.

Edmonds, J. (1965a). "Paths, trees and flowers," *Canadian Journal of Mathematics* 17, 449–467.

Edmonds, J. (1965b). "Minimum partition of matroid in independent subsets," *Journal of Research of the National Bureau of Standards Sect 69B*, 67–72.

Ehrenfeucht, A., Parikh, R., and Rozenberg, G. (1981). "Pumping lemmas for regular sets," *SIAM Journal on Computing* 10, 536–541.

Evey, J. (1963). "Application of pushdown store machines," *Proceedings 1963 Fall Joint Computer Conference*, Montvale, NJ: AFIPS Press, 215–227.

Floyd, R. (1967). "Nondeterministic algorithms," *Journal of the Association for Computing Machinery 14*, 636–644.

Fortune, S., and Wyllie, J. (1978). "Parallelism in random access machines," *Proceedings of the 10th Annual ACM Symposium on Theory of Computing*, 114–118.

Freivalds, R. (1979). "Fast probabilistic algorithms," *Proceedings of the 1979 Mathematical Foundations of Computer Science*, Lecture Notes in Computer Science 74, Berlin: Springer-Verlag, 57–69.

Garey, M., and Johnson, D. (1979). *Computers and Intractability: A Guide to the Theory of NP-Completeness*, San Francisco, CA: W. H. Freeman and Company.

Gill, J. (1977). "Computational complexity of probabilistic Turing machines," *SIAM Journal on Computing* 6, 675–695.

Goldschlager, L. (1982). "A unified approach to models of synchronous parallel machines," *Journal of the Association for Computing Machinery 29*, 1073–1086.

Greibach, S. (1981). "Formal languages: Origins and directions," *Annals of the History of Computing 3*, 14–41.

Griffiths, T. (1968). "The unsolvability of the equivalence problem for Λ-free nondeterministic generalized machines," *Journal of the Association for Computing Machinery 15*, 409–413.

Grolmusz, V., and Ragde, P. (1987). "Incomparability in parallel computation," *Proceedings of the 28th IEEE Symposium on Foundations of Computer Science*, 89–98.

Gurari, E. (1979). "Transducers with decidable equivalence problem," Technical Report, University of Wisconsin-Milwaukee, 1979. Revised version, State University of New York at Buffalo, 1981.

Harrison, M. (1978). *Introduction to Formal Language Theory*, Reading, MA: Addison-Wesley.

Hartmanis, J., and Stearns, R. (1965). "On the computational complexity of algorithms," *Transactions of the American Mathematical Society 117*, 285–306.

Hilbert, D. (1901). "Mathematical problems," *Bulletin of the American Mathematical Society 8*, 437–479.

Hopcroft, J., and Ullman, J. (1969). "Some results on tape bounded Turing machines," *Journal of the Association for Computing Machinery 16*, 168–177.

Hopcroft, J., and Ullman, J. (1979). *Introduction to Automata Theory, Languages and Computation*, Reading, MA: Addison-Wesley.

Hunt, H. (1973). "On the time and type complexity of languages," *Proceedings of the 5th Annual ACM Symposium on Theory of Computing*, 10–19.

Hunt, H., Constable, R., and Sahni, S. (1980). "On the computational complexity of scheme equivalence," *SIAM Journal on Computing 9*, 396–416.

Ibarra, O., and Rosier, L. (1981). "On the decidability of equivalence for deterministic pushdown transducers," *Information Processing Letters 13*, 89–93.

Immerman, N. (1987). "Space is closed under complementation," Technical Report, New Haven, CT: Yale University.

Hong, J. (1985). "On similarity and duality of computation," *Information and Control 62*, 109–128.

Johnson, D. (1983). "The NP-completeness column: An ongoing guide," *Journal of Algorithms 4*, 189–203.

Johnson, D. (1984). "The NP-completeness column: An ongoing guide," *Journal of Algorithms 5*, 433–447.

Jones, N., and Laaser, W., (1976). "Complete problems for deterministic polynomial time," *Theoretical Computer Science 3*, 105–118.

Jones, N., and Muchnick, S. (1977). "Even simple programs are hard to analyze," *Journal of the Association for Computing Machinery 24*, 338–350.

Jones, N., and Muchnick, S. (1978). "The complexity of finite memory programs with recursion," *Journal of the Association for Computing Machinery 25*, 312–321.

Kannan, R. (1982). "Circuit-size lower bounds and non-reducibility to sparse sets," *Information and Control 55*, 40–56.

Karp, R. (1972). "Reducibility among combinatorial problems," in *Complexity of Computer Computations*, edited by R. Mille and J. Thatcher, New York: Plenum Press, 85–104.

Kindervater, G., and Lenstra, J. (1985). "Parallel Algorithms," in *Combinatorial Optimization: Annotated Bibliographies*, edited by M. O'hEigeartaigh, J. Lenstra, and A. Rinnooy Kan, New York: John Wiley and Sons, 106–128.

Kleene, S. (1956). "Representation of events in nerve nets and finite automata," *Automata Studies*, Princeton, NJ: Princeton University Press, 3–41.

Kučera, K. (1982). "Parallel computation and conflicts in memory access," *Information Processing Letters 14*, 93–96. A correction, *ibid 17*, 107.

Kuroda, S. (1964). "Classes of languages and linear bounded automata," *Information and Control 7*, 207–223.

Ladner, R. (1975). "The circuit value problem is log space complete for P," *Sigact News 7*, 18–20.

Landweber, P. (1963). "Three theorems on phrase structure grammars of Type 1," *Information and Control 6*, 131–136.

Lesk, M. (1975). "LEX — a lexical analyzer generator," Technical Report 39, Murray Hill, NJ: Bell Laboratories.

Levin, L. (1973). "Universal sorting problems," *Problemi Peredaci Informacii 9*, 115–116 . English translation in *Problems of Information Transmission 9*, 265–266.

Lueker, G. (1975). "Two NP-complete problems in non-negative integer programming," Report No. 178, Computer Science Laboratory, Princeton, NJ: Princeton University.

Maffioli, F., Speranza, M., and Vercellis, C. (1985). "Randomized algorithms," in *Combinatorial Optimization: Annotated Bibliographies*, edited by M. O'hEigeartaigh, J. Lenstra, and A. Rinnooy Kan, New York: John Wiley and Sons, 89–105.

Matijasevic, Y. (1970). "Enumerable sets are Diophantine," *Doklady Akademiky Nauk SSSR 191*, 279–282. English translation: *Soviet Math Doklady 11*, 354–357.

McCarthy, J. (1963). "A basis for a mathematical theory of computation," *Computer Programming and Formal Systems*, edited by P. Braffort and D. Hirschberg, Amsterdam: North-Holland.

McCulloch, W., and Pitts, W. (1943). "A logical calculus of the ideas immanent in nervous activity," *Bulletin of Mathematical Biophysics 5*, 115–133.

Megiddo, N. (1981). "Applying parallel computation algorithms in the design of serial algorithms," *Proceedings of the 22nd IEEE Symposium on Foundations of Computer Science,* 399–408.

Meyer, A., and Ritchie, R. (1967). "The complexity of loop programs," *Proceedings of the ACM National Meeting,* 465–469.

Moore, E. (1956). "Gedanken experiments on sequential machines," *Automata Studies,* Princeton, NJ: Princeton University Press, 129–153.

Muller, D., and Preparata, F. (1975). "Bounds to complexities of networks for sorting and for switching," *Journal of the Association for Computing Machinery* 22, 195–201.

Myhill, J. (1957). "Finite automata and the representation of events," *WADD TR-57-624,* Dayton, OH: Wright Patterson Air Force Base.

Myhill, J. (1960). "Linear bounded automata," *WADD TR-60-165,* Dayton, OH: Wright Patterson Air Force Base.

Oettinger, A. (1961). "Automatic syntactic analysis and the pushdown store," *Proceedings of the 12th Symposia in Applied Mathematics,* Providence, RI: American Mathematical Society, 104–109.

Pippenger, E. (1979). "On simultaneous resource bounds," *Proceedings of the 20th IEEE Symposium on Foundations of Computer Science,* 307–311.

Post, E. (1946). "A variant of a recursively unsolvable problem," *Bulletin of the American Mathematical Society 52,* 264–268.

Rabin, M. (1976). "Probabilistic algorithms," *Algorithms and Complexity — New Directions and Recent Results,* edited by J. Traub, New York: Academic-Press, 21–39.

Rabin, M., and Scott, D. (1959). "Finite automata and their decision problems," *IBM Journal of Research and Development 3,* 114–125.

Ritchie, R. (1963). "Classes of predictably computable functions," *Transactions of the American Mathematical Society 106,* 139–173.

Ruzzo, L. (1981). "On uniform circuit complexity," *Journal of Computer and Systems Sciences 22,* 365–383.

Savitch, W. (1970). "Relationships between nondeterministic and deterministic tape complexities," *Journal of Computer and Systems Sciences 4,* 177–192.

Scheinberg, S. (1960). "Note on the Boolean properties of context-free languages," *Information and Control 3,* 372–375.

Schutzenberger, M. (1963). "On context-free languages and pushdown automata," *Information and Control 6,* 246–264.

Schwartz, J. (1980). "Fast probabilistic algorithms for verification of polynomial identities," *Journal of the Association for Computing Machinery 27,* 701–717.

Shannon, C. (1949). "The synthesis of two-terminal switching circuts," *Bell System Technical Journal 28,* 59–98.

Sheperdson, J. (1959). "The reduction of two-way automata to one-way automata," *IBM Journal of Research and Development 3,* 198–200.

Shiloach, Y., and Vishkin, U. (1981). "Finding the maximum, merging and sorting in a parallel computation model," *Journal of Algorithms 2,* 88–102.

Sipser, M. (1978). "Halting bounded computations," *Proceedings of the 19th IEEE Symposium on Foundations of Computer Science*, 73–74.

Solovay, R., and Strassen, V. (1977). "A fast Monte Carlo test for primality," *SIAM Journal on Computing* 6, 84–85. A correction, *ibid* 7, 118.

Stearns, R., Hartmanis, J., and Lewis, P. (1965). "Hierarchies of memory limited computations," *Proceedings of the 6th Annual IEEE Symposium on Switching Circuit Theory and Logical Design*, 191–202.

Stockmeyer, L. (1985). "Classifying the computational complexity of problems," *IBM Research Report*, San Jose, CA.

Szelepcsenyi, R. (1987). "The method of forcing for nondeterministic automata," *Bulletin of the European Association for Theoretical Computer Science 33*, 96–100.

Turing, A. (1936). "On computable numbers with an application to the Entscheidungs problem," *Proceedings of the London Mathematical Society 2*, 230–265. A correction, *ibid*, 544–546.

Valiant, L. (1973). "Decision procedures for families of deterministic pushdown automata," Ph.D. Thesis, University of Warwick, U.K.

Valiant, L. (1975). "Parallelism in comparison problems," *SIAM Journal on Computing 4*, 348–355.

Welsh, D. (1983). "Randomised algorithms," *Discrete Applied Mathematics 5*, 133–145.

Index

308